About the Editors

Professor Chih-yu Shih teaches China studies, anthropology of knowledge and international relations theory in the Department of Political Science of National Taiwan University. Determined to collect and represent intellectual heritage in Asia, he has been devoted throughout his academic career of 30 years to researching, teaching and writing on the cultural and political agency of human society in Asia, especially where the Anglophone scholarship has failed to attend. His methods are primarily field interview, oral history, cultural memory and archive research. Professor Shih's publications consistently challenge the mainstream views on the law of human behavior and gather evidence of human agency from ethnic communities, postcolonial countries, people living in poverty, and so on. In his writings, Professor Shih pays attention to cultural meanings of civilizational components such as religion, language, ecology, gender and institution. Since the beginning of the 21st century, Professor Shih has led a transnational project to compare scholarship on China from various continents, tackling the deep, ontological foundation that girds the mutual constitution of the Chinese scholar, Chinese scholarship and China. His project pays great attention to individualized trajectories of intellectual growth. For the past decade, Professor Shih and his transnational teams have carried out over 400 oral history interviews (http://www.china-studies.taipei).

Professor Prapin Manomaivibool, while working on her M.A. thesis in Thai Language Program at the Faculty of Arts, Chulalongkorn University (CU), in 1966, was selected and assigned to study for a Ph.D. in Chinese at the University of Washington (UW), Seattle, in 1967. Upon graduation, she returned with the mission to set up a Chinese Section in the Department of Eastern Languages, Faculty of Arts, CU, in 1973. Under her administration as Head of the Chinese Section, the teaching of Chinese that she pioneered steadily developed; today CU is the only university in Thailand that offers B.A., M.A. and Ph.D. programs in Chinese. Her current positions include Director of Asia Research Center at CU, Chair Professor of the Chinese Section, Faculty of Arts, CU, President of the Chinese Language Teachers' Association of Thailand under the Royal Patronage of H.R.H. Princess Maha Chakri Sirindhorn and Fellow (院士) of the Royal Society of Thailand. Dr. Manomaivibool has been honored by CU as Distinguished Teacher in Social Science and Humanities. In 2014, she was awarded an Honorary Doctor of Philosophy in Humanities by Mae Fah Luang University, and most recently was awarded Outstanding Senior Interpreter by the Translators and Interpreters Association of Thailand (TIAT).

Mariko Tanigaki (Ph.D.) is a Professor at the Department of Area Studies, University of Tokyo, with a B.A. (Asian Studies), M.A. and Ph.D. (Area Studies) from the University of Tokyo. She studied at the Centre of Asian Studies, the University of Hong Kong, from September 1986–September 1987. She also taught at Department of Civilization, School of Letters, Tokai University, as Assistant and Associate Professor. Her research interests cover Contemporary Hong Kong Studies and Southern China Studies. Her recent publications include *The Morphing South China and Contemporary Chinese Networks* (in Japanese, co-edited, 2014) and *China Studies and Views toward China in the post-war Japan* (in

Japanese, co-edited, 2018). The former book got the Japan Consortium for Area Studies Award for Collaborative Research. She is the former president of Japan Association of the South China Studies. She wrote many articles on Politics and Society of Hong Kong, and contributed to the annual report of the Institute of Developing Economies (1993–2002, 2004–2006) and the Institute of Chinese Affairs (1995–2002), and also to the bi-annual report of the Japan Association for Asian Affairs (2004, 2006, 2008).

Professor Swaran Singh is Chairman, Centre for International Politics, Organization and Disarmament (CIPOD), School of International Studies, Jawaharlal Nehru University New Delhi; president of the Association of Asia Scholars; general secretary of Indian Association of Asian & Pacific Studies; visiting professor at China West Normal University and Research Institute of Indian Ocean Economies (Kunming); and adjunct senior fellow of the Charhar Institute (Beijing), Institute of National Security Studies Sri Lanka and Sichuan University Jinjiang College. He has supervised 32 Ph.D. and 50 M.Phil. degrees, and he sits on Selection Committees for faculty recruitment. He has published in *Journal of International Affairs, Security Challenges, Journal of Indian Ocean Region, Issues & Studies, African Security, BISS Journal*, and several Chinese and Indian journals. Prof. Singh co-edited *Corridors of Engagement* (2019), *BCIM Economic Corridor: Chinese and Indian Perspectives* (2017), *Transforming South Asia: Imperatives for Action* (2013), *India and the GCC Countries, Iran and Iraq: Emerging Security Perspectives* (2013), *On China By India: From Civilization to State* (2012), *Emerging China: Prospects for Partnership in Asia* (2012) and *Asia's Multilateralism* (2012); edited *China-Pakistan Strategic Cooperation: Indian Perspectives* (2007); co-authored *Regionalism in South Asian Diplomacy* (2007); and authored *Nuclear Command & Control in Southern Asia: China, India, Pakistan* (2010), *China-India Economic Engagement: Building Mutual Confidence* (2005) and *China-South Asia: Issues, Equations, Policies* (2003).

Acknowledgment

The project has benefited from a number of research, travel and conference grants, including the Ministry of Science and Technology in Taipei (No. 108-2811-H-002 -529 and No. 107-2410-H-002 -152 -), the Contemporary China Research Base Office of the Institute of Social Science at the University of Tokyo in Tokyo, the Asia Research Center at Chulalongkorn University in Bangkok, the Center for International China Studies at the Chinese Academy of Social Sciences in Beijing, and the Association of Asia Scholars in New Delhi.

Contents

About the Editors v
Acknowledgment ix
Introduction xv

Part I Rearranged Colonial Relations — In the Eyes of the Colonized Self 1

Chapter 1 Colonial Connections through Commerce and Culture: Revisiting China Studies in India 3
Reena Marwah

Chapter 2 Exploring China Consciousness of Pre-independence India 25
Swaran Singh

Chapter 3 "Majian": Formation of the Cultural Sites through Interaction between the Chinese and Arab Cultures from the Perspective of Post-colonialism 53
Mohsen Fergani

Chapter 4 Comparing China Studies in a Decolonized State: A Case Study of Pakistan 69
Pervaiz Ali Mahesar

Chapter 5 Colonialism, Cold War and Nanyang University's Chineseness Dilemma 97
Ngeow Chow-Bing

| Chapter 6 | Embedded Anti-Chinese Orientations: The Dutch Occupation and Its Legacies
Harryanto Aryodiguno | 121 |

Part II China as Relational Other — In the Eyes of the Lost Self — 147

Chapter 7	Colonial and Post-colonial Legacies of the Intellectual History of China Studies in Korea: Discontinuity, Fragmentation and Forgetfulness *Jungmin Seo*	149
Chapter 8	Anglo-Chinese Studies in Post-WWII Hong Kong: The Perspectives of Colonial Languages *Mariko Tanigaki*	165
Chapter 9	Development of Japanese Studies in Hong Kong from the Perspectives of Chineseness and Hong Kong's Subjectivity *Chin Chun Wah*	193
Chapter 10	Colonial Relationality and Its Post-Chinese Consequences: Japanese Legacies in Contemporary Taiwan's Views on China *Chih-yu Shih & Raoul Bunskoek*	231
Chapter 11	The Imaginary of China: Sameness and Otherness from the Perspective of Macau *Cátia Miriam Costa*	257
Chapter 12	A Research Note of the French Legacies in Indochina's Scholarship: A Review on École française d'Extrême-Orient's Publications and Contributors on Sinology *Tran Tien Nguyen*	285

Part III	**Emerging Pluralist Relations — In the Eyes of Autonomous Self**	**305**
Chapter 13	The Anglo-Japanese Inter-imperial Relations and Ideas on the Future of the Japanese Empire *Hiroyuki Ogawa*	307
Chapter 14	China Studies in Aotearoa/New Zealand: Moving Beyond Postcolonialism *Pauline Keating*	339
Chapter 15	A British Legacy or Modern University Crisis? Chinese Studies in Australian Universities *Shirley Chan*	367
Chapter 16	Pondering China Studies in the Philippines as an Academic Practice and Scholarly Inquiry *Tina S. Clemente*	407
Future Agendas?		431
Index		435

Introduction

An Emerging Agenda

China demonstrates the possibility of developing without surrendering entirely to colonial modernity — e.g., by not democratizing, redefining or constructing "Chinese" models of development. China additionally provides a stable and credible platform as well as support for global, regional and national political economies to escape crises. However, this seeming power of possibility constitutes at the same time a claim to difference, which is the source of Orientalism many former colonies suffered from in their processes of becoming "Western/modern". Due to China's seemingly promising yet speculative and uncertain future, China's readily available alternative route to modernity remains plausible and perhaps even comfortable for post-colonial neighbors. This makes the selection of a perspective to study and observe China both an identity statement and a realignment strategy.

Relying on the available oral history scripts of interviews with senior China scholars in South and Southeast Asia as well as Japan that several transnational teams have already completed since 2004, we compare how British and Japanese colonial ruling, institution and values have been received and reflected upon in post-colonial localities and how encountering with the rise of China may trigger strategic, uncertain and coincidental possibilities. At the same time, these oral history scripts enable the comparison of a number of former colonial sites with regard to the different uses of China-related colonial resources that likewise are strategic, uncertain and coincidental.

On this peculiar agenda and in this book, we have together taken up a seemingly unmanageable and fruitless agenda that promises to create endless mirror images inside one another that are beyond legibility and intelligence of our limited capacity. It is about colonial construction of intellectual perspectives of the colonized population in terms of the latter's approach to China and Chineseness, directly as well as indirectly, in the modern world. However, our task is not merely a post-colonial critique of Orientalism, Euro-centrism and reproduction of hegemonic world views, but an exercise of self-reminder that any drawing of binary can be oversimplistic, each in its own way. For one simple example, the Dutch policy of zoning the Chinese residents in today's Indonesia and the Portuguese policy of mixing them in Macau render European colonialism at best an ambiguous term. We all are actually on multiple agendas at the same time. In fact, societies that experienced more than one colonial regime on our agenda include the Philippines under Spain and the US, Hong Kong and Singapore under the UK and Japan, and Indonesia under Dutch and Japan. Thus, we intend to show a way of self-understanding that does not require discursive construction of border or cultural consumption of any specific "other".

We show, in a partial way and yet maximally, these multiple routs of self-constitution and reconstitution through the use of China and Chineseness as category. Hopefully the revealed manipulation of this third category, romantically as well as antagonistically, is easier than straightforward self-reflection for us all to accept that, coming to identities and relations, none, even subaltern, is politically innocent or capable of epistemological monopoly. In other words, we are equally concerned about how our familiar lenses silence and suppress different others, in addition to how we, in ourselves, suffer silencing and suppression by legacies of former colonial relations. The caveat is possibly that we may lose sufficiently critical and emancipative agency that requires imagination of essential identities to make us self-empowering, resistant and respectable. Our remedy is to mind both the intellectual and the materialistic forces of production that create and limit the range of options in the colonial relations. Therefore, we ask how China and Chineseness constitute the self-understandings of the colonial as well as the colonized and how various colonial relations constitute China and Chineseness differently and evolutionarily.

The Themes of Their Time

We consider colonialism existing in ruling and governance that discriminate against the ruled population, especially in terms of unequal distribution of political, economic and educational opportunities. Thus, colonialism rests upon the institutionalized binary of the ruling and the ruled classes in favor of the former. According to this definition, Chinese Malaysians who can access political and educational resources and own a relatively better-off economic life despite policy discrimination are not a colonized population. In the same vein, Chinese Indonesians are not, either. Both suffer ethnic discrimination rather than colonial discrimination. For another example, Hong Kong, Taiwan, and Macau where the Chinese regimes have taken over in the aftermath of the British and the Japanese colonial regimes, respectively, do not qualify as colonial either, in the sense that no discriminative policy deprives the ruled population of equal opportunities available to the Chinese migrants even though the regime does not share power with the people.

Hegemonic, usually "Western" and colonial theories and methods are not only inevitable but also useful for self-interrogating scholars of former colonies to understand and present their own paths (Wang 2017). However, efforts to develop indigenous theories and methods are increasingly apparent and politically correct almost everywhere in post-colonial communities (Aydinli and Biltekin 2017; Shimizu 2019). The reason for this is that postcolonial actors seek to account for those conditions perceived to be forcefully re/constructed, discursively silenced or practically re/appropriated in the academic practices at post-colonial sites. However, this is actually not an experience limited to the colonized. The chapter by Hiroyuki Ogawa, for example, demonstrates how the struggle over a proper colonial policy led Japanese scholars to seek inspiration from the British counterpart, Japan's colonial officials and Chinese at different colonial sites, e.g., Manchukuo and Taiwan, to the effect of uncertainties in the colonial subjectivity. In Vietnam, according to Tran Tien Nguyen, French knowledge on Indochina engendered a bifurcative scope consciousness composed of an Indochina identity on one hand and sub-regional or national identity in Laos and Cambodia, on the other hand, resulting in China's perpetual involvement in local political balance.

The rise of China, differently felt in the world and inconsistently felt over time, exerts pressure on the intellectual community to defend or reorient their discourses on China. Such a rise has engendered both challenges and opportunities to post-colonial communities. Tina Clemente, for example, shows that the American colonial impacts on the thriving interest in China has dwarfed the history on how Spaniards had relied on the Chinese migrants to the Philippines, serving liaison with Europe in the remote past and how more recently Chinese descendants still engulfed their consciousness in the Chinese Civil War. Nevertheless, Chinese reflections, past as well as contemporary, can influence post-colonial communities, thus creating bifurcating understandings of "China" and "Chineseness" among indigenous populations continuously despite the overwhelming power rivalry between Washington and Beijing in the current century. Harryanto Aryodiguno, for example, contrarily traces the difficult choices of allying strategy by different Chinese Indonesian groups during and in the aftermath of WWII, which have been plaguing intra-ethnic relations as well as their indigenous relations in subsequent decades. Aryodiguno's sensibilities simultaneously trace the Chinese network before the anti-Chinese riots in 1965 in the current open-minded approach toward China under Joko Widodo during the rise of China.

China itself is a conceptual home to an endless array of emerging narratives, making attempts not only at self-reinterpretation but also border-crossing to the effect of complicating, if not obscuring, China as category. Relearning about China can be done in various incompatible ways. For example, Chinese resources, once acquired, could balance or even transcend former colonial legacies. Pervaiz Mahesar juxtaposes China scholarship written in English and travelogues written in indigenous Urdu to show the opening of new epistemology arising out of actual encountering of the Pakistani writers in China and eyeing readers outside of the former colonial circles. Conversely, Chinese perspectives could be disputed to strategize an exit to unwanted historiography as Chih-yu Shih and Raoul Bunskoek juxtaposes those relying on the colonial construction of Chineseness and those estranging from it. Together, they enable an undefinable Taiwan identity, which is bitterly disintegrative and yet too formidably irreconcilable and deterring for any potential future conqueror to want to tackle. In Hong Kong, according to Mariko Tanigaki, Chinese cultural resources peculiarly served the colonial system to either prevent the influence of revolution spreading from the Mainland or convince the colonized population that the ruler respected its culture.

Understanding China could thus substitute direct Western-style self-interrogation at post-colonial sites and block the process of epistemological realignment that could produce integrative post-colonial self-identifications. Jungmin Seo, for example, finds that Japanese colonialism as well as the Cold-War ally — the US — intervened in the understanding of the historically significant Other for Korea, which had been China. The ruptures they brought in turn disallow the formation of any consistent tendency in contemporary scholarship on China. A comparable trajectory in Hong Kong is noteworthy; therefore, as Chun-wah Chin argues, the colonial legacies of denationalized Chinese pedagogy under the British rule contributed to the evolution of Japan studies in Hong Kong as well as Hong Kong's economic relations with Japan, which reversely likewise provides multiple lenses on the

Chineseness of Hong Kong. A further complication emerges in New Zealand as China's rise in the recent decade has become an intervening factor in the local quest for bilateral cultural integration. Pauling Keating details the uneasy encountering of a history of decolonization and the recent call for multilateralism that is partially to calm the aversion toward the Chinese migrant community. Macau, however, has become an outlier in this regard to the extent that Cátia Miriam Costa describes it as almost an international rather than colonial site whose very early days of civilizational encountering had witnessed public publications printed in three languages in parallel — Portuguese, English and Chinese.

Given the multiple tracks under the persistent circumstance of colonial relations, whether or not to ally with someone and if so with whom, accordingly calls for a decision that either reflects a desire for change or comforts a quest for dependence. Mohsen Fergani traces the career path of a Chinese scholar who was determined to realign China and the Arab world through mutuality of their ancient classics in such a way that their mutual constitution could sideline historical imperialism and the formation of their modern self. The similar effort appeared in the Chinese

Singaporean-Malaysian community as Peter Chow Bin Ngeow reports the rise and fall of Nanyang University, especially the aborted promise of preserving a cultural legacy embedded in the practices of the significant Chinese population in Southeast Asia. Its fall reflects the tension between uncertain identities that have existed in the colonial relations left by the British, with which the university community failed to cope effectively. Shirley Chan interrogated the possibility of reviving a holistic approach to China whereby concerns for humanity connect Australia to its European identity and yet ironically preserves the Euro-centric view of China as deviant from capitalism and modernity. Such ambivalence toward China reflects Australia's undetermined choice of partnership between the West and Asia. China studies makes a quintessential statement of identity in Australia about Asia and China both being constituting components of its multiculturalism.

There are forgotten pasts, though, because they do not appear either politically correct or intellectually systematic. Portuguese Macau displays more harmonious relations than most post-colonial sites could have imagined with otherness and sameness simultaneously registered in the local views of China, according to Cátia Miriam Costa, due to a long track of international encountering taking place before bitter colonialism. The Sino-Indian connection brought forth by colonialism is a case in point. Reena Marwah collects from sporadic historical accounts of how British colonialism exploited Indian producers and Chinese population. The subaltern populations in the two societies were not aware of their relationships crafted through the East Indian Company, nor the presumably impressive and memorable joint battle they fought together against the invader during the Opium War, as Reena Marwah recollects the story. Later in the bilateral history, according to Swaran Singh, the unavailing ideal of cultural tradition promoted by Rabindranath Tagore in China, for another example, used to inspire a romantic image of China's anti-imperialism. The exploitative links in the colonial relations that had connected China and India have found shelter in the rivalry of the two rising giants.

With the Chinese authorities enthusiastically promoting China's cultural and economic charm and pampering fears toward its mounting political influence, as well as the populations of post-colonial neighbors voluntarily or involuntarily mingling with Chinese migrants, tourists and businessmen, post-colonial societies in the vicinity of China have a much broader and yet less consistent or stable range of choices to reconstitute their self-identities.

The authors were initially requested to ponder the following research questions. To begin, in what ways do colonial legacies constitute scholarship on China, and do they continue with strength or do they decline? Some chapters, for example, those on Hong Kong, Taiwan, Indonesia, Korea and Egypt, note colonial legacies as exerting influences through various vehicles such as (1) historically engendered cleavages during the independence struggle that reduce migrant Chinese to agents of outside China, (2) colonial modernity that downgrades Chinese civilization, or

(3) the common cause of anti-imperialism that lays a sense of intimacy toward China. On the other hand, colonial legacies may have appeared as losing ground in India, for example, but a cyclical recollection of pre-modern engagements is intellectually plausible if volition emerges. In New Zealand, the colonial context of Maori-Anglo bilateralism constrains, probably decreasingly, the evolution of multilateralism, partially informed by the surge of the Chinese migrant community. In Japan, for another case of declining legacies, liberal perspectives discursively overtake the colonial studies and, in Vietnam, socialism and historical traditions attend primarily to China rather than colonial France. Most noticeably in terms of declining legacies are the cases of the Philippines and Australia where, progressively, China or Chinese studies have an embedded interest in mundane affairs. Finally, a less imposing colonial legacy of Portugal has left a more integrated view on China in Macau.

Second, are postcolonial intellectuals sensitive to Chinese perspectives on China? For those in the Sinophone circles and, peculiarly, East Asia Sinologists in Korea, Japan, Macau and Vietnam, Chinese sources continue to impact upon what people read in their quest for knowledge regarding China. In contrast, the Anglophone circles such as the Philippines, Australia, New Zealand, India, Pakistan and Singapore–Malaysia, rely more on English sources to understand their China. That said, a shared policy community between China and Pakistan uniquely enables the latter to become highly sensitive to the Chinese perspectives. Learned societies in Hong Kong, Japan, Taiwan and Korea do not have one dominant linguistic source, and thus their internal communication may suffer disintegration. In practice, relying on the Chinese source is in itself a strategic statement on the partnership with China, as opposed to the former colonial networks, and hence a politically sensitive issue. This is likewise a thorny issue among Chinese Indonesians, who vastly differ toward their indigenous, *vis-à-vis*, Chinese, identities.

Third, do post-colonial intellectuals intend to bridge the gap between post-colonial, colonial and Chinese perspectives on China?

Some chapters indicate a widespread motive amongst intellectuals to act as bridge, for example, Japan between East and West, Hong Kong between China and Japan as well as China and the West, India between China and Europe, Taiwan between China and Japan, and Chinese southeast Asian scholars between China and Southeast Asia. However, no community seems to have any consensus on the merit of the bridge role conception. Alternatively, there is the potential for reconnection to the Chinese intellectual community in some chapters. India, for one, is a possible site of initiative. Egyptian Sinologists may desire an enhanced relationship. Moreover, the lure of re-Sinicization, first economically and then culturally, attained a following among some Sino-phone circles in all communities.

Based upon historical practices of colonialism, a number of different categories of former colonial sites help make up the list of chapters. The first category includes primarily former British colonies, including Egypt, India, New Zealand, and Australia. The second includes former Japanese colonies, including Korea and Taiwan. The third includes sites that were under the political control of Great Britain and Japan in sequence, including Malaysia, Hong Kong and Singapore. The fourth has to do with other European colonialisms such as Portugal in Macau, France in Vietnam, and Spain and the United States in the Philippines.

Plan and Structure of the Book

Contemporary literature has not reflected upon colonial legacies in former colonies beyond sited resistance. It is additionally ironic that resistance comes primarily from post-colonial intellectuals that have received training at former colonial establishments. Consequently, resistance reproduces Euro-centrism. A comparative agenda of wider scope is called for in order to problematize "the colonial" — its purpose, processes and undecidable consequences.

We cannot answer everything. In fact, we can only answer those in our small world, such as how such bigger questions can be approached on a particular agenda. Our project asks and compares primarily how much influence Britain and Japan still have, directly as well as indirectly, on their former colonies. Such a comparison allows us to complicate the stereotypical agenda of post-colonial resistance and understand the intellectual exchanges between the colonial and the post-colonial. The inclusion of Japan could reduce Euro-centrism although, arguably, it could also reinforce it. This multi-sited design can move the analysis beyond nationalist standpoints.

The rise of China provides an opportunity in that the rise engenders an all-round pressure of re/deconstruction to most former colonial powers, challenging all former colonies to choose between the colonial, the Chinese and the sited perspectives.

Note also that Japan has been the only colonial power with a post-colonial identity. Japanese intellectual history encompasses a conscious effort to position Japan between Europe and China, hence forming a contrast to European colonialism.

Together, the chapter authors interrogate a number of questions based upon the idea that scholarship on and understanding of China and Chinese people involves a complex identity strategy embedded in colonial relations and the improvisational readings and analyses of the historical situation each selected as the point of their intellectual engagement. Some of us explore how the evolving understandings of the Chinese nation, people and civilization at post-colonial sites mix colonial, Chinese and sited geocultural resources to reveal a fragmented relationality that constitutes the self-identity of the post-colonial site. Others compare the intellectual perspectives on China of Japan and Great Britain that are or are not reproduced and reappropriated in former colonies and why this is the case. Still others try to understand the practices that have, to a certain degree, fixed the contemporary Chinese Southeast Asians in the eyes of the indigenous population to an imagined resemblance to China or, alternatively, released them from past relations.

There are millions of ways to structure our endeavor, which can be connected differently on various different joints of engagement. The book is currently divided into three sections in accordance with a rough relational frame, depending on the major relational contexts that the respective chapter authors choose to tackle. This does not mean that their analyses are restricted to one relational context. In fact, most authors touch upon multiple aspects of colonial legacies. Neither does the structure of the book suggest that those primary cases of post-colonial society which chapter authors choose to study are associated with only one string of colonial relations each. In fact, it is not unlikely at all for one portion of a post-colonial community to engage continuously in emancipation from past colonial dominance, while another portion practices that reproduce colonial relations.

Rearranged Colonial Relations — In the Eyes of the Colonized Self

The first section of the book studies how past colonial legacies could continue to provide a meaningful reference for the contemporary to understand and study China and Chinese people. It could be a kind of memory that associates China in a shared spirit of resistance and awaits the contemporary to recollect in due course. This might require a conscious effort to prepare or a conducive event to warm it up. Indeed, a romanticized China up from imperialism inspired intellectuals everywhere, but more strongly in the post-colonial world including South Asia and North Africa. However, the reference to colonial legacies could contrarily be made of an aversive instinct that reflects the colonial segregation policy and targets a Chinese population as either an outsider or a scapegoat. Such past segregation has infused an indigenous consciousness to undergird nation building during the period of decolonization. Estrangement from the local Chinese migrants insinuates ambivalence toward China and its transformation form a Socialist state to a globalization state.

Reena Marwah points to the lesser-discussed narratives of the relationship in Chapter 1. These aspects include the British-dominated trade in opium, tea, cotton and indigo, which themselves fostered writings on China by Indian authors and critical perspectives on India by Chinese writers. It is well known that commercial connections engendered the settling of Chinese communities in India and Indian communities in China. In India, it was Calcutta (Kolkata) that provided space for a Chinese settlement in India. There was also a trend for Indian and Chinese intellectuals to forge ties that were independent of the West. While compulsions of diplomacy have perhaps obscured the study of the multi-dimensional interactions between the people of these two countries, enhanced understanding must be achieved by endeavouring to uncover the truth through a focus on dialogue and shared experience.

Swaran Singh follows up through the contemporary period. It was against this — the backdrop of China and India growing adrift — that the colonial frame of their interactions, and their regional and global diplomatic encounters as newly liberated nations, became vulnerable to cold war dynamics that was to greatly circumscribe their millennia-long civilizational equations of mutual respect and trust. Sovereign states of China and India were to now become territorial states with fixed boundaries and damaged whatever had been gained in building India's pre-independence China-consciousness. Some of these linkages were especially molded and evolved by India's iconic leaders like Tagore, Nehru, Subhash, Mahatma Gandhi as also by several other revolutionary and radical leaders of India's freedom struggle, yet the fact that China's liberation struggle was led by a violent revolution of the Chinese Communist Party and India's peaceful transfer of power happened under the leadership of largely British-trained Indian Congress leadership pushed both sides adrift.

Such mutual estrangement has never plagued Egyptian Sinologists. According to Mohsen Fergani, in general, a quick reading can reveal that they focused on two lines regarding China. One of them addressed the renaissance of China and the needs of its development, which made the period preceding the founding of the People's Republic of China in 1949 a neglected history. The other was mainly preoccupied with the history and traditions of China, without paying attention to the developments in its contemporary life in the last 60 or 70 years of its history. Starting from Majian's efforts to establish cultural sites between the Arabic and Chinese languages could lead to a possible integration point in Sinology, from an Arab perspective, representing a middle area or a third space in the history of cognitive efforts devoted to studying its literature. In fact, Majian represents the middle objective point between two extremes in the context of time, history and location. For him, legacy is connected to identity at the level of nationalism, and it is a link between the Arab-Islamic culture and the intellectual and psychological foundations of Chinese civilization. In addition, it is a part connected to the civilized world, both in the interaction between the dialogue and the major cultural centers (Euro/American) affecting the network of international relations, and in the conflict with it.

Contrary to Sino-Arabic solidarity in face of Western imperialism, Pervaiz Ali Mahesar's chapter painstakingly traces an emerging Urdu literature on China. Chapter 4 seeks to answer how China Studies were pursued in and influenced by the British colonial legacies in the decolonized Indian Subcontinent. The existing scholarship on China in the postcolonial state (Pakistan) shows remarkable growth. Interestingly, China Studies have been vehemently pursued by the post-colonial state intellectuals since many decades. Hence, this chapter examines the British English language as a sequel to the post-colonial legacy, as well as in Urdu languages with a view to understand the positioning of China Studies in English and Urdu (travelogues) in the decolonized state. This study reveals that China Studies in the English language are more dominant, whereas the post-colonial writings on China by indigenous writers in the form of Urdu travelogues seem to have less influence on the overall China discourse in Pakistan. It concluded that the growth in China Studies, either through indigenous languages or English language, even in the midst of the influence of the British legacies, has the potential to enhance a greater understanding on China at the postcolonial site.

The strongest case of colonial legacy for this book is probably in Chapter 5. Ngeow Chow-Bing reviews the history of Nanyang

University and asks the question why there is no or very little legacy of Nanyang University in the China Studies of Singapore and Malaysia, despite Nanyang University being the only Chinese university in the region from 1956 to 1980. Nanyang University could have played an important role in establishing the academic community of China Studies in Singapore and Malaysia. But the very Chineseness of Nanyang University troubled the authorities, from the British colonialists to the ruling governments in Malaysia and Singapore, and resulted in persistent tensions that led to the eventual closure of the university. Nanyang was politically incorrect both in terms of the Chinese language it adopted as official and the Chinese ethnicity of its teacher and student body. The Cold War was equally detrimental because it was believed, amid the anti-Communist atmosphere, that the Chinese intellectuals at Nanyang were potentially targets of Communist infiltration.

Indirect legacies could be powerfully negative, too. Harryanto Aryodiguno recollects the discursive condition in which Ethnic Chinese are considered alien to the extent the indigenous population sees them as more Chinese than Indonesian. The intellectual history of seeing them as mainly Chinese continues to haunt contemporary ethnic politics. Chapter 6 studies how the colonial legacies in the Dutch period may have intellectually perpetuated the alien image of Chinese Indonesian and connected them with an imagined threat of Chinese Communism of the PRC. The separation policy under the Dutch colonial governance became the origin of the discrimination of the Indonesian nation against its "own" people after Indonesia's independence. Separating indigenous with Chinese citizens was a colonial political agenda. The Dutch are afraid of unity and solidarity between the two ethnic groups. The Dutch government undertook the zoning system in which the Chinese ethnic were gathered at a place. This separation politics is an attempt to divide and differentiate between Indonesian indigenous and Chinese people, especially since at that time Indonesia had not yet known nationalism.

China as Relational Other — In the Eyes of the Lost Self

Colonialism affected the subsequent understanding of China and Chinese people most apparently among neighbors of China that had once fallen prey to colonialism. Colonialism imposed a transformation of worldview that centered on China. Colonial modernity even turned the hierarchical system of the Middle Kingdome upside down as colonies were able to achieve equal, if not a higher, level of modernity. China and its subordinating neighbors similarly subscribed to Western learning. The intellectual emancipation of the colony could be imagined in its overtaking the former cultural center, although this simultaneously reproduced its inferiority in the colonial relations. Irony existed between the enhanced sense of pride *vis-à-vis* backward China and reproduced dependence on colonial modernity as the key point of self-referencing. It was almost inevitable that China's neighbors continued to depend on the US, which substitutes for their former colonial masters to become the center of the world. The US, the former master, and China made an impossible mix or unattainable layers to undergird the post-colonial identities.

In Chapter 7, for example, Jungmin Seo provides a brief sketch of the intellectual history of China studies in Korea, focusing on the colonial and post-colonial intellectual conditions that determined Korean society's understanding of China. The most important colonial legacy of Korean understanding of China is, he argues, that the historical experiences of Korean epistemology prohibited the formation of coherent, continuous and accumulative knowledge about China. The pursuit of knowledge about China was fundamentally circumvented primarily by the difficulty of defining "Korea" under colonial conditions. Though China as the other was well established through the nation-making processes, the nature of the Chinese otherness in the Korean epistemology has always been unstable, vague and unidentifiable due to the very nature of colonialism that Koreans had to experience. Unlike the global colonial experiences that presuppose the dichotomy of "us" and "the West," colonial experiences and legacies in Korea are conditioned by a number of heterogeneous processes, the dismantlement of the Confucius worldview, the domination of non-conventional imperial power — Japan, and the beginning of the post-colonial time at the center of the global Cold War. With these conditions, post-colonial Korea's epistemology toward China is not characterized by existence of a certain colonial tendency but the lack of tendency itself in an ironic way.

Mariko Tanigaki deals with a peculiar historical situation where the British colonial government saw Chinese humanity studies functional to its rule in Hong Kong. This is the concept behind Chapter 8. How, then, had this intervened in the English environment of higher education? English is one of the most explicit British colonial legacies in contemporary Hong Kong. In fact, the establishment of the Department of Chinese in the British-style University of Hong Kong is an exceptional development. Such progress illustrates the consideration that the Hong Kong government has given to prevent the growth of anti-British sentiments. The establishment of the People's Republic of China resulted in an influx of migrant scholars to Hong Kong, which served as the foundation of the Chinese University of Hong Kong. The Cold War also contributed to changes in Chinese studies in Hong Kong. The emergence of contemporary Chinese studies in Hong Kong served as a window to the mainland. This development has four types of actors: exiled scholars from the 1910s to the 1930s, migrant scholars from the mainland in the 1950s and the 1960s. Since the 1970s, two actors played an important roles; (1) non-Chinese scholars who can understand Chinese Language and (2) English speaking Chinese scholars. The latter includes Taiwan-origin Chinese scholars and Hong Kong local-born Chinese scholars in the 1970s–1980s, as well as migrant scholars from Greater China including the mainland and Taiwan since the late 1980s.

Further complicating the post-colonial condition in Hong Kong is the practices of Japanese studies that reflect perspectives on China. In Chapter 9, Chun Wah Chin reviews this peculiar issue through the seemingly small scale of Japanese studies in Hong Kong. Nevertheless, Japan/Japanese language studies can actually be considered as the third largest area/language studies among higher education institutions. It follows China/Chinese language studies and English language studies. Such maturity is also observable in non-academic areas. Given the dynamic and diverse relationship between Hong Kong and Japan, the analysis of Japanese studies and its relation to Chineseness and Hong Kong's subjectivity may provide a new perspective on the relationship between the two entities. This chapter first reviews the general situation of Japanese studies in Hong Kong. This review is followed by a discussion on how intellectuals have started their Japanese studies because of Chineseness and how they have participated in Hong Kong society by creating narratives about Japan. Behind such participation and narratives are the sense of belongingness, identity and emotions toward the local society and nation. All of these elements create a diverse and vivid picture for the review of Japanese studies from a special perspective. To understand the development of Japanese studies and the issues related to Hong Kong's subjectivity, we examine the relations between Chineseness, British colonialism and the memory of Japanese imperialism.

Chih-yu Shih's Chapter 10 uses Taiwan to demonstrate how identity strategy cannot help but be always varied upon personal conditions and choices. He studies how colonial legacies constitute the intellectual growth of people within former colonies. This appears intuitive. The chapter contributes to this subject by first adding the empirical case of Taiwan to conventional understandings. Taiwan contributes to the subject in the sense that decolonization was not carried out by an anti- or post-colonial indigenous regime, but unconventionally by an exile regime from China instead. However, the exile regime looked down upon the colonized population, whose dignity ironically had to rely on colonial modernity as opposed to the arguably backward civilization represented by the exile regime. Since Taiwan is likewise a Chinese society, its take on colonial modernity necessarily bifurcates. The chapter thus further contributes to the production of post-colonial knowledge and the construction of post-colonial selves by complicating the categories of "China" and "Chineseness." Methodologically, the chapter contributes to a creative open agenda that allows constant reinterpretations of the empirical data by readers as well as those under study.

Macau appears, in comparison, more advantaged in sustaining self-respect and self-integrity due to its integrated kind of transnational perspectives embedded in its historically non-confrontational encountering with the world. According to Cátia Miriam Costa's Chapter 11, Macau embodies two strong cultural and social legacies, the Chinese and the Portuguese, and the vibrant Macanese space in between. This evidence also brings to light the specificity of Macau in the region and within the context of Portuguese colonialism. The territory had, from the beginning, particular characteristics in its fluid governance model of political coexistence, which gave place to a social and cultural interacting coexistence and at the same time and occasioned a "communicating hybridity" characterized by syncretism and generative interaction. From the trends of coexistence and syncretism, a creative intellectual atmosphere developed that allowed for the encounter and crossing of diverse perspectives not only on China. Chapter 11 reconstructs from the intellectual viewpoint the convergence and the diversity of the imaginary of China and the Chinese. Sameness and otherness coexist and sometimes mingled, embodying the diversity existing in the territory, which became one of the major elements of Macau's character.

Emerging Pluralist Relations — In the Eyes of the Autonomous Self

Tran Tien Nguyen treats the Chinese and the French influences in Vietnam, especially the evolution of the latter's knowledge on Indochina. He stresses that, before the French came to Indochina, Vietnam had been ruled by China for hundreds of years, and after centuries of resistance the Vietnam people threw their Chinese rulers and became independent. French then took control over the whole of Vietnam from 1887 to 1954 and influenced Vietnamese in many aspects such as their language, religion, literature as well as its cultures, laws, form of government, educational system and technological achievements. They have traditionally taken pride in what they called their civilization Français. Chapter 12 briefly examines the presence of China and French in Indochina and the French's scholarship in Indochina and, second, it examines French Indochina's scholarship on Sinology by looking at some publications of the École *française d'Extrême-Orient* and contributors on Sinology.

Would colonial relations pass more easily in one's mind in settlers' colonies or in the colonial masters' societies? This would mean the substitution of a broader, more general, and perhaps less historical self-concept to relativize the colonial history that one has either suffered or inflicted upon others. In settlers' colonies, the early migrants from the colonial powers constituted the elite strata nonetheless and remained in a relationship of goodwill with the colonial forces during decolonization. For the colonial powers, colonial history may be full of unjust relations but continue to undergird a sense of civilizational superiority. For scholars of a past colonial power, conscious adherence to certain self-reminders can contribute to the adoption of a liberal and national perspective to avoid seeing China in a prior colonial lens. For a settlers' colony, lack of historical animosity toward China can be conducive to breeding a pluralist view that China is not a civilizational alien. All this does not preclude those from an exploited subaltern colony from also adopting a less emotionally driven tendency in seeing China, except that this is relatively implausible in exploitation colonialism than in settler colonialism.

In Chapter 13, Hiroyuki Ogawa records the difficult encountering of liberal Sinologists during the colonial time of Japan and yet gradually resumed their morale after colonialism to compose a peculiar legacy in Japan's intellectual history. As the Japanese Empire expanded and became more aggressive in the 1930s, the arguments by Japan's liberal intellectuals to reform the Japanese Empire along the lines of the British Commonwealth of Nations lost much of the momentum. In reality, the Japanese Empire did not become like the Commonwealth and instead expanded from Manchuria and Mongolia to the rest of Mainland China. Particularly after the outbreak of the Sino-Japanese War in 1937, the ideology of *Großraumordnung* (large-area order)[1] was pursued based on certain versions of Pan-Asianism such as a "New Order in East Asia" (1938) and then a "Greater East Asia Co-Prosperity Sphere" (1940). In those versions of Pan-Asianism, the Japanese government and its right-wing ideologues considered Japan as a leading nation in Asia. After World War II, Yanaihara, a leading liberal Sinologist was elected to be the president of the University of Tokyo during the period 1951–1957. In post-war Japan, chairs of colonial policy studies at universities were abolished and replaced by those of new subjects such as world economy and development economics. Although Japanese liberal intellectuals faced substantial difficulties and were forced to change their opinions or lost their jobs during the 1930s and early 1940s, the trajectories of imperial universities, Yanaihara, and colonial policy studies, for instance, demonstrated Japan's transformation from the pre-war militaristic Pan-Asianist empire to the post-war "liberal" pro-Western ally of the United States.

In Chapter 14, Pauline Keating discovers a neglected parallel between Anglo-Maori bilateralism and the evolution of Chinese studies in New Zealand. The formal study of China in New Zealand universities began in the 1950s. Maori language and culture studies were introduced at approximately the same time, and this is not entirely a coincidence. Proposals to get both Asian and Maori studies into the educational curriculum had roots in post-war critiques of Western imperialism. Nevertheless, the two fields of study did not develop in tandem nor recognize a common cause until the 1990s, when the expanding discourse on race relations was exposing the deep-rooted racism that is a legacy of Britain's colonization of New Zealand. This chapter examines the

---

[1] In Germany, *Großraumordnung* was famously advocated by Carl Schmitt, when he championed Nazi Germany's external policy, which was practically intended to rule Europe.

roles played by China scholars in New Zealanders' search for a post-colonial identity. It reviews the early history of China Studies in universities and then analyzes three important developments in the late 20th century — developments that widened opportunities for China scholars to participate more actively in decolonization drives in the public sphere. First, since the 1980s, decolonization and, specifically, the displacement of anglo-centric monoculturalism have been energized by the widely respected Waitangi Tribunal and its promotion of biculturalism. Second, the New Zealand government's rapidly expanding engagement with China is giving "China knowledge" the status of a "national asset." Third, the very large growth of the Chinese community in New Zealand since immigration reforms in 1987 and 1991 has helped to widen the movement against racism and to drive the search for ways of melding biculturalism with multiculturalism.

In Chapter 15, Shirley Chan traces the transformation of China studies from a colonial to a multicultural agenda in Australia. Chinese Studies as an intellectual discipline in Australia has been a colonial phenomenon since its first establishment in the mid-20th century. At the same time, Chinese Studies in Australian universities has undergone a process of reconstruction and adjustment over the decades under the modern university system. Since Australia's independence from Britain in 1901, the dynamics of modernity and historical reality of post-colonial conditions, the contemporary political and socio-economic environments and its cultural relationships with countries in Asia, Europe and America are constantly shaping Australia's nationhood beset with complexity in its evolution. This complexity has been understood in different ways — politically, economically and culturally — which have influenced questions of our individual and collective identity and our sense of belonging; questions which are crucial for understanding the development of Chinese Studies in Australia in the last few decades. This chapter provides a brief trajectory about Chinese Studies in Australian Universities in the context of the British colonial legacy; how such a legacy is fading, and so is the traditional Sinological studies of taking China as a culture or civilization to be understood, and how the tradition is being replaced by contemporary China Studies seeking solutions for, or understanding of, China as a "political" or "economic" power to be tackled by the West.

Exceptional but nonetheless plausible is the case of China studies in the Philippines, where a disciplinary identity powerfully emerged, albeit one with a broader agenda that includes Chinese Filipino studies. Tina S. Clemente reviews the multifarious characteristics of China Studies in the Philippines in Chapter 16. First, as an academic practice in tertiary education, it is approached through varied fields and modalities such as, but not limited to, area studies, international relations, cultural/ethnic studies, history and economics. Second, as a subject of scholarship, it is inclusive in that it covers any aspect of China and its people, the Chinese diaspora, and Chinese in the Philippines as distinct streams of inquiry. This chapter attempts to interrogate contemporary China Studies in the Philippines by considering China Studies as a current academic practice and scholarly inquiry. I present areas for particular rumination using my experience at the University of the Philippines (U.P.), which is considered the Philippines' national university, and in particular, the U.P. Asian Center (U.P.A.C.), the graduate unit in which China Studies, as part of its degree programs, is formally lodged. In the succeeding discussion, I begin by locating the beginnings of the interest in studying China in the colonial historical context. The next section then discusses four aspects: China Studies in terms of academic program structure and content, pedagogical concerns, the U.P.A.C.'s journal production and the University's China-related thesis production.

References

Aydinli, Ersel and Gonca Biltekin. 2017. *Widening the World of International Relations: Homegrown Theorizing*. Routledge.

Gungwu, Wang. 2017. Keynote address Southeast Asia: Imperial themes. *International Journal of Asia Pacific Studies* 13 (2): 179–192.

Shimizu, Kosuke. 2019. *Critical International Relations Theories in East Asia: Relationality, Subjectivity, and Pragmatism*. London: Routledge.

Part I

Rearranged Colonial Relations — In the Eyes of the Colonized Self

Chapter 1

Colonial Connections through Commerce and Culture: Revisiting China Studies in India

Reena Marwah

ICSSR Senior Fellow Secretary General, Association of Asia Scholars, New Delhi, India

Introduction

The study of China has undoubtedly been impacted when viewed through the experience and understanding of British India.

It is well known that the earliest India–China exchanges were through Chinese pilgrims. Thus, the sources of information about India in China were through them. Although there were hundreds of pilgrims to India in the first millennium, the most well known among the Chinese pilgrims were Faxian, Xuanzang and Yijing, who gained fame due to their detailed travel records. By the seventh century, most of Asia, China, India and their respective spheres of influence, were fully integrated into this network of religious and commercial intercourse between India and China (Sen 2003, p. 2).

These pilgrims oriented the Chinese with Buddhist texts, knowledge on rituals and ceremonies as well as acquainted themselves with the diverse facets of Indian society. In addition, they narrated incidents of the miraculous powers of the Buddha as well as about the wisdom drawn from Buddhist teachings. China received information about Indian culture, including its languages through the translation of Buddhist texts and through the diaries of Chinese monks making pilgrimages to India. Thus, it was their travel records which provided details of this land (India) that was perceived as civilized.

A Khotanese Saka document[1] (Ch. 1.0021a) in the Stein Collection housed at the British Library in England testifies to the Buddhist traffic between India and China through the southern Taklamakan region in the tenth and eleventh centuries (Sen 2006, p. 117).

According to Tansen Sen, when this document is viewed in perspective, it is evident that the supply of north Indian products, including saffron, to the Chinese markets was undertaken by traders entering China through this Gilgit–Chilas–Khotan route, situated between Northwest India and China. This not only gives a vivid description of the markets and Buddhist communities along this route but also substantiates the fact that trade between India and China had continued even after the transfer of sugar-making technology (Sen 2006, p. 114).

After the seventh century, there was a shift from exchanges through Buddhism to exchanges of goods. The British East India Company, comprised of a few thousand capitalists, set up in 1600, initially to trade with South and Southeast Asia, ended up colonizing most parts of the Indian subcontinent as well as trading mainly with China.[2]

---

[1] Saka languages are known in documents from Khotan and Tumshuq, north-east of Kàshghar, belonging to the pre-Islamic period. To Khotan, scholars came from China to receive and study the new faith. See https://www.cambridge.org/core/books/the-cambridge-history-of-iran/khotanese-saka-literature/EC44ED443465EDBCF50C53327C6BD497 for further details. Accessed on 16 May, 2018.

[2] The East India company's encounters with foreign competitors eventually required it to assemble its own military and administrative departments, thereby becoming an imperial power in its own right, though the British government began to rein it in by the late 18th century. Before the British Parliament created a government-controlled policymaking body with the Regulating Act of 1773 and the India Act 11 years later, shareholders' meetings made decisions about Britain's *de facto* colonies in the East. The British government took away the Company's monopoly in 1813, and after 1834 it worked as the government's agency until the 1857 India Mutiny when the Colonial Office took full control. The East India

Partha Chatterjee explores how a supposed tragedy,[3] known as the "Black hole of Calcutta" in which European lives were lost, paved the ideological foundations for the "civilizing" force of British imperial rule and territorial control in India. The East India Company's monopoly was taken over completely by The British government in 1813. Chatterjee takes a close look at the justifications of modern empire by liberal thinkers, international lawyers and conservative traditionalists, and examines the intellectual and political responses of the colonized, including those of Bengali nationalists (Chatterjee 2012).

It would be appropriate to mention here that the Britishers brought about changes in the field of education, with great emphasis on modern subjects and the use of the English language. It was in 1858 that three colleges were established in the cities of Bombay, Madras and Calcutta. It was in Calcutta that the earliest nationalist movement took place, bringing together those articulating their vision of freedom in the English medium. Studying China has hence been through the writings of western scholars including the British.

India and China's shared experiences against the British are highlighted here. This engagement based on shared anti-imperialism brought together the Indian and Chinese soldiers during the Taiping Rebellion in the middle of the 19th century. The Britishers sent Indian forces to suppress the Rebellion; however, several Indian soldiers crossed over to the Chinese side and fought with them. The second incident was during the Boxer Rebellion in north China in 1900. It was an Indian — Thakur Gadadhar Singh — who expressed deep anger against the British for the

---

Company went out of existence in 1873. For more details, read http://www.victorianweb.org/history/empire/india/eic.html. Accessed on 9 May 2018.

[3] When Siraj, the ruler of Bengal, overran the British settlement of Calcutta in 1756, he allegedly jailed 146 European prisoners overnight in a cramped prison. Of the group, 123 died of suffocation. While this episode was never independently confirmed, the story of "the black hole of Calcutta" was widely circulated and seen by the British public as an atrocity committed by savage colonial subjects. *The Black Hole of Empire* follows the ever-changing representations of this historical event and founding myth of the British Empire in India, from the 18th century to the present.

atrocities committed against the Chinese. He later wrote a detailed account entitled *Thirteen Months in China,* documenting the unfair treatment meted out to them (Singh 2017).

It is also well known that British dominated trade in opium, tea, cotton and indigo, and themselves fostered writings on China by Indian authors and critical perspectives on India by Chinese writers. It was mainly commercial connections which engendered the settling of Chinese communities in India and Indian communities in China. In India, Calcutta (Kolkata) is popularly known for providing space for the earliest Chinese settlement. There was also a trend for Indian and Chinese intellectuals to forge ties, that were independent of the West (Sen 2006, p. 1).

Thus, it was a process of gradual change when Sino-Indian trading relations between the seventh and twentieth centuries transformed from Buddhist-dominated exchanges to market-centred commercial transactions, resulting in interactions among communities on both sides, development of urban settlements of migrants as well as a shared resistance to imperialist designs and hostilities (*Ibid*).

This chapter is structured in five sections: This first section — Introduction — is followed by the second which highlights the turbulent trade ties between British India and China. The third explains the two-way movement of people, the fourth focuses on perceptions of British India and China in the colonial period. The conclusion forms the last and fifth section of this chapter.

Trade Ties and Tribulations

By the eighteenth century, the East India Company, which had by then firmly established itself in India, traded woolens from Britain and cotton from Gujarat in India in exchange for Chinese tea, silk and porcelain. This marked the beginning of the triangular trade relations between Britain, India and China. During this time, it was British and even Indian traders like Jamsetjee Jejee Bhoy who made substantial profit from the cotton trade. However, it was the large volume of tea imports from China which had to be paid for in silver by the Britishers. Initially, it was the limited availability of silver which compelled the Britishers to seek other commodities for export to China.

It was then that Opium was discovered as a highly profitable product. After 1820, the primary commodity exported to China was Opium. The opium was grown initially in Bengal and Bihar, by Indian farmers, but was also cultivated in the Malwa region in India's western region. Ironically the cheaper Malwa Opium resulted in the drug being widely sold in China. Toward the end of the 18th century, there was a huge increase in the direct trade between the port of Bombay on the west coast of India and Guangzhou (Canton), initially for the export of raw cotton and, later, opium from India to China. These exports were carried both by the British East India Company as well as by private Indian and Western traders (Encyclopedia Vol. 1, p. 11).

The attempted consolidation by Britain through incorporation of China, of a new Asian and world order for global capitalism through the commodity opium linked India, China and Britain. This helped to increase consumption of British manufactures and thus contributed to British domination in the East (Karl 2002, pp. 253–254).

It was not without a closely-knit network of agents, traders, officials and merchants from Britain, India, America and China that the prohibition on opium by the Chinese could be circumvented.

The addictive and secretive nature of opium trade made it extremely difficult for the Chinese authorities to control. Although Opium was exported to China for a long time, its popularity as an addictive substance grew in the 1820s. When it was used for medicinal purposes, there were only around 2000 chests imported into China a year. But from the 1820s the number rose to more than 20,000 and then later, 40,000 chests.[4] The negative impact of the influx of Opium on the Chinese people including officials, soldiers

---

[4] Madhavi Thampi in an Interview to Shivanand Kanavi; September 21, 2010, *Ghadar Jari Hai*, Vol 4, No 1&2, Jan–June. For the interview, see http://reflections-shivanand.blogspot.in/2010/09/india-china-civilizational-interactions.html. Accessed on 6 May 2018.

and workers was immeasurable — from negative impacts on health, loss of productivity and loss of lives. When the Chinese responded with efforts to ban the trade of Opium, Britain launched the Naval attack on China defeating it in the first Opium war in 1840. The provocation for the war was when Lin, the Commissioner of the Canton ordered almost 20,000 chests of Opium from British ships to be confiscated. The first Opium war lasted for two years and also resulted in a treaty under which Hong Kong was lost by China to Britain for 150 years. In addition, five Chinese ports including Canton and Shanghai were to allow the entry of foreign traders.[5]

In India, the memory and the connection of the Opium war is not well known as the wars were fought beyond the territory of India. The Britishers wreaked havoc not only in China where thousands of Chinese people died but also on India's rural peasants and their land ownings. The first and salient India connection to the opium trade was that the poppy plants were grown in India. The cotton farmers were forced to cede their land for poppy cultivation, which was then sent for processing to Opium factories in Bihar. Ironically, while the farmers were being exploited by the Britishers, the profitable business led to Parsi businessmen amassing wealth. While Mumbai and its businessmen flourished, the poor farmers of Bihar and Bengal were ravaged.

Opium revenue was a substantial source of profit for the British in India, as these profits made up a considerable percentage of both total British revenues from India and total Indian exports. There were two economic indicators used in evaluating the opium trade: the annual record of official monies received and the number of chests exported. The Opium and Customs Departments of British India compiled the data collected on opium revenues during the period. According to John F. Richards, the data collected was mostly accurate. Over the period 1842–1880, opium revenue on an average was about 15% of India's total revenue. In 1843, opium became the second largest source of revenue for India, its

---

[5] http://www.bl.uk/reshelp/findhelpregion/asia/china/guidesources/chinatrade/index.html. Accessed on 9 May 2018.

revenue being more than that generated by customs and stamp taxes combined. From 1842 to 1859, opium comprised 31.5% of all Indian exports, after which its share declined to approx. 18.66% of all exports. Opium was the single largest contribution in generating India's export surplus. This was the second manifestation of the India connection (Richards 2002).

The third India connection in the Opium Wars was through the Indian soldiers who were used by the Britishers. Indian sepoys were also brought in to fight alongside the Britishers in the battles of Canton, Amoy, Tinghai and Chin-Kiang Fu. The role of India and Indians in amassing wealth by unleashing the opium addiction as well as the images of Indian soldiers fighting in tandem with the Britishers against the Chinese obviously left a distinct imprint on the Chinese memory, which then continued to deface India–China ties.

In the words of Mira Sinha Bhattacharjea, "When we began to oppose British in our own interest, then we looked to other supporters (example China) and we overarched the British colonial era by going back to our ancient cultural linkages. But that was the only thing that could help us to overcome colonial era. Because in the colonial era, the British were the aggressors for China and Indian soldiers, Indian policemen, Indian bureaucrats, were well-known to be servitors of the British. So their image in China was not very good. In fact mothers in Shanghai, for instance, would frighten their children by saying that bearded Sikhs (Indians) would come, certainly we were there fighting on the behalf of British."[6]

This image of the vicious Indian soldier as well as that of wealth amassing by a few private Indian families adversely impacted India's image.

The second Opium War in 1860 resulted in the Qing Government being compelled to legalise the Opium Trade. Those in India and China who know and understand the nuances of India's role in the Opium Wars study each other in a much more

---

[6] Mira Sinha Bhattacharjea in an interview to Dr. Reena Marwah, April 21, 2008; www.china-studies.taipei/act/india04.doc.

sympathetic and benign manner. (Encyclopedia Vol. 1, p. 44). Chang writes that the Opium War of 1840–1842 inaugurated China's modern century of humiliation. Chang's book places it in historical perspective and also details the day-to-day crises that led up to the hostilities. This trade in Opium, which was a source of increasing revenue for the British and was prized to the extent that wars were fought, is lucidly described by Chang through not only events as they occurred but also the tactics, motives, eye witness accounts and documents. Inevitably, it is thus an important resource on the subject which had a triangular connection (Chang Hsin-pao 1964).

The manner in which India was exploited for filling the coffers of the Britishers, through the opium trade, required more focus by Indian scholars to allay the misunderstandings between India and China. In fact, the extent to which India was ravaged, especially its states of Bengal and Bihar, which have been left way behind in the development process of the country, till the present day, finds scant attention.

Thus, the Opium Wars must be understood against the context of the British Empire's uncontrolled vested interests in which it seized the land, labor and capital resources of India to vanquish China (Choudhury 2015).

It was left to those who believe in the merit of strengthening India–China civilizational ties to decipher, document and disseminate the underlying devastation caused by the opium production in India. Many of these intellectuals (some of whom came together under the banner of the Institute of Chinese Studies in 1969[7]) have helped readers traverse the footprints of people on both sides, providing greater sensitivity to the study of India in China and China in India.

Movement of People

As referred to earlier in this chapter, prior to the occupation of Asia by colonizers, India and China interacted through traders and

---

[7] For further details, see www.icsin.org.

travelers. Especially well known and studied are the multiple voyages made by Zheng He in the 15th century when Chinese dominance in coastal networks of Asia was not only visible but significant (Sen in Ira Pande 2010, pp. 40–45).

In pre-20th century Asia, although the occupation by the Europeans retarded the interactions between India and China, as Sen further states, this was a time when there were Chinese travelers who came to British India, settled in Kolkata and other parts of India and wrote about their life as immigrants; similarly Indians also traveled to China, settled in Shanghai and wrote about how they perceived China.

Thampi provides an explanation for the stationing of Indian merchants, soldiers and others. She also writes about the complex situation of World War II during which Indian soldiers were aligned with Japan (through the Indian National Army) which was then in occupation by China. This nexus resulted in several Indians being forced to leave the Chinese mainland. For the Indian community in China then, they were adversely affected by the Nationalism revolution and civil war in China. However, for the Chinese in India life remind fairly stable till the downturn in relations of the 1960s.

Chinese immigrants in India included not only refugees or deportees but also a number of Chinese seamen who were left in India due to the War. There were others who simply crossed over the borders for legal or illegal trade. Madhavi Thampi also provides an account of the number of Chinese who seem to have come across the border illegally, often disguised as Tibetans, creating what the authorities believed was a security problem. Kalimpong[8] was seen as the epicenter of smuggling between India and China. Suspicions were expressed about the interaction of the Chinese consular and diplomatic representatives with the Chinese here and elsewhere, including their role in organizing them (Encyclopedia Vol. 1, pp. 441–457).

---

[8] Kalimpong is an Indian hilltown in the Himalayan foothills of West Bengal.

The 18th-century migration of the Chinese to various parts of India is one of the less-studied aspects of history. Some of the earliest Chinese settlements took place in the port cities of British colonial India, especially Kolkata and Mumbai. During the course of the nineteenth and twentieth centuries, Chinese migrants also settled in other places including Dehradun, Mussourie, Kanpur, Lucknow, Siliguri, Kalimpong, Darjeeling, Makum and Bangalore.

Trade through the maritime route between India and China resulted in merchants from India arriving on the China coast. In the early 19th century, it was the Parsi community and also the Baghdadi Jewish community based in Bombay and some Muslim Bohra and Ismaili traders, who went to China. Once the treaty ports were opened up after the First Opium War and following the growth of Hong Kong as a port, many Indians became permanent residents in China. In addition to the import–export trade, the interests of these communities became multi-faceted — banking, real estate, manufacturing and share brokerage became of interest. The 20th century saw increasing numbers of people from the Marwari and Sindhi communities arriving in Hong Kong and China's port cities.

There was another group of Indians who arrived to stay on in China. These were policemen and watchmen, especially from Punjab. The policemen were mainly based in Hong Kong and in the foreign concessions at Shanghai, Guangzhou, Tianjin, Hankou and so on while the Indian guards settled in both large cities and in small towns. At one time, they accounted for approximately half of the Indians in eastern China. Many among this group, along with the merchants in western China and in the Chinese ports, were sent back to India during the 1930s and 1940s (Encyclopedia Vol. 1, pp. 441–457).

The commercial connection between India and China also led to the arrival of the Chinese in India. Chinese were to be found mainly in and around Calcutta (Kolkata) and Bombay (Mumbai), but it was only in Calcutta that their numbers grew large enough to form a Chinese settlement in India. The first Chinese known to have settled in India in this period was Yang Dazhao (Atchew).⁹ He received a grant of land from the British authorities in Bengal to set up a sugar mill at the end of the 18th century. Thereafter, more Chinese continued to arrive in India throughout the 19th century. They settled mainly in the Bowbazar and Tangra areas of Calcutta. They tended to specialise in carpentry and shipbuilding, and later in the tannery and shoe-making business as well. Chinese were also brought to India's northeastern province of Assam to work on the tea plantations that the British established. Their contribution in tea cultivation and processing was used to develop an extensive tea industry in India. From the early 20th century, the turbulent conditions in China led to the arrival of larger numbers of Chinese in India, including women and children. Migration of ethnic Chinese continued up to the middle of the 20th century (Encyclopedia Vol. 1, pp. 441–457).

When Southeast Asia was occupied by Japan in late 1930s, it resulted in the migration of ethnic Chinese as refugees from Malaya to British India. Post World War II, there could have been almost 15,000–20,000 ethnic Chinese who came from different areas of Southeast Asia and China. These Chinese were engaged in different enterprises including carpentry and dentistry. In addition to the popular Chinese food, they also brought in the hand-pulled rickshaws. The community was well settled, but after the border war between India and China of 1962 and the difficulties they faced in India because of that, large numbers emigrated abroad and their numbers in India dwindled.

The port cities of Shanghai, Hong Kong and Bombay were well known for their India–China connection, with Shanghai having been the base of British expansion in China. The main contributors to the growth of Hong Kong were the well-known families including the Sassoons, the Ruttonjees, the Kadoories,

---

⁹ A small locality near present-day Budge Budge was the first Chinese settlement in Calcutta, much before Bowbazar and Tangra. The place is Achipur, named after Chinese trader Yang Dazhao (nicknamed Atchew) who arrived on the banks of the Hooghly in 1778 and has a temple dedicated to him. See https://www.telegraphindia.com/calcutta/how-a-trader-became-a-deity-200310. Accessed on 17 May 2018.

Paul Chater, H. N. Mody, Abdoolally Ebrahim & Co and others. Their contribution to infrastructure building as well as education is well known. The Sassoons, who were a Jewish family from Bombay, owned major properties in Shanghai. The emergence of Bombay as a key financial centre was largely due to its contribution to trade with China (*Ibid*).

People from both countries living alongside the border areas interacted in several ways during the period from 1939 to 1945, thus presenting a complex relationship that could neither be considered as one of friendship and brotherhood, or one of enemies, hostile to one another. What can be comprehended is the growing importance of the two countries to each other during World War II. It also portrays the initiation of modern state-to-state relations spanning diverse areas including issues of confrontation, the role of external powers as well as interactions of commerce and trade. A formulation that most accurately characterizes India–China relations in this period is that of increasingly "linked destinies" (Thampi & Sharma 2015).

India–China: Studies and Perceptions

The role of intellectuals in building India–China ties is well documented in the two volumes of the Encyclopedia on India–China Relations, a study commissioned in 2011, published in 2014.[10] In 1893, Swami Vivekananda, one of the most well-known philosophers of modern India, went to China for 3 days. He was one of the very few thinkers who visited China in those days. His writings reflect his sympathy and friendship for the Chinese people. He also predicted a great future for the Chinese people (Page 2013). Rabindranath Tagore, the poet and philosopher, is revered as the architect of Sino-India relations in the modern era. This was in 1924, when Tagore spent 50 days in China having been invited by renowned Chinese thinkers. Although there were some people who opposed him, he developed lasting associations and

---

[10] Institute of Chinese Studies, India, conducted the study.

friendships with numerous poets and writers including Xu Zhimo, Guo Moruo, Xie Bingxin, Zheng Zhenduo and Wang Tongzhao. Tagore's impact on the Chinese people continues to be celebrated not only in Cheena Bhawan in Viswa Bharati University in Shantiniketan but also all over India. It was a young Chinese scholar — Tan Yunshan — who came and stayed on in Viswa Bharati that started teaching Chinese language, initially with just five students.[11]

K.M. Panikkar, who was India's ambassador to China during the period 1948–1952, has contributed immensely in enriching China studies in India through his books. Strategic thinking in India continues to be influenced by Panikkar's writings to this day, despite him being considered a communist sympathiser in India (Bateman 2017). Some of his contributions include *The Problems of Greater India* (1916), *Indian Nationalism: Its Origins, History, and Ideals* (London: Faith Press 1920), *Asia and Western Dominance* (London: Allen and Unwin 1954), *A Survey of Indian History* (Asia Publishing House 1960), etc.

An excerpt from K. M. Panikkar's writings delineate his views on India and China's ignorance of British power. He underlines the importance of naval capabilities in no ambiguous words, when he writes,

> The Chinese Admiral who challenged the might of Britain during the First Anglo-Chinese War knew nothing about the naval strength of Britain and firmly believed that he could defeat the British Navy with his fleet of junks. The result of this ignorance of the sources of power of other nations was that India had, for a long time, to remain subject to a foreign power while China was, for over a hundred years, the whipping-boy of European nations.

---

[11] Tan Yunshan became Tagore's main collaborator and assistant in setting up what became the first centre for Chinese studies in modern India. He returned to China to raise financial and other support for the project of setting up such a centre. Eventually, it was inaugurated on April 10, 1937. With the assistance given by the Nationalist Government, the Sino-Indian Cultural Society and other supporters in China, the Cheena Bhavana as it was called, was established with its own unique building and a library consisting of a large number of Chinese works (Encyclopedia Vol. 1).

His critical assessment of India's inward looking nature (omphaloskepsis or intense introspection) are worth quoting here:

> From the earliest times, India lacked interest in the balance of power outside its own national frontiers. While China was continuously watchful of developments across its land frontiers and had developed a very efficient system of diplomatic relationship on a continental basis, the Indian idea of diplomacy was confined to states within the geographical limits of India. Within this area, at different times, India developed a system of international relations and diplomatic usage. But so far as areas outside the physical boundaries of India were concerned, we were content to live with the attitude of complacent ignorance.

In addition to Chatterjee and Panikkar, Indian authors who have written on the colonial period are few. Madhavi Thampi's edited book titled *India and China in the colonial world*, which includes several articles on the India China Relationship in the British era, is one that has enriched China studies in India. The articles show that the process of interaction in the colonial period was a complex one and cannot be simply limited to either indifference or solidarity against the colonialists or be merely encapsulated as economic and cultural interactions. What is clearly discernible is the impact of the western powers on India–China ties. The book is comprised of papers related to trade and economic interaction, the migration of Chinese to India as well as the Indian Community in China, cultural interactions and links between the national and revolutionary movements in India and China.

The paper by Asiya Siddiqui titled, "Pathways of the poppy: India's opium trade in the nineteenth century", in Thampi's edited volume highlights the role of trade in Opium in India's revenue and explains how the Chinese Government's ban of the trade impacted profits not only of the Britishers but also the India merchants who were active in this trade (Siddiqui 2010).

Sisir Das in his article titled "The controversial guest: Tagore in China", focusses on the rich cultural ties that were forged among the Chinese and Indian intellectuals with a view of understanding one another. He has written lucidly about Rabindranath Tagore's visit to China in 1924 which, though considered a major landmark in India–China ties, was followed by intense criticism by Chinese intellectuals at that time. In fact, Tagore at that time was referred to as "A Slave from a Lost country" (Das 2010, pp. 86–88).

The life and work of Tan Yun Shan who was the founder Director of Cheena Bhawan at Santiniketan devoted his life to understanding the Indian Civilization. In fact, Tan Yun Shan played a role in nudging Tagore to articulate against the Japanese aggression on China. Herein again, the intent is to project India's yearning for a free China.

Some Indian scholars have attempted to reinterpret the events as they occurred and the involvement of the Indian troops in the British army and to further delineate the role assumed for and with the Chinese peasantry — B.R. Deepak, in "The 1857 Rebellion and Indian Involvement in the Taiping Uprising in China" (Deepak 2010, pp. 142–143), has written about the involvement of Indian troops fighting alongside their Chinese counterparts against the British in the Taiping Rebellion/revolutionary war in China from 1851 to 1864). It is estimated that after the Britishers quashed the 1857 mutiny in India, 10,000 Indian soldiers were despatched to China along with the French and British troops. Troops were sourced from the Sikh regiment and Madras Regiment among others as it was these regiments who had shown their loyalties to the British in 1857.

The colonial period is one which has made a lasting imprint on India–China ties. This historical legacy, according to Thampi was largely ignored by these two countries, even as they attempted to carve out their own distinct paths and destinies. The two civilizations understood one another through a projection by the imperialist West and its scholarship. This has obviously been unhelpful in creating an atmosphere of trust and mutual sympathy. There has been little reflection on issues and events of the colonial era, possibly due to varied political leanings during the Cold War (Thampi 2005, pp. 1–18).

Liang Qichao, who was an admirer of the Indian civilization and who is known to have invited Rabindranath Tagore, in his 1901 essay writes, "I have heard of countries destroying countries, but I have never heard of a non-country destroying another". He could not understand how India could be completely taken over by 70,000 small capitalists of the East India Company" (Karl 2002, p. 160).

There were other Chinese scholars quoted in various Chinese publications too who wrote about India having become a "lost" country (Sen 2003, p. 43).

However, in sharp contrast, it was a very different picture that was painted of the Chinese revolution by Edgar Snow. In the concluding paragraph of the book published in 1937, *Red Star Over China*, he expressed certainty that the Chinese revolution would win. In his words:

> The movement for social revolution in China might suffer defeats, might temporarily retreat. might for time seem to languish, might make wide changes in tactics to fit immediate necessities and aims, might even for a period be submerged, be forced underground, but it would not only continue to mature; in one mutation or another it would eventually win, simply because (as this book proves, if it proves anything) the basic conditions which had given it birth carried within themselves the dynamic necessity for its triumph (Whiteman 1972).

Dr. Sun Yat-sen, the leader of China's Republican Revolution of 1911, was a source of great inspiration for many Indian nationalists, especially the Indian National Congress and its leaders in India. It was the Indian National Army (INA) that helped to forge links with Chinese nationalists and were against the tyranny of the British soldiers in China. Jawaharlal Nehru also expressed much appreciation for China's ancient civilization. Gandhi also became very well known in China in the early 20th century and, in fact, 27 books about him as well as his autobiography were published in China. In addition, the *Oriental Magazine* published 60–70 articles and even had a regular column on "Gandhi and New India" for some years.

Another prominent contributor to the study of Chinese culture and values is Raghu Vira. He founded the International Academy of Indian Culture in New Delhi in the 1930s. His son Lokesh Chandra's contribution to translating and disseminating the writings of Raghu Vira is well known. In 1938, he wrote *Ramayana in China*.

There were other important centres too. In the late 1930s, Fergusson College in Pune opened a centre for China studies. Scholars such as Bapat and Gokro began to make a comparative study of Sanskrit, Pali, Chinese and Tibetan Buddhist texts.

Prabodh Chandra Bagchi's contribution to China studies in India is noteworthy. Bagchi researched and taught (from 1945 to 1956), at Viswa Bharati University. His writings on the cultural interaction between India and China inspired several young scholars in India. On the Chinese side, Sun Yat-sen, Zhang Taiyan, Liu Shipei, Liang Qichao, Li Dazhao and other personalities sought to build this kind of consciousness of Asian unity through in their speeches and writings (Encyclopedia Vol. 1, pp. 12–14).

Thus, the manner in which India was perceived by Chinese travelers is noteworthy, because it provides insights regarding the subjugation of Indians by the British. It also conveys categorically that the Chinese perception of Indians changed dramatically from one of a "civilization" and a Buddhist land of great teachings in the sixth and seventh centuries to a "lost country". One article went even further to ridicule India's Buddhist legacy and the people for becoming slaves of the British. This was the image and perception of British India in the minds of most Chinese intellectuals.

Conclusion

The contributions of Indologists and Sinologists such as Professor Tan Yunshan, Raghu Vira and many others mentioned in the preceding pages as well as the establishment of China study centres in India and India study centres in China during and after the colonial period have contributed to more intense, comprehensive and objective views of each other.

An excerpt from the interview of Prof. Lokesh Chandra (Raghu Vira's son) explains this as follows:

> Monk Feng Tzu-kai, a friend of Chairman Mao wrote poems and drew pictures on Ahimsa. In the mid 1940's my father translated it in English and published the first volume. Ahimsa was a central concept in our freedom struggle. Gandhiji was impressed by this book and that the Chinese also believe in Ahimsa. My father wanted to strengthen Sino-Indian friendship on a cultural footing that could absorb the shocks of political misunderstandings. Gaps of communication could be tided over by such an approach and could generate an ambience that allows us to see beyond parochial politics.[12]

Despite this, the Sinophobes in India, not necessarily those enmeshed in the study of China or its languages, have continued to exert influence on Indian foreign policy; the 1962 war further drummed up their anti-China emotions. In a way, it was Britain that was responsible for the border dispute even as both China and India agree that the treaties and agreements are legacies of history and cannot be solved in the short or medium term and are best left for the future (Guruswamy 2017).

Interactions between India and China at present times increasingly borrow less from the rich web of relations accumulated in the past, from the trade and technology transfers to the ties of nationalism and anti-nationalism or the colonial and imperialist shared experience. What is fortunately and favorably etched in the Indian memory is the intercourse among intellectuals, political activists, writers and artists. It is this small community which captures and presents the resentment of centuries of Western dominance as a major part of the strategic psyche of both India and China.

The atrocities committed by the colonialists left permanent scars on the Indian landscape deemed to be obliterated soon after India's independence. The colonial power handholding continued to be sought, replete with business and trade dependency. In China,

---

[12] Interview of Prof. Lokesh Chandra to Dr. Reena Marwah, September 2011, India.

in contrast, the nationalist revolutionary fervor helped the polity to shake off the colonial masters' conundrum, treating the latter with both caution and skepticism.

While the positives of Sino-India relations are articulated in terms of seeking out one another through cultural and literary dialogue, writings and translations, the negatives span the misunderstandings created through the opium trade during most of the 19th century, alignment of the Indian soldiers with the Japanese forces against the Chinese, as well as the entire perception of a disunited India falling prey to a handful of capitalists, among others. Although the memory of the opium wars of the 19th century provided lessons for India, this was cursorily dismissed as "problems of another".

Another positive aspect of the early part of the 20th century, which merits mention here, was when the pace of the nationalist and anti-imperialist movements in both India and China picked up. China and Chinese political leaders provided a haven in this period to several exiled Indian political activists and nationalist organizations. It was the Ghadar[13] Party in China for almost two decades during and after the first world war that mobilized Indian soldiers as well as policemen to fight alongside the Chinese against the British.

Despite sympathy being garnered for the aggrieved by Indians in China, its fallout on India could never be comprehended in its entirety. One casualty has been the objective and contextual study of China in India, summed up in the words of A. N. Tagore,

> It is still my firm conviction that we will not be able to go ahead with Chinese studies by only teaching Chinese language. We have to have an oriental mindset in which to do things, if we still think that we have to go to Cambridge or Oxford to be educated then it is out of question. But when we will start thinking that yes to get education we have to go to Peking University, then I will agree that our students have understood what education is all about.[14]

---

[13] *Ghadar* means revolt, rebellion or revolution in Punjabi and Urdu.
[14] Interview of Prof. Amitendranath Tagore to Prof. Swaran Singh, 2008, India.

References

Bateman, Sam. 2017. *Remembering K. M. Panikkar: The Future of Western Influence in Asia*. https://www.aspistrategist.org.au/remembering-k-m-panikkar-future-western-influence-asia/.

Bhattacharjea, Mira Sinha. 2008. Interview to Dr. Reena Marwah, 2008, India. http://www.china-studies.taipei/act/india04.doc.

Chandra, Lokesh. 2008. Interview to Dr. Reena Marwah. http://www.china-studies.taipei/act/india03.doc.

Chang, Hsin-pao. 1964. *Commissioner Lin And The Opium War*. Cambridge: Harvard University Press. http://books.wwnorton.com/books/Commissioner-Lin-and-the-Opium-War/.

Chatterjee, Partha. 2012. *The Black Hole of Empire: History of a Global Practice of Power*. Princeton: Princeton University Press.

Choudhury, Avinanda. 2015. "Avinanda Choudhury's research". In *The Opium War in China: The Indian Connection*. http://indpaedia.com/ind/index.php/The_Opium_wars_in_China:_the_Indian_connection.

Das, Sisir Kumar. 2010. "The controversial guest: Tagore in China." In Madhavi Thampi (Ed.). *India and China in the Colonial World*. New Delhi: Social Science Press, pp. 85–125.

Deepak, B. R. 2010. "The 1857 Rebellion and Indian Involvement in the Taiping Uprising in China." In Madhavi Thampi (Ed.). *India and China in the Colonial World*. New Delhi: Social Science Press, pp. 139–149.

Encyclopedia of Sino-Indian Cultural Contacts. 2014. Volume 1. Ministry of External Affairs, Government of India in Collaboration with the State Council of the PRC.

Encyclopedia of Sino-Indian Cultural Contacts. 2014. Volume 2. Ministry of External Affairs, Government of India in Collaboration with the State Council of the PRC.

Guruswamy, Mohan. 2017. Why India and China's Border Disputes Are So Difficult to Resolve. South China Morning Post (December 17). https://www.scmp.com/news/china/diplomacy-defence/article/2124528/why-india-and-chinas-border-disputes-are-so-difficult.

Karl, Rebecca. 2002. "Staging the World: Chinese Nationalism at the Turn of the Twentieth Century." In Xudong Zhang (Ed.) *Whither China?: Intellectual Politics in Contemporary China*. Durham: Duke University Press.

Page, William. 2013. Swami Vivekanand's Experiences in China. Available at https://www.esamskriti.com/e/History/Great-Indian-Leaders/Swami-Vivekanand-colon-S-Experiences-In-China-1.aspx (accessed on 2 May 2018).

Richards, John. 2002. "The Opium Industry in British India." *Indian Economic & Social History Review* 39 (2–3): 149–180.

Sen, Tansen. 2003. Buddhism, Diplomacy, and Trade The Realignment of Sino-Indian Relations, 600–1400. file:///C:/Users/Reena/Downloads/%2313_Sen.pdf.

Sen, Tansen. 2006. The Travel Records of Chinese Pilgrims Faxian, Xuanzang, and Yijing Sources for Cross-Cultural Encounters Between Ancient China and Ancient India. http://afe.easia.columbia.edu/special/travel_records.pdf.

Siddiqui, Asiya. 2010. "Pathways of the Poppy: India's Opium Trade in the Nineteenth Century." In Madhavi Thampi (Ed.) *India and China in the Colonial World*. New Delhi: Social Science Press, pp. 21–32.

Singh, Gadadhar. 2017. *Thirteen Months in China: A Subaltern Indian and the Colonial World: An Annotated Translation of Thakur*. Anand A. Yang, Kamal Sheel and Ranjana Sheel (Eds.). Oxford: Oxford University Press.

Tagore, Amitendranath. 2008. Interview to Prof. Swaran Singh. http://www.china-studies.taipei/act/india07.doc.

Thampi, Madhavi. 2005. *Indians in China 1800–1949*. New Delhi: Manohar Publishers & Distributors.

Thampi, Madhavi. (Ed.). 2010. *India and China in the Colonial World*. New Delhi: Social Science Press and Orient Black Swan.

Thampi, Madhavi and Nirmola Sharma. 2015. *Catalogue of Materials Related to Modern China in the National Archives of India, 1939–1945*. New Delhi: The Institute of Chinese Studies.

Whiteman, Alden. 1972. Edgar Snow Dies; Wrote About China. https://www.nytimes.com/1972/02/16/archives/edgar-snow-dies-wrote-about-china-edgar-snow-author-on-china-is.html.

Chapter 2

Exploring China Consciousness of Pre-independence India

Swaran Singh[1]

School of International Studies, Jawaharlal Nehru University, New Delhi, India

Introduction

Expanding British colonial footprint in China and India, especially during the latter half of the 19th and early part of the 20th centuries, had *prima facie* undermined mutual connections between these two large and ancient Asian societies. As usual, most colonial societies, especially their elites, were trained by and connected closely to their metropole masters in Europe. Yet, despite this general trend, their rather sporadic yet persistent connections were to gradually expand and germinate strong mutual consciousness about their shared plight as also their shared anti-colonial strides. However, the first contention of this chapter is that even while these Asian elites were often aware about each other's civilizational history and culture, Indian elites were not the pioneers in the revival of pre-independence India's consciousness about Chinese society. Second, the initial interface between Indian and Chinese people during the British rule was facilitated by the British themselves, who were using their subjects for further consolidation and expansion of their

---

[1] Author is Professor, School of International Studies, Jawaharlal Nehru University, New Delhi. E-mail: ssingh@jnu.ac.in

grip over the commerce and territories of these Asian societies. Third is that this colonial frame of their initial interactions was to introduce an enduring new element of skepticism in their rather eulogistic mutual perceptions and policies since ancient times.

As regards initial interactions of Indian common people with their Chinese counterparts, this was to happen not as friends from a neighboring peer civilization — as had happened since ancient times — but mostly as instruments of British empire building in China. This was to greatly circumscribe the millennia-long ancient India–China traditions of mutual respect and understanding where culture, especially Buddhist monks and analects, had been the strongest bridge linking the two ancient societies. Nevertheless, this increasing mutual awareness about their shared colonial subjugation was to gradually mold their sense of shared destiny. Later, India's iconic leaders were to further highlight and fine-tune India's China-consciousness and underline its instrumentality in strengthening India's pan-Asian connections and act as a boost for India's nationalist impulses. This saw several iconic figures of India's freedom movement engaging Chinese leaders and intellectuals, resulting in revival of their linkages reflected in their publicly expressed mutual sympathies and support for their parallel anti-imperial liberation strives. But apart from sowing seeds of mutual skepticism, British colonial rule was also to leave India with several contentious colonial legacies like disputed boundaries, an issue that continues to present most formidable challenge to their efforts at building partnerships.

This chapter seeks to examine the aforementioned contentions by first elucidating the piecemeal evolution of their grassroots diasporic connections. This is followed by elucidation of various episodes of engagement of China by India's iconic leaders, locating them in their historicity by underlining several other triggers and factors that facilitated these interactions and their impact on India's pre-independence China discourses. In doing so, this chapter alludes to the impact of their colonial subjugation on India's China-consciousness, resulting in euphoric attempts to overcome it through initial China–India *Bhai–Bhai* (brotherhood) slogans which soon fell prey to their colonial legacies and cold war dynamics that explain the vulnerabilities of a newly liberated country and its leadership. This chapter is divided broadly into three sections. The first section explores into evolution of flows of Chinese and Indian diaspora into each other's society and how both their colonial experience and diaspora flows were distinct and yet resulted in similar impulses and outcomes for both sides. The second section looks at the engagement and interactions of a few iconic leaders with China that were to have a lasting influence on India's China-consciousness as well as on India's China studies. The last section alludes to various limitations of this pre-colonial China-consciousness that was dented deeply by their colonial experiences, further reinforced by cold war dynamics.

Indian Diaspora in China

To begin with, the late 1850s were to witness two big simultaneous insurrections — India's first war of independence (1857) and China's Taiping Rebellion (1851–1864) — that were to badly shake the imperial grip of Britain over these two Asian societies. These two parallel historical episodes are seen marking an inflection point in the rise of national consciousness in both Indian and Chinese societies. But these two insurrections were surely not mutually connected, and it is debatable to what extent they were even aware of and/or inspired each other; yet their occurring at same time did contribute to their sense of shared plight and shared national aspirations. As part of their colonial expansion in China, the British had, for the first time, deployed Indian troops in China during the First Opium War (1840–1842) and later again in their Second Opium War (1857–1860). The fact that these two above-mentioned insurrections, respectively, in India and China occurred in middle of these two Opium Wars makes it likely that they were surely becoming conscious about each other's struggles even if there was no coordination or cooperation between them as yet. With the knowledge of hindsight, it is now seen as perhaps partly responsible for at least few Indian soldiers of the British Opium

Wars joining the Taipings in their fight against the foreign legions and the Qing officials who were trying to put down the Taipings (Deepak 2017, p. 140). The fact that some of these Indians also stayed back in China marked the beginning of the Indian diaspora in China, which was to become the most critical source of this revival of pre-independence India's China-consciousness during British rule across the Indian subcontinent.

Even if this historic switchover of some Indian soldiers to the side of Taiping Rebellion is considered a knee-jerk reaction of individual soldiers and not a premeditated exercise, it nevertheless represented the first of many episodes to be examined later as both the cause and also the consequence of increasing China consciousness amongst Indian troops in China. The wider impact of these experiences of Indian soldiers in China were to be felt through their connections where their families and friends who were to be deeply exposed to these soldiers' stories and impressions about the contemporary Chinese society. Among these Indians, Sikhs were to become especially noticeable given their distinct appearance and enthusiasm. In fact, other than coming to China as part of two opium wars, Sikhs had also come to China as policemen (to Hong Kong in 1848 and then to Shanghai from 1884). But their presence was to germinate negative sentiments amongst locals as "wielding his baton and patrolling the streets of the foreign concessions in the treaty ports" these Sikhs were seen as empire's "the most characteristic and well recognized figure among Indians in China in the nineteenth and early twentieth century" (Kahlon 2017, p. 212). Later, Sikhs were regularly recruited for British concessions at Gulangyu (Xiamen), Tianjin, Shamian (Canton), Hankou etc. and though this was to make them the target of "the racist hostility of Chinese", they also became the strongest source of mutual consciousness between their two large and ancient societies. This is so much so that today "one of the first displays that meets visitors to Shanghai's History Museum is a wax-work Sikh traffic policeman", reflecting the centrality of India's Sikh sepoys in revival of its China's consciousness and vice versa (Bickers 2016, p. 64). Later, during the earlier part of 20th century, and especially during the World War I, North America-based radical groups like the *Ghadar* Party were to infiltrate this Sikh community in Shanghai, making China an important sanctuary for various radical elements of India's freedom fighters (Bikers 2016; Chao 2011, p. 158). Several of these Indians sepoys were to become part of Indian National Army, and many of these were to be radicalized in pursuing, just like China's communist movement, an armed struggle against British rule in India. So, the Indian diaspora in China was to germinate both positive as well as negative impulses among the Chinese and Indians as they became conscious about each other, and this has continued till date to define their mutual trust or lack of it thereof.

For the British, however, this period of two Opium Wars marked the onset of the Industrial Revolution. This was to greatly help them in reinforcing their need for colonies as well as to strengthen their grip on these two large Asian economies.[2] This was done through accelerated pace of social and physical infrastructure building, such as by introducing the English language, modernizing ports, building railways and grand trunk roads and other logistics in India (and some of it in China) to intensify their commercial exaction and political usurpation in these Asian giants; in the process, they also inscribed their piecemeal deindustrialization and misery, also triggering the irreversible nationalisms. China and India, two countries that that contributed over 30 percent to global gross domestic product till onset of Industrial Revolution in Europe, contributed less than eight percent to global gross domestic product by the late 1940s. But this consolidation of British colonial rule had also ignited nationalistic impulses in which various radical groups — often vanished or exiled by these imperial rulers — were compelled to build networks beyond their national borders laying foundations of pan-Asian connections. This made even the moderate nationalists conscious of building pan-Asian connections

---

[2] Several studies show how till the onset of Industrial Revolution in Europe, China and India are the two dominant drivers of global production of culture and commerce and the strongest pillars of global GDP. (See, for example, Pollock and Elman 2018).

among various colonized nations. In this long sojourn, episodes like the Partition of Bengal in 1905 in India that coincided with the Russo-Japanese war — busting the myth of European supremacy — greatly encouraged these pan-Asian connections and the consciousness among various leaders of India's freedom movement about their counterparts across other Asian societies, especially in Japan which hosted several Indian and Chinese revolutionaries. This interface of Chinese and Indian freedom fighters in Japan was again to reinforce Indian consciousness about how various radical leaders from India were to meet Chinese counterparts in Japan only to find that Chinese leaders like Sun Yat-sen (1866–1925) and Zhang Taiyan (1869–1936) were equally disappointed and disillusioned by constitutionalists at home (Deepak 2012, p. 148). It was from their exile in Japan that their Chinese newspapers like *Min Bao* (People's Tribune) openly supported India's freedom movement. There are inferences made of connections among several Indian and Chinese leaders who were often working underground in China or Japan with changed names; also, various Indian names in Chinese language make it difficult to establish their identities. But there are records available for several of these Indian leaders visiting Japan during the decade following the Russo-Japanese war. These included Surendra Mohan Bose (1906), Taraknath Das (1906), Dhangopal Mukerji (1908), Barakatullah (1909), Bhagwan Singh (1913), Narain Marathe (1914), Abaninath Mukherji (1915), Rashbehari Bose (1915), Lala Lajpat Rai (1915), Harambalal Gupta (1915) and M. N. Roy (1915), and most of them were in close contact with Sun Yat-sen and Zhang Taiyan (Deepak 2012, pp. 149 and 153). Their shared anti-imperial zeal was an important first trigger to germinate the revival of India's China consciousness, not just regarding their shared freedom struggles but also on their past civilizational linkages.

Chinese Diaspora in India

Unlike the flow of Indians soldiers to China, the arrival of ethnic Chinese to India began much earlier, involved larger numbers and none consisted of soldiers, although they were allowed to settle in India by the British as part of their empire building in India. In case of the Chinese diaspora in India — like most other foreign immigrants such as the Jews and Parsis during 19th and early 20th century — most of them had congregated in and around big cities, especially Calcutta, which was the capital of British India during the period 1772–1911 (Bose 2016, pp. 257–269). Calcutta was also the easiest port to access from China. The record of the first Chinese arriving in India talks of Yang Tai Chow (nicknamed Atchew) arriving in Calcutta in 1778 and being granted land for a sugarcane plantation and sugar factory by the then Governor General Warren Hastings (Xing 2010, p. 1). Atchew was to later bring several Chinese workers for his sugar factory and plantations, and within 50–60 years they had established their own unique neighborhood in central Calcutta. Then the failure of the Taiping Rebellion in the 1860s resulted in another visible flow of the Chinese, which further added to these numbers (Xing 2010, p. 2). As per the 1901 censuses of British India, 1,640 Chinese were recorded in Calcutta — mostly from Canton, Fukien and Hubei — and this number had increased to about 40,000 before India's independence in 1947. Of these, over 15,000 were residing mostly in central Calcutta, though Tangra had also emerged as small Chinatown with its unique temples, stores, restaurants and schools. Also, just like the British opened English-medium schools, the Chinese community had also set up few Chinese-medium schools in Bombay, Darjeeling, Kalimpong and Shillong (Xing 2010, p. 4). Indeed, in one of the most evocative expositions, Yin Marsh's *Doing Time with Nehru: The Story of an Indian-Chinese Family* talks of Chinese families having migrated to India since early 1800s and becoming "integral part of India's very own diverse and multi-ethnic population … because of inter-marriages with Indians over decades … the Chinese community was fluent in Assamese, Bengali, Khasi, Nepali, Hindi and English" though they had also "preserved Chinese cultural practices" (Banerjee 2015, p. 2).

Again, the first four decades of 20th century witnessed China having continuous political upheavals, civil wars and massive

Japanese invasions, all resulting in dislocations, economic deprivation and political vendetta, triggering the continuous exodus of Chinese communities to South and Southeast Asian countries (Marsh 2015, p. 63; Biswas 2017, p. 49). This stream of Chinese visitors and settlers were to be piecemeal assimilated into Indian settlements, and this merger was far more imperceptive in parts of northeast India that housed India's mongoloid ethnic communities of largely indigenous people with very flexible imaginations of sovereignty or entitlement. Like most earlier waves of other immigrants to India, most Chinese were welcome in their newfound homes. Indeed, starting from early 1920s, the Chinese community had established their first school in Calcutta called the *Meiguang* School. This was renamed in 1933 as *Meiguang Wanquan Xiaoxue* and was formally recognized by the education section of the Commission on Overseas Chinese Affairs of the Kuomintang government as *Yindu Jiacheng Sili Meiguang Xiaoxue*. The Chinese community also launched *Yindu Ribao* and some other newspapers later, though circulation of these remained limited. Initially, the medium of instructions at Chinese schools was *Hakka*, which was changed in 1940s to Mandarin when the Chinese also opened similar schools in Kalimpong and other Indian cities in North Bengal (Xing and Sen 2013, p. 218). Given their acceptability in India, the small Chinese community had also been active in influencing political discourse of China–India relations by negotiating with the British by advising Ivan Chen, the Chinese delegate to the famous 1914 Simla Conference on Tibet boundary demarcation and in 1930s by engaging KMT for building an anti-Japanese coalition. As regards India's China-consciousness, this diasporic interface though was largely inter-societal and cultural in nature.

Most of these Chinese continued to stay in India after India's independence in 1947 and liberation of China in 1949. However, except for the first decade of India's independence, these immigrations from China and the lives of the Chinese diaspora in India were to face severe limitations in view of strained China–India relations from the late 1950s and their short border war in 1962.

India's approach to these Chinese was to become prey to colonial legacies of mutual suspicions. The Chinese leadership was blaming it on India inheriting not just British institutions but also the mindset that made Mao Zedong condemn Indian leadership as a class of "Indian bourgeois middle-of-the-roaders" even when they were trying to project themselves as neutrals or nonaligned (Liu 2010, p. 219). Most of these Chinese in India therefore were to begin to leave, with only few deciding to stay back given their intermarriages and resultant trust and goodwill they enjoyed amongst Indian neighborhoods. These Chinese, of course, had also created their own enduring niche in their famed specializations in shoe making, Chinese restaurants, tanneries, dentistry and so on. Nevertheless, several of them were also exposed to rather harsh experiences, especially during the 1962 China–India war. Almost 3,000 Chinese were moved to Deoli camp in Rajasthan province of India, and some were even deported to Mainland China while many others migrated to North America, Europe and Australia. For those who stayed back, the discomfort following the China–India war was compounded by their livelihood challenges, financial constraints and internal divisions that led to further decline and closing of Chinese schools as the Chinese began sending children to English medium schools as that education was seen to have better prospects (Xing and Sen 2013, p. 222). This reflected how the colonial frame of their interface had impacted Chinese diaspora in India and therefore India's China-consciousness. Today, about 2,000 Chinese Indians live in Calcutta Chinatown and another 400 in Mumbai's Chinatown, plus a few sporadic families elsewhere, but their minuscule efforts in sustaining their newspapers has survived. The rise of China since the 1990s has however reignited interest in the Chinese diaspora and their history and culture as well as further explorations into India's China-consciousness during its pre-independence period. These explorations have highlighted how this colonial frame impacted India's consciousness about China as also India's China studies that again remained neglected for several decades following the China–India border war of 1962. This was also to result in creating a divide between India's academic experts and policy makers. Talking of general irreverence of the foreign policy community to academic experts Tansen Sen, for instance, talks of how, in spite of China being regarded today as a "significant foreign policy and security challenge for India" that should lead India to invest in China studies, "the reverse seems to have taken place with the decline of Cheena-Bhavan (Institute of Chinese Language and Culture), Visva-Bharati University, Santiniketan, West Bengal and whatever expertise that institution may have developed with regard to China" (Sen 2013, p. 27). The same can also be seen as true of several other institutions in training China experts in India, though the number of such China-focused institutions and experts have increased following China's unprecedented rise (Shih, Singh and Marwah 2012, p. 9). This week institutionalization has shifted the focus to personalities influencing India's China-consciousness and policy making which, in turn, only reinforces the centrality of India's iconic pre-independence leaders' China-connections in laying foundations of India's China-consciousness then as well as now.

India's Iconic Connections

The early part of the 20th century was to see India's global connections expanding, given the infusion of new technologies of transport and communications. The experience of India's participation in British operations during World War I was to see Indian soldiers again traveling far and wide and mingling with soldiers of several other nations. The Indian National Congress had emerged as the mainstream force in India's freedom struggle, throwing up several iconic "national" leaders. Mahatma Gandhi was to emerge as symbolic father figure, and his return to India after his experiments in non-violent protests in South Africa and his unusual connect with common people had expanded the freedom movement into a mass movement. The Russo-Japanese war of 1905 had busted the myth of European superiority and made Japan an inspiring force for Asia's freedom fighters. In 1913, an Indian — Rabindranath Tagore — was to become the first Asian to be conferred a Nobel Prize for Literature, and he soon emerged as India's global citizen triggering his extensive travels across Asia, including three visits to China. Also, a large number of younger leaders with foreign (mostly British) education and training were to bring new global consciousness to India's national narratives, and some of this was also happening in China that had witnessed the coming of the Republic under Sun Yat-sen who, along with Chiang Kai-shek, enjoyed long and close relations with several Indian leaders. Some of these iconic Indian leaders were to leave their indelible mark in the molding of India's China-consciousness during this pre-independence period.

Tagore's China connections

Rabindranath Tagore — the first Indian to be awarded a Nobel Prize for Literature in 1913 and who set up in 1921 an international university, Visva-Bharati — had been one of India's most visible global citizens with connections in several Asian countries and beyond. As regards his connections in China, in 1923, Tagore was invited by the Lecture Association of Beijing to give a lecture tour in various Chinese cities. Given that Tagore was the first Asian to ever be bestowed with the Nobel Prize for Literature, it was natural for Asia's largest ancient civilization representing a unique and evolved culture to take a strong liking to engaging Tagore. As a global citizen, Tagore had also been very keen to build contacts with the Chinese society and its intellectuals. Therefore, for his visit to China, Tagore chose a delegation to accompany him that included several stalwarts of his own and other Indian universities namely, painter Nandlal Bose, agricultural scientist Leonard Elmhirst, historian Kalidas Nag and Sanskrit scholar Kshitimohan Sen. Tagore's objective for this visit was to "learn all aspects of its life from modern China and to establish a link between China and Visva-Bharati International University" (Gupta 2011, pp. 59–60). As Elmhirst would later recall: "Tagore insisted that his Indian specialists should live with the Chinese and travel with them not only to see the ancient treasures of China but to meet and understand the Chinese at work, and at leisure in their homes. He used to say before we left India that it was vitally necessary for Indians to try and discover the aspirations of modern China" (Gupta 2011, p. 60). Tagore's visit to China, therefore, was anything but a one-stop event; it was to lay the foundations for the revival of India–China connections and mutual consciousness through building of academic exchanges and network.

Tagore's interest and awareness about China however had preceded this visit by several decades. For example, much before Tagore undertook his first 1923 visit to China, way back in 1902, he had planned to send his visiting Japanese Sanskrit scholar at his Santiniketan school, Ishiku Hori, to China. Hori-san was then expected to search and bring back to India copies various lost Sanskrit documents that were still available in Tibetan and Chinese translations. Sadly, this Sanskrit scholar, Ishiku Hori, fell sick and died in India. However, Tagore's interest in the study of China was so enduring that in 1921 he invited the well-known Sinologist of Sorbonne, Sylvain Levi, as the first visiting professor to Visva-Bharati. In this endeavor of Tagore, the Vice Chancellor of Calcutta University, Asutosh Mookerji, provided not just financial support for this visiting professorship but also sent some of his leading scholars to work with Prof. Levi at Visva-Bharati. One of these scholars from Calcutta University was Sanskrit scholar Prabodh Chandra Bagchi, who Levi trained in Chinese and Tibetan studies to materialize Tagore's project of bringing back translations of lost Sanskrit texts that were now available only in China. Some of these experts were to become India's celebrated pioneers of China studies in India just as Tagore's Cheena Bhavan at Visva-Bharati was to emerge as the first dedicated China studies center in the entire Indian subcontinent. All this marked the backdrop of Tagore's second China visit in April 1924 that was hosted by *Jiangxueshe* — a recently founded intellectual organization that had flourished during the May Fourth Movement of 1919–1920.

As regards Tagore's 1923 visit to China, several leading magazines had already published articles about this impending visit by Asia's first Nobel Prize winner for literature and his welcome aboard his ship *Atsuta Maru* as it docked at the Western shore of Huangpu (Shanghai), was historic. *Jiangxueshe* had earlier hosted eminent foreign intellectuals like John Dewey and Bertrand Russel. So, addressing a large crowd that came to welcome him at the port, Tagore explained the purpose of his visit as: "My general ideal is to advocate Eastern thought, the revival of traditional Asian Culture, and the unity of the people of Asia" (Ren 2011, p. 114). Accompanied by his King's College of London trained interpreter Xu Zhimo — who was himself a young poet and held his guest in very high esteem — Tagore saw his visit "as successful as never before on any travels" and wrote to Kshitimohan's wife, Kiranbala, how busy they were and how much was happening for "Visva-Bharati's ideal of international cooperation [as it] marked the beginning of an abiding connection between modern China and modern India" (Gupta 2011, p. 60).

In anticipation of Tagore's visit, several leading Chinese magazines had published articles on him making him a well-known name across China's intellectual circles. Tagore's interpreter Xu Zhimo was so inspired by Tagore's *Gitanjali* (collection of poems) that he had launched *The Crescent Moon Society* (1921–1931) and later the *Crescent Moon Society Journal* (1928–1931) after one of its poems. During this travel, therefore, Tagore also discussed the possibilities of opening a Department of Chinese Studies at Visva-Bharati and proposed an exchange of scholars with various universities there. However, as Tagore went around Shanghai, Hangzhou, Nanjing, Jinan and Beijing for six weeks, other than appreciation from China's intellectuals, Tagore also faced bitter criticism as "a petrified fossil of India's national past (*Yindu gouge de toushi*)" and this indeed made him even cancel his last three lectures at Beijing (Ren 2011, p. 114; Chatterjee 2011, p. 280). However, all this was not to weaken Tagore's resolve to promote China studies in India. During the same year, for example, Tagore persuaded Dr. Lin Ngo-Chiang — who was the Principal of the Chinese college at Kenmendine in Burma and who met Tagore on his way back from China in Burma to come to Santiniketan. Thus, the first teaching of Chinese language and literature begin in late

1924 itself. This was in continuation with the 1921 visiting professorship of Sylvain Levi who was followed by Prof. Guiseppe Tucci of the University of Rome and then Ngo-Chinag from Burma who was there till early 1926. In the early part of 1927, Tagore met another Chinese scholar Tan Yun-shan in Singapore and invited him to Santiniketan. After that, although Tagore visited China a further two times (in April and then in June of 1929 while going to and returning from Japan), he "avoided the spotlight and chose to put up with his friend [and interpreter of his 1924 visit] Xu and his wife Lu at their place in Shimingcun" in Shanghai where commemorating this visit a bust of Tagore was unveiled in May 2010 by visiting Indian President Mrs Pratibha Patil (Mukherjee 2010). Tagore's *Cheena Bhavan* at *Visva-Bharati* later continued to be a pioneering center for China studies and, till date, continues to be one of India's most important institutions for training young scholars in Chinese language and studies, thereby contributing to India's China-consciousness both before and after India's independence.

The Nehru interface with two Chinas

Among India's founding fathers, India's Prime Minister for its first 17 years, Jawaharlal Nehru, was a giant of an intellectual statesman with a deep sense of history and purpose. More important, he almost singlehandedly guided independent India's formulation of its worldview from the very early stages; from the 1927 Brussels Conference of Oppressed Nationalities — where he represented Indian National Congress — till his death in May 1964. During his entire term of 17 years as Prime Minister, Nehru was his own foreign minister as well. As a result, to a large extent, the Nehruvian paradigm still continues to determine India's worldview as well as most of its enduring axioms guiding its foreign relations. So, when it comes to pre-independence China-consciousness, it remaisn closely tied to Nehru's understanding and articulations. Nehru's engagement with China or his China-consciousness, was driven far more by China's history, society and culture rather than by any visits or other momentary episodes at the surface level. Among China's leaders, Nehru greatly admired Sun Yat-Sen and Zhang Taiyan for their support of India's freedom movement. While in exile in Japan, Zhang Taiyan used to translate and publish articles from Indian newspapers "to make the Chinese people aware of the Indian situation and let the voice of Indian unrest reach out of India" (Deepak 2012, p. 150). So, reciprocating to this perceived support of Chinese freedom fighters, while participating at the 1927 Brussels Conference, Nehru had "extended India's support to the Nationalist China and hoped for their success in unifying the entire China thus setting it free from the imperialist shackles" (Deepak 2001, p. 56). Indeed a "note on joint declarations duly signed by the representatives of China and India was passed by the Brussels Congress" (*Ibid*). Among other understandings, Nehru's delegation of the Indian National Congress had agreed to press the British Government at home to withdraw Indian troops from China. In his discussion with Chinese delegate Liao Huanxing, the two also agreed that Kuomintang China will open an Information Bureau in India and both sides will arrange regular exchange of high-level visits. There was an agreement to invite Chinese delegates to annual sessions of the Indian National Congress, and China wanted Indian students to visit China to study and establish enduring links between their national liberation movements. Taking this proposal forward, the Indian National Congress invited Kuomintang (KMT) representatives for its 1927 session. Sun Yat-sen's widow Song Qingling was nominated by KMT to attend this INC session of 1927. But the British government denied her permission to travel to India. This invitation to Song Qingling was repeated in 1928, but again she was denied permission by the British government to travel to India. Likewise, in 1927, KMT had also invited D.R. Thengdi, Joglekar Ghate and Nimbkar to attend a Labour Conference, but they were also denied permission by British to travel to China.

Nehru had also been an erudite author producing several books outlining Indian and world history. These were written by Nehru during his prison terms. For instance, while serving a prison sentence during 1931 Nehru wrote letters to his daughter that were later compiled as chapters for his book titled *Glimpses of World History*. Among its chapters, some of these like "A Thousand Years of China", "The Chi'ins and Hans", "The Huns Came to India", "China Flourishes under the Tangs", "Harsha-Vardhana and Hiuen Tsang", "The Age of Peace and Prosperity in China", "China in Difficulties" and "Japan Bullies China" shows his deep interest and understanding about China and its history and culture. Nehru in these cases, explained in great detail various epochs and aspects of "India's sister in ancient history — China" (Nehru 2004, p. 32). Similarly, Nehru's second most read book titled *Discovery of India* — an initial draft of which was written during an April– September 1944 imprisonment at Ahmadnagar Fort — also has a full chapter titled "India and China", and China also appears in several other chapters (Nehru 2004, p. 232). This knowledge of China was to be reflected in his visits to China as well as in his engagement with China and its leaders.

As regards Nehru's first visit to China, it was to the city of Nanking which was then capital of Kuomintang government, and this happened over 13 days starting from 20 August 1939. It is important to note that this visit took place in the middle of the Japanese aggression against China. In this, both Indian newspapers as well as the Indian National Congress were seen making appeals for sanctions against the Japanese while Mr. Atal's Indian ambulance helped in looking after the sick and wounded Chinese in their war with Japan (Roy 1993, p. 79). The story of Dr. Dwarkanath Kotnis — who was dispatched by Nehru as part of a medical mission to China and who died while helping Chinese victims of this war — was to become a legend connecting both sides (Ramesh 2005, p. 44). Therefore, despite such a difficult situation, Nehru's exuberance about his 1939 China visit can be seen from his records about this visit where he calls China "a wonderland of legend, and history, as well as of great deeds in the present" (Nehru 1939/1972, p. 82). This visit was later reciprocated by the 1942 India visit of Chiang Kai-shek that was described by Nehru as a "great event in India" (Nehru 1939/1972, p. 82). This shows Nehru's rootedness in romanticism about engaging this peer civilization in building Asia's future together. This also explains how Nehru's government became the first non-communist state to recognize Mao's People's Republic of China on December 30, 1949 and the euphoria with which Nehru later hosted first India visit by Premier Zhou En-lai in 1954 that included "eleven hours of discussion" between Nehru and Zhou En-lai (Panigraphi 2016, p. 43). Without doubt, Nehru's writings and his speeches on world affairs and foreign policy as well as his interactions with various Chinese leaders (of both the Kuomintang and Communist Party) were to singularly mold pre-independence India's China-consciousness, and this was especially much more central to the making of India's China policy after India's independence.

China connections of Subhash Bose

Like Jawaharlal Nehru, there are also records of Subhash Bose's close emotional connections with Chinese leadership. Experts have recorded Bose's "emotional involvement in this historic mission" that the Indian National Congress (INC) had organized to provide medical relief to the Chinese who were fighting against Japanese aggression in 1937. This was part of INC's efforts to build closer connections with Kuomintang — the foundations of which were laid by Nehru from 1927 — and Subhash Bose was not just an important leader of the INC but also its President during the following years of 1938 and 1939. Subhash Bose had to resign as INC President given his radical orientations that made him unacceptable to Mahatma Gandhi who had by now emerged as most important father figure of the Indian national movement. As Subhash Bose decided to leave India to raise an externally supported insurrection against the British in India, China was to be the first country of his choice before he landed in Germany and Japan to engage these Axis powers to raise his Indian National Army (Maiti 2017, p. 187). The Indian National Army of Subhash Bose was initially raised by putting together British Indian soldiers captured by Japan during World War II, but it was to be joined by several other British Indian soldiers of Indian ethnic origins in other countries like China as well.

As Subhash Bose finally left India on the night of 16th January 1941 and via Afghanistan and Central Asia finally landed in Berlin (instead of Moscow where he wanted to go), he was convinced of China and India having a shared destiny "and wanted to secure China's help in his struggle against British imperialism" (Maiti 2017, p. 187). As the story goes, in October of 1939, when Subhash Bose had finally decided to leave India, he chose to seek political asylum in China and approached the Consul General of Kuomintang in Calcutta, Dr. Huang Chao-chin, to arrange it. Subhash Bose was told by the Consul General that he was most welcome to visit China and "every facility and ovation would be given to him", yet political asylum was not possible as British were now an ally of the Kuomintang government in the World War II and it would not be proper for his government to do such a thing against the British who did not wish Subhash Bose to leave India. The British government in India had refused to issue a passport to Subhash Bose fearing that he might travel abroad and build "contacts with Russia or her nominal ally Germany" and would have surely preferred to keep him in India instead of losing him in China (Maiti 2017, p. 187). But none of this was to change Subhash Bose's views about China and his determination to engage it. As Alexander Werth of the Special India Division of the German Foreign Office during World War II was to record later, building peace and amity between Japan and China was an important priority for Subhash Bose and he "paid particular attention to the maintenance and development of good relations of India with Soviet Union and China even though he was living in Germany and Japan during the war period" (Maiti 2017, p. 187). As soon as Subhash arrived in Berlin in April 1941, he had submitted a memorandum to the German government urging Japan must arrive at "a settlement of the China Affair" thereby facilitating her "to move freely and confidently move towards the South" where Subhash Bose wanted Kuomintang government to help him liberate his motherland from the British, French and Portuguese (Hauner 1981, p. 663).

Like several other aspects of Subhash Bose's life, this also remains one of 'ifs' and 'buts' of history to think what would have been the nature of India's China-consciousness if Kuomintang government had helped India achieve its independence from the British. Nevertheless, his brief engagement with Kuomintang was instructive to the consciousness of the leadership of INC about the significance of China and its enduring connect with India's past and future. As regards Subhash Bose, his much researched global connections — and his rise as the leading light of the Indian National Army and star of his team — was to see them building close communications with several European and Asian nations including China. In the middle of World War II, Subhash Chandra Bose had undertaken a perilous journey from Germany to Japan where he was received by no less than the Japanese Emperor. Indeed, his host nation, Japan, had even recognized his provisional government in exile. So, when in November 1943, Subhash Bose visited Shanghai and Nanking he came there as a head of his government-in-exile and as a mediator to resolve China–Japan tensions so as to direct their joint efforts for India's freedom struggle. Subhash Bose arrived in China in 1943 with an appeal to the head of Kuomintang government Chiang Kai-shek to make honorable peace with Japan so that foreign troops, including Indian troops, could be withdrawn from China (Vas 2005, p. 162). This visit of Bose was at the invitation of Wang Jingwei, President of Republic of China (the so-called Nanjing puppet regime under Japanese control), which made him appear as if working for the Japanese. This visit, however, also saw Subhash Bose addressing several meetings of the Indian community and visiting Indian National Army camps in China, asking them "to work hard for Indian independence" (Cao 2018, p. 154). But given rapidly changing geopolitics of World War II — where Axis powers were now on the losing side, making Japan the villain and inside China, the Kuomintang government was losing its battle against the communist revolution — Subhash Bose "as leader of the INA" had to "work out their policies towards China, Japan, and other countries" and "whatever choices he felt compelled to make … it would be wrong to accuse Bose of having had an anti-China attitude ... he had sympathy for the Chinese people and their struggle is abundantly clear from many of his writings and actions" (Maiti 2017, p. 189). Given that non-violence became the creed of freedom struggle under Mahatma Gandhi and the fact that Axis powers lost in World War II and were demonized by the post-war history, the contributions of Subhash Bose's radical and revolutionary ideas and techniques and his Indian National Army did not receive ample attention to highlight his role in building of India's China-consciousness.

Gandhi's China connections

Mahatma Gandhi — the father of Indian nation — was perhaps singularly the most important figure to influence India's self-consciousness and its pre- and post-Independence ideological orientations and policies, yet his engagement with China had not been his primary preoccupation. Gandhi's contacts with Chinese people, however, go back to his initial experiments during early 1900s with his non-violent protests in Transvaal in South Africa where "Chinese people participated in Gandhi's movement and even threw dinners for their Indian friends in South Africa" (Jain 2014). Leaders of the Chinese community in South Africa had first met Gandhi formally as an attorney for consultations during April 1907 after the Transvaal government passed the Asiatic Act (Reddy 2016, p. 9). The same year *Indian Opinion* of Gandhi was to publish a special supplement on Chinese Community leader Leung Quinn. Gandhi's subsequent commentaries also praised Chinese for their discipline and determination surpassing that of his fellow Indians. Given his regular contact with the Chinese community in South Africa, during his farewell banquet on 14 April 1914 — when Gandhi was returning to India — The Cantonese Club presented him with a formally signed commendation that said "the Chinese Community are losing a dear friend, a valued advisor, and a source of inspiration for nobler things" (Reddy 2016, p. 44). Indeed, the Chinese had debated about Gandhi much more than Gandhi debating about Chinese affairs. In Mainland China, for instance, during his six lectures on nationalism in 1924, China's greatest leaders of times, Sun Yat-sen was to formally praise Gandhi's "achievement in uniting the Indian people" and urged Chinese to "emulate the Indian people's non-cooperation" as weapons against the British (Wei 2011, p. 19).

Sun Yat-sen's successor, Chiang Kai-shek had, in a letter dated 21st November 1939 extended an invitation to Mahatma Gandhi to visit China which he said should be a source not only of delight but also of profound education for the Chinese people. Chiang Kai-shek had even made arrangements of Gandhi's visit to China (Nair 1949, p. 32). This invitation was repeated while Chiang Kai-shek was on his visit to India. On 18 February 1942, Marshal Chiang Kai-shek and Madam Chiang held a four-and-half-hour meeting with Mahatma Gandhi in Calcutta (Mitra 1991, p. 89). Both shared their understanding on their national situation though both leaders did not hold similar ideological orientations. Gandhi promised Chiang Kai-shek to visit China after India's independence. Later in a letter to Chiang Kai-shek (published in *Hindustan Times* of 15 August 1942), Gandhi sought to explain to Generalissimo how his opposition to India's participation in British efforts during World War I — that could weaken Allied powers and strengthen Axis powers of which Japan was one and was then invading China — was not aimed at seeking India's freedom at the cost of China: "I am anxious to explain to you that my appeal to the British power to withdraw from India is not meant in any shape or form to weaken China's defense against the Japanese or embarrass you in your struggle. India must not submit to any aggressor or invader and must resist him. I would not be guilty of purchasing the freedom of my country at the cost of your country's freedom" (Karackattu 2013, p. 4).

However, with the rise of Communist Party in China, Gandhian non-violence axiom was to be pushed to the margins of Chinese mainstream discourses. However, the earlier part of the 20th century (prior to China's liberatoin in 1949) had witnessed Chinese debating Gandhi and his thoughts rigorously, which germinated a constituency of intellectuals who were keen to engage and cultivate the Indian intellectual elite. Indeed, "the unique non-violent movements led by Gandhi attracted global attention" and given "the geographical proximity between India and China, Chinese scholars followed closely the evolution of … non-violent movements led by Gandhi" (Shang 2013). Gandhi studies in China especially flourished from 1920s, resulting in the production of 27 books on Gandhi: 3 in 1920s, 16 in 1930s and 8 in 1940s (Shang 2013). This was also the period when the Kuomintang government greatly supported China studies in India, especially at Tagore's Visva-Bharati. There was also regular coverage on Gandhi in Chinese newspapers and journals like Oriental Magazine, National News Weekly, Guidance, Pioneer and China Youth, and Oriental Magazine alone published over 70 articles that included its special edition and column on Gandhi. But just as Gandhi was condemned by the 12th Party Congress of Soviet Union in 1930 as being an accomplice of Imperialism, the Communist Party of China that was following the policy of "leaning on one side" was never to approve of Gandhi's non-violence or his peaceful movements of non-cooperation and civil disobedience (Deodhar 2012, p. 45). Nevertheless, during the heyday of the Panchsheel agreement and China–India *Bhai–Bhai* (brotherhood) euphoria, Tan Yun-shan recalls Mahatma Gandhi telling him, "I long for the real friendship between China and India based not only economics or politics but on irresistible attraction. Then will be real brotherhood of man" (Khanna 2007, p. 63). It is also possible to insinuate Gandhi's influence on Nehru reflecting itself in his euphoric engagement of even Communist China and especially in his formulation of *Panchsheel* (five principles) as the basis for their inter-state relations.

Varying Trajectories of China and India

In spite of long-term visions and geo-civilizational perspectives of leaders from both sides, the rise of the Communist Party in China since the late 1930s had introduced variance in pursuits of Chinese and Indian leaderships. With the defeat of Japan marking the end of World War II in 1945, Kuomintang China was one among the victorious Allied powers. The Kuomintang China was, therefore, to fill the geopolitical vacuum that was expected from the imminent departure of colonial powers from Asia including from South Asia where the British had finally begun working on their exit strategy. But this was also the time when Kuomintang (China's Nationalist regime) stood seriously challenged by impending communist revolution at home. The victory of communists was to make mainland China instead the target of containment by the same Allied powers led by the United States. The same United States was facilitating peaceful transfer of power in India from the British. Added to this was the enduring "overarching negative impact of colonialism on China" that had "dealt a major blow to its overall capacity" and "the most devastating impact of colonialism had been on the Qing state" that had triggered half a century of uncertainties, wars and violence (Wahed 2016, pp. 24, 32). This sentiment was to become central to the Communist Party's national narrative about "century of humiliation", making successive Chinese leaders preoccupied in reclaiming its sovereign territories and status, which led to pushing China adrift into the disastrous Cultural Revolution and radicalizing its foreign relations that then fueled anti-China sentiments against the Chinese diaspora in several Asian nations.

The process of India's transition of power, on the other hand, was progressing during the 1930s and 1940s in a piecemeal manner ensuring western support to this newly independent nation's liberal democracy led by mostly western-trained power elite. This fundamental difference in their political behaviour and systems as also their political leaderships resulted in both China and India developing varying trajectories, making them competing models for smaller Asian countries. This was to greatly undermine the initial euphoria of China–India *bhai–bhai* (brotherhood) sentimentalism and push them into an enduring relationship of contestations, including a short border war, thereby truncating all efforts to promote China-consciousness or China studies that had been so meticulously evolved during the latter half of 19th century and earlier part of the 20th century. The last major interface of India with China prior to India's independence in August 1947 was to take place during March/April of that year when New Delhi hosted the first of the Asian Relations Conference. This was a culmination of anti-colonial Asian solidarity that had permeated India's consciousness about the Asian region — especially through its interface with major nations like China and Japan — from the early 1920s. This inaugural meeting was to be followed the next year by the Asian Relations Conference hosted by China. But this did not happen as China was then in the throes of its revolution and was heralding a New China. At this juncture, therefore, the Asian Relations conference not only ignited the embers of mutual anxieties given British India's special relations with Tibet, this conference invited a Tibetan delegation separately from that of Kuomintang China which perhaps sowed the seeds of Tibet becoming such a contentious issue for their successive leaderships as also for an enduring neglect of China studies in India till China's unprecedented rise was to ignite a global curiosity about this re-emerging Asian giant.

Conclusion

To conclude, therefore, credit must be laid at the door of several common Indian people, especially soldiers who had first traveled to and lived in China starting from the British Opium Wars of the 1840s. Likewise, the British had also allowed and encouraged ethnic Chinese to settle in India, which was equally central to construction of pre-independence India's China-consciousness that evolved in a piecemeal manner driven by the central trait of assimilation of India's diverse and multi-ethnic society. Later, some of these linkages were especially molded and evolved by India's iconic leaders like Tagore, Nehru, Subhash Bose and Mahatma Gandhi as well as by several other revolutionary and radical leaders of India's freedom struggle. Yet the fact that China's liberation struggle was led by a violent revolution of the Chinese Communist Party and India's peaceful transfer of power happened under the leadership of the largely British-trained Indian National Congress leadership was to push both sides adrift.

Against this the backdrop of China and India growing adrift that was driven by their colonial frame guiding their interactions, their follow-up regional and global diplomatic encounters as newly liberated nations, were to became vulnerable to cold war dynamics of great powers thus greatly circumscribing their millennia-long civilizational equations of mutual respect and trust. Sovereign states of China and India were to now become territorial states with fixed boundaries, and their rigid positions on their complex and contested borders were to become the most formidable challenge for their national elites. Their short war in 1962 especially damaged whatever had been gained in building India's pre-independence China-consciousness. Successive decades were to see discouraging trends for the understanding of China, especially Chinese history and culture. It is their rise in recent decades that has reignited the explanations regarding their mutual interactions, with scholars now revisiting the evolution of pre-independent India's China-consciousness and how that can provide different answers to their persistent difficulties in building bridges of much desired developmental partnership.

References

Banerjee, Payal. 2015. "Introduction." In Yin Marsh (Ed.). *Doing Time with Nehru: The Story of an Indian-Chinese Family*. New Delhi: Cuban.

Bickers, Robert. 2016. "Britain and China, and India, 1830–1947." In Roberts Bickers and Jonathan J. Howlett (Eds.). *Britain and China, 1840–1970: Empire, Finance and War*. London: Routledge.

Biswas, Debarchana. 2017. The Chinese Community of Kolkata: A Case Study on Social Geography. *IOSR Journal of Humanities and Social Sciences* 22, 8, Ver. 15 (August): 48–54.

Bose, Arpita. 2016. *The Kuomintang in India, 1900–1962*. New Delhi: Sage.

Cao, Yin. 2018. *From Policemen to Revolutionaries: A Sikh Diaspora in Global Shanghai: 1885–1945*. Leiden: Koninklijke Brill.

Chatterjee, Partha. 2011. Tagore, China and the Critique of Nationalism. *Inter-Asia Cultural Studies* 12, 2: 271–283.

Deepak, B. R. 2001. *India-China Relations in the First Half of the 20th Century*. New Delhi: APH Publishing Corporation.
Deepak, B. R. 2012. The Colonial Connections: Indian and Chinese Nationalists in Japan and China. *China Report* 48, 1 & 2: 147–170.
Deepak, B. R. 2017. "The 1857 Rebellion and Indian Involvement in the Taiping Uprising in China". In Madhavi Thampi (Ed.). *India and China in the Colonial World*. London: Routledge.
Deodhar, P. S. 2012. *Cinasthana Today: Viewing China from an Indian Eye*. New Delhi: Tata McGraw-Hill.
Gupta, Uma Das. 2011. "Sino-Indian Studies at Visva-Bharati University: Story of Cheena-Bhavana 1921–1937." In Tan Chung et al. (Eds.). *Tagore and China*. New Delhi: Sage, pp. 59–73.
Hauner, Milan. 1981. *India in Axis Strategy: Germany, Japan and Indian Nationalists in the Second World War*. Stuttgart: Klett-Cotta.
Jain, Ankur. 2014. Why Mahatma Gandhi Is Becoming Popular in China. *BBC News*, 1 February. https://www.bbc.com/news/world-asia-india-25942584 (accessed on 6 January 2019).
Kahlon, Swarn Singh. 2017. *Sikhs in Asia-Pacific: Travels Among the Sikh Diaspora from Yangon to Kobe*. London: Routledge.
Karackattu, Joe Thomas. 2013. *The Economic Partnership Between India and Taiwan in a Post-ECFA Ecosystem*. New York: Springer.
Khanna, Tarun. 2007. *Billions Entrepreneurs: How China and India are Reshaping Their Futures and Yours*. Boston: Harvard Business School Press.
Liu, Xiaoyuan. 2010. *Recast All under Heaven: Revolution, War, Diplomacy and Frontier China in the 20th Century*. London: The Continuum International Publishing Group.
Mahatma Gandhi and China. https://www.mkgandhi.org/articles/mg-and-china-1920-1970.html (accessed on 6 January 2019).
Maiti, Girish Chandra. 2017. "Subhash Chandra Bose's Perspective on China." In Madhavi Thampi (Ed.). *India and China in the Colonial World*. New York: Routledge, pp. 184–192.
Marsh, Yin. 2015. *Doing Time with Nehru: The Story of an Indian-Chinese Family*. New Delhi: Cuban.
Mitra, Asok. 1991. *Towards Independence: 1940–1947: Memoirs of an Indian Civil Servant*. Bombay: Popular Prakashan.
Mukherjee, Bivash. 2010. Tagore in China. *Hindustan Times* (New Delhi, May 08). https://www.hindustantimes.com/india/tagore-in-china/

story-CWmtIuVZq1vjOoOHDyOVxK.html (accessed on 3 January 2019).
Nair, V. G. 1949. *Short Studies on China & India*. Shantiniketan: Stanford Libraries.
Nehru, Jawaharlal. 1939/1972. *Selected Works of Jawaharlal Nehru*, First Series, 10. New Delhi: Oriental Longman.
Nehru, Jawaharlal. 2004. *The Discovery of India*. New Delhi: Penguin Books.
Nehru, Jawaharlal. 2004. *Glimpses of World History*. New Delhi: Penguin Books.
Panigraphi, Devendra. 2016. Nath *The Himalayas and India-China Relations*. London: Routledge.
Pollock, Sheldon and Benjamin Elman (Eds.). 2018. *What China and India Once Were: The Pasts that May Shape the Global Future*. New York: Columbia University Press.
Quanyu Shang. 2013. Mahatma Gandhi in Mainland China: Early 1920s–Late 1970s. *Gandhi Marg* 35, 2 (July–September): 245–261.
Ramesh, Jairam. 2005. *Making Sense of Chindia: Reflections on China and India*. New Delhi: India Research Press.
Reddy, E. S. 2016. Gandhi and the Chinese in South Africa. *Occasional Paper 3*. New Delhi: National Gandhi Museum and Library.
Ren, Chao. 2011. Revisiting Tagore's Visit to China: Nation, Tradition and Modernity in China and India in the Early Twentieth Century. *Asia Network Exchange*, Vol. XVIII, 2, (Spring): 112–133.
Roy, Meenu. 1993. *Thousand Days of Indo-US Diplomacy: The Kennedy–Nehru Era*. New Delhi: Deep & Deep Publications.
Sen, Tansen. 2013. Is There a Need for China Studies in India? *Economic & Political Weekly*, Vol. XLVIII, 29: 26–29.
Shih Chih-yu, Swaran Singh, and Reena Marwah. (Eds.). 2012. *On China, By India: From Civilization to Nation-State*. New York: Cambria Press.
Vas, Eric A. 2005. *Subhas Chandra Bose: The Man and His Times*. New Delhi: Lancer Publishers.
Wahed, Mohammad Shakil. 2016. The Impact of Colonialism on 19th and Early 20th Century China. *Cambridge Journal of China Studies* 11, 2: 24–33.
Wei, Liming. 2011. "Historical Significance of Tagore's 1924 China Visit." In Tan Chung *et al.* (Eds.). *Tagore and China*. New Delhi: Sage, pp. 13–43.

Xing, Zhang and Tansen Sen. 2013. "The Chinese in South Asia." In Tan Chee-Beng (Ed.). *Routledge Handbook of the Chinese Diaspora*. New York: Routledge, pp. 203–224.

Xing, Zhang. 2010. *Preserving Cultural Identity Through Education: The Schools of the Chinese Community in Calcutta, India*. Singapore: Institute of Southeast Asian Studies.

Chapter 3

"Majian": Formation of the Cultural Sites through Interaction between the Chinese and Arab Cultures from the Perspective of Post-colonialism

Mohsen Fergani

Faculty of Al-Alsun, Ain Shams University, Cairo, Egypt

Is it feasible to study the efforts of the Chinese intellectual, translator and pioneer of Islamic Chinese studies, Majian, in his translations of "Chinese-Arab Cultural Legacy" or in his entire cultural activity in the second half of the 20th century, from the perspective of "post-colonialism"?

Of course, his cultural project can be put forth in the context of the descriptive concept of "post-colonialism", the side which focuses on examining the relationship between the colonial center and the other parts. The Chinese intellectual and translator Majian (Muhammad Makin, 1906–1978) appeared in the third phase of the Chinese modernization process, which started in the middle of the 19th century in response to the Western threat to China.[1]

---

[1] The first phase (The middle of the 19th century — 1895) aimed at modernization based on Chinese sciences, while at the same time deriving inspiration from western sciences. It has been followed by the second phase (1895–1911) where intellectuals played a significant role in the reform process, and going a step forward beyond Westernization. The third phase (1911–1949) witnessed the rise of the Chinese republic, also witnessed the varied visions of Chinese intellectuals of westernization methods and the widespread

He studied both English and Arabic at the Shanghai Teachers' School after moving from a remote area in Yunnan in 1929 and specialized in Arabic language and legacy. He graduated with honors and then traveled to Egypt for a scholarship at Al-Azhar in 1931 from where he graduated after four years. He continued his studies in the Department of Arabic Language in the Faculty of Teachers, Cairo University until 1939.

It is noteworthy that this study plan, which began with Al-Azhar as a conservative religious educational institution that then moved to a modern civil university, followed the same course of many of the Arab enlightenment intellectuals at a time when Egypt was under the British occupation. The cultural process there monitored the objectives of development against the different circumstances of the two cultures. The Arab cultural sites witnessed diversity in their vision of modernization, with some of them foreseeing solutions that were close to the aspirations of the Chinese cultural scene. Perhaps, he met there with Dr. Taha Hussein, his colleague who moved from Al-Azhar to the civil university, and who later became one of the most important founders of an Arab cultural site that deemed Westernization as a solution to the Arab society backwardness. This was the same logic that made the liberal Chinese intellectual Hu Shi, who belonged to the third generation in the Chinese modernization process, see the "Westernization" of Chinese thought as a gateway to renaissance. However, there was some difference because Taha Hussein was influenced by the French culture while "Hu Shi" was a believer in American pragmatism and a student of John Dewey. Perhaps Majian also met in Cairo with his colleague at the Department of Philosophy — Fouad Muhammad Shibl — the first to translate and write about Chinese philosophy in Arabic in a way that highlighted early awareness of the British colonial influence in reading Chinese thought.

---

westernization. Most of these visions took as its target establishing a fruitful model of modernization erected on a solid national basis.

In the introduction of his book, "Hikmat Al-Sin" (Chinese Wisdom), Shibl stated "In the late 19th century, the colonial British poet Rudyard Kipling stated in some of his poems which glorified the British Empire that the East was the East and the West was the West and that they would never meet. Nowadays, this view proved to be incorrect, because modern innovations brought the parts of the world near to one another. My study on Chinese philosophy derives from four sources: 1. Chinese sources translated into English, in the libraries of China; 2. European and American references; 3. Discussions on philosophy with Chinese and foreign scholars 4. My own impressions following repeated visits to China (Chebel 1967). If Majian moved from Al-Azhar to the civil Egyptian university for academic reasons related to his project of studying Arabic in ways that would later help him open departments of Arabic in Chinese universities, as discussed in this research, another Egyptian Sheikh from Al-Azhar, Mustafa Abdul-Razek, had moved to the Egyptian university before him. The latter moved to it as a professor of philosophy (1935) after he was engaged in a political struggle that made the political power angry with him. Ironically, both Sheikh Abdul-Razek and Majian had an influential role in Islamic culture through working for an Islamic charity. They also contributed, without any coordination and without even meeting, to translating the book *Risalat Al-Tawheed* (Message of Monotheism), authored by their professor Muhammad Abdou, the pioneer of religious reform. Abdul-Razek translated that book into French with the help of his friend Bernard Michel, while Majian translated it into Chinese, with the help of his teacher, Sheikh Ibrahim al-Jibali, and this translation was published by the commercial press in Shanghai.

French was more welcomed by the reform intellectuals in Egypt than English, because it was the means of civilized communication with the West since the establishment of the modern Egyptian state (Muhammad Ali 1805) for all economic, military, social and cultural aspects. However, English started to play its role after the British occupation of Egypt. Although it was imposed in the stages of education from 1881 to 1908, its role in the translation of literature did not give it real value in the eyes of the men of reform, who saw in the material aspects of civilization an advantage in the renaissance project (Dunne 1968). In general, the Egyptian generation of modernization in the early 19th century was in many ways similar to its counterpart in China in the middle of the same century in terms of its preoccupation with benefiting from the Western technology. This is found in the translation project initiated by Muhammad Ali (Al-Alsun School), "where the purpose of the translation was transferring the Western systems and laws in the army, the fleet, the schools, administration and modern science in general. The translation movement was confined to the scientific, medical, military and sports techniques" (Al-Zayat 2017).

The researcher notes that the Chinese modernization policies from 1861 to 1894 were also concerned with benefiting from the Western technology under the banner of "Self-Support Movement and Foreign Affairs Support Movement" (自强运动, 洋务运动). Its objectives included protecting the national integrity against threats and supporting the dominant role of Chinese culture against the destructive influences of Western thought. In fact, most of China's modernization trends, especially since the early 20th century, supported the idea that traditional Chinese culture was an essential part of the national identity to the extent that the great geologist Ding Wen Jiang (1887–1937), who studied in London and occupied the position of general manger in Shanghai in the 1920s, deemed some of the classical Chinese scientific and intellectual legacy as superior to modern scientific achievements. For example, he considered that the ancient Chinese geographer Xu Xiake (1586–1641), had far superior knowledge than recent Western European geography. Moreover, Hu Shi, who was known for his support of Westernization, called for "a revolution in literature" stemming from creative roots existing in classical Chinese (Meisner 2006). The researcher does not believe that he is diverted away from one of the aspects of the definition of post-colonial studies. Edward Said's book *Orientalism*, as a basic source in this subject, considered that studying the unbalanced relationship between the

West, the Middle East, the Islamic World and the East is considered to be the appropriate theoretical input to create awareness of the civilizational self after the demise of the colonial state. That imbalanced relationship assumed similarity in the development of the block of eastern colonial sites that suffered from colonialism and had liberation experiences at different levels, including liberation from colonial patterns of thought through language.

During the various stages of modernization, Chinese cultural sites supported the idea of identity rooted in the traditional culture. This led to rise of the need for a national language to protect the element of cultural power and to develop national education for the purpose of creating awareness of the cultural personality and redefining and reshaping the self by possessing equivalent power characteristics. The aim was to also create an evolution path that could determine the relationship between local characteristics and the network of world powers, large parts of which were under the domination of the ancient colonial powers. Hence, Majian's return to China in the early 1940s to teach Islamic culture in Shanghai, and open and teach Arabic in Beijing University in 1946 represented awareness of the importance of language in rediscovering and reshaping the traditional cultural identity within the modernization project. For him, language was to play its role as a post-colonial cultural site, in the following two respects:

1. Translating the aspect of excellence in the Islamic cultural legacy (translation of "the Quran") to end the monopoly of the sources of great cultural relations by the Western colonial culture and present himself as a substitute for it, especially that Islamic cultural studies have a distinguished history in China. China had by that time absorbed the religion coming from the Arab region as part of the trade exchange. The belief that came from West Asia was not a colonial legacy; rather, it was a cultural current absorbed by China according to its pre-Islamic features represented in Confucianism, Taoism and Buddhism.[2] In a recent period of history, the Hui

---

[2] China did not know a fixed name for Islam because the Arabs did not propagate it there. In the book 唐书, Islamis attributed to a ruler in Central Asia. However, what is said about the

nationality was formed, with its ancestors being the Arabs, while its spirit was the legacy of the Chinese people. The most important national rules of the Hui Muslims were based on the principle of the wise old man, Wang Dayu, namely "True integrity is loyalty to the emperor, while fulfilling God's right." (正教真论·真忠)[3] A long time before Majian, the efforts of Chinese Muslim scholars to establish a connection between Chinese and the Arab-Islamic culture had preceded what was translated from the Western culture, when the two old men — Ma Dexin and Ma Anli — translated "A-Burda" of Al-Busayri (天方诗经) into Chinese. It was published in 1848 in "Cheng Du" (成都) eight years before publishing the first edition of the French novel "The Lady of the Camellias". Because the Chinese-Islamic cultural sites were characterized by harmony between religious belief and national loyalty, they inspired non-Muslim Chinese scholars to engage in some aspects of Islamic scientific issues, until "Tie Zheng" (铁铮) published a translation of the Qur'an from Japanese in 1927 which was published by 中华书局出版社 publishing house in Beijing. However, the value of Majian's translation of the Qur'an was that it represented an addition to the importance of cultural site for a Chinese intellectual belonging to a national minority that represented the richness and diversity of the cultural features of the Chinese personality. At the same time, it reflected continuity of the Islamic scientific traditions in Yunnan, determined by the following two aspects:

First, respecting the traditions of classical Islamic studies, which were based in part on their translations rooted in the Chinese intellectual concepts (Confucianism, Taoism, Buddhism).[4]

---

word "Islam" in the historical references of the Song Dynasty states that the name of the Prophet of Muslims, "Muhammad" had various forms. For example, he is called 麻霞勿 and even 佛 in one of the contexts.

[3] 先贤王岱舆认为"忠于真主，更忠于君父，方为正道"忠君的实质就是爱国。

[4] Wang Daiyu, Liu Zhi, Ma Zhu and Ma Dexin, among others, have been those Muslim-Confucians who borrowed Confucian, Buddhist and Daoist, and particularly Confucian, concepts to elaborate on Islamic religion in delicate Chinese, introduce and study the culture of Islam, and made enormous contribution to the survival and development of both Islamic religion and culture in the Chinese environment (Ding 2018, p. 129).

Second, respecting the traditions of Chinese cultural studies, and here he was like other intellectuals of the generation of reform and modernization who were keen to protect the dominant role of the Confucian cultural site due to its importance in preserving the national identity, in the face of the growing "Westernization". We notice that Majian's translation of the Qur'an was in modern Chinese, one of the fruits of cultural sites created by the movement of cultural modernization, after May 4, 1919. His translation of the Qur'an reflected his affiliation with a new generation seeking to enhance the national cultural sites. Besides using modern Chinese, the translation was an attempt to form awareness of the one identity by removing the enormous differences among the Hui people in understanding the text of the Qur'an. For example, he says in his introduction to the first part of the Qur'an, published in 1949, that "The sons of Hui could not understand the Qur'an deeply, and therefore they could not reach identical ideas derived from their understanding of the teachings of the same text, which, if achieved, could lead to unity among them based on correct understanding and synergy, and creating their cultural awareness for serving the people." The translation was his main project, or one of two major cultural projects in his life, as he explicitly told his friend, "Na Zhong"纳忠, stating that the goal of the translation was creating a homogeneous spirit and synergy. His language was closer to that of the modern Chinese intellectuals of the 1920s, with their national goals, which for the most part expressed the main course of the Chinese nation in its attitude toward the colonial threat of modern times, rather than the language of a translator of religious texts. After his return from Egypt in 1939, he devoted his time to his translation and completed the first part of it after ten years. However, he stopped for 20 years for complicated reasons. During that period, he established another cultural site as his second project — the opening and development of Arabic language departments in Chinese universities. I will discuss this point in the following section.

2. In 1946, he managed to introduce Arabic into universities, and this was the first time when Arabic moved from the non-government school education to government education. This was perhaps a

far-reaching step when analyzed from the perspective of the influence of the Chinese modernization generation. Language was considered a cultural icon that played a national emotional role in addition to its practical function in the development of education and realization of traditional power elements, in a society whose identity was sustained in the millennium civilization through language.

He also introduced Arabic into the Department of Oriental Languages at Beijing University. The name of the department indicates the influence of the western linguistic methodologies, because the term "East" was not used by China for the Arab region throughout their historical relations. However, benefiting from the Western civilization at the level of cultural studies was commonplace. China tried to benefit from the western achievements when the national need for development rose. For example, in the late Ming era, Chinese scholars benefited from the methodology of mathematical induction from Euclid's book, which was brought by some Jesuit missionaries from Europe. Although those missionaries came from an anti-reform background in their countries, that was against the modern ideology of the emerging bourgeoisie and the modern scientific revolution that accompanied the growth of capitalism, they carried to China medieval ideas rather than advanced scientific knowledge (He 1991). There are many examples of this matter in the early stages of cultural exchange between China and the West. In China, they were received with a very warm welcome as they brought science, astronomy, calendaring, mapping and fragments of the Ptolemaic theory in the division of geographical regions. The scientific engineering knowledge brought by them caused the transfer of Chinese mathematical concepts from their function as a theme of the sorcery (existing in the Taoism tradition) to modular mathematical statistics that formed the features of modern science. What happened in Egypt was close to that seen, despite the different circumstances and details, when American schools were introduced into Egypt with the emergence of schools of foreign communities as early as 1875, as they introduced the English language to the Egyptian middle class, which had known only French on a large scale (Dunne 1968).

When Majian introduced the Arabic language into the teaching content at the university level for the first time in China, this brought about a great cultural leap unknown to the Arab–Chinese relations, during the communication periods in previous eras. He benefited from Arabic teaching methods at Al-Azhar and authored the first Arabic–Chinese dictionary. In addition, he carried out contrastive linguistic studies, establishing a curriculum for teaching Arabic at the university level, and a distinct cultural site that contributed to the following:

1. Achieving the communicative ability of the modern Chinese language at an early stage in building a modern identity of China after the new cultural movement.
2. Achieving harmony in the national cultural diversity within China, and the Hui identity had the advantage of participating in the development of the Han language communication abilities, as a historical language for the Chinese people.
3. Enhancing the ability to eliminate the dominance of a Western language like English to assume the role of lingua franca during colonial times, a situation that was not escaped by some Arab countries (Maghreb countries, for example, under the French colonization).

Here, the national language, as a tool of identity confirmation, connection of the society with the age, and the exchange with the Arabic language, worked as a tool of external communication without passing through the colonial bridge. Majian mastered English and Persian, both of which stood for cultures that transferred civilization. English represented a Western culture with a Greco-Roman legacy, and Persian represented the Islamic culture as the bearer of a glorious Middle Eastern legacy and a bridge of contact with the Arab region. This concept was included in the definition of Homi Bhabha of the "Third space" as language then represented different cultures that converge in a common dialogue so that each party could have hybrid identity models so as to avoid the "cultural clash" posed by Samuel Huntington.

However, there are additional cultural sites created by Majian's experience during his efforts in "translation" and "teaching Arabic" which influenced communication paths in a seemingly good manner. For example, he contributed to the formation of an important base for the creation of "Chinese studies science" in the Arab region, through his translations of some of the most important books of Chinese legacy into Arabic like "The Book of Analects" (论语) and the "Chinese Book of Proverbs" (中国格言谚语). Thus, his efforts can be seen as an in-between cultural site whose first value is preventing the western monopoly of this scientific topic. Its second value is that it provides knowledge bases for an Arab base emerging from a true vision presented by the Egyptian publisher Muhib Al-Din Al-Khatib in the preface to the Arabic translation of "The Book of Analects" published in Cairo (1933). He states: "I did not want the Arabic language to miss the opportunity of Muhammad Makin's (Ma Jian) stay among us, so I entreated him to translate "the Book of Analects" into Arabic, because I knew that he was accurate in his literary works, that he placed things in their correct places and that he was efficient to do that task, because the wisdom of the nations translated into Arabic through foreign translations is so distorted that its people can hardly recognize it" (Ma 1935).

After the publisher's preface, Ma Jian states in his introduction: "Concerning the religious duty, during the summer vacation I translated Risalat Al-Tawheed (The Message of Monotheism) into Chinese last year. Concerning the national duty, one day the Honorable Sheikh Ibrahim Al-Jabali, asked me about the wisdom of the Great Wise Man of China (Confucius), and I promised to translate his words into the Arabic language. Unfortunately, I did not have the time for it. However, later I was asked by Mr. Muhib Al-Din, owner of Al-Fateh Publishing House to acquaint his readers with China's wisdom and literature. I accepted that valid request, to fulfill the old promise. I also took the opportunity of the general strike at Al-Azhar University and proceeded to carry out this national duty." He signed his name as "Muhammad Makin Al-Sini". Perhaps he wanted to link his sense of national belonging with mentioning his national identity after his name. In addition, he was linking the "strike" at Al-Azhar, one of the modern civil life features in the national confrontation, with "translation" as a national duty in the features of the cultural legacy of the Chinese nation. Thus, there is a link between the two cultural sites, one in the form of the Chinese nation Min Zu (民族) when it is present as a cultural conscience in the background of the national event of the educational institution in Egypt, in the modern civil sense Guojia (国家). The other is the publishing house and "paper" in the Arab–Egyptian context, as a cultural and historical benefit from the legacy of exchange with China. The social and cultural roles of the Arab publisher and Al-Azhar teacher are defined in the framework of "Islamic cultural work" with its background derived from the spirit of the Islamic nation of the other, Arabs (他者的民族), in its relation with the intellectual component of the unique cultural site of the Confucianism as a cultural capital of the Chinese State (中国国家).

Here we note that the two parties appeal to the terms of a civilized exchange that derived its legitimacy from legacies. Majian is the Confucian who accepts Islam as a believer and scholar, and both Sheikh Jabali and the publisher Al-Khatib (the Arab intellectual and merchant) represent the Arab Muslim side that interacts with China — the hub of wisdom and knowledge — as conceived by the Arab legacy. The researcher may be tempted to visualize historical echoes of such a pattern of China–Arab encounters by approaching the dialectical interaction with the Chinese sea journeys led by Admiral Zheng He (郑和) between China under the reign of the Ming Dynasty and the Arab region, particularly Egypt. By those journeys, I mean the seven expeditions carried out by the Chinese Admiral Zheng He (1371–1433 AD) under the reign of the Ming Dynasty in the 15th century to the different regions in Asia, East Africa and Egypt. The marine route had evolved over generations, but Zheng He used marine navigation techniques of Muslim origin. He was accompanied by Muslim sailors, assistants and surveyors because he belonged to a Muslim family. He was said to have visited Mecca and performed Hajj. Surprisingly enough, both he and Ma Jiang came from the same area called Yunnan, and the end of both their journeys was Egypt. Zheng He went to Egypt accompanied by his sailors and interpreters on an official visit ordered by the Chinese State (Emperor Yong Le), which recognized the role of Islam and Confucianism in subjugating the Mongol legacy. The Chinese State Guojia explored the marine routes and sought sovereignty through its harmonious national philosophical legacy Minzu after the land roads were developed by the "Mongol" colonial legacy for some time. Five centuries later, he was followed by the intellectual and scholar Majian, who was accompanied by members of an educational mission representing the Chinese state (国家), which was derived from the harmony between Confucian and Islamic legacies formulated in a spirit consistent with the Chinese nation's identity (汉化的回族). Both journeys were aware of the need to overcome the crisis of civilizational weakness.

During the first journey, the State of Ming was just emerging from the legacy of Mongols; at the time of the second journey, the modern Chinese state was suffering from the effects of Western colonization, while the Arab region was seeking a new modern identification of its existence. China faced a difficulty in finding a "geostrategic" dimension that could move it from the romantic version of the state/central empire of Zheng He to a realistic identification of a civilized state with a modern concept of security, foreign relations, political alliances, national interests and sovereignty, "noting that 'sovereignty' as a legal concept invented in the aftermath of the Peace of Westphalia in the Christian West, is the enemy of Confucian harmony (Shih 2013). However, Chinese political literature in the modern era, specifically in the late 1970s expanded in response to the call of "Deng Xiaoping" in China's reading of the world situation from the perspective of the Statist reading rather than ideological analysis. Nevertheless, the national interest "Minzu" and the main national interest Guojia did not become China's main policy until the beginning of the twenty-first century." The first official definition of national interest, contained in the White Paper on National Defense in 2002, includes territorial integrity, economic development, social stability, the socialist system and regional order. The notion of core national interest had appeared in the academic writings in the mid-1990s, but the active use of it by narrators of FPA began only after 2010 (Shih 2013). In any case, an attempt to understand the post-colonial cultural conditions in relation to the Arab region and the world can be clearer if we can envisage the continuation of the philosophy of the Chinese state Tianxia, associated with the traditional Confucian legacy. In fact, it was the former Chinese President Hu Jintao who introduced the term harmony into political discourse in place of the ideology of the post-1949 class struggle. This supports the idea that a combination of Confucianism and other traditional Chinese philosophies constitutes a traditional intellectual base of China's foreign policy nowadays in a way that is slightly different from what existed in Zheng He's journey to East Africa and Egypt in the 15th century. This in turn may confirm an earlier statement by scholar Lucian Pye, who stated: "China is only a civilization pretending to be a nation-state, Chinese foreign policy is incomprehensible unless we first penetrate into this pretense" (Shih 2013). The Majian project, in the context of the cultural interaction between China and the Arab region, was of importance at another point, as a final complement to his efforts, and it was related to the intellectual introduction required for establishing an intellectual base for "Chinese studies" formulated in an Arabic spirit that had an indirect role in fueling its causes.

If we review his word in the preface to the translation of "The Book of Dialogue," we find that he highlighted two important things: first, the presence of national awareness in his cultural mission and second is the presence of the interactive situation between two civilizations in taking a first step in a reciprocal project, accomplished through translation by the Chinese side and thorough examination by the Arab side. If the publisher explained the Arab cultural role in the examination of the origins because he was skeptical of the value of translation from the "western legacy" as he put it, the Chinese side represented in Majian presented in the first attempt to transfer the necessary intellectual resources a research attempt in Sinology.

The researcher believes that the value of Majian's contribution to the establishment of an Arab trend in Chinese studies by translating some of the basic intellectual sources in Confucianism does not stem from impaired awareness of the cultural differences between the Chinese and the Arab cultural contexts. However, the investigation of cultural equivalences would not go through a bitter conflict or contrast; rather perhaps cultural diversity between the two contexts called for understanding of the peculiarities within the context of difference rather than discrimination. Moreover, this does not deny the fact that much of the effort to translate ancient Chinese intellectual legacy through European languages was successful in producing objective knowledge of the Chinese culture. Nor does it deny that a common ground between Confucianism and Christianity was sought by the Jesuit project through translation of the Confucian legacy. This produced the same problems and distortions in reading the Chinese thought as those produced by the middle area between Islam and Confucianism, created by the Chinese Muslims and intellectuals in their project to establish a cultural link between the Arab and Chinese cultures. Perhaps it was the value judgments of the results of Sinology in its European and American versions that made Edward Said include them in the "postcolonial" subjects. In general, a quick reading can reveal that they focused on two lines regarding China. One of them addressed the renaissance of China and the needs of its development, which made the period preceding the founding of the People's Republic of China in 1949 a neglected history. The other was mainly preoccupied with the history and traditions of China, without paying attention to the developments in its contemporary life in the last sixty or seventy years of its history.

The researcher believes that starting from Majian's efforts to establish cultural sites between the Arabic and Chinese languages could lead to a possible integration point in Sinology, from an Arab perspective, representing a middle area or a third space in the history of cognitive efforts devoted to studying its literature. In fact, Majian represents the middle objective point between two extremes in the context of time, history and location. For him, legacy is connected to identity at the level of nationalism, and it is a link between the Arab-Islamic culture and the intellectual and psychological foundations of the Chinese civilization. In addition, it is a part connected to the civilized world, both in the interaction between the dialogue and the major cultural centers (Euro/American) affecting the network of international relations, and in the conflict with it.

References

Altschiller, Donald. 1994. *China at the Crossroads (Reference Shelf, Vol 66, No 3)*. New York: The H.W.Wilson Company.

Al-Zayat, Latifa. 2017. *The Literary Translation Movement from English to Arabic in Egypt between 1882–1925 and Its Relevance to the Press of this Period* (حركة الترجمة الأدبية من الإنجليزية إلى العربية فى مصر فى الفترة ما بين 1882–1925 ومدى ارتباطها بصحافة هذه الفترة). Cairo: National Center for Translation.

Budetti, Domini. 2016. *Form Silver to Opium: A Study of the Evolution and Impact of the British Trade System from 1780–1842*. Virginia: Marymount University.

Chebel, Mohamed Fouad. 1967. *The Wisdom of China* (حكمة الصين). Cairo: Dar Al Ma'aref.

Ding, Jun. 2018. The Studies of Heavenly Land in China: From Wang Dai to Ma Jian. *The Second International Conference on Muslim Studies* (September 3–6), Lanzhou, Northwest University of Nationalities.

Dunne, Heyorth. 1968. *An Introduction to the History of Education in Modern Egypt*. London: Frank Cass Publishers.

Ge, Zhaoguang. 2008. Opening the Post-Mongolian Age in East Asia: An Exploratory Talk on a Critical Period in East Asian History (*kaiqi hou dongya de hou menggu shidai: shi tan dongya shi de yige guanjian shiqi*). Presented at *Multiple Perspectives on Ming–Qing History of China*. (January 15) Shanghai: Fudan University. Available at http://www.guoxue.com/?p=48068.

He, Zhaowu. 1991. *An Intellectual History of China*. Beijing: Chinese Academy of Social Sciences, Foreign Languages Press.

Ma, Mohamed Jian. 1935. *The Analects of Confucius* (كتاب الحوار لكونفوشيوس). Cairo: Mahbuddin Khatib.

Ma, Zhixue. 2008. Postscript for the Newest Edition and Preface for the Third Edition of Mr. Ma Jian's *Translation of General History of the Arab World* (*Ma Jian xiansheng yizhu alabo tong shi san ban xuyan ji zuixin ban houji*). *Studies on the Arab World* 5: 75–81.

Meissner, Werner. 2006a. China's Search for Cultural and National Identity from the Nineteenth Century to the Present. *China Perspectives* 68:41–54.

Meissner, Werner. 2006b. Identity from the Nineteenth Century to the present. *China Perspectives*. Available at http//china perspectives.revues.org/ 2006.

Sawant, Batta, G. 2011. Perspectives on Post-colonial Theory: Said, Spivak and Bhabha. *Research Gate*. Available at https://www.researchgate.net/publication/271633479_Perspectives_on_Post-colonial_Theory_Said_Spivak_and_Bhabha.

Shih, Chih-yu. 2013. *Sinicizing International Relations: Self, Civilization, and Intellectual Politics in Subaltern East Asia*. New York: Palgrave Macmillan.

Wang, Ning. 2006. *Translation of Culture and Interpretation of the Classics* (*wenhua fanyi yu jingdian chanshi*). Beijing: China Bookstore.

Wang, Ning. 2008. *Translating Global Cultures: Towards Interdisciplinary (Re)constructions*. Beijing: Foreign Languages Teaching and Research Press.

Zhu, Zengpu. 1993. *On Cultural Communication* (*wenhua chuanbo lun*). Beijing: Chinese TV Broadcasting Press.

Chapter 4

Comparing China Studies in a Decolonized State: A Case Study of Pakistan

Pervaiz Ali Mahesar

*Department of International and Strategic Studies, University of Malaya,
Kuala Lumpur, Malaysia
Department of Political Science, University of Sindh, Sindh, Pakistan*

Context of the Study

China, as a civilizational state coupled with visionary leadership, strong economic management and, thriving on the philosophical orientation of harmonious world, has magnetized China watchers around the world. The evolving studies and discourses related to China have itself produced its identity in Asia. As one of the China experts asserted in his study: understanding of China and self-understanding are no more separate from each other (Shih *et al.* 2018). However, these studies have witnessed a great boom and have swung between social sciences and area studies in the post-World War II era that has primarily focused on the concerns related to humanity in traditional Sinology (Shih *et al.* 2012). The current studies have also posed one of the most important questions that ruminate upon how intellectuals understand China and Chineseness in the 21st century. Their study argues that most of the intellectuals' studies on China reflected not only humanism but also pragmatism (Shih 2017).

Interestingly, the rise of China and its rapid economic growth have wider implications for the decolonized states in the Indian Subcontinent. Since 1979, the meteoric rise of China and its economic development point to a great transition toward planned market economy (Lin and Rosenblatt 2012). The current scholarship on China, in the field of International Relations, gravitates around the rise of China that is coincidental with its political, economic and military power, and its active cooperation and participation in various regional organizations indicates its influence in the Asia-Pacific region (Lo 2018). With the increasing growth of power and influence, the studies on China have taken a great leap forward since its agenda for reforms and transformation in 1978. It offers up specific knowledge that could commensurate with critical thinking, so that an overall understanding of China could be developed.

However, the scholarship on British colonialism generally focuses on the nature and approach of how colonial masters controlled and exploited colonized states in their favor. In connection to this, scholars like Kelly and Altbach (1984) came up with the argument that colonial masters extended their domination through an economic exploitation, penetrated by assimilating through the education system. In this way, education introduced by the British, invariably, kept colonized people away from learning through indigenous methods. However, the exploitative nature of the British legacies is still haunting the memories of the colonized and has largely affected indigenous knowledge, learning and understandings in decolonized states like Pakistan. Apart from this, the study of Quijano (2000) showed that the process or the way of European invasion in America was also exploitative in nature. Further, his study observed that besides material exploitation, the British masters also had a motivation for their cultural domination. He concludes that the roots of colonialism can be traced back to economic, political and cultural spheres (Quijano 2000). Similarly, Mignolo (2000a, 2000b, 2003) also argued in his study that colonial mentality was based on the discrimination and biases that thrived on the epistemic and ontological motivations in order to validate/legitimize or extend their hegemony and superiority, by invalidating what the colonized believed was their knowledge, experiences and rights.

Therefore, Ronald Horvath defined colonialism as a form of domination to control individuals or groups, their behavior and territory (Horvath 1972, p.47). However, domination, exploitation and imposition of culture have remained dominant elements of colonialism. Contemporary studies on the colonialism also reflect on the exploitative nature and its impact, even today, over the distribution and sharing of burdens, benefits and responsibilities at the decolonized sites. The existing inequalities and discrimination are being attributed to the colonial legacies at the decolonized locations (Brydon 2000).

Hence, the British colonialism was marked by trade and economic pressures, territorial acquisition, extension of military bases, creating political conflicts among the local population and continuity in English language dominance over the Indian Subcontinent. Language as an identity strategy has remained an integral part of values and cultures at the local level throughout the decades. It has been the main source of communication for rulers and the ruled, in the given mechanism, in a multi-ethnic social structures and in the world. To conduct a research in one's own language is considered a basic human right (Segota 2001). The studies on the scope and importance of language have remained under the eye of rigorous scholarly discourse (Fromkin, Rodman and Hyams 2018; Song 2018; Bracken and Oughton 2006; Welch and Welch 2008; Chen Geluykens and Choi 2006). However, a similar nature of discourses on languages also exists among the decolonized states like Pakistan (Abbas 2018; Mahboob and Jain 2017; Waseem 2014; Rahman 1998; Shamim 2008). The current state of English language in Pakistan is due to colonization of the united South Asian Subcontinent by the British.

The British had left an indelible footprint in the shape of its legacies, and these legacies are still haunting the memories and state institutions of the decolonized Indian Subcontinent. This chapter does not focus on the British imperialism or East India Company rule or China–Pakistan relations or India–Pakistan relations, but explores how China Studies was pursued by intellectuals in the post-colonial state and how these studies were influenced by the British legacies, i.e. English language. In this chapter, the study demonstrated that in spite of colonial influences in the decolonized Indian Subcontinent, China Studies have evolved and flourished not only in the English language, but also in indigenous languages (Urdu).

Therefore, in this chapter, I make six points: first, I examine, how the Britishers introduced their English language; second, how English language influences studies on China in the decolonized states; third, briefly explain how China is making efforts through its soft power to enhance Studies on China; fourth, highlight China Studies in Pakistan written in English language; fifth, examine travelogues on China written in Urdu (native language) and, finally, compare studies on China written in English and Urdu languages in Pakistan.

UK's English Language Legacy and Its Impact

The historical accounts affirm that the British English language legacy (BELL) had influenced the post-colonial state structures. For instance, the loss of Persian, the end of the indigenous system of education, formation of hybrid identities, segregation in society and the establishment of elite institutions. These issues are still plaguing the education system in present day Pakistan. The Western colonization process started in the 16th century. The Renaissance had led to the emergence of national consciousness and to the philosophy of mercantilism in Britain, which entailed self-reliance in areas of defense, governance, economy, navigation and in arts and literature.

Regions like Africa, the Far East and Asia also embraced political and commercial systems. These areas were supposed to offer a huge magnitude of raw material that was beneficial for the British factories. By doing so, such trade provided lucrative, "markets for the manufactured products of the home country". It was also pushed by factors like Industrial Revolution

(Southgate 1953, cited in Waseem 2014). Apart from this, the colonies provided a space where the British could dump the outcasts and experiment with social as well as educational programs. It was, according to Kipling, "White Man's Burden", not motivated by a welfare-oriented service, but had a beneficial aspect, as an imperialist power.

In the words of Robins (2017), the British East India Company (BEIC) was considered to be mother of the modern-day multinational companies. Its trade encapsulated an entire world besides importing Asian luxuries, for instance, spices, textiles and teas. The irony of the fact was that the company had applied force and fraud. For example, in China, the British had introduced an opium trade. Therefore, the way with which EIC ruled was filled with violence, and it was very shocking to the outside world (Robins 2017).

The British East India Company (BEIC) had been working in the Indian Subcontinent for almost a century. However, officially, the British government took control only after Bahadur Shah Zafar, the last ruler of Mughal Empire, handed over power to them. It was believed that the decline in the power and prestige of the Mughal Dynasty could strengthen the power of the British in the region in the year 1764. However, it was in 1818 that the British had completely taken command and control of India (Baumgardner 1993). As a matter of fact, the British took benefit from the heterogeneity of the Indian masses, and this situation went in favor of the British.

Additionally, the British had introduced the policy of Divide and Rule through which they attempted and managed to control the Indian Subcontinent. In this context, Shah (1990) stated that "the Subcontinent was conquered by Indian arms, Indian men and Indian resources". The British introduced the educational reforms only when they knew that they had politically controlled the Indian region. This policy still exists in the planning sector of the ex-British colonies.

The British took many steps aimed at political control of India. The first step, among others, was political control. After gaining control at the political level, the British had decided to create a situation in which vanquished people could voluntarily accept their inferior status. This phenomenon was favorable to the British. In connection with that, Antonio Gramsci (1971) cited in Liguori (2015), has termed it "submission by consent". It means that people under slavery or subjugation accept their status of inferiority. The way with which the British controlled certain areas was the reflection of their domination through the show of power and coercion. They believed that their power can only last longer if they had the cooperation of the local people. This approach or way of domination or control has been characterized by Gramsci as "hegemony" in 1930s. They had adopted three tools, education, church and media, as the apparatus for any ideological states (Althusser 2014).

The British colonial records showed that the EIC had formally engaged in education sector of India in 1781. In that context, the Charter Act of 1813 was regarded as a founding stone in laying down an educational structural system. Shah (1990) argued that there were two main objectives behind the launching of reforms and major changes in regard to the British role in the Indian Subcontinent. One, it took responsibility of education system of India and offered them one lakh rupees (Shah 1990). The way by which education was introduced to Indian was based on the oriental traditions, and it was further strengthened by bringing the education system on par with Western education system.

There were two Schools of thought in Britain: Orientalists and Anglicists. Both these schools of thought had taken contradictory approaches toward an education system that was expected to be imparted to Indian people. In this regard, the Orientalist School of thought preferred an indigenous education system which was based on Persian, Arabic and Sanskrit as the medium of instruction. By doing so, they believed that sympathies and loyalties of the local could be gained and ensured. On the other hand, the Anglicists, supported the Western education system. The purpose behind this agenda was to produce a class of individuals who could look after the British agenda. Experts like Rahman (1999) acknowledge that the both agendas of the British regarding education were politically driven. Their political desire to aggrandize their power and prestige was obvious (Rahman 1999).

English language teaching was introduced in such a way that could ensure them political and social control (Ashcroft *et al.* 1995, p. 425). The British structured the English subjects and these were taught in the English language. Major focus was given to the English text for it was believed that it was an embodiment of universal values, while others were considered by the Britishers as barbaric and uncivilized (Ashcroft *et al.* 1995, p. 426).

The above discussion implies that the British education policy framing was not philanthropic in nature, but it was based on political, economic and military domination. Moreover, experts like Shah have rightly observed that "on grounds of practical and administrative convenience, the government wanted English educated subordinates and the people wanted jobs ... essentially the idea of duty to the people seemed to coincide with interests of trade and government" (Shah 1990, pp. 45–46).

The Current State of China Studies

There is a growing trend toward China Studies in this contemporary period. The rise of China and its economic development coupled with exchanges at the regional and global levels speak volumes about the evolving shape of these studies in the post-colonial states including Pakistan. Further, China is also promoting its language through its International Council — Hanban. The increasing ratio of Chinese language institutes and Confucius institutes around the world, and particularly in the post-colonial states (Pakistan), shows that it is extending its role and stature at the global level. Moreover, the rise of China with its innovative ideas, trade and investment, and soft power has remained the talk of the town almost everywhere, including in the decolonized Asian region.

Apart from the British English language legacy in the post-colonial states, China is focusing on its language component so as to develop an understanding on China in the decolonized states. It would be no exaggeration to say that the subject of Chinese language is proliferating like a wildfire at the global level. Many studies (Forrest 1948; Wang 1973; Wen 1997; Chao 1948; Yajun 2003; H. C. Chen and Tzeng 1992; and Ding and Saunders 2006) provide enough evidence to show the increasing popularity of the Chinese language. The Chinese language promotion is being facilitated through Confucius institutes and language centres. The location of these institutes could be found in the higher education institutions of the decolonized states.

In addition to this, China launched the Belt and Road Initiative (BRI) in 2013. The purpose of this grand initiative was to build a trade and infrastructure network, connecting Asia with Europe and Africa along the ancient trade routes. The Confucius Institutes, since their establishment 13 years ago, have produced millions of the students who could speak Mandarin even in the decolonized states.

President Hu Jintao in 2006 began his focus on China's image, credibility and its influence by promoting the cultural and traditional values of China. The study showed that China in 2010 had clearly announced how they are going to introduce soft power through cultural means. Therefore, it would not be an exaggeration to say that the Chinese government is diverting its efforts aimed at promoting China Studies in order to neutralize Western biases against China. The Chinese language institutes are described in two different ways: First, they can be understood as an instrument of China's soft power (Lien, Ghosh and Yamarik 2014; Shi 2015; Liu 2017), second, Chinese language institutes can be understood as an instrument of China's public and/or cultural diplomacy (Gil 2017).

The purpose of introducing these studies at decolonized sites was to promote soft power. Nye (2004) defined the soft power in the following words: "The ability to get what you want through attraction rather than coercion or payments", and it stems from "the attractiveness of a country's culture, political ideas, and policies". The other way to attract the general public is through public diplomacy (Nye 2004, p. 95). With the evolving agenda for Harmonious World, the field of China Studies seems to have broadened its scope at the decolonized sites.

China Studies in English Language by the Post-colonial Communities

For a man, language is a means of communication and interaction with the society. Our patterns of thinking and ideas get influenced and conditioned by our actions. It is also a means to express and transfer our sociocultural norms and values (Lovelyn 2004; Sirbu 2015, p. 405) To promote China Studies and their learning could pave the way for more understanding on China in the post-colonial Indian Subcontinent. The Chinese desire for the peaceful development and cultural promotion possesses the potential to render her to lead from the front for the developing countries. Keeping in view the rapid growth in China Studies in the decolonized states, this section has also explored studies done on China by the postcolonial communities. However, all these studies were written in English language. Thus, Table 1 shows studies on China in English language.

The former colonies of the British remained under its control for more than two centuries. Given the longevity of their rule over the Indian Subcontinent, they left an indelible footprint. Their power, glory and influence are still visible in the form of state institutions and political, constitutional, educational and economic systems in each of the decolonized sites. This section examines how the British English language legacy influenced China Studies in one post-colonial state, Pakistan.

As mentioned earlier, the British had introduced English language as a tool to extend their power and influence. In connection with this, they had introduced various policies through the East India Company. Their newly introduced education system that was said to have been based on the divide and rule policy created haves and have-nots, and those who learned English language were supposed to be given perks and privileges in the civil services. Gradually, the British extended their control through their power and influence in the Indian Subcontinent. It was obvious that Pakistan as a former colony of UK has inherited their laws and systems. Pakistan's existing education system, bureaucracy, Army and almost all institutions are still carrying the

Table 1: China studies in English language by the post-colonial state intellectual communities in Pakistan.

China Studies in English Language	Year	Author
Muslim China	(1949)	Ali, Ahmed
Relations between Pakistan and the People's Republic of China. In Foreign Policy of Pakistan — An Analysis: A Group Study	(1964)	Aziz, Qutbud-Din
China, India, Pakistan; (Documents on the Foreign Relations of Pakistan)	(1966)	Hasan, K. Sarwar
China and Pakistan: Diplomacy of an Entente Cordiale	(1974)	Syed, H. Anwar
Communist China and South and Southeast Asia	(1975)	Niloufer Wajid Ali
China and World Powers: A Case study of Manchurian Crisis, 1931–1933	(1975)	Nazir A. Mughal
Visit to China	(1976)	Abdul Ghani
China's Policies: Other Side of the Picture	(1976)	Abu Imran
Administrative Reforms, Chinese Communes, and Local Government: A Report on the Training of Divisional and Tehsil Level Officers	(1976)	S. M. Haider (Ed)
China and Pakistan: A Political Analysis of Mutual Relations	(1977)	Rasul Bux Rais
Rural Industrialization: A Maoist Model	(1977)	Yousaf Kamal
Pakistan's Relations with China, 1947–1979	(1980)	Samina Yasmin
Pakistan, China and America	(1980)	Latif Ahmed Sherwani
Reflections on China: An Ambassador's View from China	(1986)	Mohammad Yunus
Human Records on Karakorum Highway	(1995)	Dani, Ahmed Hasan
Sino-Pakistan Relations: Future Prospects	(1996)	Bhatti, A. Maqbool
Chinese Central Asia: An Account of Travels in Northern Kashmir and Chinese Turkistan	(1998)	P. C. Skrine
Sino-Pakistan Relations: An "All Weather" Friendship	(2001)	Ahmed, Khalid
Pakistan–China Economic Relations: Forging Strategic Partnership in the 21st Century	(2001)	Akhtar, Shaheen
Chinese Soft Power Code	(2014)	Syed Hassan Javed

Table 1: (Continued)

China Studies in English Language	Year	Author
China's Success Stories: How China Has Transformed in the Past 40 Years	(2015)	S. M Hali
Awakened China Shakes the World and is Pakistan's Mainstay: Memoirs a Diplomat	(2015)	M. Younas
China of Today and Tomorrow: Dynamics of Relations with Pakistan and Handbook of Pakistan–China Relations	(2010 and 2015)	M. Akram Zaki
Rise of China and the Asian Century	(2016)	Syed Javed Hassan.
China–Pakistan Relations: A Historical Analysis	(2017)	Ghulam Ali

Source: Compiled by the author.

colonial laws, besides having the English language as a part of the British legacy. Pakistan is a multilingual, multiethnic and multicultural state. However, it has introduced, officially, English language besides its native languages, for teaching, writing and speaking.

Keeping in view this context, many studies/books on China could be found written in English language. The writings on China by the post-colonial state intellectuals seem to be of great importance. The main theme as mentioned in Table 1 reflects the different perspectives on China. The studies on China by post-colonial intellectuals came into the limelight after 1966. The focus of Pakistani China scholarship was on how China acts in the region and the world at large. Further, their focus also remained on policies pursued by China for reforms and modernization and its interactions with the decolonized states in the region.

The Chinese administrative and local systems were also the subject of writing and discussions by the intellectual community. Their major focus was on how China is approaching the level of the developed and developing countries, Chinese foreign policy, its relations with great powers, its economic dynamism, its political and economic relations with neighbouring countries and its rise at the regional level.

Thus, it is obvious that though Pakistan has inherited the British institutions, systems and their laws, its people have preferred pursuing their studies on China. It shows that the growing epistemology on China significantly contributes to the new learning and understanding on China in the post-colonial state.

Interestingly, apart from the studies on China pursued in English language, the author has explored some travelogues written on China in Urdu language in Pakistan. The writings on China in one of the native languages also manifest how the post-colonial indigenous writers were attracted to China. The following section briefly examines travelogue writings on China in Urdu language, in Pakistan.

Travelogues on China in Indigenous Language by the Post-colonial Communities

Travelogues have assumed great importance in the contemporary period. It is considered to be a part of literature. The nature of travelogue writings can be attributed to adventure, exploration and acting as a guide book for the people. For a long time, it has been the natural urge of the people to travel from one place to another. The purpose of such traveling could be political, religious, economic or diplomatic. Travelers make different kinds of observations on whatever comes their way. Their life experiences and on sight information could be valuable and informative for the general public.

Looking into the past, those people who left their travelogue writings behind were a great source of information and acted as guides. For instance, the travelogue writings of Chinese pilgrims like Fa-Hsein and Huen Sang, Taverrnier, Bernier, Marco Polo, Batuta and Alberuni, etc. as well as a few other names like Aldous Huxley, Graham Greene, V. S. Naipaul, etc. are famous. The main purpose behind keeping diaries or writing travelogues was to note down proper and accurate information about the places to be visited. In this way, one can pen down historical places, traditions, and the political and economic outlook of that specific country (Smrutisikta 2014).

The purpose of writing Urdu travelogues on China was to produce information so that people may be properly guided about various places, locations and systems. The early travelogue writers in Urdu were well aware and conscious about provision of information they were supposed to incorporate in their writings (Abbas *et al.* 2016).

It is to be noted here that literary writers dive deep into the world of literary traditions. They are well aware of the others traditions, and such a type of self-consciousness seems to be important, as was written by T. S. Eliot in his essay "Tradition and the Individual Talent". In this way, one can get inspiration from what is described as a literary trend and tradition. In addition to this, what motivated T. S. Eliot was to be well aware of one's traditions rather than to follow them blindly (Joshywashington 2009).

Urdu travelogue writings have focused on multiple factors. These factors have been noted properly and consciously. Travelogue writers portrayed almost everything, for instance, celebrations, fairs as well as occasions of rejoicing and mourning. Further, they have highlighted information related to buildings of the areas. Apart from this, their writings also inform about other countries and their architecture, different shrines and their ancient and modern buildings (Qureshi 1996). Two of the few important and famous travelogues on China in Urdu language were *Ishtaraqi Chin* and *Basti Basti Nagar Nagar*. These travelogues were written by Irshad Ahmed Haqani. His travelogue contains information about his sojourn to China, Hong Kong, Libya and Turkey. Basically, he was a journalist, and his writing style was similar to that of newspaper columns (Haqani 1989). Something very similar was written by Jamiluz Zaman in his travelogue *Chistan e Chin*. His travelogue focuses on Chinese economy and talks at a great length on industrial institutes. He further informs about the civilization, education and traditions of Chinese society.

Studies on China in the form of Urdu travelogues have been of immense importance and have become part and parcel of the Urdu literature since many decades. The growth of travelogue writings has been due to a number of factors. One of the major factors is the booming travel industry. The improvements in transportation and communication have further facilitated and promoted the travel industry. In this way, it has attracted the attention of people who belong to all walks of life to go to various destinations with an intention to visit places and understand the political, economic and cultural life of the country visited. Keeping in view this broad perspective of travelogue writings and their purpose, in this section, the study has explored Urdu travelogues as a part of China Studies in the post-colonial state, Pakistan. A number of Urdu travelogues have been written on China, but a few of them are examined here.

Table 2 shows that various travelogues in Urdu language have been written on China by the post-colonial state intellectuals. These studies are examined briefly in this section. The travelogue writings on China have now considerably become a part and parcel of literature in Urdu language as it is based on the various observations and experiences. The travelogue writing in Urdu language started from the 19th century. The travelers who lived in the post-colonial state traveled almost everywhere. They saw and experienced different types of circumstances in that specific country. With the passage of time, many travelogues have been produced in Pakistan since its establishment in 1947. Since then, travelogue writings in Urdu language have gained wide coverage and attained high standards in modern-day literature. Table 2 is briefly reviewed in the following.

A few of the famous travelogues on China written in Urdu language are analyzed briefly. The first and the most important travelogue written in Urdu language was *Nai Diwar-e-Cheen* (New China Wall). It was written by Ibrahim Jalees. During the second anniversary of the China revolution, Ibrahim Jalees was given invitation by the Vice Chief Minister of China. The cities he visited were Canton, Beijing, Shanghai, Hong Chao, Nanking and Tennyson. The writings of Ibrahim Jalees on China reflect the Chinese culture and their political dynamics. He was also inspired

Table 2: Studies on China through Urdu travelogues by the Post-colonial communities in Pakistan.

China Studies in Urdu Language	Year	Author
Nai Diwar e Cheen (New Wall of China)	(NF)	Jalees, I.
Chaltay Ho to Cheen Ko Chaley (Lets Go To China	(1973)	Insha, I.
Ishtaraqi Cheen (Socialist China)	(1957)	Ahmed, I.
Basti Basti Nagar Nagar (From Village to Town)	(1989)	Haqani, I. A.
Lahore Say Cheen Tak (From Lahore to China)	(1989)	Kamal, A.
Muhabaton Kay Darmiyan (Among the Lovers)	(1992)	Nadeem, A.
Rasham Rasham (Silk Silk)	(1993)	Amjad, I. A.
Parvasni (Providence)	(1995)	Atif, P.
Cheen Hay Too Cheen Main (Cheen is in China)	(1976)	Langhah, T. M.
Chistan e Cheen (China and China)	(1977)	Zaman, J.
Aagy Mor Judai Ka (Ahead is Turn of the Separation)	(1994)	Aasi, S.
Tasrat e Cheen (Memories of China)	(1956)	Badayoni, A. H.
Safarnama e Cheen (Travelogue on China)	(1957)	Hashmi, A. Q.
Ni Hao (Hello China)	(1990)	Khawja, K.
Tazkara e Cheen (Recalling of China)	(1984)	Ahmed, G.
Qisa Cheen Janey Ka (Story of a China Tour)	(1996)	Qureshi, M.

Source: Compiled by the author.

and impressed by the new laws introduced during his time of travel. He has incorporated the names of various Chinese personalities in his book (Jalees, nf).

Similarly, there was another one on China by one of the famous writers Ibne Insha. His famous travelogue was *Chaltay Ho To Cheen Ko Challay* (Let's Go To China). Although Ibne Insha had written many travelogues, this was about China. On his visit to China, he was accompanied by his friends like Pir Hassam ud Din Rashdi, Professor Waqar Azeem, Ibrahim Kha, Kawi Jaseem ud Din, Dr. Inaam ul Haq, Ijaz Batalvi and Dr. Waheed Qurashi. They visited many cities in China like Beijing, Shanghai, Dahon, Canton and Socho. Ibne Insha had a different style of writing. His writings were mostly consisted to be of humorous style. Besides that, they were informative. His writing also comprises details on Mao's long March and has he translated his seven poems. His travelogue was full of cartoons and pictures (Insha 1973/2016, p. 163).There is no denying that travelogues are very informative and contain deep knowledge. Travelogues provide important information and act as a guide to the other travelers who wish to travel to China.

In addition to that, Irshad Ahmed had also written a travelogue on China in the year 1952, the name of which was *Ishtraqi Cheen* (Socialist China). He had visited many new places of China and learned about different types of developments. The areas which he had visited were Beijing, Canton, Urumqi and Xinjiang. People from different professions, like journalists, also had accompanied Irshad Ahmed during his visit to China. What was impressive to them was the revolution in China and reforms introduced. His travelogue on China informs the readers about the agricultural system, industry, political system, religion and medical facilities (Ahmed 1957/2016, p. 164).

Similarly, another famous travelogue writer Irshad A. Haqani was accompanied by the then President of Pakistan, Zia-ul-Haq. Irshad, during his travel to China, Libya and Turkey, wrote various travelogues. He was basically a journalist. His writings were very much attractive from the political, economic system and socio-cultural harmony points of view. The name of his travelogue was *Basti Basti Nagar Nagar* (City Township). Moreover, his travelogues focused on the president's visit to China and other countries (Haqani 1989). It was obvious that such type of writers could belong to any profession. Given the different nature of their professions, they can offer different insights to the reader about the areas they visited during their time. The travelogue writers act like explorers, doctors, scholars and missionaries. Their personalities are reflected through their writings. Their writings are based on onsite or first-hand knowledge about the areas or cities they have visited. In fact, the travel writings can be linked or attributed to the history, exploration and adventure as part of their non-literary exposition. Similarly, their literary writings could be linked to their exposition to autobiography and experience. Moreover, during their traveling, some people are in the habit of keeping diaries with them because wherever they go on a trip or a tour, they note down some basic information of that particular area visited. Similarly, Aslam Kamal was also one of those people who maintained diaries during traveling. One of his famous diaries was *Lahore Se Cheen Tak* (From Lahore to China). During his visit to China, Aslam Kamal was accompanied by Arbab Niaz and Begum Arbab Niaz. They traveled around cities like Beijing, Shanghai and Canton. The main focus in his diary was how he lived in China, including accommodation, meals and breakfasts. He visited beautiful gardens besides historical places. He loved to join many functions and exhibitions. Moreover, he loved the art and paintings he saw during his visit to China (Kamal 1989/2016, p. 164).

In the travelogue *Muhabton Kay Darmiyan* (Among the Loved Ones), Ashraf Nadeem also visited various places in China. He went to China along with the delegation of trainees of PAS (Pakistan Administrative Staff). This delegation had visited cities like Beijing, Shandong, Haikou and Canton. The purpose behind this visit was to know and understand the agricultural reforms in China and also observe how they have developed their agricultural system. The writer has offered the reader a great insight into his personal attachment and feelings related to life in China. He explains that the cultural and ethical values and rich past and historical places were one of the important things that moved his feelings (Nadeem 1992/2016, p. 164). It is worth noting here that for any tourist who starts his/her journey to any part of the world, he would wish to see each and every surrounding of that city.

What comes to the immediate observation of a visitor are events and circumstances. They collect the facts and figures and then turn these into their observations and experiences. The travelogue *Rasham Rasham* (Silk Silk) was written by one of the famous poets Amjad Islam Amjad. He was not only a poet but also a great dramatist. He holds great prestige among the Urdu literary writers. He visited China in 1991. He was accompanied by many distinguished poets and writers. His writings were filled with love and emotions coupled with life experiences of the Chinese way of life. These writings were basically written in a humorous pattern. One can enjoy reading his travelogues, including the one on China (Amjad 1993/2016, p. 164).

As a representative of PWH (Pakistan Women Hockey), Pervin Atif, toured not only Japan, but also China, India and Holland. During her visit to various countries, she had written travelogues and diaries. One of her famous travelogues was *Parvasni*. She highlights her meetings with the literary personalities of China. Further, she explained about social issues in societies in the different countries she had visited. These travelogues were written in the form of a monologue (Atif 1995/2016, p. 164). Another writer, Taj M. Langah, has pointed out correctly about China. The title of his travelogue was *Cheen Hay Too Cheen Main* (Cheen is in China Country). He had visited many countries including China, Korea and Hong Kong. He was accompanied by Z. A. Bhutto. They visited China in 1975. In his travelogue, the friendship between Pakistan and China is highlighted. One of the important things about his travelogue was that he has clearly depicted the political, economic, social, and literary life of the Chinese people. The interactions with many literary figures were also noted in his travelogue (Langhah 1976/2016, p. 164). Nevertheless, the travelogue by Jamil uz Zaman was a bit different from that of Taj. The name of his travelogue was *Cheestan-e-Cheen*. In his travelogue, details about cities like Beijing, Canton, Shanghai, Nanchang and Shiyan are explained in detail. He also included an economic survey of China in his travelogue. He had also visited various industrial zones and institutions and somehow touched upon the political reforms introduced in China. His travelogue was very informative (Zaman 1977/2016, p. 164).

In 1992, Saeed Aasi visited China. During his visit to China, he was the part of Parliament delegation. He has written a travelogue on his visit to China and explains about the activities of his delegation in China. His travelogue provides the reader with a beautiful pictorial view of his visits. The name of his travelogue was *Aagay Mor Judai Ka* (There is a Turn of Separation Ahead) (Aasi 1994/2016, p. 165). It could be said that writings during traveling seem to be a productive genre for they turn the attention of the huge public toward China. Credit also goes to the travel and tourism sector and improvements in transportation that have facilitated people. There is a growing sense of the people to visiting important historical places and locations in order to observe and witness the political, economic, social and cultural lifestyles of different countries.

Similarly, A. H. Badayoni has beautifully given his impressions on China. The name of his travelogue was *Tasrat-e-Cheen* (Impressions on China). His writings mention about his meetings with the religious scholars and different personalities he met in China. His impressions mainly portray the social, economic and religious life of Muslims in China (Badayoni 1956/2016, p. 165). However, similar impressions on China and the Chinese Muslims have also been given in the travelogue *Safarnama-e-Cheen* (Travelogue on China), by A. Q. Hashmi. He made an extensive tour to China including such destination as Canton, Beijing, Shanghai and Xinjiang. A. Q. Hasmi was the part of the delegation from the Pakistani side who were invited by the "Jamiat e Islamia e Chin". His writings provide a good account of the lifestyle of Muslims in China. His travelogues contain not only information on religious activities but also on agriculture. What further inspired them was education, industry and the rich past history of China (Hashmi 1957).

In addition to that, K. Niazi, along with the delegation of Nusrat Bhutto, visited China in 1972. His travelogue *Aik Hafta Cheen Main* (One Week in China) provides ample information about various activities and their participation. These activities were well documented in the form of a travelogue. His travelogue entails information about history, geography, politics and administration system of China (Niazi, cited in Javeed *et al.* 2016, p. 164). Kokab Khawaja also traveled to China in 1984. She lived along with her husband in China for about three years. Her travelogue was known as "NIHAO". She explains in her travelogue about the Chinese culture, festivals, religions, health, food and places to visit (Khawja 1990/2016, p. 165). Similarly, another travelogue with a similar writing style was *Qisa Cheen Jany Ka* (Story of Visiting China) by M. Qureshi. In fact, he had toured

China for around 15 days. His visit was filled with joy and happiness for he visited Shanghai, Shiyan and *Hangchow*. He explains about the various cultural activities and attended conferences. Thus, his travelogue informed about the Chinese literature, culture and history (Qureshi 1996/2016, p. 166).

It is a fact that many travelogues in Urdu language have been written by the post-colonial state intellectuals. Their way of writing and recollections were different. Writers' visits to China have been either through political, religious, media delegations or an individual journey. They have presented all those activities through their delegations and provided the readers with their pictorial view of China. Their writings encompass the broad cultural, political, social, economic, reforms agenda, revolution, religious state of Muslims and civilization of China. All these travelogues are rich with knowledge on China. This first-hand information about China could pave the way toward greater and new understanding on China in Pakistan. All these travelogues were written during different periods influenced by various political events in the decolonized Indian Subcontinent. In fact, simple and easy to understand, these travelogues were written in the national language (Urdu). The deeper understanding on China has the potential to change the perspectives of the people.

Comparative Perspective on China Studies in the Post-colonial State

With the elapsing of three decades after the Reform and Opening Up agenda (1978), China has remained under the constant scrutiny of intellectuals. The growth of power, influence and economic dynamism reflects how China has attained rapid transformation. There is no denying that the ascendancy of China at the regional and global level has not been a piece of cake. Its journey began with drifting into uncharted waters; witnessed and experienced troubles, turmoil and the Century of Humiliation; and now is moving toward its great power destiny. Thus, the contemporary scholarship on China indicates how the post-colonial intellectual communities are showing their keen interest on China.

The epistemology on China in Pakistan is increasing, though at a snail's pace, yet carries a lot of importance in the midst of the western legacies and their influences. However, the approach and policies of China are perceived differently as compared to the British policies. China has launched Confucius institutes and language centres in the post-colonial states. Their way of promoting culture, values and ideas have attracted the attention of the general public. The concept of Harmonious World coupled with Soft power dynamics is pushing the postcolonial communities toward learning and understanding China.

As a matter of fact, the Indian Subcontinent remained under the British colony for more than two centuries. The policies and approach of East India Company was different. They introduced their language to the local communities. It was considered as a tool to aggrandize the British power and influence. The local population was asked to learn the English language. By doing so, they were offered incentives in the civil services. The British policies were adopted with an intention to divide and rule. The Persian language of the natives was abolished. Poverty, unemployment, illiteracy and dual political systems were some of the characteristics of the British style of ruling in the Indian Subcontinent.

Generally, people consider English language as a linguistic imperialism at the postcolonial sites. In such a dramatic scenario, the British legacies had left a deep impact on the peoples' way of life besides political, economic and social fabric. Even in the aftermath of the British deep-rooted legacies, many studies were conducted on China in English language too.

The intellectual contributions further substantiate the fact that China has attracted many people even in the post-colonial states. Indeed, this learning on China would play a significant role in understanding and strengthening Pakistan's relations with China. The upward trend in China Studies came in the post-colonial state (Pakistan) in the year 1966. Since then, the focus of the intellectual communities has been on how China has opened up to an outside world and its relations with neighbors.

Studies on China were not only conducted in the English language, but also in the indigenous language. Urdu is the national language of Pakistan. Many people, at the individual level, have written travelogues on China, in their native language. Their writings on China have been influenced by their personal visits, and some of them had accompanied different delegations. These travelogues on China inform about how China has developed within a short span of time. The major source of attraction for the travelers was the Chinese hospitality, traditions, architecture, infrastructure, and their political, economic and educational systems. China, being a civilizational state, with strong economic and trade mechanism, has invited the attention of many tourists. The Pakistani Urdu writings on China have contributed to a new understanding on China, and it is a guide book for the next visitors. The sharing of their observations and experiences obviously points to the fact that there was a renewed spirit among the post-colonial intellectual communities in countries like Pakistan to undertake studies on China. Table 1 shows that from 1949 to 2017, the growing trend toward writings on China in Pakistan were influenced by the British English language legacy. However, the Urdu travelogues on China from 1956 to 1996 were written intermittently. These writings are considered to be the second largest in the post-colonial state of Pakistan.

These contributions and writings — either in Urdu or English languages — show that the Pakistani intellectual community was magnetized toward China. Thus, the growing trend toward China Studies in the post-colonial state showed that the intellectual community did not necessarily resist colonial perspective on China. It is an acknowledged fact that the postcolonial communities seem to have taken a leaf from the Studies on China by the Chinese experts, their official or unofficial visits. The influence of the British policies on the post-colonial communities cannot be avoided, yet their studies on China are less influenced by the colonial legacies.

Conclusion

The sustainable economic growth, political and military strength, magnificent outreach to the world and technological advancement seem to be the catalyst for China rise. The policies and approaches of Chinese leadership toward regional and global powers, inevitably, point to how China is growing rapidly. Therefore, studies on China at the post-colonial sites reflect that trend toward understanding China and its cultural values are increasing. In connection with this, this chapter compared studies on China in English language and travelogues written in the native language.

It was observed that the British had left many legacies — political, economic, constitutional and education systems — in the post-colonial states. This study highlighted how the English language legacy influenced China Studies at the post-colonial sites; further it explained, in great detail, about how China Studies was pursued by the post-colonial state intellectual communities. In addition to that, it explained about travelogue writings on China in one of the native languages (Urdu); and finally, the different studies on China were compared. The findings of this chapter show that Studies on China pursued in English language seem to be dominant, whereas the travelogue writings in Urdu language on China are more prevalent but were expected to have less influence on the overall discourses on China in the post-colonial state.

Although the influence of the British policies and its legacies in the shape of English language cannot be overemphasized, it does not mean that the intellectual contributions/knowledge on China in the post-colonial communities were entirely influenced. Many of these studies on China have taken a leaf from China scholars and official and unofficial visits, rather than be influenced by colonial scholarship on China. The interesting thing is that the growth in China Studies, either through indigenous languages or English language, contains a potential to enhance the understanding of China in Pakistan.

References

Aasi, Saeed. 1994. *Aagy Mor Judai Ka*. Lahore: Sange Meel Publications. Cited in Javeed, M. A. *et al*. 2016. Travelogues of China in Urdu

Language: Trends and Tradition. *Journal of Applied Environmental and Biological Sciences*, 6, 9: 163–166.

Abbas, Qaisar. 2018. Cultural Identity and State Oppression: Poetic Resistance to Internal Colonialism in Pakistan. *Pakistaniaat: A Journal of Pakistan Studies*, 1–32.

Abbas, Qamar, Dua Qamar, Mujahid Abbas, Farooq Ahmad, Zafar Abbas and Ghazala Zia. 2016. The Travelogue Writing in Urdu: Its Technique and Tradition. *Journal of Applied Environmental and Biological Sciences* 6, 12: 181–185.

Ahmed, Irshad. 1957. *Ishtaraqi Cheen*. Lahore: Aaina e Adab. Cited in Abbas. Q, *et al*. 2016. Travelogues of China in Urdu Language: Trends and Tradition. *Journal of Applied Environmental and Biological Sciences* 6, 9: 163–166.

Althusser, Lousis. 2014. *On the Reproduction of Capitalism: Ideology and Ideological State Apparatuses*. Verso Books, Karachi Oxford University Press.

Amjad, Islam, Amjad. 1993. *Rasham Rasham*. Lahore: Sange Meel Publications. Cited in Javeed, M. A. *et al*. 2016. Travelogues of China in Urdu Language: Trends and Tradition. *Journal of Applied Environmental and Biological Sciences* 6, 9: 163–166.

Ashcroft, Bill, Gareth Griffiths and Helen Tiffn (Eds.). 1995. *The Postcolonial Studies Reader*. London: Routledge.

Atif, Perven. 1995. *Parvasni*. Lahore: Sange Meel Publications. Cited in Abbas. Q, *et al*. 2016. Travelogues of China in Urdu Language: Trends and Tradition. *Journal of Applied Environmental and Biological Sciences*, 6, 9: 163–166.

Badayoni, Abdul Hamid. 1956. *Tasrat e Cheen*. Karachi: Jamiat Ulma e Pakistan. Cited in Abbas. Q, *et al*. 2016. Travelogues of China in Urdu Language: Trends and Tradition. *Journal of Applied Environmental and Biological Sciences*, 6, 9: 163–166.

Baumgardner, Robert. J. 1993. *The English Language in Pakistan*. Oxford University Press, Karachi Oxford University Press.

Bracken, Louise. J., and E. A. Oughton. 2006. "What Do You Mean?" The Importance of Language in Developing Interdisciplinary Research. *Transactions of the Institute of British Geographers* 31, 3: 371–382.

Brydon, Diana. (Eds.). 2000. *Postcolonialism: Critical Concepts in Literary and Cultural Studies*. Routledge, London and New York.

Lo, Catherine, Yuk-Ping. 2018. "China's Rise and the US Pivot to Asia: The Implications of Trans-Pacific Partnership on the Regional

Economic Architecture." In Stefan Froehlich and Howard Loewen. (Eds.). *The Changing East Asian Security Landscape*. New York: Springer, pp. 83–103.

Chao, Yuen-ren. 1948. *Mandarin Primer: An Intensive Course in Spoken Chinese*. Harvard University Press, Karachi Oxford University Press.

Chen, Hsuan Chih and Ovid J. L. Tzeng (Eds.). 1992. *Language Processing in Chinese. Advance in Psychology* 90. Elsevier, North-Holland.

Chen, Stephen Ronald Geluykens and Chong Ju Choi. 2006. The Importance of Language in Global Teams: A Linguistic Perspective. *Management International Review* 46, 6: 679–696.

Ding, Sheng, and Robert A. Saunders. 2006. Talking Up China: An Analysis of China's Rising Cultural Power and Global Promotion of the Chinese Language. *East Asia* 23, 2: 3–33.

Forrest, R. A. D. 1948. *The Chinese Language*. London: Faber & Faber.

Fromkin, Victoria, Robert Rodman, and Nina Hyams. 2018. *An Introduction to Language*. Boston, USA: Cengage Learning.

Haqani, Irshad Ahmed. 1989. *Basti Basti Nagar Nagar*. Lahore: Jang Publisher.

Hashmi, Abdul Qudoos. 1957. *Safarnama e Cheen*. Karachi: Maktaba e Neem Roz.

Horvath, Ronald, J. 1972. A Definition of Colonialism. *Current Anthropology* 13, 45–57.

Insha, Ibne. 1973. *Chaltay Ho to Cheen Ko Chaley*. Karachi: Maktaba e Daniyal. Cited in Javeed, M. A. *et al*. 2016. Travelogues of China in Urdu Language: Trends and Tradition. *Journal of Applied Environmental and Biological Sciences*, 6, 9: 163–166.

Javeed, Muhammad Afzal, Qamar Abbas, Mujahid Abbas, Farooq Ahmad, Dua Qamar. 2016. Travelogues of China in Urdu Language: Trends and Tradition. *Journal of Applied Environmental and Biological Sciences*, 6, 9: 163–166.

Javeed, Muhammad Afzal. 2016. Travelogues of China in Urdu Language: Trends and Tradition. *Journal of Applied Environmental and Biological Sciences* 6, 12: 181–185. Link accessed on 12.4.2018. https://www.textroad.com/pdf/JAEBS/J.%20Appl.%20Environ.%20Biol.%20Sci.,%206(9)%20163-166,%202016.pdf.

Joshywashington. 2009. The Importance of Connecting with Travel Writing throughout History. Available at https://matadornetwork.com/notebook/the-importance-of-connecting-with-travel-writing-throughout-history/. Accessed on April 5, 2018.

Kamal, Aslam. 1989. *Lahore Say Cheen Tak*. Lahore: Maqbool Academy. Cited in Abbas. Q, *et al*. 2016. Travelogues of China in Urdu Language: Trends and Tradition. *Journal of Applied Environmental and Biological Sciences*, 6, 9: 163–166.

Kelly, Gail P. and Philip G. Altbach. 1984. "Introduction: The Four Faces of Colonialism." In Gail P. Kelly and Philip G. Altbach (Eds.). *Education and the Colonial Experience*. New Brunswick: Transaction, pp. 1–5.

Khawja, Kokab. 1990. *Ni Hao*. Lahore: Feroz Sons. Cited in Javeed, M. A., *et al*. 2016. Travelogues of China in Urdu Language: Trends and Tradition. *Journal of Applied Environmental and Biological Sciences* 6, 9: 163–166.

Langhah, Taj Muhammad. 1976. *Cheen Hay Too Cheen Main*. Lahore: Irtaqa Publications. Cited in Javeed, Muhammad Afzal., *et al*. 2016. Travelogues of China in Urdu Language: Trends and Tradition. *Journal of Applied Environmental and Biological Sciences* 6, 9: 163–166.

Lien, D., Ghosh, S. and Yamarik, S. 2014. Does the Confucius Institute Impact International Travel to China? A Panel Data Analysis. *Applied Economics* 46, 17: 1985–1995.

Liguori, Guido. 2015. "Conceptions of Subalternity." In Mark McNally (Ed.). *Antonio Gramsci*. New York: Springer, pp. 118–133.

Lin, Justin Yifu, and David Rosenblatt. 2012. Shifting Patterns of Economic Growth and Rethinking Development. *Journal of Economic Policy Reform* 15, 3: 171–194.

Lo, Catherine Yuk-Ping. 2018. "China's Rise and the US Pivot to Asia: The Implications of Trans-Pacific Partnership on the Regional Economic Architecture." In Stefan Forhlich and Howard Loewen (Eds.). *The Changing East Asian Security Landscape*. Wiesbaden: Springer, pp. 83–103.

Lovelyn, Ani Ebere. 2004. The Importance of Language Education in National Development. *International Journal of Emotional Psychology and Sport Ethics* 6, 1: 87–90.

Mahboob, Ahmar and Rashi Jain. 2016. "Bilingual Education in India and Pakistan." In Ofelia Garcia, Angel Lin, and Stephen May. (Eds.). *Bilingual and Multilingual Education*. Switzerland: Springer International Publishing, pp. 233–246.

Mignolo, Walter (Ed.). 2000a. *Local Histories/Global Designs: Coloniality, Subaltern Knowledge, and Border Thinking*. Princeton, NJ: Princeton University Press.

Mignolo, Walter. 2000b. The Many Faces of Cosmopolis: Border Thinking and Critical Cosmopolitanism. *Public Culture* 12: 721–748.

Mignolo, Walter. 2003. *The Darker Side of the Renaissance: Literacy, Territoriality, and Colonization* (2nd ed.). Ann Arbor: The University of Michigan Press.

Nadeem, Ashraf. 1992. *Muhabaton Kay Darmiyan*. Islamabad: Atiq Publishing House. Cited in Javeed, M. A., et al. 2016. Travelogues of China in Urdu Language: Trends and Tradition. *Journal of Applied Environmental and Biological Sciences*, 6, 9: 163–166.

Niazi, Munir. *Aik Hafta Cheen Main*. Cited in Javeed, M. A., et al. 2016. Travelogues of China in Urdu Language: Trends and Tradition. *Journal of Applied Environmental and Biological Sciences*, 6, 9: 163–166.

Nye, Joseph S. 2004. *Soft Power: The Means to Success in World Politics*. Cambridge: Public Affairs.

Quijano, Anibal. 2000. Coloniality of Power, Eurocentrism, and Latin America. *Nepantla: Views from South* 1: 533–580.

Qureshi, Masood. 1996. *Qisa Cheen Janey Ka*. Lahore: Feroz Sons. Cited in Javeed, M. A., et al. 2016. Travelogues of China in Urdu Language: Trends and Tradition. *Journal of Applied Environmental and Biological Sciences* 6, 9: 163–166.

Rahman, Tariq. 1998. Language and politics in Pakistan. *Language* 133: 9.

Robins, Nick. 2017. *The Corporation That Changed the World: How the East India Company Shaped the Modern Multinational*. London: Pluto Press.

Segota, John. 2001. Board of Directors Reaffirms Position on Language Rights. *TESOL Matters* (February 6).

Shah, S. G. M. 1990. *Legacy of the British: A Brief History Educational and Cultural Survey of British Rule in India*. Karachi: Sindhi Kitab Ghar. Cited in Filza Waseem. 2014. The Legacy of the Colonial Project of English Education in Pakistan. *International Journal of Business and Social Science* 5, 11, 1: 138–141.

Shamim, F. 2008. Trends, Issues and Challenges in English Language Education in Pakistan. *Asia Pacific Journal of Education* 28, 3: 235–249.

Shi, Lu. 2015. *Analysis of the Network Communication Approach to Public Diplomacy: Case Study of the Confucius Institute at Carleton University*. M.A. Thesis, University of Ottawa, Ottawa, Canada.

Shih, Chih-yu, Prapin Manomaivibool and Reena Marwah (Eds.). 2018. *China Studies in South and Southeast Asia: Between Pro-China and Objectivism*. Singapore: World Scientific.

Shih, Chih-yu, Swaran Singh and Reena Marwah (Eds.). 2012. *On China By India: From Civilization to Nation State*. New York: Cambria Press.

Shih, Chih-yu (Ed.). 2017. *Producing China in Southeast Asia: Knowledge, Identity, and Migrant Chineseness*. London: Springer.

Sirbu, Anca. 2015. The Significance of Language as a Tool of Communication. *"Mircea cel Batran" Naval Academy Scientific Bulletin* 18, 2: 405–406.

Smrutisikta, Mishra. 2014. Travelogues: An Innovative and Creative Genre of Literature. English IJEL-Travelogues, cited in Meena, S. 2017. Indian Writing in English in the Wake of Travelogues. *International Journal of Research in Humanities, Arts and Literature* 6, 1: 17–24.

Song, Sooho. 2018. *Second Language Acquisition Theories: Second Language Acquisition as a Mode-Switching Process*. New York: Springer, pp. 9–36.

Wang, William S-Y.1973. *Human Communication: Language and Its Psychobiological Bases: Readings from Scientific American*. San Francisco: WH Freeman & Company, 1–12. Accessed on August 8, 8, 2019. http://www.ee.cuhk.edu.hk/~wsywang/publications/chinese_lang.pdf.

Waseem, Filza. 2014. The Legacy of the Colonial Project of English Education in Pakistan. *International Journal of Business and Social Science* 5, 11: 1.

Welch, Lawrence and Denice Welch. 2008. The Importance of Language in International Knowledge Transfer. *Management International Review* 48. 3: 339–360.

Wen, Xiaohong. 1997. Motivation and Language Learning with Students of Chinese. *Foreign Language Annals* 30, 2: 235–251.

Yajun, Jiang. 2003. English as a Chinese Language. *English Today* 19, 2: 3–8.

Zaman, Jamil uz. 1977. *Chistan e Cheen*. Lahore: National Book Foundation. Cited in Javeed, M. A., *et al.* 2016. Travelogues of China in Urdu Language: Trends and Tradition. *Journal of Applied Environmental and Biological Sciences* 6, 9: 163–166.

Chapter 5

Colonialism, Cold War and Nanyang University's Chineseness Dilemma

Ngeow Chow-Bing

Institute of China Studies, University of Malaya, Kuala Lumpur, Malaysia

Introduction

Singapore today boasts the most developed China studies academic community in Southeast Asia. The East Asian Institute (EAI), attached to the National University of Singapore (NUS), is a world's renowned research institute specializing in contemporary Chinese affairs. Other than the EAI, the S. Rajaratnam School of International Studies (RSIS), of Nanyang Technological University (NTU), has an influential China Program, which actively participates in the research of Chinese foreign and security policy. Other than the EAI and RSIS, other academic or research institutions, such as Yusof Ishak Institute of Southeast Asian Studies (ISEAS), Singapore Management University, Lee Kuan Yew School of Public Policy (of NUS), Nanyang Centre of Public Administration (of NTU), also have at least some degree of China expertise of various fields (ranging from sociology to economics to international relations).

As a result of this well-developed academic community of China Studies in Singapore, there is a growing literature devoted to the study and analysis of the beginning, evolution, achievements and challenges of China Studies in Singapore, but the literature almost exclusively focused on the EAI, and its major intellectual leaders — Wang Gungwu, John Wong and Zheng Yongnian (Yew 2016; Shih 2018; Shin 2014; Chen 2011; Guo 2008). It is clear what is the mission of the EAI — it is to supply the best and most accurate information and intelligence on contemporary China's developments in the service of Singapore's government. To this end, the EAI recruited mostly *foreign* talents (usually western-trained nationals of the People's Republic of China). Professor Wang Gungwu, who has deep connections to, and understanding of, the region, was appointed chairman of EAI's Board, in a way ensuring EAI's direction would remain rooted. But otherwise, excellent scholars recruited from overseas (such as John Wong, Yang Dali, Zheng Yongnian) supplied the main research and intellectual leadership of the EAI. In fact, one could say that the "EAI model" was emulated by Singapore's other institutes later when they developed their programs of China Studies.

As Shih Chih-yu (2018) has sharply noted, in a way the EAI has been somewhat operating in isolation from the rich (but dwindling) Sinological traditions and resources of Singapore. Despite the full adoption of English as the main medium of instruction in all schools (primary, secondary, tertiary) in the 1970s and 1980s, Singapore retained many Chinese-educated intellectuals, who were mostly humanists with deep appreciation of Chinese culture, language, literature, history, philosophy and arts (Wong *et al.* 2015; Shih and Lee 2015; Chang 2015). These were scholars of "cultural China," in contrast to scholars of "contemporary China" that the EAI (and other institutions) employs.[1] Wong and his co-authors (2015, pp. 15–16) noted that within Singapore's intellectual community (divided implicitly along the English-educated and Chinese-educated), there are

> … those intellectuals who regard China as "other," [who] will have a certain tendency in the construction of knowledge on China. They are more concerned with contemporary China and

---

[1] "Contemporary China" and "Cultural China" are similar to the concepts of "state perspectives" and "civilizational perspectives" on China that Professor Chih-yu Shih proposed. See Shih 2014.

want to understand contemporary Chinese politics and economics to determine the actual situation of the "theory of the China threat" and the "theory of a peaceful rise," as well as the evaluation of the Chinese market and economic trends. Therefore, to some extent, they ignore the cultural China as if having no practical value. On the other hand, those scholars who believe in Chinese culture and Chinese identity ... are certainly positive of the importance of cultural China. The knowledge on China they constructed is built on the basis of traditional Chinese literature, history, and philosophy. In our opinion, a comprehensive knowledge on China should be contemporary China complemented by cultural China. Lacking either one will lead to a deviation in one's knowledge on China. Therefore, in the reconstruction of knowledge on China in Singapore, the key lies in a comprehensive understanding of "China." One must fully understand cultural China and contemporary China, with both aspects used to build a relatively comprehensive Chinese knowledge.

Why then did Singapore *not* have an indigenous group of scholars specializing in the knowledge "of contemporary China complemented by cultural China," despite the rich Sinological resources, and the existence of a large Chinese-speaking community? The same question could be posted to Malaysia too (Ngeow, Ling and Fan 2014), given the common colonial background, similar social makeup and the entangled history of both countries.

This chapter contends that there was once such a possibility. In Singapore, a Chinese-medium university, Nanyang University, once existed, from 1956 to 1980. Although located in Singapore, the university should not be seen as exclusively Singaporean. It was meant to be a university for the Chinese in the Nanyang (Southeast Asia) region. The students (predominantly Chinese-educated ethnic Chinese) mostly came from Malaya and Singapore, with some others from Indonesia, Borneo, Thailand and the Philippines. Its faculty, especially in the early years, was mostly staffed by intellectuals and scholars from Taiwan and Hong Kong. Had Nanyang University survived, it could have produced China scholars equipped with the knowledge of both "contemporary China" and "cultural

China" to serve in the academia or think tank sector in Malaysia and Singapore. It could have played a pioneering role in the development of China Studies in Malaysia and Singapore.

However, the history of Nanyang University was full of controversy and struggle. It had a difficult beginning under the colonial administration, went through a turbulent period in the context of ideological politics of the Cold War, continued to struggle to justify its own existence in the face of official skepticism /semi-acceptance/unacceptance in both Singapore and Malaysia, and ultimately could not escape its tragic end of being closed down, by Singapore Prime Minister Lee Kuan Yew and his People's Action Party (PAP) government. Its history, in a way, illustrated the complexity of preserving and maintaining a Chinese higher education institution, and the dilemma of negotiating its "Chineseness," in this region.

Nanyang University: A Chinese University Outside of China[2]

The beginning: The idea of a Chinese University outside of China

It is often said that outside of the Greater China area (Mainland, Hong Kong and Macao, Taiwan), Chinese education is best maintained in Malaysia, and to a lesser extent Singapore, owing to the existence of a large number of Chinese primary and secondary schools.[3] Their existence also testified to the great demand for Chinese education, because of the large number of Chinese who migrated to Southeast Asia, especially during the late 19th century and early 20th century, when the British colonial government in Malaya and Singapore imported Chinese laborers to work in

---

[2] Unless specifically mentioned, the following section is drawn from these materials: Nanyang University Alumni Association of Malaysia 1990; Ku 1994: 169–196; Ku 2003; Lei 2008.

[3] After its independence from Malaysia in 1965, Singapore's government, under Prime Minister Lee Kuan Yew, opted for an English-first policy, and gradually all its schools became English-medium schools, and the level of Chinese education today in Singapore is inferior to Malaysia's Chinese schools.

plantation estates and mines. The British colonial government did not support Chinese education, but also did not fully obstruct the development of Chinese schools, at least not strongly. Hence, Chinese schools expanded as the number of Chinese migrants and their descendants increased significantly. However, the existence of these schools did not sit comfortably with the indigenous Malay nationalist political circle, who saw this as a threat to national integration and the superior position of the Malay language.

After the Second World War, if the graduates of these Chinese schools, which were at the primary and secondary levels only, wished to pursue tertiary-level education, they could go to the universities in China. Chinese schools also recruited teachers from China. But that option became untenable after the Chinese Communist Party won the civil war with the Nationalists in 1949. The British colonial authorities started to close off interactions between China and the Chinese in Malaya and Singapore, and students who still went to universities in China after 1950s would probably not be allowed to come back because of the fear of spreading communism. The British colonial government established a University of Malaya[4] to train a class of English-speaking elite, but this University could not accept the graduates of the Chinese schools. The small Department of Chinese Studies of the University of Malaya could not and would not be able to meet the demands for tertiary level of education by the Chinese-educated students. It was under this context that the call for establishing a university for the Chinese-educated students emerged.

Tan Lark Sye and the founding of Nanyang University

Tan Lark Sye 陳六使[5] was a wealthy Singapore-based Chinese businessman, a protégé in, and eventually the successor to,

---
[4] University of Malaya was originally established in Singapore in 1949. A branch campus in Kuala Lumpur was established in 1959. The Singapore campus eventually became the University of Singapore in 1962, while the Kuala Lumpur campus retained its name as the University of Malaya.
[5] For more on Tan Lark Sye, see Ong, Lim and Ng 2015.

Tan Kah Kee's 陳嘉庚 rubber business empire. He was also the leader of various Chinese organizations such as Singapore Chinese Chamber of Commerce and Hokkien Guild Association of Singapore. Tan initiated and led the efforts to establish this Chinese university, which was eventually named Nanyang University (in Chinese abbreviation is called Nantah 南大, which remains the popular term to refer to the University; throughout this chapter the term "Nantah" will sometimes be used also). In establishing Nantah, Tan Lark Sye was inspired by his mentor Tan Kah Kee. Tan Kah Kee was best known for his spirit of "bankrupting one's own fortune to revive learning" (*huijia xingxue* 毀家興學), who spent a lifetime devoted to the advancement of education, and almost single-handedly founded Xiamen University and Jimei University in China. But by the 1950s, founding a university in China was no longer practical or necessary, and with the communist takeover of Mainland China, the Chinese in the Nanyang region slowly realized that they would have to settle in this place for long, if not permanently. Hence, establishing a Chinese university to meet the needs of the local Chinese population became a mission for Tan Lark Sye.

Tan initiated the idea formally in a committee meeting of the Hokkien Guild Association of Singapore in January 1953, and by February, through the platform of Singapore Chinese Chamber of Commerce, a Preparatory Committee for the Establishment of Nanyang University, comprising delegates from all major Chinese associations and organizations in Malaya and Singapore, was formed. In April 1953, the Preparatory Committee issued a Declaration, which outlined four major reasons for establishing Nantah and its two distinguishing characteristics. Accordingly, the four main reasons were: 1) to provide an avenue for the graduates of secondary schools (especially Chinese schools) to pursue tertiary-level education; 2) to groom teachers for the secondary schools; 3) to nurture specialized knowledge and skills for the country; and 4) to meet the needs of the growing population in Malaya and Singapore. In addition, there are two distinguishing characteristics of Nantah. It is worth reproducing the whole passage of this part of the Declaration here, for it illustrated the kind of vision that guided the establishment of Nantah (cited in Ong, Lim and Ng 2015, pp. 149–152):

> First, as the bridge between the ancient Eastern culture, which is profound in breadth and depth, and the brilliant Western culture, which is deeply rooted and widely influential. Together, they form the main framework of world culture. Singapore is situated at the pivotal point of the confluence of these two cultures. For this reason, an important agenda of universities in Singapore should be to serve as a conduit for both cultural systems to mingle and prosper. This is where Nanyang University can complement the University of Malaya. While the University of Malaya emphasizes English, Nanyang University would place equal emphasis on Chinese, English and Malay to meet the practical demands for academic research, so that scholars may be well grounded in the local languages without fear of failing behind international level. In this way, Nanyang University can function as the bridge linking both Chinese and Western cultures.
>
> Second, as a center for developing the Malayan culture. Malaya is a land where the Chinese, Malays and Indians live in harmony while having frequent social and cultural interactions. A distinctive feature of Nanyang University will be the study of these ethnic cultures and the amalgamation of their essences into a Malayan culture that shall have its pride of place in history. For this reason, Nanyang University will focus its research efforts in subjects such as the geography, history, economy, language of the various ethnic groups in Malaya.

Hence, although Nantah was a Chinese-medium university, the Declaration made it clear that it was more than just a "Chinese" university.[6] By declaring its embrace of inter-cultural interactions and local cultural development, it wished to address the potential criticisms that this would be a university promoting Chinese "chauvinism."

---

[6] In fact, there were always some non-Chinese students studying at Nantah throughout its history.

British colonial hesitation

The proposal to establish Nantah garnered substantial support from the entire ethnic Chinese community in Malaya and Singapore. Tan Cheng Lock 陳禎祿, President of the Malayan Chinese Association, which was a component party of the ruling Alliance coalition in Malaya, pledged full support. However, the British colonial authorities were not very supportive about the project. Registration of Nantah as a university failed, and instead the university had to register as a company to gain legal recognition. Construction of Nantah's campus ran into technical and bureaucratic resistance. No financial assistance from the government was granted, and the government refused to guarantee recognition of the diplomas/degrees offered by Nantah. As T. H. Wong (2005) pointed out, this was in contrast to the more relaxing policy in another British colonial territory — Hong Kong. There, the development of the Chinese University of Hong Kong, a university with a similar nature of Nanyang University, gained no obstacles from the British colonial government in Hong Kong.

There were several reasons for this resistance from the colonial authorities. First, the British still had to be sensitive about the sentiments of the majority ethnic group in Malaya and the implications for racial politics. The idea of a Chinese University in Malaya/Singapore, in most cases, was not well received by the Malay politicians and intellectuals, and instead generated strong Malay opposition, or at least uneasiness. They claimed that this university would "create little Beijings and little Nanjings" in the land of Malaya (cited in Wong 2005, p. 204). Endorsing the establishment of Nantah ran counter to the efforts of the colonial government to foster a common Malaya identity (Ong 2015, p. 75).

Second, the British suspected of the communist infiltration through Nantah. Nantah was founded on the strong Chinese sentiment of preserving Chinese education and culture, which could be sometimes mixed with anti-colonial, anti-imperialist, left-leaning or even communist ideologies. The Communist Party of Malaya was supportive of Nantah, and the British were worried that the communists could exploit the cultural sentiments of the students in Nantah and recruited them and developed them into committed communists.

Third, the British did not want to see its preferred university having to compete for the rich financial resources of the ethnic Chinese business community. The University of Malaya was just established in 1949, with substantial financial donation from the local Chinese business community. But the Chinese business leaders, including Tan Lark Sye, were disappointed that the University of Malaya basically did not care about Chinese-educated students; hence, these leaders turned their resources into funding the new Chinese university.

Nevertheless, the colonial government eventually acquiesced, and gave its reluctant blessing to Nantah. Two factors were mainly at play here. First, the persistent and overwhelming support of almost the entire ethnic Chinese community in Malaya and Singapore, and the status and reputation of Tan Lark Sye, meant that the British could not overtly suppress it, notwithstanding the risk of negative reactions from the Malay community. Second, and more importantly, the United States played a crucial role in convincing the British that Nanyang University could be turned into its advantage, especially in countering the threat of communism.

Lin Yutang episode, cultural cold war, and the involvement of the United States

Tan Lark Sye and his colleagues were acutely aware of the sensitivity of a Chinese university in the region, especially in the context of the emerging Cold War in Asia. Communist China just fought to a standstill with the United States and its allies in the Korean War, and had been supportive of the communist movements in Southeast Asia that presented serious threats not only to the British interests but also to the emerging indigenous nationalist elite. The fact that members of the communist movements in Southeast Asia, especially in Malaya and Singapore, were predominantly ethnic Chinese added to the suspicious that the

Chinese people were more likely to be sympathetic to the cause of communism. This was especially the case among the Chinese-educated Chinese (in contrast to the English-educated Chinese), because the Marxist and communist propaganda materials were predominantly circulated within the Chinese-reading circles. In the eyes of the British colonial authorities and the Malay nationalists, allowing a Chinese University to be established was tantamount to allowing a base to spread communism to be set up in the region.

To assuage these fears, Tan Lark Sye and his colleagues had to appoint a scholar who could not and must not be seen as sympathetic toward the communist or at least the leftist "cause" as the Chancellor of Nantah. After failing to secure the appointment of Hu Shih 胡適 and Mei Yiqi 梅貽琦, Tan and his colleagues were able to persuade Lin Yutang 林語堂, a famous Chinese linguist, essayist, philosopher and translator, to take up the position as Chancellor of Nantah. Lin grew up in a Chinese Christian family, had always been an anti-communist and liberal, and enjoyed a good relationship with the Chiang Kai-shek government in Taiwan and with the United States, and thus seemed to be the ideal candidate to lead Nanyang University.

However, differences between Lin Yutang and Tan Lark Sye soon became irreconcilable, and both sides parted on bitter terms, even before Nanyang University formerly commenced its classes in 1956.[7] After Lin's departure, he published a highly disparaging remark on Nantah in an American magazine, accusing the university to be a front for Beijing's communist operations, without offering substantiating evidence. This drew a rebuttal from Tan Lark Sye and others. Nantah eventually commenced without a Chancellor, and operated under the leadership of an administrative committee (headed by a Vice Chancellor) until 1969, when Dr Rayson Huang 黃麗松 was appointed as Chancellor.

Little was known then that the whole "Lin Yutang Episode" was very much part of the "Cultural Cold War" that involved the

---

[7] These differences included visions of the university, budget, management style, etc. On the differences between Lin Yutang and Tan Lark Sye, see Ong 2015; Chen 2015.

United States (Saunders 1999). A former CIA agent operating in Southeast Asia revealed in his memoir that his mission did include the "monitoring" of Nantah and there was a secret meeting between him and Lin Yutang. Lin was indeed the ideal candidate most acceptable to the Americans, British, and Taiwan's Chiang Kai-shek government. Lin's resignation was a seen as a serious concern although Washington was unable to convince him to stay on, but the CIA agent managed to convince Lin to write the disparaging article on Nantah (Smith 1976, pp. 199–201). The Cultural Cold War in Southeast Asia was about how to win the "hearts and minds" of the overseas Chinese for the cause of anti-communism. After the Korean War, the US was particularly worried about the sizable ethnic Chinese population in Southeast Asia, fearing that communist China could mobilize this population or at least win the allegiance and support of the overseas Chinese youth. The US and the British colonial government had different views on and policies toward Nanyang University and overseas Chinese education in general. Whereas the British adopted a more passive approach, in which case they neither supported nor overtly suppressed Nantah, the Americans adopted a more proactive approach, in which they saw the potential of mobilizing the nationalism of overseas Chinese *against* communism. While the British were afraid that Nantah would be a breeding ground for communism, the Americans thought that it did not have to be so — with proper ideological guidance, including American assistance in designing and preparing program curriculum, Nantah could evolve into a non-communist, if not actively anti-communist, intellectual center for the overseas Chinese. Another difference between British and American attitudes toward Nantah concerned national identity and racial politics. The British, still as the colonial governing authority, displayed more sensitivity toward Malay nationalism, whereas the priority of the United States was to foster an anti-communist overseas Chinese base, without much consideration for local racial and ethnic dynamics (Zhang 2015, pp. 119–120). The issue of overseas Chinese education was taken very seriously by the Unites States government, reaching the level of Operations Coordinating Board, a body under the National Security Council that comprised Assistant Secretary of State, Assistant Secretary of Defense, Director of Central Intelligence Agency (CIA), Director of United States Foreign Operations Administration and a representative from the White House (Zhang 2015, p. 118).

It was under this context that the US played a proactive role in persuading the British to eventually acquiesce to the establishment of Nanyang University, and secretly supported Lin Yutang's appointment as Nantah's Chancellor. The departure of Lin Yutang reinforced the United States' concerns that the Chinese communists were winning the Cultural Cold War, notwithstanding the fact that Lin's personal differences with Tan Lark Sye were far more important in causing Lin's separation from Nantah. The US Department of Defense even conducted a study of Nanyang University after the "Lin Yutang Episode." It concluded that Nantah was a lost cause, and advocated two proposals to move forward — constructing a high-quality university in Taiwan for the overseas Chinese, or constructing another similarly anti-communist university in the East Asia region. Although neither proposal materialized, the United States' support and funding for the Chinese University of Hong Kong (and its predecessors) did increase (Zhang 2015, pp. 124–125).

Nevertheless, the United States ultimately disengaged itself from the issue of overseas Chinese education. With more countries achieving independence, indigenous nationalism was rising throughout the region, and the US, just like the British colonial authorities, risked alienating the indigenous populations if a policy of actively supporting overseas Chinese education was continued, even for the cause of anti-communism. In addition, with China achieving diplomatic successes in the Bandung conference in 1955, the US felt that securing the support from the newly independent states became a more important policy goal, compared to supporting overseas Chinese education for anti-communism. Encouraging national integration between the non-Chinese indigenous population and the overseas Chinese now served the interests of the US. Sympathy of the US toward overseas Chinese education and Nantah was essentially instrumental, for the purpose of the Cultural Cold War. It eventually lost interest and no longer cared about the fate of Nantah.

Student politics and reorganization of Nanyang University

Nantah formally commenced its classes in 1956, but it soon ran into problems with the Singapore government. Once Nantah was established and commenced its classes, the British also gradually let the autonomous government of Singapore handle the issue, without much direct intervention. The Labor Front government, elected in 1955, refused to give official recognition to Nantah's degree, or at least not consistently, with only the degrees of the first batch recognized and the subsequent batches would have to wait for relevant legislation. Two commissions (Prescott Commission and Gwee Ah Ling Commission) were appointed in 1959 to evaluate the academic standard of Nantah, and both Commissions published unfavorable reports, although such reports were widely seen by supporters of Chinese education as biased, deliberately negative and contained the purpose of trying to change Nantah as a Chinese university.

The People's Action Party (PAP) government, which came into power in 1959 (until today, PAP is still the ruling party of Singapore), continued the policy of reluctant acceptance of Nantah. Using the Commissions' reports, Singapore's government forced Nantah to enter into negotiation to reform, reorganize and restructure itself to gain official recognition. With unfriendly or obstructive attitudes of the PAP government disappointing the supporters of Nantah, many Nantah supporters actively campaigned for the opposition party (Socialist Front) in the 1963 General Election, which incurred further wrath from the PAP government, and Tan Lark Sye was even stripped of his citizenship.

Within Nantah's campus, especially from 1956 to 1965, student activism was indeed prevalent, and most of the student activists were indeed radicals inclined and sympathetic toward the communists. The powerful Nanyang University Students Union (NUSU) was the most ideological of all. According to a foreign teacher at Nantah (Van Der Kroef 1964, pp. 112–113).

> from the start the Malayan Communist underground, since 1955 committed to development of united front activity, sought to manipulate Nanyang student opinion through NUSU; indeed, there is little question, as the Malaysian Government's "White Paper" on Communism in Nanyang University, published in June 1964, makes plain, that the impulse behind the founding of NUSU was taken by the leaders of the Communist controlled Singapore Chinese Middle School Union (subsequently proscribed) when they entered Nanyang University.
>
> ... A not inconsiderable number of NUSU activists thus had themselves been participants in, or were closely identified with, the violent agitation of Chinese middle school associations and as they continued to maintain close ties with the "Old Boys" associations, i.e., organizations of graduates of these Chinese middle schools; NUSU and many of the "Old Boys" associations came to constitute an amalgam of significant agitational value to the Singapore Communist underground in subsequent years. NUSU's constitution, according to the earlier cited "White Paper" was framed by the pro-Communist group for their exploitation and has become in their skilled hands an instrument of 'democratic centralism' denying representation and power to any but their own nominees.

Van Der Kroef's observation was certainly biased against the students, but his view was widely shared by the authorities in Singapore. Lee Kuan Yew himself remarked that "a situation is developing which if left unchecked will make it more a University of Yenan than of Nanyang" (cited in Van Der Kroef 1964, p. 96). This was also the period of vast political change with the future of Singapore still in flux. For a few brief years, Singapore went through autonomy under British colonialism (until 1963), Malaysia merger (1963–1965) and Singapore independence (1965). Regardless, there were remarkably converging attitudes among the British, Malay and PAP rulers toward Nantah, and that was to limit, restrict, coopt and reorganize it. Fundamentally, they sat uncomfortable with the idea of a Chinese university outside of China, especially a communist China. Students' activism only confirmed their uneasiness and strengthened their resolve to control and change Nantah. Student activism at Nantah was therefore met with a series of political repression measures by the PAP government, including the arrest of student activists within campus, banning of campus publications, the stripping away of Tan Lark Sye's citizenship and the eventual forced dissolution of NUSU.

That the students tended to be (but not always) "leftist" in orientation was not unexpected. Nanyang Chinese yearning for the preservation for cultural autonomy and development, the sense of injustice suffered by the Chinese because of colonialism and later, racialism, the intellectual ties fostered between the overseas Chinese intellectual leaders and the progressive ideas from the May Fourth movement in China, the fashionable worldwide trend of leftist-student movements (that began years later in the United States and Europe but was already forming) resulted in a prevailing ethos among students of Nantah of supporting anti-colonialism, anti-imperialism, social justice, progressive culture and, to the fear of the rulers, a sympathy for Chinese communist revolution (Qiu 2006).

Students' political activism, interestingly, contrasted sharply with the conservatism of the faculty of Nantah. Especially during the beginning years, most faculty members were recruited from Taiwan or Hong Kong, and understandably they were averse to communism, radicalism and student activism. There were a few exceptions, such as the famous writer Han Suyin, who was more sympathetic to the activist students, and these exceptions tended to have deeper ties and lived longer in the region. Nevertheless, by and large, the faculty of Nantah was apolitical and ideologically indifferent.[8] Jin (2015), in his study of the faculty of Chinese Studies

---

[8] They were very little studies of the faculty of Nantah (in contrast to its students, its leaders such as Tan Lark Sye, and its relationship with different authorities), so it was harder to have a full picture of what these refugee intellectuals (they were refugee intellectuals fleeing from Mainland China) thought about this Chinese University outside of China.

Department of Nantah, noted that the faculty members tended to be indifferent to the developments in Nantah, especially its politics, sometimes with even a sense of disdain. Many saw their stay in Nantah as temporal, attracted by a good pay that was not the case in Taiwan, and understood that eventually they would leave the region. Nevertheless, they were excellent scholars who received the best training in classical Chinese learning. One can surmise from the curricula structure that was put in place that these scholars performed their teaching and research very seriously in their years at Nantah.

From Chinese University to English University: The End of Nanyang University

The Singapore government finally was able to take more direct control over Nantah in 1965, after the Wang Gungwu Report was issued, in which a drastic reorganization of the university and promotion of more widespread use of English was recommended. A new legislation was passed in 1966 that allowed the government to have more representatives in the university's board. After the reorganization, Nantah finally was able to appoint a full-time Chancellor, Professor Rayson Huang, in 1969, and Nantah also began a graduate school in 1970. A period of professionalization, stability, but also de-radicalization ensued. Although Nantah now became much less ideological and was in full control by the authorities, the PAP government's mission of turning it into an English University continued. In 1973, the government adopted the policy of common admission of students between University of Singapore and Nantah, which deprived Nantah from recruiting prospective good students, and also forbade Nantah from recruiting students from Malaya, effectively cutting off perhaps the most important source of students for Nantah. In 1975, the government appointed Lee Siow Mong, an official from the Ministry of Education, as the new Chancellor, to implement measures that were aimed to turn Nanyang University into an English University. Although he had to resign abruptly in the middle of his term due to opposition to his reform plans, the "English-ization" of Nantah was already underway. Finally in 1980, the government forced a merger of University of Singapore and Nanyang University into a National University of Singapore (NUS), effectively closing down Nantah. The campus of Nantah was later reopened as Nanyang Technological Institute, an English polytechnic, which was later upgraded to be a full-fledged university — Nanyang Technological University (NTU). NTU, despite having a similar name as Nantah, however is not Nantah's successor; it is a completely separate university. Nantah, the only Chinese university that existed outside of greater China area, ended in 1980.[9]

Nanyang University's Chineseness and Its Dilemma

Nanyang University's complicated and tortured relationship with the government, and its eventual demise, illustrated the different kinds of Chineseness and also different imaginations and responses. These differing perspectives on Nantah never reconciled among themselves, resulting in persisting tensions. For Tan Lark Sye and his supporters, the idea of Nanyang University was one simply for fulfilling the wish of the overseas Chinese to continue their own education and culture in the Chinese language and within Chinese intellectual tradition. For them, the struggle to maintain Chinese culture and civilization among the ethnic Chinese in Southeast Asia was not a form of chauvinism, but was often seen as such by the non-Chinese opposed to Chinese education. It was simply a basic right of an ethnic group to preserve its own culture, and Nanyang University fundamentally embodied that right. It was mostly a culturalist understanding of Chineseness that Tan Lakr Sye was promoting. For the Malay nationalists, such Chineseness was a threat, or at least a serious concern, to the agenda of national

---

[9] In the late 1990s, a number of higher education institutions supported by the Chinese community in Malaysia began to emerge, and they include Universiti Tunku Abdul Rahman, New Era University College, Han Chiang University College of Communication and Southern University College. To an extent, they could be said to be the extension of the defunct Nantah.

integration, especially an integration not built on the vision of multiculturalism but based on Malay supremacy, with minority groups assuming a subordinate role. Nanyang University, whether it was communist or anti-communist (as commonly expressed in their discourse, they did not want either Beijings or Nanjings in Malaya), was an obstacle to this national agenda.

For the British colonial government, its colonial policy arguably resulted in the situation that drew rising demand for Chinese education. Yet it sensed that the very Chineseness embodied by Nantah could undermine its interests, and its sensitivity to the Malay concerns meant that it was never fully supportive and enthusiastic about the project. For the United States, Nantah was a strategic opportunity; its Chineseness was to be used as a weapon to fight communism in the Cultural Cold War. But as soon as this goal came into conflict with the larger strategic priority of maintaining a positive relationship with the governments of the newly independent countries in Southeast Asia, Nantah was no longer supported by the US. For Nantah's students, their understanding and imagination of Chineseness was filled with emotion and the pursuance of anti-colonialism and social justice. Contrasting to the Chineseness of Tan Lark Sye, to the radical students, Chineseness was a political and politicized concept. It embodied progressive and revolutionary ideals.

For Nantah's faculty, many of them refugee intellectuals coming from Taiwan and Hong Kong, Nantah seemed to be only an aberration, a curiosity in a land marginal to the Chinese civilization yet full of enthusiastic overseas Chinese to learn about their own culture and history. The faculty, especially among the Chinese Studies Department faculty, felt that Nantah's Chineseness symbolized the vibrancy and vitality of Chinese culture and civilization, and for some of them, the passing on of the great Chinese intellectual traditions to the Nanyang Chinese was perhaps indeed worth pursuing.

The PAP government has had a mixed and very torturous relationship with Nantah. Singapore in many ways is a manifestation of the legacy of British colonialism. It is a state carved out by the colonialists as its special settlement, resulting in an entity comprised mostly of ethnic Chinese but surrounded by the much larger Malay and Indonesian peoples. The post-colonial government has to try very hard to convince its neighbors that Singapore is not the third "China," not a front of either Beijing or Taipei (especially Beijing). In addition, it has to grapple with the issue of national identity as a multi-ethnic society. For the PAP government, the best way was, and still is, to downplay sectarian or ethnic identity of all groups, promote English as the common language (but not official language), and keep somewhat of a distance from China. Although the PAP government recognized that certain values of traditional Chinese culture and Confucian philosophy could be promoted, mainly for the purposes of maintaining social order and morality, it has always been ambivalent with the notion of Chineseness. For these reasons, the very existence of Nanyang University, no matter how much it symbolized only cultural and not political aspirations (in the views of Tan Lark Sye and supporters of Chinese education), undermined the efforts by Lee Kuan Yew and his PAP government to construct a non-sectarian Singapore national identity. Although Nantah enjoyed wide support, and its tenacity and struggle to protect and preserve Chinese culture and education even earned the grudging respect of Lee Kuan Yew, the very Chineseness of the institution needs to be curbed and undermined to preserve the vision of national cohesion of the PAP government.

Conclusion: On the (Lack of) Nanyang University's Legacy in China Studies

A number of Nantah alumni eventually became well-known and accomplished scholars, including scholars working on various aspects of modern and contemporary China, such as Chang Chak-Yan 鄭赤琰, Yen Ching-Hwang 顏清湟, Leo Suryadinata 廖建裕, Yong Chin Fatt 楊進發, Toh Lam Seng 卓南生, Shee Poon Khim 徐本欽, Tan Kok Chiang 陳國相 and others.[10] With the exception of Leo Suryadinata, none of them however, for various reasons, chose

---

[10] A majority of them have been subjects of oral history interview for the Intellectual History of Chinese Studies led by Professor Chih-yu Shih.

to stay in Singapore or Malaysia for long-term development of their professional and intellectual career. Had they decided to remain, they could have formed a strong cohort and foundation for China Studies in Singapore and Malaysia. Had Nantah survived, one can surmise that it could have produced more scholars of this caliber to supply and sustain the development of China Studies in Singapore and Malaysia as well. If that had been the case, the scene of China Studies in Singapore and Malaysia perhaps would be very different today. There would be more local-origin and deeply rooted scholars on contemporary China, but with a background in cultural China, due to their locally rooted Chinese education. Their views of and research on China would not be detached from this particular background. There could even be a "Nantah School of China Studies."

Nevertheless, had Nantah survived as a Chinese university, but otherwise with the political views of the governments of Singapore and Malaysia unchanged, there would still be difficulties. The PAP government would perhaps still prefer foreign-origin scholars. For them, Chineseness has to be somewhat "foreign," otherwise it would be inconsistent with their own view of Singapore's national identity, and so the recruitment of scholars from a foreign country — China, perhaps would still be preferable to local scholars, unless the local scholars come from the mainstream English educational background. The PAP government would have uneasiness with scholars from Nantah as the major China scholars in Singapore. In Malaysia, decades of Malay supremacy ideology has permeated deep into the political and academic institutions, and China scholars with Nantah background perhaps would also not be easily accepted into the mainstream academic and policy circles.

Nanyang University could have played a pioneering role in the establishment of a vibrant academic community of China Studies in Singapore and Malaysia, but its very existence troubled the politics of identity in Singapore and Malaysia, and the geopolitics of survival for Singapore, all of which could be said to be the legacy of British colonialism. At the end, it met its tragic fate, and its potential in the field of China Studies was never realized.

References

Chang, Pi-Chun. 2015. Rewriting Singapore and Rewriting Chineseness: Lee Guan Kin's Diasporic Stance. *Asian Ethnicity* 16, 1: 28–42.

Chen, Chang-Hong 陳昌宏. 2011. *Xinjiapo Zhongguo yanjiu de zhishi mima: Huayi liqunzhe de shenfen celue yu nengdongxing zhanxian* 新加坡中國研究的知識密碼: 華裔離群者的身份策略與能動性展現 (The Knowledge Code of Singapore's China Studies: Identity Strategy and Agency Expression of Chinese Diaporic Scholars). Taipei: Guoli Taiwan daxue zhengzhi xuexi Zhongguo dalu ji liangan guanxi jiaoxue yu yanjiu zhongxin.

Chen, Yulan 陳煜爛. 2015. Chushen lishi yu shengcun zhihui: Lin Yutang Nanyang daxue qijian de xingwei jiantao 處身立世與生存智慧: 林語堂南洋大學期間的行為檢討 (Living Rightly and the Wisdom of Living: An Examination of Lin Yutang's Behavior during the Nanyang University Period). *Minnan shifan daxue xuebao* 閩南師範大學學報 (Journal of Minnan Normal University) 4: 17–23.

Guo, Jiajia 郭佳佳. 2008. *Lisanzhe de Zhongguo minzu zhuyi: Huayi xuezhe Zhao Suisheng, Zhengyongnian miandui Zhongguo de shenfen celue* 離散者的中國民族主義: 華裔學者趙穗生, 鄭永年面對中國的身份策略 (The Chinese Nationalism of Diasporic Scholars: The Identity Strategy of Ethnic Chinese Scholars Zhao Suisheng, Zheng Yongnian). Taipei: Guoli Taiwan daxue zhengzhi xuexi Zhongguo dalu ji liangan guanxi jiaoxue yu yanjiu zhongxin.

Jin, Jin 金進. 2015. Lengzhan, nanlai wenren yu xiandai Zhongguo wenxue: Yi Xinjiabo Nanyang daxue zhongwenxi renjiao shizi wei taolun duixiang 冷戰, 南來文人與現代中國文學: 以新加坡南洋大學中文系任教師資為討論對象 (Cold War, Southbound Literary Writers, and Modern Chinese Literature: A Case Study of the Faculty of the Department of Chinese Studies of Singapore's Nanyang University). *Wenxue pinglun* 文學評論 (Literary Commentary) 2: 147–158.

Ku, Hong-ting 古鴻廷. 1994. *Dongnanya huaqiao de renting wenti: Malaiya pian* 東南亞華僑的認同問題: 馬來亞篇 (The Identity Issue of the Overseas Chinese in Southeast Asia: Malaya). Taipei: Lianjing.

Ku, Hong-ting 古鴻廷. 2003. Xinjiapo Nanyang daxue de gaige yu guanbi 新加坡南洋大學的改革與關閉 (The Reform and Closure of Singapore's Nanyang University). *Nanyang wenti yanjiu* 南洋問題研究 (Southeast Asian Affairs) 1: 1–30.

Lei, Xie 雷瀣. 2008. *Nanda chunqiu* 南大春秋 (History of Nanyang University). Kajang: Fengxia wenshi gongzuoshi.

Nanyang University Alumni Association of Malaysia. 1990. *Nanyang daxue shiliao huibian* 南洋大學史料彙編 (Compilation of Historical Materials of Nanyang University). Kuala Lumpur: Nanyang University Alumni Association of Malaysia.

Ngeow, Chow Bing, Tek Soon Ling, and Pik Shy Fan. 2014. Pursuing Chinese Studies Amidst Identity Politics in Malaysia. *East Asia: An International Quarterly* 31, 2: 103–120.

Ong, Senghuat 王琛發. 2015. Lin Yutang de Nanyang daxue enyuan: huozai lixiang yu zhengzhi jiuchan zhijian 林語堂的南洋大學恩怨: 活在理想與政治糾纏之間 (Lin Yutang's Bitterness in his Nanyang University Career: Academic Idealism and Political Entanglement), *Mintai wenhua yanjiu* 閩台文化研究 (Fujian-Taiwan Cultural Research) 3: 67–81.

Ong, Chu Meng, Lim Hoon Yong, and Ng Lai Yang (Eds.). 2015. *Tan Lark Sye: Advocator and Founder of Nanyang University.* Singapore: World Scientific.

Qiu, Shuling 丘淑玲. 2006. *Lixiang yu xianshi: Nanyang daxue xueshenghui zhi yanjiu 1956–1964* 理想與實: 南洋大學學生會之研究 1956–1964 (Ideals and Reality: A Study of Nanyang University Students Union 1956–1964). Singapore: Bafang Wenhua.

Saunders, Frances Stonor. 1999. *The Cultural Cold War: The CIA and the World of Arts and Letters.* New York: The New Press.

Shih, Chih-yu. 2014. Introduction: Humanity and Pragmatism Transcending Borders. *East Asia: An International Quarterly* 31, 2: 93–102.

Shin, Chih-yu. 2018. "Crafting a Bridge Role Through Chinese Studies without Sinology: Lessons of South Asian Think Tanks for Singapore." In Chih-yu Shih, Prapin Manomaivibool, and Reena Marwah (Eds.) *China Studies in South and Southeast Asia: Between Pro-China and Objectivism.* Singapore: World Scientific, pp. 225–252.

Shih, Chih-yu and Celine Yi-Chin Lee. 2015. Between a Subject and an Object: Representation of China in Kuo Pao-kun's Singapore and Denny Yung's Hong Kong. *Asian Ethnicity* 16, 1: 43–58.

Shin, Chueiling. 2014. Understanding Chinese Economy Accurately: John Wong and His China Research. *East Asia: An International Quarterly* 31, 2: 157–169.

Smith, Joseph B. 1976. *Portrait of a Cold Warrior.* Toronto: Longman Canada.

Van Der Kroef, Justus M. Nanyang University and the Dilemmas of Overseas Chinese Education. *The China Quarterly* 20: 96–127.

Wong, Sin Kiong, Ruixin Wang, Zhuo Wang and Shihlun Allen Chen. 2015. Producing and Reconstructing Knowledge on China in Singapore: Perspectives from the Academics and Mass Media. *Asian Ethnicity* 16, 1: 8–27.

Wong, Ting-Hong. 2005. Comparing State Hegemonies: Chinese Universities in Postwar Singapore and Hong Kong. *British Journal of Sociology of Education* 26, 2: 199–218.

Yew, Chiew Ping. 2016. The Evolution of Contemporary China Studies in Singapore: From the Regional Cold War to the Present. *Journal of Chinese Political Science* 22, 1:135–158.

Zhang, Yang 張楊. 2015. Lengzhan qianqi Meiguo dui Dongnanya huawen gaodeng jiaoyu de ganyu yu yingxiang: Yi Nanyang daxue wei gean de tantao 冷戰前期美國對東南亞華文高等教育的干預與影響: 以南洋大學給個案的探討 (American Interference and Influence in Chinese Higher education in Southeast Asia during the Early Cold War: An Inquiry Based on the Case of Nanyang University). *Meiguo Yanjiu* 美國研究 (America Studies) 3: 114–132.

Chapter 6
Embedded Anti-Chinese Orientations: The Dutch Occupation and Its Legacies

Harryanto Aryodiguno

Department of Political Science, National Taiwan University, Taipei, Taiwan and School of Humanities, President University, Bekasi, Jawa Barat, Indonesia

Introduction

Ethnic Chinese are considered alien to the extent the indigenous population sees them as more Chinese than Indonesian. The intellectual history of seeing them as mainly Chinese continues to haunt contemporary ethnic politics. This chapter studies how the colonial legacies in the Dutch period may have intellectually perpetuated the alien image of Chinese Indonesian and connected them with an imagined threat of Chinese Communism of the PRC.

The discrimination that happened to the ethnic Chinese in Indonesia during the Dutch colonial period, before and after Indonesia's independence, remains an exciting record to study, even today. Although there have been many changes to the life of Chinese Indonesians after the tragedy of May 1998, discrimination against ethnic Chinese in Indonesia still exists, whether in social life or at the level of nation and state. The most recent discrimination against Chinese identity is what happened in the Jakarta elections in 2017, where indigenous and non-indigenous ethnic identities were raised again for the sake of voting.

About discrimination against ethnic Chinese, this may not be because of high indigenous spirit among indigenous ethnic people. If indeed the indigenous spirit is high, why are only the Chinese attacked? And why aren't the people of Arab descent and Indian ethnicity, who in fact are also foreign descendants, targeted as well? In fact, the hatred toward the Chinese people has stretched long from the history of the Indonesian state, from the VOC (Verenigde Oost-Indische Compagnie or the Dutch East Indies Company) era to the New Order (1967–1998) era. Also during the reform era, hatred toward the Chinese people slowly began to disappear, although it is still strong because most Chinese people have a different religion from the majority of the indigenous population in Indonesia (Aziz 2018). Bear in mind that sometimes the ethnic riots in Indonesia not only targeted the Chinese, but the indigenous peoples themselves often clash with each other because of religious issues and sentiments. The experts consistently point out one reason for why the ethnic and religious riots to happen so easily in Indonesia. It is that it is the legacy of Dutch colonialism — they applied "Divide et Impera"[1] politics to divide the nation of Indonesia.

Especially for the riots that often occur against the Chinese Indonesians. Chinese people are considered exclusives, they do not want to mingle with the native population and feel like a superior race. Then the indigenous people and leaders of Indonesia also doubted the loyalty of the Chinese toward the state of Indonesia. And, the history of hatred against the Chinese and the Chinese loyalist doubt that it was a profound imprint on the indigenous Indonesian. Hatred is easily evoked through political issues wrapped in religion and anxiety over ethnic mastery of one against another. The community of Chinese people was in Java centuries

---

[1] Divide and rule (or divide and conquer, from Latin *dīvide et imperā*) in politics and sociology is gaining and maintaining power by breaking up more significant concentrations of power into pieces that individually have less power than the one implementing the strategy. The concept refers to a plan that breaks up existing power structures and especially prevents smaller power groups from linking up, causing rivalries and fomenting discord among the people. It was heavily used by the British Empire in India and elsewhere.

ago, but they still cannot be considered as indigenous as other immigrants in Indonesia. The history of Indonesia noted that the Chinese nation has been in Indonesia since before the Sriwijaya Kingdom that was seen between the 6th and the 12th century AD (Mackie 1976, p. 4). Interestingly, although it has surpassed several generations in Indonesia, the Chinese ethnicity has never been fully accepted as an integral part of Indonesia. The anti-Chinese sentiment is still strong everywhere, both in the real world and in cyberspace. Some use specific terms to express anti-Chinese sentiments, such as the term "Asing and Aseng"[2]. Take for instance, President Jokowi himself: many Indonesian politicians use ethnic sentiments, such as the word "Asing and Aseng" henchmen to address him and incited people by saying that "Asing, Aseng, and PKI" would rise in Indonesia (Nicholas 2017). This accusation happens for various reasons, and one of them is the next presidential election in 2019, followed by some issues with China, mainly related investment and agreement between Indonesia and China. Discriminative sensibilities are higher wherever people perceived as Chinese are involved. For example, being reminded of the Chinese threat, the Indonesian authorities did not drown the illegal vessels from China that caught fish in Indonesian waters, while other foreign ships caught were immediately drowned (Detik Finance 2015). As another example, the arrest of many drug smugglers especially from China and Taiwan is publicized *(The Straits Times*, 2018). Economic exchanges provide reasons to fear, too, including the giving of the Jakarta–Bandung high-speed rail project to a China consortium and the Jakarta bay reclamation to a Chinese-Indonesian developer, which was followed by a hoax news about 10 million workers from China (Interview with

---

[2] The "Asing" word refers to foreigners or non-local residents, while Aseng is intended to insult ethnic Chinese and people from China who stay in Indonesia. Aseng is a man's nickname with Chinese characters 阿成. While the Communist Party of Indonesia (PKI) is a political party in Indonesia that has been disbanded, the PKI was the largest non-ruling communist party in the world after Russia and China before the PKI was finally demolished in 1965 and declared a forbidden party the following year.

Dr. Sunardi Mulia, 2015).[3] People thus wonder if all sectors of the economy are dominated by China, from the elite to the worker class, and thus ask then as Indonesian people what do we get in our country? So, all this showcases how Chinese people are still despised and still cannot be accepted entirely and remain the primary tool/weapon to weaken the political enemy in Indonesia. Also, the lower strata that is easily influenced by anti-Chinese issues is also proof that anti-Chinese sentiments are so easy to use to provoke them into harassment and violence against the Chinese.

History notes not only the socioeconomic gap but also political rivalry and commercial competition can often be the root causes behind cases of racism and anti-Chinese violence, as occurs in Medan, Solo and other cities. But as has been the case for every riot and conflict among the people in Indonesia, the end has always led to mass riots against ethnic-Chinese, such as the "Malari" incident (Fourteenth of January Incident), which was originally a demonstration of the State visit by the Japanese Prime Minister, Tanaka Kankuei, to Indonesia between 14 and 17 January 1974 that ended with anti-Chinese riots in Jakarta (Aliansyah 2014). Even so, this does not mean there is always a dispute between the local and the Chinese community. In West Kalimantan, where I was born, I saw and felt that the Chinese relationship with the local people is quite good and harmonious, like a frame of symbiotic mutualism. There are even many indigenous people who can speak Chinese.

I find that anti-Chinese sentiments in Indonesia primarily originated from the political discrimination applied by the government regime so far, (Kosasih 2010, pp. 1–79) especially since the Dutch colonial rule reached its climax during the New Order era when the Chinese were only used as an object of extortion and as scapegoats. This is because ethnic Chinese are always asked for material donations for public and government events, for security and nationalist reasons. They are considered a scapegoat, because if there is a clash going on, the Chinese are always the weaker ones,

---

[3] Interview with Dr. Sunardi Mulia, 2015 by The Research & Educational Centre for Chinese Studies and Cross-Taiwan Strait Relations, Department of Political Science, National Taiwan University.

always considered not to acculturate with the local population, arrogant, and always the cause of the clash problem. It should be noted that the May riots in Jakarta were not the beginning of anti-Chinese violence in Indonesia. Dozens of times anti-Chinese sentiments have erupted in the form of violence in this country. For example, the largest anti-China riot occurred in 1740 known as genocide ("The slaughter of the Chinese") in Batavia. At that time, more than 10,000 Chinese lives have drifted (Windoro *et al.*, Kompas on the web, 2016). Many historians suspect the brains of this genocide is the VOC or the Dutch East Indies Company because China is considered a strategic competitor in the economic. In the New Order period, the Chinese suffered quite a bit, and since they were accused of being behind the scenes of the PKI (Communist Party of Indonesia), anti-Chinese campaigns and eradication have continued to be systematic. To this day, some groups still associate Chinese with communism, although many of them are anti-communist. This is an anti-Chinese campaign, not only in the physical sense but also in the form of destruction of all things Chinese, including its culture and religious tradition, and this is a part of the irony and dark history of the Indonesian nation.

Anti-Chinese sentiment in Indonesia occurs at almost every level, from lower society to middle class to even upper-class society. Politicians have always used the issue of "Chinese influence" and the rise of "communist China" to bring down their opponents. Likewise, many of the academicians in Indonesia always remind people of the dangers of China and the ethnic Chinese, the danger of China beginning to claim the territories of the South China Sea and the Natuna waters, as well as the dangers of the Chinese-Indonesian who have started to participate in politics in Indonesia. Maybe we can understand if this anti-Chinese issue occurs in the lower circle only, but why is the anti-Chinese movement in Indonesia able to influence academics and intellectuals? Intellectually, these are all negative "images" implanted by the Dutch colonialists against the Chinese in Indonesia. The Dutch had considerable influence in making Chinese people remain as a Chinese nation in Indonesia, and unfortunately, this Dutch policy was adopted by Suharto to perpetuate his power. In this chapter, I will discuss anti-Chinese riots in every government regime and its effect on the views and the treatment of the indigenous ethnic and the Indonesian government's policy on Chinese ethnicity in Indonesia.

History: Anti-Chinese in Indonesia During the Dutch East Indies

When the Dutch started to enter the Nusantara (a Javanese term for the Indonesian Archipelago), Java was one of the prosperous islands. At the time the Dutch explorer Cornelius de Houtman arrived in Java in 1596, one of the most famous ports was "Sunda Kelapa" or "Jayakarta," where many Chinese were already living. After the Dutch arrived in Indonesia, the original "Sunda Kelapa" or "Jayakarta" was changed to Batavia as its power increased (Arsip Nasional Republik Indonesia 2016). The Dutch slowly made Batavia into a more planned city, which has a spectacular wall (Benteng). The Chinese lived in the wall, and the Indonesian locals lived outside the wall. In addition to building a city in the port of "Sunda Kelapa," the Dutch also opened a trading company — the "V.O.C/Vereenigde Oostindische Compagnie" — the origin of the Dutch East Indies.[4]

In the history of pre-independence and post-independence of Indonesia, anti-Chinese riots are not uncommon. Even before the Republic of "Indonesia" was established, anti-Chinese riots occurred in the "Nederland Indische" era, for example between October 9 and 11, 1740 Overseas Chinese against the Dutch East Indies government. This confrontation was considered to be the first "Genocide" in the history of Indonesia. About 10,000 ethnic Chinese were slaughtered, and their bodies were thrown directly into the gutter of the city of Batavia, turning the whole gutter blood

---

[4] Arsip Nasional Republik Indonesia, Khazanah Arsip VOC abad ke 17 dan 18, 22 May 2018, https://sejarah-nusantara.anri.go.id/id/hartakarunmaincategory/4/.Latest update 2 July 2018. (National Archives of the Republic of Indonesia, VOC treasures archives of the 17th and 18th centuries.

red, so this incident was also called "Tragedy of red gutter" (Peristiwa Angke).[5] The outbreak of unrest started under the Dutch East Indies Governor Adrian Valckenier (1737–1741), and it continued to open up Fujian's immigrants and opened the well-educated overseas Chinese in the early days. However, many criminals who committed crimes in China also subsequently immigrated to the Dutch East Indies. Because many immigrants lacked job opportunities, this lead to conflicts between overseas Chinese and the colonial government. As 50 Europeans died in Batavia on October 4, 1740, the Dutch East Indies government began to kill these rebellious overseas Chinese. Most of the overseas Chinese fled across the cities of Java. In Mataram, overseas Chinese were protected by the Sultan Mataram, so they cooperated to declare war on the Dutch government (Windoro *et al.* 2016). The war was often considered by Indonesian scholars to be the first time that the Chinese and the Indonesians cooperated against Dutch imperialism.

Besides that, in 1777 the Chinese established the "Republic of Lan Fang" in West Kalimantan, Indonesia, against the Dutch government. At that time, there were three Malay kingdoms in Kalimantan, Sambas, Pontianak and Mempawah sultanates. In the middle of the 10th century, West Kalimantan unearthed gold mines, and the Chinese were hired by the Sultan Sambas to open the gold mines. Later, these Chinese workers organized a company for their rights. The company was called "Lan Fang Company" or "Lan Fang Kongsi," and they elected Lo Fong Pak (Luo Fang Bo) as the leader. As this company flourished, it later led to the formation of a "new village." The local Sultan did not care much about how the Chinese in the new village were living. The local Chinese were free to follow their habits, cultures and festivals. The most important thing was to pay taxes to the Sultan on a regular basis. According to the research of Indonesian scholar La Ode, they

---

[5] *Angke* is a Hokkianess word which means "red gutter"; in 1740, the colonial government carried out ethnic cleansing of Chinese. More than 10,000 Chinese in Batavia and 60,000 Chinese outside Batavia were killed. Their blood flows and makes the river around red. Since then, the river is called *"kali Angke"*/red gutter.

later resisted the Sultan Sambas and began to refuse to pay taxes because the influence of the Lan Fang Republic became stronger; however, this incident caused the Sultan to lose patience with the Chinese and declare war with them. After eight days of the war, the Chinese were defeated, but the Sultan did not give Lan Fang any punishment. They still had to follow the same the old rule, that is, paying taxes to the Sultan (La Ode 2013, p. 105). The Republic of Lan Fang has a very long history in West Kalimantan. They were established in West Kalimantan for 107 years and had conducted 13 leaders' elections. Because of their growing power, they were wiped out by the Dutch East Indies Company in 1884. The surviving Chinese people immigrated to other islands. According to Indonesian history, half of the immigrants started a new life in a new place. This place is now called "Singapore" (Poerwanto 2005, pp. 137–138).

In the colonial period, in fact, the Chinese did not show their identity. They knew that they were a different ethnic group from Indonesians, Dutch people or other races. Chinese people stayed in their communities in their living habits. This was because, at that time, the Colonial government specified that the Chinese had to live in a specific area, in other words, the Chinese couldn't live in a place along with other race. This regulation is the so-called Zoning System or "Wijkenstelsel." However, this situation remained until Indonesia's independence. After Indonesia's independence, this condition was not so obvious. Although there was no zoning system in Indonesia after independence, the Chinese needed to apply for a "Surat Keterangan Jalan" or "passenstelsel" to go from one place to another.[6] It was not until 1912 or after the founding of

---

[6] In 1910, the Dutch government determined that if Chinese people wanted to go abroad or go to other areas, they must apply for approval from the Dutch government; this rule was fundamentally invalid after Indonesia's independence. However, because Indonesian law was entirely inherited from the laws of the colonial government, some local officials used the loophole in this law to make money. Until the Suharto era, Chinese people who wanted to go to other islands or other provinces and cities had to file what is called a "Travel Pass" (Surat Keterangan Jalan) in the "Kelurahan" (Urban Village office). Currently, the "Travel Pass" is only needed for foreigners who want to enter areas in Indonesia that are categorized as "dangerous" or "riotous"; such as "Papua," Aceh and other restive regions.

the Republic of China that the identity of Chinese politics in the Dutch East Indies began to form. In 1917, some Chinese living in Semarang City, Central Java, publicly declared that they did not want to participate in local politics to maintain their status as the Chinese nation. Also, they rejected the Dutch government's (Nederlandsch Onderdaanschap) citizenship law and considered themselves as belonging to the Chinese nation. The Indonesian nationalist movement at that time also contributed to the identity and political thinking of the Chinese in Indonesia, and the political movements of the Chinese also expressed their identity (Suryadinata 2005, pp. 3–4).

According to Charlotte Setijadi citing Amy Chua's research, the story of the Chinese Indonesian is one that has fascinated scientists and observers for years. This is a classic example of what Amy Chua calls "Market dominant minority," as since the Dutch colonial era, Chinese-Indonesians were generally considered economically strong but politically weak. Furthermore, their inability to claim indigenous tenure modes in Indonesia means that Chinese-Indonesians have been continuously seen as foreigners and their national loyalties always questionable. This precarious situation makes them victims of racial violence during episodes of political or economic instability. An example is the frequent racial riots against ethnic Chinese in Indonesia (Setijadi 2016, p. 3).

The zoning system made by the Dutch government increasingly separates ethnic Chinese from indigenous Indonesians, leading to frequent misunderstandings between these two ethnicities. The same opinion was also raised by Professor Dahana, a Chinese expert from Binus University Indonesia: Although the Chinese community in Indonesia has existed for ages and can be called an inseparable part of Indonesian society, during the last century they faced various problems in being accepted as Indonesian. This was caused mainly by the policy of Dutch colonialism, which created what nowadays can be said as a segregation policy. The system separated Chinese from local people, which was called "Pribumi" in the past. This separation was created by several factors like employment, settlement, legal status, politics, and other regulations.

The policy was established disregarding the fact that there were cultural orientation differences between the Peranakans-Chinese and the Totoks-Chinese.[7] Consequently, there had been no mutual understanding between the two groups, and the only communication only took place in the "market." As a result, there had always been mistrust between the two groups (Dahana 2015).

Sukarno: The Concept of the Chinese Nation in Indonesia

After World War II ended and Indonesia's independence was achieved, what was the position and status of the Chinese nation in Indonesia? Were they still regarded as Indonesian or Chinese? To find out exactly the twists and turns of the Chinese people's life in Indonesia after the Indonesian independence era, we need to first look at the structure of Chinese society in Indonesia both before and after Indonesia's independence. To understand this problem, I will trace the different class of society during Dutch rule in Dutch East Indies. The Chinese at that time were separated from the two racial groups, respectively, the Dutch or European Class, and the indigenous Indonesians or inlander/pribumi. The Chinese minority at that time were not classified as "Peranakan" or "Totok." In the colonial era, the rise of Chinese nationalism was intimately connected with the spread of Chinese nationalism at China. Political identification with China, however, emerged clearly after the establishment of the Republic of China in 1912. The ethnic Chinese felt that the colonial government considered their culture, customs, and ethnicity at that time as the bottom class, so they united to establish the Chinese Association or "Tiong Hoa Hwee Koan."

---

[7] Peranakan or Peranakan Tionghoa is a term used to refer to the Indonesian-born Chinese who use Malay or indigenous dialects as their medium of communication. Culturally, they were partly adapted to the indigenous community. Totok is a term used to refer to China-born Chinese residing in Indonesia. Totoks still speak a Chinese language (Mandarin or other Chinese dialect).

At that time, the Chinese community was divided into three groups. The first group tended to identify with China and believed they were always Chinese and must be loyal to the motherland. This group established the "Tiong Hoa Hwee Koan" on March 17, 1901, and are often referred to as "Sin Po group" in Indonesian history. The founder of the Tiong Hoa Hwee Koan believed that Chinese Confucianism was critical to Chinese residents in the colonial land. Therefore, they advocated that Chinese culture could be conveyed through education. However, it was Sin Po — a Peranakan daily newspaper — that spread information related to the China national movement. It also strengthened the political loyalty of the Chinese in Dutch East Indies to the home country. During the Sino-Japanese war, the Chinese in Dutch East Indies launched donations to support the anti-Japanese movement in China (Gu 2017, p. 31). Although the primary purpose of "Sin Po" was to spread Chinese culture in the Dutch East Indies and support Chinese nationalism, this newspaper was also the first newspaper to use "Indonesia" as a term to refer to "Netherlands East India," and it was the first one that used Malay language. In 1964, because the newspaper supported Sukarno and opposed the anti-communist media, when Sukarno was overturned, the newspaper suffered closure (Sudibyo 2001).

The second faction consists of the Dutch-educated and wealthy Chinese that were in support of Dutch nationality. One of their representatives, Kwe Tek Hoay, believed that the Chinese should actively participate in the Volksraad (People's representative of the colonial government). Even though the Indies Chinese are China's citizens, the Indies Chinese must accept the reality that the area in which the Chinese live is part of the Dutch territory and thus they must comply with the "law of Dutch East Indian citizens" (Wet op het Nederlandsche Onderdaanschap) (Suryadinata 1994, p. 41).

The third group is the Indonesia-oriented group. For them, Indonesia is the homeland and country of the Indies Chinese, but they wish to retain their Chinese identity. This group led by Liem Koen Hian and Kwe Kwat Tiong established the Indonesian Chinese Party (PTI) in East Java on September 25, 1932. In contrast, one of the members of the Indonesian Independent Review Committee (BPUPKI) — established during the Japanese occupation of Indonesia — Oei Tjong Hauw, insisted that after Indonesian independence the Chinese should remain Chinese citizen. But Liem Koen Hian objected, and his reason was that Chinese were born, lived and died in Indonesia. Therefore, the Chinese should also have a standard position as the Indonesian natives (Jahja 1995). The contribution of PTI does not mean that the Indonesian society can genuinely accept Chinese Indonesians. Though the purpose of this party was to work together with Indonesian national activists for Indonesian independence and indeed to contribute to Indonesia's independence, Suharto completely denied the contribution of the Chinese to the Indonesian nation after he took office.

According to Leo Suryadinata on the concept of the Indonesian nation and the ethnic Chinese, before World War II, most Indonesian nationalists (except leftists and communists) did not include Chinese ethnic groups in the Indonesian nationality. The concept of the Indonesian nation is actually a continuation of colonial formation of the Dutch (Adiputri 2014, pp. 1–8). However, some Indonesian nationalist figures sparked the concept of the Indonesian nation based on political concepts. But, Sukarno argues that the concept of the Indonesian nation includes all people who live in all parts of Indonesia, so according to Sukarno's opinion, the Chinese people can be categorized as part of Indonesia. However, Sukarno did not clarify anymore about this. And according to the study of Suryadinata, the Indonesian leader after Indonesian independence, who still based his views on the indigenous race as the Indonesian nation, the Peranakan Chinese cannot be indigenous if they have not "merged" into the life of the native people. During the era of "Guided Democracy" the debate about the concept of this nation was not completed. But in 1963, Sukarno sparked the concept of "the Indonesian nation is the whole Indonesian indigenous race coupled with Peranakan Chinese" (not Totok Chinese). Sukarno argues that the Chinese Peranakans have become part of the Indonesian nation and need not "melt" into the indigenous population group again. Moreover, the concept of the nation of Sukarno did not last long, in addition to being challenged from various parties. After Sukarno lost his government seat, Suharto took Sukarno's position firmly and did not include ethnic Chinese as part of a group of Indonesian nation, because Suharto defined the Indonesian nation as Indonesian indigenous (Suryadinata 2010, pp. 249–251).

Actually, Sukarno himself always wanted to solve the problem of Chinese citizenship, but the issue of citizenship or nation concept also cannot be viewed as a problem on the Indonesian side only. Because of the issue of overseas Chinese, the People's Republic of China and the Republic of China both claim that all overseas Chinese belong to the Chinese citizen. This is also one of the reasons hindering the relationship between the Indonesian government and the Chinese government. The Indonesian government has blurred the views on the status of overseas Chinese, the identity of overseas Chinese and even the relations between Indonesia and China. Regarding the nationality of the Chinese, the Indonesian government did not have a distinct "law," and the People's Republic of China declared that the overseas Chinese are, by the basic principle of "Ius Sanguinis," Chinese citizens. At the Asian–African Conference in Bandung in 1955, Zhou Enlai believed that overseas Chinese should be loyal to the motherland. Although Mao Zedong promoted the policy of recognizing overseas Chinese as a part of the Chinese, there were many anti-communist Chinese in Indonesia who were not willing to admit to being Chinese (PRC) citizens and would not accept Indonesian nationality too. They would rather maintain the status of the Republic of China (Taipei), but because Indonesia has no formal diplomatic relations with the Republic of China (Taipei), these overseas Chinese were listed as "stateless persons" (Chen 1989, p. 38).

With the end of the Second World War, Chinese who were recognized as having the identity of the Chinese nation established the "Persatuan Tionghoa (The Chinese Unity)" organization in 1948, and later changed the name to "Partai Demokrat Tionghoa

Indonesia (Chinese Democratic Party of Indonesia)" in 1950. The purpose was to preserve Chinese culture and Chinese identity, and in the end, it was changed to "Baperki" in 1954[8] (Suryadinata 2005, p. 8). After the independence of Indonesia, the Chinese identity fragmented into two types; the first consists of those with a cultural and political orientation toward China and those who maintain their Chinese identity, while the other group chose to be close to Indonesians without alienating themselves from its ethnic identity. Although the political ideology and identity of the two groups were different, most of them chose to study in the Chinese style of education. In general, Chinese who chose to study at the Chinese school were relatively familiar with the concepts of Chinese consciousness (regardless of them being either pro-Beijing or pro-Taipei); on the contrary, those Chinese who chose to study at the English school or a Dutch school were more pro-Indonesian.[9] The "Baperki" actively played a role in the multiculturalism of Chinese in Indonesia. Then there was another Chinese organization supported by the Indonesian Army, the "Institute for the Development of National Unity" (Lembaga Pembina Kesatuan Bangsa, LPKB). The former favors a multicultural policy, emphasizing that the Chinese be a part of the Indonesian nation, while the latter fully supports the separation from Chinese identity and overall assimilation. The struggle between the two Chinese organizations ended on September 30, 1965. Following the failure of the coup by the Indonesian Communist Party, Baperki, which was suspected of plotting with the Indonesian Communist Party, was banned by the New Order government.

---

[8] Badan Permusjawaratan Kewarganegaraan Indonesia (Baperki) was an organization founded in Indonesia in 1954 by an Indonesian of Chinese descent. The organization sponsored schools including Res Publica University (1960). The group was associated with the Indonesian Communist Party (PKI). After the 1965 coup attempt in Indonesia, Res publica was burned down and replaced by a new school, Trisakti, and this group was banned.

[9] Interview with Doctor Leo Suryadinata, at the Research and Education Center for China Studies and Cross Taiwan-Strait Relations, Department of Political Science, National Taiwan University on April 4–5, 2007.

De-Sinicization in the Suharto Era

After the "9.30 incident"[10] broke out in 1965, the anti-China and-Chinese atmosphere began to increase. In particular, after the Army controlled the media, unbalanced news often appeared. Anti-China campaigns continued to occur, including incidents such as rushing into Chinese embassies and burning Chinese stores and housing. Both Baperki and LPKB want to integrate into the larger Indonesian society. However, the first disappeared after Sukarno lost power. The latter was supported by the Indonesian military and actively participated in the anti-communist movement. Although LPKB wanted to show its loyalty to the Indonesian government, they were also actively protesting against the Baperki. Some of these Chinese, such as the Catholic Party Secretary Harry Tjan, also played an essential role in the "KAP-Gestapu" (Anti-Communist groups). He and Soe Hok Gie from the Faculty of Arts at the University of Indonesia and also the Catholic University Student Association led by Bim Koen/Sofjan Wanandi organized the Indonesian Students Action Forum (KAMI) against the Communist and Sukarno regimes (Coppel 1994, p. 131).

In order to eliminate the Communist Party and begin the anti-China movement, Suharto's new order regime announced that "the People's Republic of China interfered with Indonesia's internal affairs and supported Indonesia's leftist coup." The rumors of China's support for the Indonesian Communist Party's *coup d'état* eventually led to long-term harm to Chinese Indonesia. The "9.30 Incident" profoundly affected Indonesian mainstream society's understanding of China and the Chinese Indonesian. After the incident, Indonesia's internal affairs and foreign policy thus restricted local people's understanding of China and the Chinese. Although the New Order Government is anti-China, it also recognizes that the role of the Chinese Indonesian in the economy

---

[10] On the evening of September 30, 1965, known as the 30 September movement, six of Indonesia's top military Generals were captured and executed by the group of militants. The movement proclaimed itself as Sukarno's protectors, issuing a preemptive strike to prevent a possible coup by the "anti-Sukarno," pro-Western council of Generals.

is vital. If it is to overthrow the Chinese economy, it is tantamount to overthrowing the country's economy. Under this consideration, the government believes it is necessary to use the "strength" of the Chinese to assist the government in building the entire national economy. Therefore, the new order regime adopted two kinds of measures for the Chinese Indonesian in political economy. On the one hand, it tried its best to use the Chinese's economical to promote the construction of the country. On the other hand, the monopoly policy restricted the economic activities of the Chinese, so that Indonesian people can slowly catch up and even replace the economic status of the Chinese Indonesian. All in all, the New Order regime upholds Indonesianism and hopes that one day Indonesia's indigenous people will replace the Chinese's economic status and allow the New Order Bureaucracy to get the highest profits. This kind of situation suppresses the Chinese people. If an economic crisis occurs in Indonesia, the Chinese will be accused of being the primary source of economic problems. Anti-Chinese riots may occur at any time.

Before the Asian financial turmoil in 1997, most of the Indonesian society had been dissatisfied with the domestic economic performance. Most of the communities that were dissatisfied with the Chinese Indonesian had already staged anti-Chinese protests in the early 1990s, including Medan in 1994, Tasikmalaya in 1996, and Jakarta in 1997 (Schwarz 1997, pp. 119–134). The monetary crisis of 1997 made Indonesia become more democratic and also caused massive anti-Chinese riots. These riots have awakened the Chinese in Indonesia and caused them to question their identity status and choices. Did they leave Indonesia or continue to become Indonesian? In February 1998, demonstrations led by students from University of Indonesia demanded that the government solve "corruption, collusion between government and business, and nepotism" (Korupsi, Kolusi dan Nepotisme), eliminate the dual functions of the military (Dwifungsi ABRI) and force President Suharto to step down. The demonstrations of these university students resulted in the constant occurrence of civil–military conflicts. The student demonstration in 1998 was different from that in 1965, when they received full support from the army. In the 1998 demonstration, students even clashed with the police and the army. Clashes between students and police/army on May 12, 1998, resulted in the death of four Trisakti University students, this incident spread into a massive riot against the ethnic Chinese.

The "May Riot" that occurred in 1998 was the most significant Chinese riot in Indonesia since the independence. Anti-communism and Chinese people in 1965 were not riots that directly targeted the Chinese. At that time, besides the Chinese people suffering the highest damage, many Indonesian natives were implicated in the killing. In contrast, the riots in 1998 were purely against the Chinese in Indonesia. Also, because China's state property in Indonesia was not harmed, the Beijing authorities reacted with indifference. Contrary to the active protest in 1965, this time China even shut down information about the Chinese exclusion in Indonesia.

The main reason why Indonesia often has a Chinese expulsion movement is that the gap between the rich and the poor is enormous. Whenever the regime changes in Indonesia, the Chinese often are the victims. Although many Indonesian Chinese people don't speak the Chinese national language or dialect, most of them have been separated from Chinese culture. The targets of anti-Chinese riots in 1998 were all the Chinese people in Indonesia, not to mention groups that were pro-assimilation or pro-China were also targeted, as well as people from mainland China and the Taiwanese.

"Reformasi" and Discrimination

President Suharto announced his resignation on May 21, 1998. Habibie, who replaced Suharto after the riots, began to change the Chinese Indonesian policy. At that point, Indonesia entered a new era called the "Reformasi" era (reform era). Habibie believed that Indonesia should learn from historical experience, so it started by abolishing the clauses that discriminated against the Chinese and repealed the laws and regulations that prohibited the Chinese from participating in politics, celebrating Chinese cultural festivals or banning the use of Chinese language. Therefore, Indonesia's next President Abdurahman Wahid also lifted many laws that are unfavorable to Chinese.

With the democratization of Indonesia, the first political party was founded by the Chinese Indonesian Lieus Sungkharisma, the Chinese Reform Party of Indonesia, on June 5, 1998. He was followed by Muhammad Yusuf Hamka, a Chinese Muslim, who established the Assimilation Party of China Indonesia (Party of Indonesian Assembly). The former had no political experience at all, while the latter was a supporter of Suharto's assimilationist policy; neither of them could attract the Chinese to join with them. Thung Ju Lan explains why Chinese people do not participate in politics: it is because they are afraid to participate in politics since the September 30, 1965 incident, especially something related with China. Because anti-communism has caused ethnic Chinese to be victims, parents of Chinese families want their children to avoid politics. In addition, Chinese Indonesians are often consciously strangers, so they often choose not to interfere in things unrelated with them, resulting in the impression of aborigines against Chinese, that Chinese people do not want to communicate with indigenous people and that Chinese people refused to integrate into local communities. The indigenous ethnic also believe that all Chinese recognize themselves as superior. Thung Ju Lan further explained that Chinese organizations such as the Chinese Society (INTI) and the Chinese Hundred Surname Association (PSMTI), established after 1998, stressed that their organizations are cultural organizations and do not interfere in politics. In fact, regardless of the formation of a cultural or social organization, once an organization is established, it is a political activity. Moreover, the Chinese did not dare to report the losses caused by the riots. The reason for Thung Ju Lan's analysis is that Chinese people feel that they are not accepted as citizens and that Chinese people have low confidence in the government and believe that discrimination is always there (Ju Lan 2005).

In fact, it is difficult to blame the attitude of the Chinese because the decisions made by the government are often not based on the principle of "justice and equality." For example, Vice-President Jusuf Kalla on October 24, 2004, stressed that by Presidential Decree no. 16 of 1994, the central and district governments must distinguish the economically weak (pribumi) and the Chinese; this declaration of the Vice-President was considered a discriminatory declaration by Chinese business people. Also, a severe problem exists in the city of Pontianak in West Kalimantan. The city's mayor ordered in 2008 that the Lantern Festival celebrated by Chinese people be restricted to specific areas, and stated that the riots in 2007 were since (the first elected West Kalimantan vice-governor was Chinese. The first elected Vice-Governor, Christiandy Sanjaya, was a non-Muslim governor. After his election, Chinese houses, temples and cars were burned to the ground (Thung 2005, pp. 3–11).

Although many regulations and discrimination laws have been abolished, it does not mean that anti-Chinese discrimination in Indonesia is automatically resolved. Observers take the example of the election candidate battle of the Special Capital Region Governor of Jakarta, Basuki Tjahaja Purnama or Ahok who wanted to fight to continue retaining his seat as the governor also gets a black campaign. According to senior researcher Sri Yuniarti, the opponents used the issue of ethnic identity and the insulting point of the Quranic verses to attack Ahok, and he said the election campaign in Jakarta was "unhealthy." Because in the battle the drive contains a language that points to ethnic identity, it mobilizes Muslim militant groups, who then pose a threat to Muslims who choose non-Muslim leaders; if they die, they will not be disallowed according to the Islamic religion (Suryowati 2017).

Political discrimination has begun to fade, but there are still many Indonesian aborigines and Islamic believers who find it hard to accept non-Islamic leaders. Take the case of Basuki Tjahaja Purnama, the Governor of Jakarta, as an example. During the election campaign in Jakarta, the statement of "Cina," non-Muslim and non-indigenous people were often used to attack him." Ahok, a Christian of Chinese descent, angered religious conservatives after he referenced a verse from the Islamic holy book, Al-Maidah

51 of the Qur'an, on the campaign trail in September. Ahok instead boldly told voters they should not be duped by religious leaders using the verse to justify the claim that non-Muslims should not lead Muslims (*The Guardian* 2016).

When Ahok quoted a passage from the Qur'an, he was attacked by political opponents cruelly. The video of his speech was edited, and a part of the speech was deliberately omitted. Then Ahok was accused of insulting the Qur'an and desecrating Islam; this incident also caused mass protests. He is also accused of slandering Muslims. Although he has publicly explained the truth of his speech after the incident and expressed his apologies to Muslims throughout the country, the Indonesian Police Headquarter upgraded Ahok's status to "suspect," because of pressures of the "radical" protest on November 16, 2016. However, on May 9, 2017, the Jakarta District Court convicted Ahok as guilty and he was "sentenced for one year and suspended for two years" (BBC News 2016).

When interviewed by BBC reporters on the reaction of Indonesian Chinese to Basuki Tjahaja Purnama or "Ahok," Dr. Thung Ju Lan, an academician of the Indonesian Institute of Sciences, said that the Indonesian Chinese community today is different from the period between 1965 and 1998. Ahok's sentence caused fear and worry in Indonesian Chinese that was different from the events that occurred between 1965 and 1998. In 1965, Chinese Indonesians were worried about being connected with the Communist Party. In 1998, they were worried about social unrest. Dr. Thung told the BBC that after the social unrest in 1998, Indonesian Chinese saw a glimmer of hope of participating in politics, but when Ahok was sentenced, they knew that there was still discrimination in Indonesian society. Owing to the incident of Ahok, most Chinese dare not participate in politics, and Thung said that she does not worry about this kind of thing. She further went on to say that everyone's ideas and thoughts about ways to do things are different. For those Chinese who dare to integrate into society, they have many demands. Those Chinese who dare not integrate into society are always cautious and hesitant.

They used to have many expectations in the past, and now they are starting to retreat (BBC News 2017).

Conclusion

This recollection of discrimination against Chinese ethnicity in Indonesia traces its course to the Dutch colonial government, which had succeeded in compartmentalizing the "indigenous" and "Chinese" nations. And this was a strategy by the Dutch to maintain their existence in Indonesia. Moreover, this also became the origin of the discrimination of the Indonesian nation against its "own" people after independence. Separating the indigenous from the Chinese citizens was a colonial political agenda. The Dutch were afraid of unity and solidarity between the two ethnic groups. The Dutch government undertook the zoning system in which the Chinese ethnics were given a separate place to live in. This separation politics is an attempt to divide and differentiate between the indigenous Indonesian people and the Chinese people, especially since at that time Indonesia had not yet known nationalism.

It is important to remember that the tragedy of Jakarta in May 1998 was not the beginning of anti-Chinese violence in Indonesia. There have been dozens of times that anti-Chinese sentiments have erupted in the form of violence in this country. After this nation became independent, especially during the Suharto period, ethnic Chinese experienced the peak of suffering. Ever since they were accused of being behind the scenes of the PKI (Communist Party of Indonesia), anti-Chinese campaigns and eruptions continue to be systematic. Even today, some groups still associate Chinese with communism, although many of them are anti-communist too. This anti-Chinese campaign is not only in the physical sense but also in the form of an annihilation of all things Chinese, including its culture and religious tradition. This is part of the irony and dark history of the Indonesian nation.

The May 1998 riots were the turning point of the "fate" of ethnic Chinese in Indonesia. After the May 1998 riots, no one group has benefited, especially the lower classes, and after that, there have been better relations and communication, and better interaction between indigenous groups and Chinese. Many Chinese Indonesians are now actively involved in political activity — a field they have avoided during the New Order government. The Chinese are now considered part of the Indonesian nation in the Indonesian society. However, I believe that discrimination still exists in this vast nation of tribes. One example is the punishment of Basuki Tjahaja Purnama, whose "impressed be forced," can be used as a real example, at least in some parts of Jakarta's community there is still anti-Chinese sentiment. In addition, there was a foul campaign against President Joko Widodo ahead of the 2019 presidential election, saying that Joko Widodo is a descendant of Chinese and Chinese henchmen, "Asing and Aseng" (foreign and Chinese) henchmen, PKI (communist) henchmen, etc. All these blackening of the campaigns not only aim to corner President Joko Widodo but also indicate that the anti-Chinese sentiment still a strong issue that "consumes" the nation.

References

Indonesian:

Aliansyah, Muhammad Agil. 2014. "Malari, perlawanan terhebat pertama terhadap Orde Baru." https://www.merdeka.com/peristiwa/malari-perlawanan-terhebat-pertama-terhadap-orde-baru-hariman-dan-malari-1.html. Latest update 26 June 2018. (*Malari*, The first Great disobedience to the New Order Government).

Arsip Nasional Republik Indonesia, Khazanah Arsip VOC abad ke 17 dan 18, 22 May 2016. https://sejarah-nusantara.anri.go.id/id/hartakarunmaincategory/4/, Latest update 2 July 2018. (National Archives of the Republic of Indonesia, Hidden treasures of the 17th and 18th century VOC Archives).

Aziz, Munawir. 2018. "Tionghoa, Antara Sasaran Kebencian dan Ketimpangan Sosial." https://nasional.kompas.com/read/2018/02/22/14163721/tionghoa-antara-sasaran-kebencian-dan-ketimpangan-sosial. Latest update 25 June 2018. (Tionghoa, between Hate and Social Inequality Target).

BBC News. 2016. "Pidato di Kepulauan Seribu dan hari-hari hingga Ahok menjadi tersangka." http://www.bbc.com/indonesia/indonesia-37996601. Latest update 9 July 2018. (Speeches in the Thousand Islands and days until Ahok became a suspect).

Coppel, Charles. A. 1994. Tionghoa Indonesia Dalam Krisis. Jakarta: Pustaka Sinar Harapan. (Indonesian Chinese in Crisis).

Detik Finance. 2015. "Lainnya Ditenggelamkan Kapal Maling Ikan Asal China Ini Hanya Dituntut Rp 200 Juta." https://finance.detik.com/berita-ekonomi-bisnis/d-2866366/lainnya-ditenggelamkan-kapal-maling-ikan-asal-china-ini-hanya-dituntut-rp-200-juta, Latest update 15 November 2015. (The others drowned, The Chinese Fishing Vessel Only Demands 200 Million Rupiah).

Jahja, Junus. 1995. "Partai Tionghoa Indonesia 'Manfaatnya bagi Keturunan Cina' 50 Tahun Indonesia Merdeka." Kompas, 25 Juli. (Indonesian Chinese Party "The Benefits for Chinese Descendants" 50 Years of Independent Indonesia).

Ju Lan, Thung. 2005. "Dari Objek menjadi Subjek." In Leo Suryadinata (Ed.). *Pemikiran Politik Etnis Tionghoa Indonesia 1900–2002*. Jakarta: Pustaka LP3ES Indonesia, 3–11. (From Objects to Subjects. In Political Thinking of the Indonesian Chinese, *ed.* Leo Suryadinata).

La Ode, M. D. 2013. *Politik Tiga Wajah*. Jakarta: Yayasan Pustaka Obor. (The Three Faces of Politic).

Nicholas, Manafe. 2017. "Jokowi: Masih Banyak yang Teriak Antek Asing, Aseng dan PKI Bangkit." http://wartakota.tribunnews.com/2017/11/20/jokowi-masih-banyak-yang-teriak-antek-asing-aseng-dan-pki-bangkit. Latest update 26 June 2018. (Jokowi: There are still many who shout out foreigners, *Aseng* and *PKI* rise).

Poerwanto, Hari. 2005. *Orang Cina Khek dari Singkawang*. Depok: Komunitas Bambu. (Hakka Chinese People from Singkawang).

Sudibyo, Agus. 2001. "Pers Tionghoa, Sensibilitas Budaya, dan Pamali Politik." Kompas, 1 Juni. (Tionghoa's Media, Cultural Sensibility and Political Abtinence).

Suryadinata, Leo. 2010. *Etnis Tionghoa dan Nasionalisme Indonesia: Sebuah Bunga Rampai 1965–2008*. Jakarta: PT. Kompas Media Nusantara. (Chinese Ethnicity and Indonesian Nationalism: A Collection of Story).

Suryadinata, Leo. 2005. *Pemikiran Politik Etnis Tionghoa Indonesia: 1900–2002*. Jakarta: Pustaka LP3ES Indonesia. (Political Thinking of the Indonesian Chinese).

Suryadinata, Leo. 1994. *Politik Tionghoa Peranakan di Jawa*. Jakarta: Pustaka Sinar Harapan. (*Peranakan* Chinese Politics in Java).

Suryowati, Estu. 2017. "Peneliti Senior LIPI: Pilkada DKI Jakarta, Pilkada yang tidak Sehat," Kompas on the web, 03/05/2017. https://nasional.kompas.com/read/2017/05/03/18124191/peneliti.senior.lipi.pilkada.dki.jakarta.pilkada.yang.tidak.sehat. Latest update 16 June 2018. (LIPI Senior Researcher: DKI Jakarta's Election, Unhealthy Local Election).

Windoro, Adi, Helena F Nababan, Pingkan Elita Dundu. 2016. "Kali Angke, Aliran Kemelut Sejarah Kelam Jayakarta." Kompas on the web, 28/11/2016. Available at https://megapolitan.kompas.com/read/2016/11/28/17000011/kali.angke.aliran.kemelut.sejarah.kelam.jayakarta. Latest update 6 June 2018. (*Angke's* River: The Darkness History of Jakarta).

English:

Adiputri, Ratih D. 2014. The Dutch Legacy in The Indonesian Parliament. *Journal of Political Science and Public Affairs* 2 (2): 1–8.

Dahana, A. 2015. Indonesian Peranakan Chinese: The Origin and Their Culture. http://chinese.binus.ac.id/2015/02/18/indonesian-peranakan-chinese-the-origins-and-their-culture-by-prof-a-dahana/. Latest update 5 July 2018.

Kosasih, Luciana Sani. 2010. *Chinese Indonesians: Stereotyping, Discrimination and anti-Chinese Violence in the context of Structural Changes up to May 1998 Riots*. Master Thesis in Conflict Studies and Human Rights, Utrecht University, Netherlands.

Mackie, J. A. C. 1976. *The Chinese in Indonesia*. Australia: Thomas Nelson (Australia) Limited.

Schwarz, Adam. 1997. Indonesia After Suharto. Foreign Affairs Vol. 76, No. 4, July/August.

Setijadi, Charlotte. 2016. Ethnic Chinese in Contemporary Indonesia: Changing Identity Politics and the Paradox of Sinification. *Perspective* 2016 (12): 1–11.

The Guardian. 2016. Jakarta governor Ahok's blasphemy trial: All you need to know. https://www.theguardian.com/world/2016/dec/12/jakarta-governor-ahoks-blasphemy-trial-all-you-need-to-know. Latest update 9 July 2018.

The Straits Times. 2018. Indonesia sentences eight Taiwanese drug smugglers to death. https://www.straitstimes.com/asia/se-asia/indonesia-sentences-eight-taiwanese-drug-smugglers-to-death. Latest update 15 November 2018.

Chinese:

Author n.a. 2017. Zhong Wanxue Sentenced Two Years (ZhongWanxue-panxing liang nian). Available at http://www.bbc.com/zhongwen/trad/world-39897347. Accessed on July 9, 2018.

Sunardi Mulia. 2015. Interview: The Research & Educational Centre for Chinese Studies and Cross-Taiwan Strait Relations. Department of Political Science, National Taiwan University. Available at http://www.china-studies.taipei/comm2/Sunardi%20Mulia.pdf (last update 15 November 2018).

Gu, Chang-yong. 2017. *Indonesia Have Changed Entirely* (Yinni zhengti gaibian). Kaohsiung: National Sun Yat-sen University Press.

Chen, Yi-ling. 1989. *The General Conditions of Chinese Overseas in Indonesia* (Yinni Huaqiao Gai Kuang). Taipei: Zheng Zhong Bookstore.

Part II

China as Relational Other —
In the Eyes of the Lost Self

Chapter 7

Colonial and Post-colonial Legacies of the Intellectual History of China Studies in Korea: Discontinuity, Fragmentation and Forgetfulness

Jungmin Seo

Department of Political Science and International Studies,
Yonsei University, Seoul, South Korea

Introduction

This chapter provides a brief sketch of intellectual history of China studies in post-colonial Korea where domestic and regional conditions disallowed continuity, unity and legacy in academia. The chapter summarizes those conditions in two sections: the colonial conditions that prohibit knowledge-accumulation and/or knowledge-transmission regarding classical and contemporary Chinese texts, and the post-colonial conditions in which knowledge production regarding China has been almost impossible.

When Korean academia searches for the way to understand China and to interpret what happened in China, the dilemma emerges not only from the problem of identifying what China is but also from the difficulty of identifying what Korea means for those intellectuals. Unlike the orientalist strategy of the West that reifies the Chineseness in the process of dual identity formation — defining non-West to define the West — (Said 1978) and unlike the Japanese dilemma that Japanese intellectuals had to construct "Japan's Orient" through dual departures from the classical East Asian civilization and from the West as the new source of epistemology, (Tanaka 1995) Korean intellectuals had to go through radical epistemological transformations under the conditions of the dismantlement of the classical world and the Japanese colonization that prohibited the formation of "modern self" (Schmid 2002).

The purpose of this chapter is to delineate the conundrum of Korean intellectuals in the conditions that I have mentioned above, while suggesting that the pursuit of knowledge about China was fundamentally circumvented primarily by the difficulty of defining "Korea" under colonial conditions. Though China as the other was well established through the nation-making processes, the nature of the Chinese otherness in the Korean epistemology has always been unstable, vague and unidentifiable. This impossibility ultimately determined the nature of post-colonial Korea's epistemology toward China.

From "Chosun versus Tianxia" to "Colonized Korea versus Semi-Colonized China"

The pre-modern pursuit of knowledge about China in the Chosun dynasty (1392–1910) was almost identical to the universalistic inquiry about civilization. Similar to Latin in Medieval Europe, classical Chinese as a written language system was not understood as "Chinese language" but as the signs of universal knowledge and moral inquiries. Many Chosun intellectuals positioned themselves as hegemonic members of the Confucius world order, while being the ruling class of the Chosun dynasty. For Chosun intellectuals, China was the civilizational center rather than a foreign country.

The first effort of otherizing China in Chosun was made by a few scholars in the 18th century in the name of "Northern Studies (*bukhak*)" (Baek 2012, p. 569). Ironically, many Confucius scholars in Chosun dynasty, soon after the collapse of the Ming Dynasty by the Qing dynasty, did not recognize Qing, or the Manchus, as the orthodox inheritor of the Chinese Civilization and maintained a paradoxical conceptual framework toward the Qing. While recognizing Qing's political superiority, they refused to accept the centrality of the Qing dynasty in the Confucius moral world order. A few of those scholars genuinely believed that Chosun became the cultural center of the Confucius world order as Ming was destroyed by barbarians. With inherently pejorative attitudes toward Qing, they called Qing not "Middle Kingdom (*zhongguo* or *zhonghua*)" but "the Northern State (*beiguo*)." From this context, the inquiry about Qing was slowly distinguished from the inquiry about civilization in general and labeled as "the Northern Studies" by mid-18th century. Compared to classical studies, the Northern Studies focused on non-traditional academic subjects such as astronomy, engineering, mathematics and others, the majority of those being a part of the early Western knowledges popular in Beijing. Despite its potential to become a part of Chosun's academia — as *Rangaku* (Dutch Learning) did in Japan — Northern Studies was never integrated into Chosun's academic institutions and remained as the intellectual hobby of a few adventurous aristocrats. In the early 19th century, some of those curious scholars became associated with forbidden Christianity and were brutally suppressed. Since then, the tradition of the Northern Studies could not effectively survive until the end of the Chosun dynasty.

The Chosun Dynasty slowly collapsed due to two forces: the exhaustion of the pre-modern dynasty that lasted for more than five centuries and the incessant invasions from imperial powers, especially Japan. The Kanghwa Treaty (1876), the first modern but unequal treaty, between Chosun and Japan forced the hermit kingdom to enter into the modern world system without much preparation. The treaty meant for Chosun's intellectuals that the tianxia, the universalist world system, was over. The status of Qing or China was drastically downgraded from the center of the universal order to a decaying empire. The rulers of the Korean peninsula had witnessed many dynastic transitions in the Chinese continent. Yet, the collapse of the Qing Empire was different from the precedents. There was no replacement that functioned as the center of the universal order. Qing was relativized as one state among many. Nevertheless, Chosun scholars could not identify alternatives. The conundrum naturally led to the pursuit of national studies (*guoxue*) as an important part of nation-building efforts.

Even today, there is no consensus regarding the character of the period between the Kanghwa Treaty in 1876 and the forced annexation by Japan in 1910. In spite of the anecdotal depiction of this period as a gradual Japanese colonization of Korea, Japanese political dominance was seriously challenged by two sets of regional balances — Japan versus China (until 1895) and Japan versus Russia (until 1905). That means the Chosun dynasty and the Chosun aristocrats had few chances to gain relative freedom against powerful neighbors through solid nation-building processes.

While the Chosun's court and political aristocrats struggled to manage their dominant status in the Korean peninsula, a new type of intellectuals emerged — "enlightenment intellectuals" who tried to find a way to establish a Korean nation through enlightening its population. Nevertheless, their tasks were enormously complex. They had to negate the worldview formed by the tributary system and the traditional Confucius morality world so that the population in the peninsula could see themselves as a distinct/homogenous entity. To be distinct, the Korean language and culture had to be reinvented as modern ones. To be homogenous, the feudal hierarchy had to be replaced by the modern concept of "we, the people." By the end of the 19th century, Korean written script, which was invented in the 15th century and primarily used by women and commoners, was revived as the national script that quickly became the standard means of instruction in hundreds of newly found modern educational institutions. Non-establishment intellectuals who did not belong to the decaying royal educational systems diligently wrote Korean national history books that largely accommodated Social Darwinist worldview.

The newly re-formed Korean national script and the construction of Korean national history were the two most important steps toward "otherizing China." The rise of the Korean texts over the classical Chinese texts vitiated the supremacy of the feudal aristocrats/literati who maintained the Confucius worldview throughout the Chosun dynasty. New knowledge from the West was translated from English, Japanese and Chinese to Korean. That meant that traditional literati's monopoly of knowledge and information was diminishing fast. By the end of the Chosun dynasty, classical Chinese texts that were pivotal to the universalist Confucius world order became "foreign" at last, though Chinese characters remain as an important component of Korean linguistic practice till today. The formation of Korean national history, on the other hand, meant that the history of the peninsula was carved out from the history of "tianxia." For this task, the world had to be reinterpreted as a constellation of independent sovereign nations, which resulted in the relativization of China. Yet, this conceptual transformation could not happen over one generation.

The era between the Kanghwa Treaty and the Annexation could be best characterized as uneven penetration of heterogeneous modernities. The western modernity was imbued into the peninsula through Christian missionaries and Christianity-based educational institutions such as Yonsei University (1885), Ewha Women's University (1886) and Sungsil University (1897). Those institutions created intellectual lineages in Korean society through the import of the western disciplinary academic system and creating a small group of intellectuals who eventually spent significant time in the United States. Jaephil Suh, the founder of *Dongnip Sinmun* (Independent Newspaper, the first Korean language newspaper found in 1896) and Syngman Rhee, the first president of the Republic of Korea, who received a PhD from Princeton in 1910, might be exemplary. Meanwhile, Japanese political penetration into the peninsula resulted in not only violent and repressive invasions but also vast interactions between the two societies. Many saw the enemy's modernity as the only way to redeem the decaying Korean feudal society and went to Japan for study. The Meiji Restoration was especially admired by many Korean royalist aristocrats and perceived as the only way to preserve the dying dynasty in the peninsula.

If the search for the Korean way of modernization was for nation-building in the peninsula, the process was aborted by the annexation that left numerous fragmented and discontinued intellectual enterprises. Modern Korean script was still imperfect and incomplete. Korean national history was still under circulation among non-establishment intellectuals. Yet, the traditional knowledge system was already destroyed beyond the point of no return. The classical world was over, yet the new national identity was still under construction. Against this situation, the Japanese colonialism started in 1910.

During the colonial era, academic inquiry about China in the peninsula was integrated with Japanese academia, so-called "*Jinagaku* (支那學)." The most influential academic institution in colonial Korea was Keijo Imperial University (京城帝國大學: KIU), founded in 1924 as the sixth imperial university in the Japanese Empire. Following other imperial universities in Japan, KIU set up departments of literature, history and philosophy. Classical studies based on Confucianism were absorbed into those three departments (Seo 2016, p. 42). Whatever contents did not fit into those departments or those that could not be accommodated in the modern disciplinary knowledge system, were discarded as "non-academic," and left as subjects of private non-establishment inquiries.

Chinese history became a subject of the department of history's subfield, East Asian (*toyo*) history, and Chinese philosophy the department of philosophy's subfield, East Asian philosophy. Being contrasted with national (Japanese) history, national (Japanese) literature or national (Japanese) philosophy, China studies in Seoul was institutionalized as a part of East Asian studies. Treating China as a foreign entity was a consistent trend of Korean intellectuals from the late Chosun era. The problem was that to perceive China as a foreign entity, those intellectuals had to simultaneously construct their own epistemological subjectivity. Nevertheless, the colonial situation gave them a deep paradox. In the Japanese educational system that was transplanted into Seoul, China as the foreign entity and object of academic inquiry was contrasted with another foreign entity (Japan) as the subject of inquiry. Similarly, while Japanese history and literature was considered national, Korean history and literature was a part of "East Asian studies" along with China studies. For Korean intellectuals under colonial rule, their academic practice led to the removal of their own identity as the subject of inquiry. In this situation, China studies in KIU and in the peninsula in general were primarily delimited in the realm of positivistic inquiries without making those intellectuals' critical/ontological questions; "what are the meanings of Chinese history, literature and culture for Koreans?" (Seo 2016, p. 366). With this fundamental limitation, China studies under Japanese colonial rule were inherently sterile.

Under the Japanese colonial rule, Korean intellectuals were forced to make a choice between the acceptance of the Japanese epistemological stances through the colonial state's educational and research institutions and to find a Korean way of academic modernization based on nationalistic consciousness. The former meant the denial of Korean identity in performing academic inquiries while the later had to be pursued without formal/official institutional support. China studies in the peninsula shared the same fate. For Korean intellectuals, the images of China were deeply divided through the transplantation of the Japanese image of China, the Korean nationalists' construction of China in the context of national liberation movement and the fragmented legacies of the classical studies.

Interpreting China in Post-Colonial Korea

The liberation of Korea came suddenly, at least for the majority of Koreans living in the peninsula. Japanese colonialism in Korea was rather different from the West's colonialism. Among many differences, one that matters to this discussion would be the deep penetration of the colonialism into the everydayness in the peninsula. Whereas there were about two thousand French living in the Indochina region, over a million Japanese lived in Korea and formed the upper skeleton of the colonial society. The French left vast routine businesses of colonial management to local elites and intellectuals. The Japanese colonial government, nevertheless, mobilized hundreds of thousand Japanese and Korean collaborators in the management of local administration, education and economic management. When the French exploited agricultural products from Vietnamese landlords, the Japanese colonial government directly "owned" a significant portion of lands in Korea. When those Japanese escaped the peninsula in a hurry immediately after the end of the Second World War, they left vast institutional structures, both official and non-official. The Korean academia had to make a start from the pre-existing institutional legacies.

KIU was absorbed by the newly formed Seoul National University (SNU) that was coordinated by the United States Army Military Government in Korea (USAMGIK). The Department of History maintained its basic structure while Chosun history became the national history major, and the national history major became the Japanese history major. The Chinese language and literature major under the Department of Literature became an independent department, and the Chosun language and literature major became the Department of National Language and Literature. Other major educational institutions that were heavily suppressed by the colonial government during the total mobilization period (1937–1945) reopened in 1945 and proactively adopted the American educational and academic systems. Nevertheless, the Korean intellectual scenes under USAMGIK were chaotic. Hundreds of thousands of Koreans who were drafted as workers or soldiers returned from Japan and warfronts across Asia. An equal number of Korean emigrants returned from Manchuria, China and Japan. Many Korean teachers and researchers in the colonial systems remained in their positions. Thousands of underground/nationalist intellectuals emerged as the legitimate voices of the liberated discursive spaces. A small number of English-speaking intellectuals who had rare experiences of education in the United States before the end of WWII found ample opportunities to promote their positions. Inexperienced Americans were hastily reorganizing the Korean educational systems without knowing much about the complexity of the post-colonial social spaces. In these chaotic situations, the Cold War came to the Korean peninsula suddenly, claiming millions of lives through incessant insurgents, mass killings and war in the following years.

The Cold War in Korea fundamentally reshaped or, to be precise, eliminated the intellectual landscape. The deepening Cold War forced scholars to take positions between left and right, before the newly independent society could contemplate on how to construct academia. Those in China studies were not exceptions. For instance, Taejun Lee, one of only three *Jina* (Chinese) literature majoring Korean students from KIU was the first scholar who attempted the comparative literature that systematically and formally separates Korean literature history from Chinese literature history, meaning both had to be carved out from the classical literature (Baek 2012, p. 578). He might be one rare figure who would bridge the *Jinagaku* in the KIU and the post-liberation China studies in newly established Korean higher educational institutions. Nevertheless, he was involved in the left-wing political organizations after the liberation and summarily executed in 1947 by the Korean police, thus preventing him from leaving a significant intellectual legacy in Korean academia. Myungsun Lee, another graduate from KIU, also majoring in *Jina* literature, became one of the first professors of the newly formed Seoul National University in 1945. Nevertheless, his pursuit of historical materialism in literary studies led him to be removed from his teaching position and to join to the North Korea. After a brief appearance in public as the figure in charge of the Seoul National University under the three-month long communist occupation of Seoul, he disappeared, presumed to be dead, in the process of the communist retreat from Seoul during the Korean War. His name and works had been entirely removed from Korean intellectual scenes until the recent publication of his works in 2007 (Lee 2007).

After the Korean War between 1950 and 1953, the South Korean intellectual spaces were irreversibly deformed by two factors. The first was, as anyone would easily expect, the elimination of any subject related to the leftist ideology. Throughout the fields of philosophy, literature and history, "unhealthy" topics including, but not limited to, current affairs of the People's Republic of China, Marxism, Communist history, and progressive literature were included in this category. Korean independent movements in China were scarcely and selectively introduced in Korean history textbooks due to their close relations with the Chinese Communist Party. The works of scholars who chose to move to or stay in North Korea were all banned regardless of their ideological orientations. Even gray areas were not permitted. For instance, publications of Lu Xun's works were not allowed until the late 1980s. All the information and interpretation regarding leftist academic subjects — as defined by the South Korean authorities — were monopolized by a few government organizations such as the Korean Central Intelligence Agency, the Ministry of Culture and numerous anti-Communist agencies in the police and military.

The second factor that reinforced the first factor, anti-communism, was the dictatorial regulation of society by the state, symbolized by the National Security Law (1952). It not only outlawed any free discussion regarding leftist ideas but also banned criticism against the incumbent government, especially the presidents. Hence, the authorities arbitrarily applied the National Security Law to suppress the demands of freedom of speech or freedom of publications while frequently labeling those demands as communist conspiracies.

Until the shock of the Nixon–Mao dialogue in 1971, inquiries about China in Korea were strongly delimited into only one dimension: reading the sophisticated classical Chinese texts in a positivistic way without leaving room for social or political implications (Ha 1989). In other words, the study of China was not about China as an existing entity but about a cultural construct called China that does not have any meaningful link to the existing People's Republic of China (PRC). A small group of scholars in the Department of Chinese Language and Literature at SNU replicated the Taiwanese or Japanese studies on Chinese classical texts and isolated themselves from rest of the academic society. Contemporary China, which was conquered by communism, was not regarded as China proper but as a temporary decay from sophisticated antique

China. Limited inquiries about contemporary China in relation to anti-Communist South Korea's foreign policy and military strategies were scarcely performed within the strict boundary of "communism studies" (Kang 2004, p. 155). In short, meaningful academic inquiries about China in post-liberation Korea did not exist in the Cold War environments. Despite historical and cultural ties for centuries, South Korean intellectuals could not perceive the contemporary China as a tangible entity. The two decades' absence of China discourse in the South Korean academia was slightly altered by the historic event between the United States and PRC.

The détente between the United States and China was an important watershed for Chinese studies in Korea. While Mainland China remained as one of the prime communist enemies, which deeply intervened in the Korean War, it became a subject of academic inquires with a certain degree of endorsement of the authoritarian South Korean government. Two pioneering research institutions, China Research Center at Hanyang University and the East–West Center at Yonsei University were set up in 1972 with direct and indirect government support. Both institutions aimed to construct an interdisciplinary research agendum in the framework of comparative socialist studies. In other words, Korean scholars, under the government's enthusiastic endorsement, started to distinguish PRC from other communist countries, especially from the Soviet Union and North Korea. They were not forced to use official sovietology to analyze PRC, and allowed to build infrastructure for China Studies in Korea. For instance, major universities in Korea started to establish the Department of Chinese Language and Literature; Korea University in 1972 and Yonsei University in 1974. Furthermore, in 1970s, Korean academia began to witness the return of Taiwan-educated young scholars. They rejuvenated the lost interest in Chinese literature and history while also bringing in the Taiwanese way of China studies, though it was deeply constrained by the Cold War mentality. In the 1970s, a group of scholars who initiated China studies in various disciplines, then, can be categorized as the first generation of China scholars in post-liberation Korea, though their realms of research were still restricted by the Cold War situation and supposed to serve the government's policy goals.

China's Reform since 1978 further strengthened Korean academia's interests and accessibility to China. Departments of Chinese language and literature were opened in many local universities. Meanwhile, the Korean society experienced a dramatic democratization process in 1980s, lifting the ban on leftist publications and research topics. Young scholars who started their research on China after the beginning of détente entered into the academic job market in the mid-1980s. In the mid and late-1980s, Korean societies witnessed a plethora of academic discourses about China, and that became the ground for second-generation China studies (Yi 2013).

Compared to the first generation of China scholars who were trained in Taiwan or in domestic academic institutions, the second-generation China scholars took diverse routes to pursue their academic career. Since the diplomatic normalization between Korea in 1992, hundreds of Korean students entered into elite Chinese educational institutions' graduate program and emerged on the Korean academic job market from the early 2000s. Dozens of students, including myself, went to American graduate programs where China studies were well established. Thanks to the strengthened faculty in the domestic program on China Studies, domestically trained scholars also became important candidates on the academic job market.

Currently, Korean intellectual discourses on China are produced in a number of heterogeneous groups without much communications among each other. Of those, however, the American academic hegemony is obvious in social scientific studies on China, as I have discussed elsewhere (Seo and Lee, 2019). In humanities, three major groups from domestic, American and Chinese/Taiwanese academic institutions are maintaining a delicate balance. Yet, the Korean state's top-down evaluation policies upon academic performance that prefer publications in English eventually produced a controversial hierarchy of scholars, reinforcing American academic hegemony throughout the fields.

Conclusion

As partially mentioned above, the post-colonial conditions in Korea are rather complex and not easily generalizable for a number of reasons. First of all, Korea was one of very few colonies that are colonized by non-Western power and by a neighbor — Japan — not offshore imperialists such as Great Britain or France. Second, due to its lateness of colonization (1910), the modern Korean nation was in the process of formation with an aggrandizing sense of national identity, national script and national history when it became a colony though the full colonization occurred before the completion of the modern Korean nation. Third, the southern part of the post-colonial Korea was academically and intellectually dominated by the global hegemony of the United States.

For those characteristics of Korean colonial experiences, scholarship in Korea is not very enthusiastic about the vocabularies related to post-colonialism which in part pre-supposes the nation-making under colonial conditions. In the Korean mainstream historiography, the modern Korean nation undoubtedly existed well before the Japanese colonialism. The colonial period is understood as a frozen time in which Korean modernity is seized, suppressed and denied. With this historiography, the year of "*gwangbok* (restoration of sovereignty)" means the national clock that was forced to stop in 1910 is now moving forward again. Nevertheless, when the national clock stopped, epistemologically, Korea was struggling to escape from the Chinese universalistic world order and to enter the modern world comprised of 'nations.' When the national clock restarted, the imagined community of Korean nation was divided in the very beginning of the Cold War and vividly experienced the fast transition of the global hegemonic order. In this turbulent process, the images, discourses and perceptions of China became fragmented and inconsistent.

As described above, the intellectual/academic discourses on China in South Korea can be characterized as non-accumulative and fragmented. The radical and forced departure from pre-modern society to colonial modernity and toward the post-colonial schizophrenic conditions forced the Korean society, despite geographical, cultural and historical proximity, to imagine China as a remote and alien entity until recently. The diplomatic normalization alongside globalization and the emergence of regional economy facilitated human interactions between Korea and China. China has now become the biggest trade partner and the most popular oversea travel destination for Koreans. Yet, the production of knowledge regarding China in Korean academia still needs institutional and intellectual maturity.

References

Baek, Wondam. 2008. Asia Jiyeok Yeong ui Munhwa Jeongchihakjok Jeonhwan Munje (The Problem of Asian Regional Studies' Cultural/Political Transformation). *Jungguk Heondae Munhak* (Chinese Modern Literature) 55: 127–162.

Baek, Youngseo. 2012. Junggukhak ui guejeokkwa bipanjeok jungguk yeongu (Trajectories of China Studies and Critical China Studies: Korean Experiences). *Daedong Munhwa Yeongu* (East Asian Cultural Studies) 80: 563–608.

Ha, Sebong. 1989. Hanguk dongyangsahakkye e daehan bibanjeok geomto (A Critical Reflection of Studies of East Asian Histories in Korea). *Yeoksa Bibyeong* (Critical Review of History) 5: 219–241.

Im, Gyuseop. 2007. Hanguk ui Jungguk Yeongu: Eoje wa Oneul (China Studies in Korea: Pasts and Presents). *Atae Yeongu* (Asian Pacific Studies) 14, 2: 161–180.

Jeong, Jaeseo. 2008. Je 3 ui Junggukhak eon Ganeunghanga (Is the third Chinese Studies possible?). *Jungguk Munhak* (Chinese Literature) 54: 1–18.

Kang, Junyoung. 2004. Hanguk esoui Junggukhak e gwanhan gochal (A Reflection on China Studies in Korea). *Hanguk Kukje Jiyeokhakhoebo* (International Regional Studies in Korea) 3 (August): 143–164.

Kim, Dohui. 2006. Hanguk ui Jungguk Yeonju: Sigak kwa Jaengjeom (China Studies in Korea: Perspectives and Controversies). *Donga Yeongu* (East Asian Studies) 50 (February): 55–89.

Kim, Dohui. 2010. Jungguk ui Jungguk Yeongu: Miguk ui Jungguk Yeongu Ddarajapki wa Neomeoseogi (Chinese Studies in China: Catching up and Overcoming American China Studies). *Heondae Jungguk Yeongu* (Modern China Studies) 12, 1: 1–29.

Kim, Gyobin. 1996. Haebang ihu Hanguk esoui Jungguk Chorhak Yongu Dongyang kwa Cheonmang (Trends and Prospects of Research on Chinese Philosophy in post-liberation Korea). *Chinese Studies* 36: 137–155.

Lee, Myungsun. 2007. *Lee Myungsun Jonjip* (Writings of Lee Myungsun). Seoul: Bogosa, pp. 1–4.

Min, Beonghui. 2010. Geundae Haksulchegye esoui Dongasia Inmunjeontong e daehan jeopkun pangsik kwa Junggukhak (Modern Academic System's approaches to East Asian traditions of humanities and China Studies. *Jungguk Hakbo*, 71: 385–409.

Said, Edward W. 1978. *Orientalism*. New York: Pantheon Books.

Schmid, Andre. 2002. *Korea Between Empires: 1895–1919*. New York: Columbia University Press.

Seo, Kwangdeok. 2016. Hanguk ui Junggukhak Yeoksa wa Hyeonhwang (History and Current Situation of China Studies in Korea. *Oneul ui Munyebipyeong* (Today's Literary Critics) (September): 241260.

Seo, Jungmin and Hwanbi Lee. 2019. "Indigenization of International Relation Theories in Korea and China: Tales of Two Essentialisms." In Kosuke Shimizu (Ed.). *Critical International Relations of East Asia*. New York: Routledge.

Tanaka, Stefan. 1995. *Japan's Orient: Rendering Pasts into History*. Berkeley, CA: University of California Press.

Yi, Gyutae. 2016. Kukje Jiyeok Yeongu roseo Junggukhak ui Yeongu Bangbeomnon e gwanhan Gochal (A Study on China Studies' Research Method as International Regional Studies. *Junggukhak Yeongu* (Chinese Studies) 49: 1–30.

Yi, Mun'gi. 2013. Han'guk daehak junggukhakkwa ui kyoyuk hyeonhwang e daehan bunseok kwa jeon (An analysis of educational situations of China studies departments in Korean colleges and a few suggestions). *Jungguk Yeongu* (Chinese Studies) 58: 41–64.

Yi, Ukyeon. 2014. G-2 Sidae Jungguk Jisikin ui "Jungguk" Jaebalgyeon kwa Hanguk Inmun Junggukhak ui Gwaje (Chinese Intellectuals' Re-Finding of China and the Tasks of Korean China Studies in Humanities in the Era of G2). *Junggukhak Yeongu* (China Studies) 43: 383–436.

Chapter 8

Anglo-Chinese Studies in Post-WWII Hong Kong: The Perspectives of Colonial Languages

Mariko Tanigaki

Department of Area Studies, University of Tokyo, Tokyo, Japan

Seeing British legacies in the daily life of Hong Kong is difficult. Hong Kong does not have a historical square like the Senado Square in Macau. Hong Kong has a group of Eurasians represented by a famous tycoon named Robert Hotung. However, the Macanese people, descendants of Portuguese by blood or culture, still inhabit present-day Macau. These Macanese people worked in the civil service and kept the law and records written in Portuguese. The British Legacies could be observed in the software of contemporary Hong Kong, such as the implementation of rule of law, the circulation of Hong Kong dollars and the wide usage of the English language.

This chapter aims to interpret the development of Chinese studies with special reference to the usage of language. The Department of Chinese Studies is an exceptional existence in the British-style university in Hong Kong. Its connotation could be observed in such progress with reference to the British administration over the Chinese people. The establishment of the People's Republic of China (PRC) affected the development of Chinese studies in Hong Kong. Hong Kong received a big influx of migrants from Mainland China, including the scholars. The Cold War also contributed to the changes in Chinese studies in Hong Kong. This function as a window to the mainland led to the emergence of contemporary Chinese studies in Hong Kong. We must also examine the changes in Chinese studies since 1997.

Chinese Studies Inside the British-Style University

Pre- and early colonial education in Hong Kong

Under the Qing Dynasty and prior to the Opium War, Hong Kong was a part of Xin'an county 新安縣 in Guangdong Province. Hong Kong's education system was similar to the education systems in the rest of the province (Lu 2003, pp. 11–12). A young boy, for instance, would begin his studies with the *Three Letter Classic* 三字經, moving on to the *Hundred Family Surnames* (百家姓) and the *Thousand Letter Classic* (千字文). At the next stage, he would study the *Four Books* (四書) and *Five Classics* (五経). A more ambitious and smarter student would continue his studies in preparation for the imperial civil service examination (Lu 2003, pp. 14–16).

In the early British colonial days, Hong Kong had two educational streams. One was the traditional style stated above, while the other was the Western style of education (Lu 2003, pp. 33–39). Most of the children received traditional education. After they finished the basic course, most of them started working and helped at home by earning money. Some were sent to the mainland and continued the traditional style of education. A small portion of students stayed in Hong Kong and studied English at the missionary schools or government schools. The number of government schools increased to 3 in 1848 and 20 in 1860 (Lu 2003, p. 36). In 1862, the government schools in urban areas were united into the Central School (Lu 2003, pp. 37–38). Given that the head area of Kowloon Peninsula was ceded to the United Kingdom, the Hong Kong government started cultivating bilingual talents and served the Hong Kong government and the Sino-British trade business. Those educated in the government and missionary schools played the important role of mediators that bridged the Chinese society, the Western officials and the business firms. By the late 19th century, Hong Kong consolidated its unique position. Hong Kong trained these bilingual talents, and these talented people found their positions not only in Hong Kong but also in Mainland China.

The University of Hong Kong was established in such an environment in 1912, which was a year after the overthrowing of the Qing Dynasty and the first year of the Republican era. The University of Hong Kong was designed to provide a British-style education to Chinese students for the modernization of China (Development and Alumni Affairs Office 2002, p. 25). The basic concept of the University of Hong Kong was "the university serves as a British university in Hong Kong for China."

In the university's early years, expatriates were very dominant. Except the lecturers in Chinese, all academic staff members were of non-Chinese origin. As a British-style university, the University of Hong Kong used English as a medium of instruction. Inside the English-speaking university, the course for Chinese was fairly exceptional. Lai Jixi (Lai Chi His, 賴際熙) taught Chinese History, and Ou Dadian (Au Tai Tin, 區大典) taught Chinese Literature (Fang and Xiong 2007, p. 227). Lai and Ou served for the Imperial Academy and settled in Hong Kong as exiles after the 1911 Xinhai revolution. Both were from Guangdong. The course was designed to have two divisions such as History and Literature. In the History division, the students read selections from the classics such as *Twenty-four Histories* (二十四史), *Zizhi Tongjian* (資治通鑑), *Tongjian, Zizhi Jilan* (資治輯覽) and historical records of the Song 宋, Yuan 元 and Ming 明 Dynasties. In the Literature division, the students read the *Four Books* (四書) and *Five Classics* (五経) with selections from the Commentaries of Zhu Xi (朱熹) and others. Literature was taught as a subject to enable students to study the Confucius classics, which was suitable to be called *Jingxue* 經學 (University of Hong Kong 1914, p. 77).

From the syllabus, it could be observed that the Chinese Studies pursued in the department stayed inside the framework of

Classical Chinese. Although time was already in a new Republican era, Chinese studies at the University of Hong Kong put emphasis on Classical Chinese. When the University was established in 1912, the imperial civil service examination had already been abolished in 1905. The reason for sticking to Classical Chinese might be interpreted from the consideration that the Hong Kong government has given to prevent the growth of anti-British sentiments. After seven years, the May Fourth Movement was launched in the mainland. The concept of democracy and sciences was emphasized, and the Colloquial Novels (白話文學) were also advocated by Hu Shi (胡適); and Lu Xun (魯迅) also published colloquial novels. These activities were deeply related to the emergence of nationalism in the Republican era. On the contrary, the emphasis of Classical Chinese in the colony could be interpreted as a political challenge for the new Republican government.

Introduction of a New Tide of Republican China

In the mid-1920s, a change occurred in the attitude of the Hong Kong government toward Chinese education. The May 30th Movement in 1925 stirred up the anti-British feeling in China and led to the boycott in Hong Kong and Guangzhou in 1925–1926. In this difficult moment for Britain, Cecil Clementi was appointed to the 17th Governor of Hong Kong. He served in Hong Kong twice before taking up the position of Governor and had a good command of both Cantonese and Mandarin. To ease the anti-British feeling, Clementi took the strategy of promoting Chinese education in Hong Kong and opened a government Chinese school in 1926 (Fang and Xiong 2007, pp. 198–199). In 1926, a Wellington Delegation from Britain visited Hong Kong and made an assessment of the education at the University of Hong Kong (Fang and Xiong 2007, p. 227). The delegation advised that the university should have a new meaning to its Chinese education.

Lai and Ou responded very actively, wrote a reform plan in the curriculum and launched an idea for the establishment of a Chinese Department (School History, n.d.). The Chancellor of the

University and previous Governor of Hong Kong, Cecil Clementi, agreed to the proposal and Lai went to Southeast Asia to seek donations for a new department with the then Vice Chancellor of the University (School History, n.d.; Fang and Xiong 2007, p. 227). Thus, the Chinese Department was officially established in 1927 (History of School of Chinese, n.d.). The department started without its own building and library. The facility was strengthened rapidly with endowments from overseas and local Chinese. Kuala Lumpur-born Chan Wing donated twenty thousand dollars to the Department, and the Cheng Yung Library 振永書藏 was established. From the Hong Kong local community, Deng Zhi'ang (Tang Chi Ngong 鄧志昂) contributed a building that is known as the Tang Chi Ngong School of Chinese 鄧志昂中文學院. In 1932, Feng Pingshan (Fung Ping Shan 馮平山) contributed a building for the library, known as the Fung Ping Shan Library 馮平山圖書館.

The 1930 University of Hong Kong Calendar showed that the curriculum for the Chinese Department was increased compared with the university's early stage in 1914. By that time, the academic staff increased in number at the School of Chinese Studies; four positions made up the permanent staff: Reader in Chinese History Dr. Lai Jixi; Reader in Chinese Classics, Dr. Ou Dadian; Chinese Translator Lin Dong ([Lam Tung] 林棟, B.A.) and Adviser on Chinese Studies, Re., H. R. Wells). (University of Hong Kong 1930, p. 168; Fang and Xiong 2007, p. 228).

A new change occurred again in the 1930s. When Hu Shi, one of the leaders of the New Culture Movement in 1919, was awarded an honorary degree of law at the University of Hong Kong in 1935, Hu highlighted that the Chinese Studies Department in the University of Hong Kong refrained from accepting the influence of a new Republican era. Hu asked the University to find a suitable person to the head the Department of Chinese Studies. The requirements included being a professional in Chinese Studies, being fluent in English, having the management capability and originating from Guangdong, if possible (Fang and Xiong 2007, p. 228).At the end, Hu recommended Xu Dishan (Hsu Ti-shan, 許地山), and Xu accepted this declaration to become the head of the Department of Chinese Studies in 1935.

The 1935 University Calendar suggested that Hu's comments had already led to some changes. The department was divided into two groups, Groups 6 and 7 (University of Hong Kong 1935, pp. 116–120). Both Groups had Translation as a subject. Group 6 was described as English and Chinese, while Group 7 was described as Chinese Studies. Group 6 put emphasis on the Chinese Literature. These groups studied Chinese Philosophy in the second year and Chinese History in the third year only. In the Group 7, students needed to study Chinese Philosophy, Chinese History, Chinese Literature and Translation through all the four years. The name Classics no longer appeared in the syllabus. Classics were replaced by Chinese philosophy. At the top of syllabus, English was listed as a subject. The emphasis on English could be interpreted as the need for bridging together the two cultures.

In the 1940–1941 University Calendar, Chinese Studies was classified into Group C. Group C had three divisions, namely, Chinese and English, Chinese History and Chinese Philosophy (University of Hong Kong 1940–1941, pp. 53–54). Under the syllabus of Chinese and English, students needed to study Chinese Language and Literature, Translation and Comparison. The content of the Literature division was not limited to prose and poetry since the 1930 calendar. Xu had already talked about the Colloquial Novels (白話文學) to the students in September 18,1935 (Xie 2004, pp. 187–188).

Xu's concept of four basic divisions included Chinese Language and Literature, Chinese History, Chinese Philosophy and Translation.

Language in the Classroom

The department was undeniably like a showroom inside the British-style university as if it indicated that Chinese culture is honoured in Hong Kong, a place with the majority of the population. Until 1932, the University authority did not allow the issuance of degrees to the graduates of the Department of Chinese Studies. The graduates could take a certificate indicating that they finished the course. Students might feel dissatisfied with it, and so left the university or transferred to other departments (Fang and Xiong 2007, p. 228).

The basic concept of the University was "the university serves as a British university in Hong Kong for China." The university was planned to provide a British-style education to the Chinese students for the modernization of China (Development and Alumni Affairs Office 2002, p. 25). The University of Hong Kong may be considered as a colonial university only serving for the British administration in Hong Kong. However, historical records indicate the university played the role of a modern educational institution in the region, including Hong Kong, Macau, Guangzhou, Northern China and Southeast Asia. The students and graduates were more diversified in terms of their origin. In the pre-war years, one-third of the students came from Guangzhou and Northern China. Another one-third came from the British and Dutch colonies in Southeast Asia (Development and Alumni Affairs Office 2002, p. 26).

The opening of Mandarin classes could be also interpreted as a will to fit the whole situation, including the assistance for China's modernization. The university's provision of Mandarin classes would be necessary. From the beginning, Lai and Ou were expected to be Cantonese speakers. Given that Lai and Ou served for the Imperial Academy and were expected to be able to speak Mandarin, Lai offered the same content of the subject Classics in Mandarin (School History, n.d.).

The continuous development of the university brought forth a need to recruit a new type of academic staff when the Department of Chinese Studies was established. The above-mentioned requirements for the head of Department showed a change. Xu Dishan was a person eligible for the following conditions: being professional of Chinese Studies, being fluent in English, having the management capability and originating from Guangdong, if possible (Fang and Xiong 2007, p. 228). Xu was born in Tainan,

Taiwan in 1893 and his family moved to the mainland after Taiwan was ceded to Japan. Xu is famous as a novelist, translator and folklorist. He first taught in a Chinese school in Myanmar. Subsequently, he studied in Yanching University in Beijing and joined the May Fourth Movement in 1919. After that, he furthered his studies at Columbia University and Oxford University.

Simultaneously, the existence of Translation as a subject also showed the characteristics of the Department of Chinese Studies under the British-style university. In 1934, Chen Junbao (Chan Kwan-Po 陳君葆) took position as Lecturer and Tutor in Translation in the Department of Chinese Studies. Lin Dong died because of an accident in 1934, and Chen filled the vacancy (School History, n.d.). Chen graduated from the Faculty of Arts at the University of Hong Kong. The appointment of local graduates to significant positions in the Faculty of Arts were exceptional cases, as the expatriates dominated the positions compared to Faculty of Medicine and the Faculty of Engineering (Development and Alumni Affairs Office 2002, p. 58).

From this article, we can observe the importance of the capability of English. Translation was an important subject in the University of Hong Kong. Given that the medium of instruction was English, students were naturally forced to expose themselves to English. Translation must build a bridge between the English and Chinese languages within the department and definitely had the elements of comparative studies. At this pre-war period, the Department of Chinese Studies was a multi-disciplinary department, and the subjects were not limited to Chinese Literature and Language.

During this period, those who were associated with the Department of Chinese Studies were from Guangdong province. Lai and Ou were from Guangdong Province. Chen Junbao was also native in Cantonese. Lai and Ou were bilingual in Mandarin and Chinese. Xu and Chen were also capable of speaking Mandarin.

Chinese Studies During the Cold War

A great influx of immigrants fled to Hong Kong to escape the chaos of Mainland China caused by the 1946–1949 Civil War. These immigrants worried about the life under the Communist regime and crossed the border. Many capitalists, the Chinese Nationalist Party (KMT) and supporters of KMT and intellectuals existed. The intellectuals were a new type of migrant scholars. With a great influx of migration, institutions also migrated from Mainland China. In such a circumstance, Hong Kong became a base for China Watching later during the Cold War.

The Migrant Scholars and their Institutions

The Chinese University of Hong Kong (CUHK) is a good example of one of institutions that migrated from the mainland. The university was formed from the amalgamation of three colleges: New Asia College (新亞書院), Chung Chi College (崇基學院) and United College (聯合書院).

All three colleges were established by migrant scholars and had different characteristics. New Asia College was founded in 1949 by famous scholars from the mainland such as Qian Mu (Ch'ien Mu, 錢穆) (History of New Asia College 2013). The founding objective was to establish an educational institution which combined the essence of the scholarship of the Song and Ming academies and the tutorial system of Western universities.

Chung Chi College was established in 1951 by the representatives of Protestant Churches in Hong Kong (Aims and Brief History of Chung Chi College 2015). The founding objective aimed to provide higher education in accordance with Christian traditions, using the Chinese language as the primary medium of instruction. The college housed the Department of Theology from the beginning.

United College was founded in 1956 by the amalgamation of five private universities originally located in Guangzhou: Canton Overseas (廣僑), Kwang Hsia (光夏), Wah Kiu (華僑), Wen Hua (文化) and Ping Jing College of Accountancy (正平會計專科學校) (History and Mission of United College 2017). These private universities were strong in social sciences and business management studies and supported the roles of raising the human resources to serve for civil service.

Among the colleges, New Asia College played an important role in Chinese Studies. New Asia College began as the Asia Evening College of Arts and Commerce (History of New Asia College 2013) and rented three classrooms from a middle school in Kowloon. General History of China was taught by Qian Mu, Introduction to Philosophy by Tang Junyi (T'ang Chun-I, 唐君毅), Economics by Zhang Pijie (Tchang Pi-kai, 張丕介) and Politics by Cui Shuqin (Tsui Shu-chin, 崔書琴).

New Asia College was a direct import educational institution from the mainland. The founders of New Asia College were the prominent migrant scholars. The subjects taught were considered to pursue the orthodoxy of Chinese Studies. The quality of subjects attracted the attention of the outside world to New Asia College.

A development style of New Asia College pushed Chinese Studies as its academic frontline. Later, CUHK also established the Institute of Chinese Studies (中國文化研究所) (Institute of Chinese Studies n.d.). Under the institute umbrella were the Art Museum, Research Centre for Translation, T.T. Ng (吳多泰, Wu Duotai) and the Chinese Language Research Centre. Later on, the institute umbrella included the Centre for Chinese Archaeology and Art, the Research Centre for Contemporary Chinese Culture and the D.C. Lau (劉殿爵, Liu Dianjue) Research Centre for Chinese Ancient Texts. Compared to the CAS, the institute put more emphasis on Humanities related to traditional China.

The Emergence of Contemporary Chinese Studies

The Cold War transformed Hong Kong into a base for China Watching. After the United Nations troops crossed the 38th parallel and fought with the People's Volunteer Army in the Korean Peninsula, the external environments of PRC deteriorated. Given the ban issued by the United Nations, Hong Kong lost its roles as an *entrepôt* to Mainland China. However, the situation was different from Taiwan, whose relations with the mainland were totally banned. The mainland was blocked by the Bamboo Curtain while

Hong Kong people could send letters to relatives and friends in the mainland.

For the overseas visitors, Hong Kong became the only window for Western countries to observe mainland affairs. The overseas correspondents were thus stationed at Hong Kong and wrote reports on the mainland. The main sources of information were interviewing those who fled from the mainland. At that time, even illegal immigrants from the mainland could get the right of abode, if they reached the border and got in contact with their relatives or friends.

In those days, Hong Kong withdrew attention as "preserve China."[1] Hong Kong was under the British administration and naturally could escape the influence of the Chinese revolution in 1949 and socialization afterward. The visitors expected that the traditional Chinese culture could be observed in Hong Kong while the traditional culture was seriously damaged in the mainland, especially during the Cultural Revolution. As long as the mainland was isolated from the Western world, those who wanted to study about China chose to go to either Taiwan or Hong Kong. For example, Hong Kong's rural area, also known as the New Territories, attracted many cultural anthropologists.

During the 1960s, many China Watchers visited two places in Hong Kong, the University Service Centre of Chinese Studies 大學服務中心 and the Union Research Institute of Chinese Studies 友聯研究所. These two institutions had good collections of mainland newspapers.

The Universities Service Centre opened in 1963[2] to the Western academics engaged in the study of contemporary China. The Centre

---

[1] Apart from universities, a private endeavor by a Hungarian Jesuit, Fr. Fr. László Ladányi's "China News Analysis" was also available to receive local news and information of China between 1953 and 1998, with the exception of the year 1983. It was published first every week, then every two weeks, and finally twice a month, and it published analyses of the current situation in China.

[2] It is said that the Centre was originally funded by CIA to gather the information on China in the 1950s. The reestablishment of Sino-US diplomatic relations might lead to the closure of the Centre.

had one of the most extensive collections on contemporary China. The Centre became a part of CUHK in 1988 and was renamed the Universities Service Centre for Chinese Studies later in 1993. It had more than 250 provincial and national newspapers and close to 1,500 periodicals from the early 1950s; over 1300 constantly updated regional and statistical yearbooks; a collection of provincial, city, county and village annals, including volumes on special topics; over 80,000 Chinese and English titles of books on China and electronic data sources (Universities Service Centre for Chinese Studies 2016, Xiong 2017).

The Union Research Institute of Chinese Studies also had a good collection on contemporary China. The Institute collected clippings from newspapers and periodicals between 1950 and the 1970s. Apart from newspapers published in PRC, the institute also paid attention to newspapers published in Hong Kong and Southeast Asia. During the 1990s, Hong Kong Baptist University Library staff continued to add clippings to this collection, concentrating on Hong Kong newspapers and using the same indexing system established by the Union Research Institute. An area that received in-depth attention was information related to the transfer of sovereignty of Hong Kong to China. The collection includes 14,000 clippings from newspapers and periodicals, 6500 monographs and working papers (Contemporary China Research Collection 2019).

Apart from these two institutions, the two universities in the mid-1960s simultaneously established new institutions for Chinese Studies. As stated above, the CU established the Institute of Chinese Studies. The University of Hong Kong established the Centre of Asian Studies (CAS) in 1967 (Centre of Asian Studies 2015). One year later, the Cultural Revolution was launched, and the Hong Kong riot occurred. The establishment of CAS initially aimed to bring together those with research interests in Asian Studies and get in touch with people outside the university. The establishment of CAS also aimed to attract university scholars in the field of Asian Studies. The Centre was the first unit where

Contemporary Chinese Studies could be conducted inside the universities in Hong Kong.

CAS published and sponsored the results of the research with the cooperation of the University of Hong Kong Press. From the structural point of view, the establishment of CAS consolidated a financial base for the promotion of the Asian Studies and could appoint Research Associates. The CAS conducted research in the fields of Contemporary and Traditional Chinese Studies, Hong Kong Studies and East, South and Southeast Asian Studies. The report of the CAS activities during the period 1968–1970 was under the first full-time Director Frank H. H. King. Under King's directorship were one research officer, three Senior Research Assistants, four Research Assistants and one Junior Research Assistant (Centre of Asian Studies 1970 pp. 1–2).

Different Academics Dealing with Chinese Studies

During this period, the different types of academics contributed to Chinese studies. We can observe (1) the direct import of the mainland academics, (2) non-Chinese scholars who can understand the Chinese language and (3) English-speaking Chinese scholars.

(1) Direct import of the mainland academics
The first type could be observed in New Asia College. The academic staff members originated from mainland China and were direct imports of the mainland academics. The Department of Chinese Studies was exceptional at the University Education of Hong Kong. This department adopted Chinese as the medium of instruction. The Chinese language has many dialects. Some dialects are very different from other dialects, and Mandarin is a standard spoken dialect. For instance, Cantonese is very difficult to understand for non-Cantonese speakers. Thus, in the Hong Kong situation, if an academic could not speak Cantonese, then they used Mandarin or English. These academics' Mandarin sometimes had their own dialect accents. (Interview Record of Wong Yiu Kwan 2018).

(2) Non-Chinese Scholars who can understand the Chinese language

The second type could be observed in the situation seen at the University of Hong Kong. As stated above, Frank H. H. King 景復朗, the founding Director of CAS, belonged to this group. King was famous for his studies on the development of Hong Kong and Shanghai Banking Corporation, but Frederick Seguier Drake 林仰山 could be also a good example. Drake left Chee-loo University 齊魯大學 in Shandong, stopped over at Hong Kong on the way back to UK and finally succeeded in becoming the chair of the Department of Chinese Studies in 1952 (Xu 2015, p. 177). Drake stayed as a professor of the Department of Chinese Studies until 1964. During his professorship, he consolidated the foundation of the Department of Chinese Studies. At first, he recruited 10 prominent scholars such as Luo Xianglin 羅香林 and Yao Zongyi (Jao Tsung-i 饒宗頤) into the Department (Xu 2015, p. 182). Drake increased the number of subjects taught in the Department of Chinese Studies and increased the diversity of the studies conducted in the Department (University of Hong Kong 1951, pp. 87–89). Drake also opened a way to expose the studies of the Department to the international academic society through dealing with the Institute of Oriental Studies (IOS) actively. IOS published the *Journal of Oriental Studies* 東方文化 and presented an academic base for the Department of Chinese Studies and the migrant scholars.

(3) English-speaking Chinese scholars

The third type of academic staff has been observed since the 1970s in CU. After three Colleges were amalgamated into CU in 1963, each college gradually lost autonomy. The migrant scholars arrived at Hong Kong in the 1940s and left the scene in the 1970s. Qian Mu's moving to Taiwan in 1977 was symbolic. He left Hong Kong and settled in Taiwan.

New human resources from Taiwan filled the vacancy. In the 1970s, when the Department of Government and Public Administration was newly established in the United College, the department needed new blood appropriate to CU, that is, academics who could read and speak Chinese and give lectures in English. The possible human resources would be from Taiwan where Chinese was the mother tongue and they could give lectures in English if they had Ph.D. degrees from the United States. Weng Songran (Byron Song-jen Weng 翁松燃) was the first scholar of Taiwan origin at the Department of Government and Public Administration. He took up his position in 1972 and designed the entire curriculum of the course for the next year. He also decided to recruit two other scholars of Taiwan origin, Liao Guangsheng (Liao Kuang-sheng, 廖光生) and Li Nanxiong (Peter Lee Nan-shong, 李南雄), separately in 1974 and in 1976 (Interview record of Byron Weng 2009, 2018; Interview record of Liao Kuang-sheng 2009; Interview record of Peter Lee Nan-shong 2009).

Another type of English-speaking Chinese Scholars could be observed in the University of Hong Kong. Localization of staff occurred in the University of Hong Kong. Especially after the 1967 Hong Kong Riot, the vacancies of expatriate staff who evacuated Hong Kong were filled with the locally born staff. By the mid-1970s, the first generation of Hong Kong-born scholars grew up. For example, at CAS, after Frank H. H. King, the chair was succeeded first by Chen Kunyao (Edward K. Y. Chen, 陳坤耀, 1979–1995) and then by Huang Shaolun (Wong Siu-lun, 黃紹倫, 1995–2009). The second and third directors were both Hong Kong-born Chinese scholars. Chen was known for his studies on the Hong Kong economy, whereas Huang's work on Shanghainese immigrant entrepreneurs gave him a good reputation.

Hong Kong as an Open Academic Sphere

Chinese Studies in Hong Kong gradually showed a new change when the time came close to the date of expiration of the Lease of the New Territories. The 1997 issue increased Hong Kong people's attention toward mainland China. Simultaneously, the Open Door Policy, receiving great attention in Hong Kong, came naturally. For non-Hong Kong local academics, Hong Kong continued to provide an open academic sphere.

As the importance of Chinese studies increased, Hong Kong received more non-local Chinese academics. Hong Kong started to receive the mainland academics. For example, the CU welcomed Jin Guantao (金觀濤) and Liu Qingfeng (劉青峰), and Jin and Liu launched the academic journal "Twenty-First Century (二十一世紀)". They built the "Database for the Study of Modern Chinese Thought" (1830–1930) during their stay in CUHK between 1989 and 2008 (Jin Guantao's introduction in UBC 2018). Later, Wang Shaoguang (王紹光) also taught at Hong Kong. He completed his Ph.D. in Political Science from Cornell University in 1990 and taught at Yale University during 1990–2000. He then moved to the Department of Government and Public Administration at the CU (Wang 2015).

When 1997 came to a close, the number of universities suddenly increased in Hong Kong. The number of universities and institutions admitted to grant degrees was 2 before 1991, 3 during 1991–1993, 6 in 1994 and 13 at present, including two private universities, one Open University and one Academy of Performing Arts. Inside the Department of Chinese Studies, the mainland academics speak the Standard Chinese, Putonghua. If these academics belong to another department, then they might use English as a medium of instruction. The Language situation was similar to the cases of direct import of the mainland academics in the 1940s, and also from that of Taiwan-origin Scholars in the 1970s.

Present Situation of the Department of Chinese Studies in Hong Kong

The Department of Chinese Studies or a similar department must be the place where the mainland academics can be expected to be found. The author of this chapter chose ten institutions: the University of Hong Kong, CU, Hong Kong University of Science and Technology, Hong Kong Polytechnic University, City University of Hong Kong, Baptist University, Lingnan University, Open University of Hong Kong, Education University of Hong Kong and

Hong Kong Shue Yan University. Although its degree is admitted by the Ministry of Education of the Republic of China, Hong Kong Chu Hai College of Higher Education is still not admitted as a degree-granting institution in Hong Kong.

Table 1 examines nine degree-granting institutions, all ten institutions stated above excluding the Open University of Hong Kong but including the Hong Kong Chu Hai College of Higher Education. With the exception of Hong Kong University of Science and Technology, all the institutions have an independent department equivalent to the Department of Chinese Studies.

Among 10 department heads, four department heads completed their first degrees in institutions in Hong Kong. Three graduated from the CU, and one was from the Hong Kong Chu Hai College of Higher Education. Of the remaining six department heads, four were from mainland China and one was from Taiwan.

Among the 10 institutions, the author especially chose six universities, the University of Hong Kong (HKU), the CUHK, City University of Hong Kong (CityU), Hong Kong Baptist University (BU), Lingnan University and Hong Kong Shue Yan University and summarized the educational background of academic staff with tenure.

(1) The School of Chinese, the University of Hong Kong
The School of Chinese of the University of Hong Kong (HKU) has the longest history among all the institutions. The name of the department symbolizes that the department was essentially multi-disciplinary and not limited to the Chinese Literature and Language Studies. The number of staff members was the largest among the six institutions.

Among 28 academic staff members, 26 were of Chinese origin. Similar to Drake's period, we could see the non-Chinese staff members.

Among 26 staff members, 12 obtained their first degree from Hong Kong local institutions: eight from HKU, two from the University of CUHK, one from the Hong Kong Baptist University and one from City University. The majority took their first degrees

Table 1: Department of Chinese in universities in Hong Kong.

	University of Hong Kong	Chinese University of Hong Kong	Hong Kong Polytechnic University	City University of Hong Kong	Hong Kong Baptist University	Lingnan University	Hong Kong University of Science and Technology	Education University of Hong Kong	Hong Kong Shue Yan University	Hong Kong Chu Hai College of Higher Education
Independent department (English)	School of Chinese	Department of Chinese Language and Literature	Department of Chinese and Bilingual Studies	Department of Chinese and History	Chinese Language and Literature	Department of Chinese	✗□	Department of Chinese Language Studies	Department of Chinese Language and Literature	Department of Chinese Literature
Independent department (Chinese)	中文學院	中國語言及文學系	中文及雙語學系	中文及歷史學系	中國語言文學系	中文系	✗□	中國語言學系	中國語文學系	中國文學系
Major program	○	○	○	○	○	○	△*1	○	○	○
Minor program	○	○	○	○	○	○	○	○	○	✗□
M.A. program	○	○	○	○	○	○	○	○	✗□	○
M.Phil program	○	○	○	○	○	○	○	○	○	△*2
Ph.D. program	○	○	○	○	○	○	○	○	○	△*2

Note: From website of each institution.

*1 indicates B.Sc. in Global Chinese Studies: Humanities and Social Science (Language and Literature Research Option), *2 indicates open at the Research Institute of Chinese Literature and History (中國文學研究所).

from local institutions. Among the eight HKU bachelor holders, six members completed all degrees up to Ph.D. at HKU, and two finished their graduate education at Kyoto University (京都大学) in Japan.

A considerable portion of staff members must show the existence of non-local scholars with Chinese ethnicity. Five graduated from universities in mainland China. They all obtained their Ph.D. degrees from English-speaking universities, including one who received it from the HKU. The Head of the School was also from the mainland. She obtained her B.A. from Hangzhou University, M.A. from Nankai University and Ph.D. from Melbourne University. In addition to being of mainland origin, two graduated from universities in Taiwan (Fu Jen Catholic University and National Taiwan Normal University). One member was from Southeast Asia. (Academic Staff, School of Chinese 2018).

(2) The Department of Chinese Language and Literature, Chinese University of Hong Kong (CUHK)

The CUHK's Department of Chinese Language and Literature is a continuation from New Asia College composed of migrant scholars. The three courses available are Classic Text (古代文獻), Classical Literature (古典文學) and Contemporary Literature (現代文學). All eighteen members were of Chinese origin.

In the Classic Text course, four members completed all degrees from CUHK. The Head of the Department also belonged to the Classic Text course and completed all degrees at CUHK. One member obtained all degrees from Peking University.

In Classical Literature, five members finished their first degrees at CUHK, one graduated from the National Taiwan University, and two were graduates from the universities in mainland China. Among five CUHK bachelor holders, three obtained all degrees from CUHK, and two finished graduate education overseas, separately in Kyoto University and Edinburgh University.

The Contemporary course 現代文學 showed diverse results. Among six members, three took their first degree at CUHK but two studied at Mainland China (Peking University and Jinan University). The famous poet Bei Dao (北島) was also a faculty member.

Compared with HKU, CUHK's case showed the tendency to raise their staff members inside their departments.[3] The smaller portion of staff members had experience studying overseas in comparison with HKU's case. Those who studied overseas do not comprise the majority. Despite the strong presence of CUHK alumni, we could observe the academics both from the mainland and Taiwan.

(3) Hong Kong Baptist University (HKBU)., Department of Chinese Language and Literature
In 1956, (HKBU). was founded by the Baptist Convention of Hong Kong as a post-secondary college committed to the provision of whole person education. In 1983, (HKBU). became a fully funded public tertiary institution. It gained university status in 1994 and was renamed "Hong Kong Baptist University." HKBU has a strong reputation in its humanities. For example, the Department of History has a good reputation in Republican China History research.

Among 14 members, two were of non-Chinese origin. Four, including the Head of Department, finished their first degree in mainland China. Furthermore, three were related to Nanjing University including the Head of Department.

Five members received their first degree from local institutions in Hong Kong, four from HKBU and two from CUHK. Among HKBU bachelor holders, two completed their M.A. and Ph.D. at HKBU, and the two finished graduate school overseas. Two CUHK bachelor holders were locally educated: one completed all degrees

---

[3] According to a graduate from the Department of Chinese, HKU, the former Department Head Kam Louie launched a policy not to invite HKU alumni as academic staff members to the Department of Chinese, the University of Hong Kong. This graduate continued his studies further at the Australian National University and earned a position in the Department of Chinese, National University of Singapore. I gathered this information from a source on June 2, 2018, at Chulalongkorn University, Bangkok.

from CUHK, and another bachelor holder earned his Ph.D. from HKU (Teachers 2011).

BU's case showed more similarity with CUHK's case than HKU's case. HKBU alumni were welcomed by the mother department, and this tendency also admittedly raised the staff members inside BU. Those who studied overseas do not comprise the majority. HKBU appears to have a strong academic network with CUHK, as well as with Nanjing University.

(4) City University of Hong Kong, Department of Chinese and History

The City University was originally established in 1984 as City Polytechnic of Hong Kong and became a degree-granting university in 1994. The City University of Hong Kong launched the Department of Chinese and History in 2015.

All the members were of Chinese origin. The Head of the Department, Li Hsaio-ti was from Taiwan, finished his B.A. and M.A. in National Taiwan University (NTU) and earned his Ph.D. in Harvard University. Among five professors and three associate professors, five had educational experience overseas. As a first degree, three were bachelor's degree holders of HKU and two were bachelor's degree holders from CUHK and NTU.

Among nine assistant professors, only one was born in Hong Kong with a B.A. from NTU, M.A. from Chicago and Ph.D. from Wisconsin. Two earned all degrees in the United States. Four acquired their first degree in mainland China (two from Peking University and two from Fudan University). All of these professors finished their Ph.D. in the United States, either from Harvard or Yale[4] (Academic Staff 2018).

The City University case showed more diversification. Among 16 staff members, only one was a City University graduate and was also associate head. The majority received experiences studying overseas and receiving higher education through English.

---

[4] One did not disclose his first degree information but completed his M.A. from Beijing Normal University and Ph.D. from City University.

The overseas educational experience heavily concentrated in the United States as a result. The CityU also received more academic staff members of Taiwan origin than HKBU and CUHK.

(5) Hong Kong Shue Yan University, Department of Language and Literature

Shue Yan University was established by Dr. Henry H. L. Hu and Dr. Chung Chi Yung in 1971. Hu and Yung were former diplomats of Republican China and chose not to return to the mainland in 1949. They donated a private fund and established a school. Shue Yan College was formally registered as a tertiary education institution in 1976. In 2006, Shue Yan College became the first private university in Hong Kong after it was renamed Hong Kong Shue Yan University (About n.d.).

Among thirteen members, five were fully or partially Hong Kong-educated. Two finished their first degree at Shue Yan, and both furthered studies in the mainland and acquired their PhDs separately at Fudan University and Sun Yat-sen University. One member received all degrees from CUHK. One completed his first degree at HKBU, and M.A. and Ph.D. from New Asia Institute of Advanced Chinese Studies. Another member earned her first degree at Chu Hai College of Higher Education, and M.A. and Ph.D. at New Asia Institute of Advanced Chinese Studies.

Four members had their education on the mainland. Two members had educational backgrounds in Taiwan, one of those members served for National Cheng Kung University and had experience as a Dean of College of Liberal Arts. One member obtained all the degrees from University of Macau (Teachers 2018).

Apparently, the educational backgrounds of academic staff differed from the above-mentioned four institutions. No staff had overseas educational experience except the Acting Head of the Department. He earned his B.A. from Jinan University, M.A. from Peking University and Ph.D. in Arizona. More than one-third of them were fully or partially Hong Kong-educated. There were many staffs originating both from the mainland and Taiwan. More than the number of members, the Shue Yan University kept steady relations with Taiwan academics. The Chu Hai College of Higher Education and New Asia Institute of Advanced Chinese Studies are both Hong Kong institutions with strong relations with Taiwan. New Asia Institute of Advanced Chinese Studies was established in 1953 by Qian Mu of New Asia College as abovementioned (History of New Asia College 2013). Similar to the Chu Hai College, the Institute was also approved by the Ministry of Education, ROC.

Beyond 1997, Toward 2047

In this chapter, the development of Chinese Studies and the change of language environment in the classroom could be traced. English is one of the most explicit British colonial legacies in contemporary Hong Kong. Inside the universities in Hong Kong, English has been the main medium of instruction. On the contrary, the Department of Chinese Studies has maintained exceptionality on the educational scene of Hong Kong. It has been a place where the Chinese language could enjoy a major status as a medium of instruction.

The reunification with China brought in a few changes in the scene of Chinese Studies in Hong Kong. Two articles in Basic Law are related to language. Article 9 states that English may also be used as an official language by executive authorities, legislature and the judiciary of Hong Kong. (Hong Kong e-Legislation 2018). In the Hong Kong Special Administrative Region, English can be treated as an official language but cannot be treated fully equally as Chinese. In the daily lives of Hong Kong's citizens, Cantonese, a dialect of Chinese language, apparently is an official language, especially in the colloquial scene. The strong presence of Cantonese could be another colonial legacy.

The language policy gradually changed in Hong Kong after 1997. Before the reunification, Education Report No. 6 advocated the importance of a mother tongue education, which the Hong Kong government originally planned to implement in the 1950s. At that time, the number of Chinese Medium Instruction (CMI) schools was higher than that of English Medium Instruction (EMI) schools. In the 1970s, parents started to show a preference for sending children to EMI schools because of compulsory education. Launching the compulsory education program in 1998 suddenly decreased the number of EMI schools from 300 to 100 (Poon and Lau 2013, pp. 136–137). Through 12 years of mother tongue education, Hong Kong amended and fine-tuned the compulsory Mother Tongue Education into a policy. Under this policy, secondary schools could not be categorized as CMI or EMI schools. Instead, EMI, partial EMI and CMI classes were available. Simultaneously, secondary schools were requested to provide an English environment to students (Poon and Lau 2013, pp. 137–138).

Promoting Chinese subjects taught in Putonghua (普教中) is another issue. Since the curriculum was amended in 1999, the Hong Kong government promoted Chinese-related subjects taught in Putonghua. The term Putonghua was used in this promotion to emphasize Hong Kong's integration to the PRC as a whole.

One finding remains untouched. From the analysis of the educational background, the author found that Japan is one source of non-English graduate education. Zhou Jiarong (周佳榮, Chow Kai Wing), the HKBU Emeritus Professor of the Department of History, stated in an interview that the scholarship offered by the Japanese government pushed him to study in Japan. He pursued his studies on Republican China at Hiroshima University and received his M.A. there (Zhou Jiarong 2018, pers.comm., 6 June). Huang Yaokun (黃耀堃, Wong Yiu Kwan) made a similar comment when asked about his experiences as a student in Japan (Huang Yaokun 2018, pers.comm., 15 March). Some academics in the Japanese Department pursued research topics related to cross-border topics related to Japan, Hong Kong, Mainland China and Taiwan at the same time. Qiu Shuting (邱淑婷 Kinnia Yau Shuk-ting) published a book on cinema exchange between Hong Kong and Japan. Her research topics include World War II on Japanese, Chinese and American Screens, Cinema Exchange between Hong Kong and Korea, and Media Influences on Japanese Attitudes toward China (Kinnia Yau Shuk-ting 2018).

References

Centre of Asian Studies, *Report of Activities 1968–1970*, University of Hong Kong. 1970/1994. *Report of a review of the Centre of Asian Studies*, LY/li/CAS.PRT. Hong Kong: University of Hong Kong.

Centre of Asian Studies, University of Hong Kong. 2015. http://www.hkihss.hku.hk/en/about_hkihss/about_us/cas/ (accessed on 18 March 2015).

Chung Chi College, Chinese University of Hong Kong. 2015. Aims and Brief History. http://www.ccc.cuhk.edu.hk/index.php?option=com_content&view=article&id=71&Itemid=42&lang=en (accessed on 12 March 2015).

Contemporary China Research Collection, Hong Kong Baptist University Library. Date n. a. http://library.hkbu.edu.hk/sca/ccrc_about.html (accessed on 18 March 2015).

Department of Chinese and Bilingual Studies. *Who We are*. 2013. http://www.cbs.polyu.edu.hk/we.html (accessed on 25 May 2018).

Department of Chinese and History, City University of Hong Kong, 2018. *Head's Message*. http://cah.cityu.edu.hk/about/message.php (accessed on 25 May 2018).

Department of Chinese Language and Literature, Hong Kong Baptist University. Date n. a. *Teachers*. http://chi.hkbu.edu.hk/teachers/tin (accessed on 26 May 2018).

Department of Chinese Language and Literature, Hong Kong Shue Yan University. Date n. a. https://chinese.hksyu.edu/home/ (accessed on 26 May 2018).

Department of Chinese Language and Literature. 2015. *Breeze of Spring over the Toro Harbour: Fifty Years of Learning at the Department of Chinese Language and Literature, CUHK* (*Tulu chun feng wushi nian, xianggang zhongwen daxue zhongwen xi tushi wenji* or 吐露春風五十年'香港中文大學中文系圖史文集). Hong Kong: Chinese University of Hong Kong.

Development and Alumni Affairs Office. 2002. *Growing with Hong Kong — The University and Its Graduates, The First 90 Years*. Hong Kong: The University of Hong Kong Press.

Fang, Jun (方駿) and Xiong Xianjun (熊賢君) (Eds.). 2007. *A History of Education in Hong Kong* (*Xianggang Jiaoyu Tongshi* or 香港教育通史). Hong Kong: Ling Ji.

History and Mission of United College, Chinese University of Hong Kong. 2017. http://www.uc.cuhk.edu.hk/index.php?option=com_content&view=article&id=20&Itemid=62&lang=en (accessed on 26 May 2018).

History of New Asia College, Chinese University of Hong Kong. 2013. http://www.na.cuhk.edu.hk/en-us/aboutnewasia/history.aspx (accessed on 12 March 2015).

History of School of Chinese, University of Hong Kong. Date n. a. http://www.chinese.hku.hk/main/school-history/ (accessed on 6 March 2015).

Hong Kong e-Legislation. https://www.elegislation.gov.hk/hk/cap5 (accessed on 25 May 2018).

Hong Kong Shue Yan University. Date n. a. *About* https://www.hksyu.edu/en/ (accessed on 26 May 2018).

Jin, Guantao. Date n. a. The Centre for Chinese Research, The University of British Columbia. https://ccr.ubc.ca/jin-guantao/ (accessed on 9 February 2019).

Lee, Peter Nan-shong. 2009. The Research and Educational Center for China Studies and Cross Taiwan-Strait Relations. *Interview records*. http://politics.ntu.edu.tw/RAEC/act02.php (accessed on 18 March 2015).

Liao, Kuang-sheng. 2009. The Research and Educational Center for China Studies and Cross Taiwan-Strait Relations. *Interview records*. http://politics.ntu.edu.tw/RAEC/act02.php (accessed on 18 March 2015).

Lu, Hongji (陸鴻基, Bernard Luk Hung-Kay). 2003. *From the Banyan Tree to the PC — A Story of Education in Hong Kong* (*Cong Rongshu xia dao Diannao qian* or 從榕樹下到電腦前——香港教育的故事). Hong Kong: Stepforward Multimedia Publisher.

Poon, Anita Y. K. and Lau Connie M. Y. 2016. Fine-Tuning Medium-of-Instruction Policy in Hong Kong: Acquisition of Language and Content-Based Subject Knowledge. *Journal of Pan-Pacific Association of Applied Linguistics* 20 (1): 135–155.

School of Chinese, University of Hong Kong. *Academic Staff*. http://www.chinese.hku.hk/main/staff/academic-staff/ (accessed on 26 May 2018).

University of Hong Kong, Date n. a. *School History*. http://www.chinese.hku.hk/main/school-history/ (accessed on 12 February 2017).

University of Hong Kong. 1914. *University Calendar 1914–1915*, Hong Kong.

University of Hong Kong. 1930. *University of Hong Kong Calendar 1930*, Hong Kong.
University of Hong Kong. 1940. *University of Hong Kong Calendar 1940–1941*, Hong Kong.
University of Hong Kong. 1955. *University of Hong Kong Calendar 1955–56*, Hong Kong.
Universities Service Center for China Studies, Chinese University of Hong Kong. 2016. http://www.usc.cuhk.edu.hk/Eng/Default.aspx (accessed on 26 May 2018).
Wang, Shaoguang. 2015. CV. The Chinese University of Hong Kong. http://www.cuhk.edu.hk/gpa/wang_files/BIO.htm (accessed on 9 February 2019).
Weng, Byron. 2009. The Research and Educational Center for China Studies and Cross Taiwan-Strait Relations. *Interview records.* http://politics.ntu.edu.tw/RAEC/act02.php (accessed on 18 March 2015).
Xie, Ronggun (謝榮滾) (Ed.). 2004. *Diary of Chen Junbao* (*Chen Junbao ri ji quan ji* or 陳君葆日記全集). Hong Kong: Commercial Express.
Xiong, Jingming, (熊景明, Jean Hung). May 31, 2017. Universities Service Center for China Studies: How "Mecca for China Studies" was established? (Xianggang Zhongwen Daxue Zhongguo Yanjiu Fuwu Zhongxin: "Zhongguo yanjiu de Maijia" shi zenmeyang jiancheng de?) http://news.ifeng.com/a/20170531/51186826_0.shtml (accessed on 12 November 2019).
Xu, Zhenxing (許振興). 2015. *Northern China Studies Transplanted in the South and the University of Hong Kong* (*Beixue Nanyi yu Xianggang Daxue* or 北學南移與香港大學) In Bao Shaolin (鮑紹霖), Huang Zhaoqiang (黃兆強) and Ou Zhijian (區志堅) (Eds.). *Northern China Studies Transplanted in the South — the Origin of Literature, History and Philosophy of Hong Kong and Taiwan, Volume Culture* (*Beixue Nanyi—Gangtai Wen Shi Zhe Suyuan Wenhua juan* or 北學南移──港台文史哲溯源 文化卷). Taipei: Xiuwei Zixun Keji 秀威資訊科技.
Yau, Kinnia Shuk-ting. 2019. http://www.jas.cuhk.edu.hk/profile/prof-yau-shuk-ting-kinnia (accessed on 12 November 2019).

Chapter 9

Development of Japanese Studies in Hong Kong from the Perspectives of Chineseness and Hong Kong's Subjectivity

Chin Chun Wah

Department of Area Studies, The University of Tokyo, Tokyo, Japan

Introduction

Japan has influenced Hong Kong society in the areas of trade and investment as well as the everyday life of the people since the last half of the 20th century, with the effects strengthening even after the 1980s. The acceptance of Japanese popular culture in Hong Kong has changed Japan's image in the eyes of Hong Kong's youth, that is, from a memory of occupation to a positive image. For those born in the 1980s until the 1990s, Japanese popular culture has become a collective memory because of massive broadcasts of animation in public TV channels.

Therefore, understanding why two large-scale departments of Japanese studies (the University of Hong Kong (HKU) and the Chinese University of Hong Kong (CUHK)) were established in 1985 and 1991, respectively, is simple.[1] Taken together, these

---

[1] Another reason is that immigration had become an option for many Hong Kong people worrying about the future due to the foreseeable handover in 1997. To cease the trend or such worries, elite education in universities had become unsuitable. In the last half of the 1980s to the early 1990s, more universities opened for young people (see *Honkon daigaku nihon kenkyu gakukei*, 2000, p. 28).

changes and developments explain why Japanese popular culture has become one of the mainstreams in Japanese studies in Hong Kong.

Popular culture is a famous field in Japanese studies among the academic fields covered by major and minor programs provided by Hong Kong universities. One of the reasons for its popularity is that the public is comfortable with and accepting of Japanese studies because of their familiarity with Japanese products, including cultural items and food and home appliances, among others.

Intellectuals of Japanese studies take advantage of this familiarity to transition from academia to public writing or commentary. Some of them are active not only in the academe but also in local mass media, including books, newspapers, magazines, radio and social media. They act as consultants when local citizens have questions about Japan, or they actively provide their opinions on issues concerning Japan through various media. Considering their role, we suggest that those intellectuals of Japanese studies be called "Japan Hands intellectuals." They use their profession to express ideas and attract a broad audience because they present their ideas through Japanese elements.

Behind these vibrant and localized developments of Japanese studies in present-day Hong Kong, Chineseness was a prime mover. From the postwar period to around the 1980s, intellectuals contributed to the earlier development of Japanese studies because of their strong sense of responsibility and sense of belonging toward Chinese culture. It is easy to understand why those intellectuals paid attention to Japan — Japan is a neighboring country with bonds and enmity with China, as clearly reflected in its history and current environment.

Nevertheless, along with the recent tension between Hong Kong and Mainland China, intellectuals have joined the discussion at a different extent on the basis of their special roles and tools, professional knowledge of Japan and easy access to information about Japan. It shows another perspective of the development of Japanese studies in recent years relative to the characteristic of Chineseness.

Previous studies about the development of Japanese studies in Hong Kong have focused on academic topics. However, these studies might have overlooked the impact of Japanese studies (in a broad sense, from academic to non-academic) on Hong Kong society. This chapter aims to avoid the stereotype in which the diversity of Japanese studies in Hong Kong is simplified. Specifically, this study aims to review the potential role of Japanese studies in relation to present-day Hong Kong and Mainland China from a new and unique perspective. First, this chapter provides an overview of the general situation of Japanese studies in Hong Kong universities. Second, on the basis of a case study by Benjamin Ng Wai-ming (吳偉明), Chair of the Department of Japanese Studies in CUHK, this chapter shows how Japanese studies connect with Chineseness and with Hong Kong's subjectivity and how narratives related to Japan issues have been created and used to interpret Japan, Hong Kong and China, along with their cultural meanings to Hong Kong's subjectivity. Finally, colonial legacy is examined to understand how Chineseness and the memory of Japanese imperialism and the policies of British Hong Kong have influenced the development of Japanese studies and Hong Kong's subjectivity.

General Situation of Japanese Studies in Hong Kong

Table 1 shows that CUHK and HKU established departments for Japanese Studies which offer undergraduate and postgraduate programs. HKU provides Japanese Studies as a major comprising two programs of study. CUHK provides one major program, five of eight University Grants Committee (UGC)-funded universities offer minor programs, and three taught programs offer master's degrees. All of the universities provide Japanese language courses. In addition, six institutes offer Japanese/Language Studies to those who opt for subdegree programs (Table 2). These scales make Japanese/Language Studies the third largest area/language studies among the system of higher education institutions and in comparison with other area/language studies, such as French, German or Korean. It follows China/Chinese language studies and English language studies.

Table 1: Degree of Japanese studies (including Japanese Language) offered by UGC-funded universities in Hong Kong (2018).

	HKU	CUHK	City University of Hong Kong	The Hong Kong Polytechnic University	Lingnan University	Hong Kong Baptist University	Hong Kong University of Science and Technology	The Education University of Hong Kong
Independent department	Department of Japanese Studies (under the Schools of Modern Languages and Cultures, Faculty of Arts)	Department of Japanese Studies (under the Faculty of Arts)	NA	NA	NA	NA	NA	NA
Major program	Japanese Studies (Japan Studies Programme/ Japanese Language Programme)	Japanese Studies	Business Administration (Honours) in International Business — Japan Studies Language Studies (Japanese) Non-UGC funded	NA	NA	NA	NA	NA

Development of Japanese Studies in Hong Kong   197

Exchange program for students majoring in Japanese studies (universities in Japan)	Voluntary	Required	Voluntary	NA	NA	NA	NA	NA
Minor program	Japanese Language Japanese Culture	Japanese Studies	Japanese Studies	Japanese	NA	Japanese Language	NA	NA
Number of courses offered by the major and minor programs	78	74	33	16	NA	6	NA	NA
Language courses	✓	✓	✓	✓	✓	✓	✓	✓
Master's degree	NA	Japanese Studies	NA	Japanese Studies for the Professions Japanese Media and Communication	NA	NA	NA	NA
Number of courses offered by the M.A. program	NA	21	NA	31	NA	NA	NA	NA

(Continued)

Table 1: (Continued)

	HKU	CUHK	City University of Hong Kong	The Hong Kong Polytechnic University	Lingnan University	Hong Kong Baptist University	Hong Kong University of Science and Technology	The Education University of Hong Kong
M.Phil.	Japanese Studies	Japanese Studies	NA	NA	NA	NA	NA	NA
Ph.D.	Japanese Studies	Japanese Studies	NA	NA	NA	NA	NA	NA

Sources: **HKU**: Course List of Major Programmes in Japanese Languages: http://www.japanese.hku.hk/programme/jlcourses.html (accessed on 10 May 2018). Course List of Major Programmes in Japanese Studies: http://www.japanese.hku.hk/programme/jscourses.html (accessed on 10 May 2018). **CUHK**: Course List of Major Programmes in Japanese Studies: http://www.jas.cuhk.edu.hk/en-GB/programmes/undergraduate-programme/major-programmes/course-list (accessed on 10 May 2018). Elective Course List of Minor Programmes in Japanese Studies: http://www.jas.cuhk.edu.hk/en-GB/programmes/undergraduate-programme/minor-programmes/elective-course-list (accessed on 10 May 2018). 2018–2019 Admission Brochure, Master of Arts in Japanese Studies: http://www.jas.cuhk.edu.hk/images/content/programmes/postgraduate_programmes/MAJS_Brochure_201819.pdf (accessed on 10 May 2018). **City University of Hong Kong**: Course List of Major Programmes in Bachelor of Business Administration (Honours) in International Business — Japan Studies: http://www.cityu.edu.hk/ug/201112/Programme/BBAIBJ.htm (accessed on 10 May 2018). Course List of Major Programmes in Bachelor of Arts with Honors in Language Studies (Japanese): http://www.cityu.edu.hk/ug/201112/Programme/BAJS.htm (accessed on 10 May 2018). Course List of Minor Programs in Japanese Studies: http://www.cityu.edu.hk/ug/201718/Minor/MNR-JAPS.htm (accessed on 10 May 2018). **The Hong Kong Polytechnic University**: Course List of M.A. in Japanese Studies for the Professions: http://www.cbs.polyu.edu.hk/majsp-cur.php?subjCode=CBS5100#elective (accessed on 10 May 2018). Course List of M.A. in Japanese Media and Communication: http://www.cbs.polyu.edu.hk/MAJMC-cur.php?subjCode=CBS5078#comp (accessed on 10 May 2018). Course List of Minor Programmes in Japanese: http://www.cbs.polyu.edu.hk/doc/4yr-cur/Minor%20programmes%20for%204-YC%20-%20japanese.pdf (accessed on 10 May 2018). **Lingnan University**: Course List of Additional Languages Courses (Free Electives) in Japanese: https://www.ln.edu.hk/ceal/courses/addlang.php (accessed on 10 May 2018). **Hong Kong Baptist University**: Course List in Japanese Language Minor: http://lc.hkbu.edu.hk/minor_foreign/ (accessed on 10 May 2018). **Hong Kong University of Science and Technology**: Course Introduction: http://cle.ust.hk/ug/languages/japanese/ (accessed on 10 May 2018). **The Education University of Hong Kong**: Course List of Minor in "Language and Society": https://www.eduhk.hk/lml/en/page.php?mid=13 (accessed on 10 May 2018).

Table 2: Subdegree of Japanese studies (including Japanese Language Studies) offered by non-UGC-funded higher educational institutes.

CUHK — School of Continuing and Professional Studies	HKU — HKU SPACE Community College	City University of Hong Kong — Community College of City University/UOW College Hong Kong	Hong Kong College of Technology	Lingnan University — Lingnan Institute of Further Education	The Open University of Hong Kong — Li Ka Shing Institute of Professional and Continuing Education
Higher Diploma Programme in Applied Japanese Language	Associate of Arts in Languages and Humanities (Japanese Studies)	Associate of Arts in Bilingual Communication Studies (Japanese and Chinese)	Higher Diploma in Language and Corporate Communication (Japanese)	Higher Diploma in Japanese Language and Communications Programme	Higher Diploma in Japanese Studies
		Associate of Arts in Bilingual Communication Studies (Japanese and English)			
		Associate of Arts in Japanese Studies			

Source: Information Portal for Accredited Post-secondary Programmes (iPASS) run by the HKSAR: https://www.cspe.edu.hk/en/ipass/index.html (accessed on 10 May 2018).

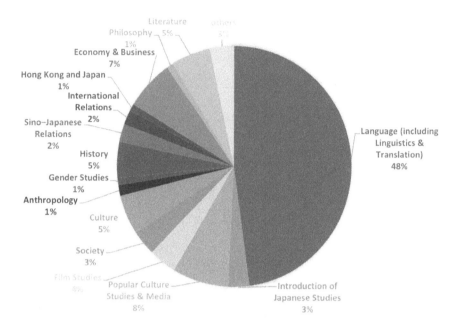

Figure 1: Courses offered by major and minor programs in Japanese Studies/Japanese Language Studies.

Figure 1 shows that excluding language courses, Popular Culture Studies and Media account for the largest percentage, followed by courses in Economy and Business. These trends are similar to the actual situation of Hong Kong–Japan interactions.[2]

To explain the socio-cultural circumstances of the formation and development of Japanese studies in Hong Kong, as well as the creation and operation of narratives about Japan and how they relate to Chineseness and Hong Kong's subjectivity, we closely examine the case of Benjamin Ng Wai-ming on the basis of the literature and the interviews conducted by the author and Tanigaki Mariko on 7 June 2018 (Chin, Tanigaki and Ng 2018). To understand the case of Benjamin Ng, we also examine the work of Tam Yue-him (譚汝謙), a famous scholar of Japanese studies. The analysis of

---

[2] The proportion of each field in Japanese Studies is similar to the findings of a research conducted by Matsuoka Masakazu (2012, pp. 93–103).

Tam is based on an interview conducted by Lin Shao-yang in 2013 (Lin and Tam 2013). The cases of two other Japan Hands intellectuals, namely Kengo (健吾) and Tong Ching-siu (湯禎兆), are reviewed to supplement the discussion as the case of Ng may not be comprehensive enough. Japan Hands intellectuals whose works have been widely recognized, published and popularized in the media are actually a small group of people among general intellectuals who conduct Japanese studies. Ng, Kengo and Tong are the most representative cases when we consider their profiles.

Case Study on Benjamin Ng Wai-ming

Benjamin Ng Wai-ming (吳偉明) is a representative Japan Hands intellectual in Hong Kong. He was born in 1962 in Hong Kong. In 1980, he entered New Asia College, CUHK, majoring in History with a concentration in Japanese History. After graduating from CUHK, he studied at the University of Tsukuba for his postgraduate degree from 1985 to 1988. He attended Princeton University for his second master's degree and, subsequently, his Ph.D. He was a visiting scholar in several universities in Japan, including the University of Tokyo, and he taught at the National University of Singapore. Since 2001, he has been with the CUHK, where he became a Professor in 2007. Ng has published numerous works on Sino-Japanese intellectual history and Hong Kong–Japan popular culture written in English, Chinese and Japanese. His research, especially on the Sino-Japanese interaction of intellectual history and his excellent studies on the interaction between Hong Kong and Japan in the area of popular culture, has significantly enriched the extant literature.

Connection between Japanese Studies and Hong Kong Society

According to Ng, as the Chair and Professor of the Department of Japanese Studies in CUHK, popular culture is the most famous field in Japanese studies in Hong Kong (Ng 2013, p. 194). Interestingly,

Japan Hands intellectuals, such as Ng, were influenced by Japanese popular culture in their youth (Sing Tao Daily 2016). The same is true for young people today. When Ng conducted Japanese studies, he mainly focused on Sino-Japanese studies. Gradually, he also developed a long series of popular culture studies. Such an effort proves that popular culture is an important driver of intellectuals in conducting relevant studies. Students who are also influenced by popular culture are thus likely to be interested in taking relevant courses. Ng said in the interview that many undergraduate students from his department choose Japanese studies because of their enthusiasm toward Japanese popular culture (Chin, Tanigaki and Ng 2018). Ng emphasized that Japanese popular culture is a springboard for students to broaden their horizon toward Japan. This relation renders popular culture as an important motivation for Japanese studies. Japanese studies can be relatively and easily accepted by the public in comparison with the other areas of studies and academic disciplines because of popular culture.

On the basis of this notion, some intellectuals who conduct Japanese studies set out to transform into public writers or commentators. As the latter, they could still practice their profession and express their ideas, but they do so to a large audience (in comparison with their audience during lectures or publishing of academic papers) because of their proficiency in using public/online media and presenting their ideas through Japanese elements.

Additionally, we note that other local Japan Hands intellectuals, similar to Hong Kong people in general, are concerned about their society and owning a Hong Kong identity to a different extent. Therefore, "Hong Kong elements" are added into Japanese studies instead of only raising the case of Mainland China in making comparisons or examining international relations (Ng 2010, p. 90). They also join the discussion on social and political issues in Hong Kong or Mainland China through the "Japan Narratives."

Japan Narratives

Japan Narratives are narratives about Japan that carry an instrumentality that influences the subjectivity or nationalism of certain entities or nations to be strengthened or cultivated by defining the "other" or making linkages between entities. People either intentionally or unintentionally create Japan Narratives. In the case of China, Taiwan or Hong Kong, especially for those who possess a stronger sense of belonging toward China, Japan Narratives usually treat Japan as the "other" and link China with Japan. For present-day Taiwan or Hong Kong, especially for those who have a low sense of belonging toward Mainland China or a strong sense of belonging toward Taiwan or Hong Kong, Japan Narratives tend to treat Mainland China as the "other" or render Taiwan or Hong Kong as a subject to link with Japan directly. The sense of belonging toward China and that toward Taiwan or Hong Kong are not mutually exclusive. Hence, actual case studies are needed to show the diversity of Japan Narratives.

We can trace the early works of Japan Narratives in China back to the late 19th century when Huang Zun-xian (黃遵憲), a famous Chinese official and reformist in the late Qing period, wrote a series of books examining Japan. One of the current states of Japan Narratives in modern-day Taiwan is reflected by the 2014 baseball film *Kano*, which depicted the identity and essence of Taiwan. In Hong Kong, Lo Wai-luen (盧瑋鑾), known as "Xiao Si" (小思), is a famous writer and educator who studied at the Department of Chinese Language and Literature in CUHK. Her books *Ri Ying Xing* (日影行) (*Walk with the Shadow of Japan*) (1982) and *Yi Wa Zhi Yuan* (一瓦之緣) (*The Fate of a Piece of Tile*) (2016) can be considered Japan Narratives that express her deep emotions toward China on the basis of her experience as a student in Kyoto University.[3]

---

[3] Lo Wai-luen, born in 1939, was raised in Hong Kong and completed her undergraduate studies in New Asia College. When she was a secondary student, she became determined to study in New Asia College because of her admiration for New Confucianism's intellectuals, such as Tang Chun-i. After being advised by Tang and Zuo Shun-sheng, she decided to study in Kyoto University mainly to conduct research on traditional Chinese text. She taught in CUHK from 1979 to 2002. As an intellectual, educator and essayist, Lu has numerous contributions in the field of Chinese literature and culture. She also applied "Japan Discourse" in her books 日影行 (1982) and 一瓦之緣 (2016). Rather than linking with Hong Kong's special identity, she showed what China should learn from Japan and expressed her love toward China. She has complicated emotions toward Japan, including alertness to militarism and appreciation for Japan. She likewise used "we" to refer to China and "they"

Ng is also a representative example of creating Japan Narratives in Hong Kong. Interestingly, his Japan Narrative reflects the changing Hong Kong society and its surfacing identity crisis. In 2005, along with the explosion of anti-Japanese demonstrations in Mainland China and Hong Kong, Ng established a blog site called "The Corner for Understanding Japan" (知日部屋) (Nippon.heiya) to promote the concept of "getting to know Japan than being against it or being a maniac" (反日哈日不如知日) (Nippon.heiya 2005a). It focuses on popular culture (Nippon.heiya 2005b). For instance, 150 of the 217 articles in 2005 discussed popular culture in terms of animation, comics, TV drama, film, game, food and travel. Oftentimes, Ng presented Japan as a good example for Hong Kong and made suggestions for comparison. For example, he introduced Kyoto's taxi system, Japan's general educational system and the light pollution policy as references for Hong Kong in 2007 (Nippon.heiya 2007a, 2007b, 2007c). In the interview in 2018, he described that the tendency to look at Japan and make a reflection and comparison is a manifestation of the looking-glass self, a sociological approach (Chin, Tanigaki and Ng 2018).

Several articles have also discussed and updated Sino-Japanese relations. These articles aimed to balance the anti-Japanese and Japanese mania. Ng criticizes Japan's right-wing and extreme nationalism in Mainland China. However, readers can feel the author's emotions toward China between the lines. For example, in 2008, a poisoned dumpling incident (food safety problem) occurred in Japan. The food was found to be made in China. The Japanese government issued an official complaint to the Chinese government, and supermarkets and restaurants in Japan consequently banned the sale or use of Chinese food commodities (Nippon.heiya 2008a). Ng stated that he was saddened by the incident. However, he

---

to refer to Japan. One of her students is Tong Ching-siu, who has published more than 20 popular books about Japanese culture and society. In reviewing the genealogy like Tang Chun-I, Zuo Shun-sheng, Lu Wei-luan and Tong Ching-siu did, the historical continuity and the changes in the utilisation of "Japan Narratives" can be likely understood from the context of Chinese nationalism to recall Hong Kong's special status and character (Xiao Si n.d. 2016, 1982, 2018; Tong 2007).

commented that Japan overreacted because only one child was poisoned and was soon discharged from the hospital. Ng further stated that Japan is supposed to conduct a safety check. Therefore, holding China fully accountable for the incident was unfair (Nippon.heiya 2008a). The occurrence of heavy winter storms in China is another example. In his blog, Ng commented that Japanese media were less concerned about the disaster and more concerned about the food poisoning incident. He further claimed that after the reunification, Hong Kong benefited from Mainland China. Hence, helping our compatriots (i.e. the Mainland Chinese) is timely (Nippon.heiya 2008b). Ng evidently takes responsibilities toward China similar to traditional Chinese intellectuals who were always concerned about their country.

We could also refer to another interview conducted in 2014 (Zhang 2014), when Ng declared that "I like China, so I have started to study Japanese history." He also said that he yearns for the spirit of New Asia (新亞精神) which spreads traditional Chinese culture in a difficult environment. He emphasizes that he studied in New Asia College rather than in CUHK, saying that teachers and students from the New Asia College have a deep affection for Chinese culture and always hope to do something for China and pave a road for the enrichment of Chinese culture (Zhang 2014). Ng expressed the same sentiments to the author during the interview in 2018 (Chin, Tanigaki and Ng 2018).

Chineseness: Legacy of New Asia

To explain why Ng has such outlook and beliefs, we trace his experience as an undergraduate student. According to the interview in 2018, when Ng was still a secondary school student, he had passion for history and read books about Chinese history written by Ch'ien Mu (錢穆), known as one of the greatest historians and philosophers of 20th century China and as one of the founders of the New Asia College (Chin, Tanigaki and Ng 2018). Ng was inspired by Ch'ien's writings, and it became one of the reasons why he decided to study history in New Asia College. Although

Ch'ien had already retired before Ng entered college, Ng was still strongly influenced by Ch'ien indirectly.

The starting point of Ng's career in Japanese studies was during his second year at the New Asia College when he met Tam Yue-him, a teacher whom he greatly respected. Ng was stimulated by Tam while learning Japanese history that he consequently raised many questions. Ng described himself as a kind of student who likes asking questions, and such behavior made him seem like a troublemaker for teachers. Only Tam was patient enough to answer his questions. "If there was no Prof. Tam, I might not to be a scholar and study Japanese history," said Ng. Tam also recommended that Ng study in Japan to build a solid foundation of the fundamentals and then go to the United States for further studies.

Tam majored in English in New Asia College, but he still learned considerably from Ch'ien Mu and Tang Chun-I (唐君毅), also known as one of the greatest modern Chinese philosophers and one of the founders of New Asia College. Tam loves traditional Chinese music and plays the erhu and the yangqin. Ch'ien emphasized the importance of music (樂), equivalent to rites (禮) in traditional Chinese culture. Ch'ien encouraged Tam to establish a music society and sometimes invited Tam to his home to have dinner. These interactions helped them establish such a good relationship. Ch'ien and Tang suggested that Tam should study Asian culture further. They pointed out that modern China was facing Western power that made China ignore her neighboring country. They believed that this imbalance was not favorable for the Chinese nation and might cause China to lose power in representing oriental culture (Tam 2014). Tam then decided to study Japanese culture. Ch'ien also helped Tam to enter Indiana University for his postgraduate degree in Japanese Studies.

Tam chose Japanese studies because he found that most teachers in New Asia College had been influenced by Japan. According to Tam, Japanese scholars' books were always included in the required reading list of Chinese philosophy and literature. Moreover, the writings of Japanese authors are always deeper but easier to understand compared with their Chinese counterparts. In his early years, Ch'ien translated a Japanese book about *I Ching*. Tam remembered that Tang enjoys noh performance and Tang has expressed his desire to move to Kyoto when he retires: "When I come to Japan, I feel like I'm back to my hometown."

Tam has become a famous scholar of Japanese studies. He even contributed to the establishment of the Department of Japanese Studies in CUHK. He believes that studying about Japan can break through the blind spot of Chinese scholars who study about China without examining other Asian countries.

Benjamin Ng was influenced by Tam Yue-him. Tam, in turn, was influenced by Ch'ien Mu and Tang Chun-I. Ng inherited the way of "studying China through Japan" as well as the spirit of New Asia, which centers on the Chinese nation and aims to protect and enrich Chinese culture with broad insights.

Spirit of New Asia and Hong Kong's Subjectivity

Although the above review shows Ng's original aspiration toward China, we note in our analysis that another perspective of Ng emerged around the 2010s. The Facebook page "Nippon.heiya FB" was established in 2012. From 2012 to 2013, Ng's Facebook page and blog site were updated. However, the number of articles posted on his blog site decreased starting from 2014, with only nine and three articles posted in 2015 and 2016, respectively. In 2017, no new posts were recorded (in comparison with the 53 articles written in 2013). Moreover, his concern toward Hong Kong society had become relatively obvious in his posts on Facebook, although they still exude a "traditional Chinese intellectual" aura.

As the Chair of the department since 2015, Ng explained that the principle of the design of the master's program in Japanese Studies (part-time study mode established in 2012) aims to improve the level of Japanese studies among Hong Kong people. Thus, he opposes the idea of changing the program from part-time to full-time. In fact, profit would probably increase because of the market of Mainland China. In general, Mainland students would not apply for part-time degrees in Hong Kong because they may not get a visa issued by the Hong Kong government. Therefore, they prefer a full-time degree. This condition may lead to an imbalance between local and Mainland students, hence Ng's suggestion of a part-time study mode despite the limited profit. Ng also emphasized the importance of the internationalization of the department instead of "Mainlandization." According to him, candidates would be accepted to the postgraduate research program or teaching post regardless of their origin if they are competitive enough.

Furthermore, several residents consider that Hong Kong faced pressure from the Chinese government, especially after 2010. This pressure increased the country's efforts to curb democratic development. In 2012, the proposal for a moral and national education was criticized as "brainwashing." The overflow of tourists from Mainland China and the changing of society also caused some people to worry about the future of Hong Kong. As a form of resistance, those Hong Kong residents reemphasized their identity.

In the interview in 2018, Ng was asked by the author, "Where is 'China' in your heart?" Although he still emphasized his Chinese identity and his passion toward China, he had second thoughts but answered, "It's a good question but I don't know" (Chin, Tanigaki and Ng 2018).

Considering the abovementioned social and political situation in Hong Kong, Ng also said, "We are bullied ... Hong Kong has no 'one country, two systems' now ... We can see the media, the rule of law, universities fall one by one." As a Japan Hands intellectual, Ng appears to have unintentionally initiated Japan Narratives in another way.

Analysis of Japan Narratives

In this section, we review three kinds of operation of Japan Narratives. The first one analyzes Ng narratives to show how Japan Narratives influence the treatment of China as the "other." The second part takes Kengo's case as an example to show how

Japan Narratives are contributed and reproduced by netizens. The third one takes into account the works of Tong Ching-siu to understand how the approach of the looking-glass self, being typical of Japan Narratives, does not treat Mainland China as the "other" but still reverifies Hong Kong's subjectivity through the direct linkage with Japan. Three Japan Hands intellectuals all use their knowledge and effective access to information on Japan to directly or indirectly comment on or interpret issues related to Hong Kong and/or China and recall the special identity, essence and character of Hong Kong unwittingly. The analysis of the Japan Narratives with concrete examples is provided in the following sections.

Treating China as the "other"

(a) Japanese information or one's experience in Japan is used in the reappearing special culture and identity of Hong Kong. In early May 2018, the website of the Hong Kong Education Bureau uploaded an academic paper by Song Xin-qiao (宋欣橋), a scholar from Mainland China who claims that the "mother tongue of Hong Kong Han Chinese is Chinese language (Hanyu)." He said that Cantonese is a dialect and "a dialect cannot be seen as a mother tongue" (Song n.d.). However, Song's idea is different from the general understanding, including that of the Hong Kong government itself. For example, Hong Kong Census and Statistic Department shows that, "It was estimated that a total of some 5623400 persons were aged 6–65 at the time of enumeration. Analysed by mother tongue, 88.1% reported Cantonese, 3.9% Putonghua, 3.7% other Chinese dialects, 1.4% English and the remaining 2.8% other languages" (Census and Statistics Department 2016, p. 88). Different from other cities in Mainland China, Cantonese is "a Chinese language spoken in the south of China and used as an official language in Hong Kong" (Cambridge Dictionary n.d.). Apart from English, Cantonese is used as a spoken language in the government, Legislative Council and the judiciary and education systems.

Song's arguments brought about a strong opposition over Hong Kong society. Ng also posted his disagreement on the Facebook page "Nippon.heiya FB" on 3 May. He referred to the difference between "mother tongue" (母語) and "home country language" (母国語) in the context of the Japanese language. Ng also showed a related picture of an article in *Asahi News* (one of the national newspapers in Japan). He argued that people who misunderstanding such an easy distinction are probably ignorant, if not malicious. Finally, he emphasized that Cantonese is his mother tongue and that Hong Kong is his homeland: "All [his] memory and sense of identity are in Hong Kong" (Nippon.heiya FB 2018d). In April 2018, Ng posted his "registered user card for automated gates" issued by the Japanese government. He said in the post that his "nationality is Chinese rather than Hong Kong, Chinese. I have a slight feeling that something is wrong (違和感)" (Nippon.heiya FB 2018c).

(b) Othering Mainland China is influenced by the sharing of certain news which are usually about scandals involving Mainland Chinese in Japan. In 2018, Ng shared on a Facebook post a news item reporting that a Mainland Chinese woman with insufficient equipment climbed a snow mountain in Japan, got lost and was rescued by the Japanese government. Ng criticized the woman and said, "This Mainlander does not thank Japan or make any self-reflection; instead, she thanks the great motherland for putting pressure on Japan and is proud of being Chinese. It's sick" (Nippon.heiya FB 2018b).

(c) When Hong Kong social movements, political controversy or general conditions were cited, Ng usually referred to opinions provided by the Japanese media. This notion depicts a bond between Hong Kong and Japan. These opinions are largely from the standpoint of Japan Hands intellectuals. For example, during the Umbrella Movement in 2014, Ng shared a link of an article which discussed the Umbrella Movement from *Japan Times*. Ng also commented that *Japan Times* basically reports Japan issues only. This instance marked the first time that a topic unrelated to Japan was published, as described by

Ng (Nippon.heiya FB 2014). In 2015, he shared the exhibition of the Umbrella Movement on a talk show held in Shibuya, Tokyo (Nippon.heiya FB 2015). In 2017, Ng shared a Japanese news article produced by Shinchosha (*Foresight*) which reported that three participants (Wong Chi-fung [黃之鋒], Law Kwun-chung [羅冠聰] and Chow Yong-kang [周永康]) of the Umbrella Movement were sentenced. They were the first political prisoners who emerged in the midst of Hong Kong's gradual shift to "one country, one system," said the author of the news article. Ng shared the article and said that it "hit the nail on the head" (一針見血) (Nippon.heiya FB 2017). In 2018, Ng shared a book titled *Honkon Henkan 20nen No Sōkoku* (香港返還 20 年の相克) (*Hong Kong: Rivalry of Handover After 20 Years*) (2017) written by Yukawa Kazuo, a professor in Hokkaido University. Ng noted, "It hits the point that the 'one country, two systems' remained but reality is gone … After reading the book, it made me sigh" (Nippon.heiya FB 2018a). Another Facebook user responded: "Hong Kong gave up being an international city of the world but fully serve one country; how can it not fall?" (Nippon.heiya FB 2018a).

Although Ng criticizes some issues related to Mainland China and worries about Hong Kong, he pays attention to avoid being offensive in his narratives. He also mentioned in the interview in 2018 that he would hide several netizens' comments which are too offensive or agitating in his Facebook page (Chin, Tanigaki and Ng 2018). Furthermore, misunderstandings are likely. That is, to consider someone who recalls or examines Hong Kong's identity, character and essence is equal to "pro-independence." Ng himself disagreed with "pro-independence" people. He said he does not like those people and has no business talking to them. He criticized that they are one dimensional and are quick to give a "like" if someone opposes or blames Mainland China regardless of the actual content. Ng emphasized that though he sometimes criticizes or satirizes Mainland China, he has a deep emotion toward China and would not deny his Chinese identity.

It is improper to say that Japan Hands intellectuals intend to use Japan Narratives to link to Hong Kong's uniqueness and identity. However, this effect is brought by their narratives, especially in Hong Kong. Some people feel that Hong Kong's uniqueness in political, legal and social aspects is in danger. One process of recalling such uniqueness is to treat China as the "other" by Japan Narratives, although the belief is that people are not aware of the creation and effects of Japan Narratives. We should also note that the appearance of the Japan Narratives cannot be produced by a few Japan Hands intellectuals but by the reaction of the people. Such reactions have caused Japan Narratives to shift from personal to a relatively open area. Thus, although the case of Ng can also show the relevant phenomenon, another Japan Hands intellectual, Kengo's example is more obvious.

Interaction and reproduction

IP Kin-ho (葉鍵濠), pen name Kengo (健吾), was born in 1980. He graduated from CUHK's School of Journalism and Communication in 2002. Afterward, he studied in the University of Tsukuba. He has been a DJ since 2007. Currently, he has his own radio program called "903 國民教育" (903 is one of the channels provided by Commercial Radio and 國民教育 means "national education") in Commercial Radio Hong Kong. He is also an instructor in the Department of Japanese Studies, CUHK. Compared to Ng, Kengo is more active in media, although he is not active in the academic field of Japanese studies. His articles have been widely published in different magazines and newspapers, including *Nikkei* (Chinese version, 日經中文網), *Mingpao* (明報) and *Weekend Weekly* (新假期). He has published more than 30 books, most of which are related to Japan's culture and society. In 2016, he established Japhub, an online platform that provides diverse information on Japan and is updated daily.

His Facebook page (Kengopage) has over 237,000 followers as of October 2018 (Ng's Nippon.heiya FB has around 22,000 in the same period). His Japan Narratives oftentimes consists of a few words with a photo, but it typically evokes resonance among readers. His posts have received thousands of "likes." For example, on 12 March 2016, a day after the fifth anniversary of 3/11 (marking the Tohoku earthquake and tsunami disasters), Kengo shared a Japanese text advertisement which read "Truly thankful for Hong Kong" (Kengopage 2016).[4] (As a background information that we should know, according to *The Asahi Shimbun*, the Japanese Red Cross Society received JPY720 million total donations for 3/11 from Hong Kong, which ranked ninth worldwide in terms of total donations, excluding personal donations; such feat is impressive given that Hong Kong has a population of only 7 million (*The Asahi Shimbun* 2013)). Kengo commented on the post and said, "An ad knows what Hong Kong people are doing for 3/11, so do not blame Hong Kong people who like Japan" (Kengopage 2016). This comment neither included any obvious metaphor nor explained who blames the Hong Kong people. Nevertheless, it earned over 8,000 "likes." People immediately gave meaning to the post through their comments. A user replied: "Without the need to discuss history, Japan is a country that knows gratitude … unlike in Hong Kong, where a brainwashing song is broadcasted and students are forced to study national education … Also, unlike some citizens in a country who say no but act honestly … They always say something nonsense, such as if we did not come to spend, then your country would have already been finished" (Kengopage 2016). Another user said, "Eastern China flood, Sichuan earthquake, Longmarch (a long charity march to benefit poor children in Mainland China), Project Hope (aims to provide educational opportunities for poor children in Mainland China) … Hong Kong has donated generously to China, and the result? How do the Chinese treat Hong Kong people? They bite the hand that feeds them, repay good with evil, have the hearts of wolves and the lungs of dog (cruel and unscrupulous)" (Kengopage 2016).

---

[4] The advertisement is made by the Consulate General of Japan in Hong Kong, the Hong Kong Japanese Chamber of Commerce & Industry, the Hong Kong Japanese Club and the Hong Kong Japanese School (Kengopage 2016).

Surely, Kengo does not represent these kinds of comments, and his own narrative is short and general and lacks any particular intention or guide. It is also obvious that those comments are emotional and probably overgeneralized. For instance, those who have benefited from the donations given by the Hong Kong people may probably be different from those criticized by such Facebook users.

Nevertheless, as indicated by the above analysis, Japan Narratives, which are not provocative, were first produced by Japan Hands intellectuals and then reproduced by numerous ordinary people who tend to emotionally criticize Mainland China. That is, they reproduced Japan Narratives and linked it to the effect of othering Mainland China.

The looking-glass self

Japan Narratives are not necessarily related to the effect of treating Mainland China as the "other." They have other perspectives in Hong Kong, such as the case of Ng who applies "looking-glass self" to make reflections from Japan to Hong Kong in terms of taxi system, general educational system and light pollution policy. In comparison with Tong Ching-siu (湯禎兆), Ng performs much more detailed and academic comparison studies of cultural exchange between Hong Kong and Japan. However, Tong's works are for the public and non-academics. He deeply and widely reads Japanese books that introduce the current Japanese local social and cultural issues to Hong Kong readers. That is, raising the case of Tong in discussing how Hong Kong reviews Japan's local social and cultural issues to reflect herself would be better.

Tong Ching-siu graduated from the Department of Chinese Language and Literature in CUHK. He is a secondary school teacher who is also known as a famous Hong Kong writer who has published more than 20 popular non-academic books about Japan which are mainly in the field of cultural studies and film studies. Tong was awarded the "Award for Best Artist" (Arts Criticism), Hong Kong Arts Development Awards from the Hong Kong Arts Development Council in 2013.

First, the approach of "looking-glass self" is a basic formation of Tong's Japan Narratives. Tong always mentions Hong Kong in his articles. In his book *Riben Zhongdu* (日本中毒) (*Poisoning of Japan*) (2009), Tong mentions a kind of "diseases of affluence," including "smartphone addiction" and "convenience store addiction" in Japan (Tong 2009, pp. 19–22). According to Tong, those who have the "addiction" in Japan have been studied in detail, interviewed and reported by columnists for a long time so that the general public can know about the social problem (Tong 2009, pp. 19–22). By contrast, as Tong argues, Hong Kong media do not spend much time and effort in conducting interviews and research; thus, the level of the discussion on "diseases of affluence" in Hong Kong is not well developed (Tong 2009, pp. 19–22).

The writer intentionally connects Japan issues to Hong Kong, and the approaches to selling and reading are the same. The cover page of *Riben Zhongdu* reads "to expose Japan and to save Hong Kong." The back cover of *Riben Jinhua: Liuxing Wenhua Jiedu* (日本進化: 流行文化解毒) (*Evolution of Japan: To Detoxify Popular Culture*) (2012) reads "the today of Japan, the future of Hong Kong." The back cover of *Renjian Kaiyan: Cong Xiaoshuo Yu Yingxiang Kuishi Xialiu Riben* (人間開眼: 從小說與映像窺視下流日本) (*Open Eye of the World: To See the Lower Class in Japan from Fictions and Films*) (2013) reads "let Japan's phantom reflect Hong Kong's ghosts to discover the same root of the fall."[5] Moreover, as indicated in the foreword in *Riben Jinhua*, Simon Shen Xu-hui, a Professor in CUHK, believes that Japanese studies render Japan as a reference for Hong Kong; hence, it can help Hong Kong nip in the bud different social problems, and the localization of Japanese studies can maintain Hong Kong's international vision (Tong 2012, p. 18). That is, the whole system of

---

[5] Apart from the traditional Chinese versions published in Hong Kong, some of his books were also published as simplified Chinese versions in Mainland China. Some parts of the content might have been edited. The way of selling would also change to fit the market of Mainland China. For example, in the cover page of the simplified Chinese version of 日本中毒, "to expose Japan, to warn China" is written. However, given the fact that the original version of Tong's writings was published mostly in Hong Kong and given his Hong Kong writer's identity and the contents of his works, it is suitable to perform a text analysis under the context of Hong Kong.

Tong's works provides a platform for looking back at Hong Kong and guides readers to reflect Hong Kong through Japan.

Second, although restrained, the writer's emotion toward Hong Kong is embedded in his works. In *Riben Zhongdu*, Tong introduces the industry of love hotel and its cultural meanings in Japan. Then, he quotes the song *Langman Jiulongtang* (浪漫九龍塘) (*Romanic Kowloon Tong*), produced by a young indie band in Hong Kong called "My Little Airport." Kowloon Tong (九龍塘) is located in Kowloon, Hong Kong, and is known for its wide array of love hotels. Therefore, the song uses Kowloon Tong as the name of the song and talks about the subtle feeling of two people who are in a love hotel. The first sentence of the lyric goes, "I want to sing you a song, about me and you went to Kowloon Tong, we have to be very strong, if we want to do something very wrong." Tong explains that love hotels in Japan have been well developed and show various differences; however, he wonders whether this development is really a civilized improvement (Tong 2009, pp. 67–72). At the same time, he said that he misses the purity and honesty behind the voice of the song and that time really belongs to Hongkongers' memory (Tong 2009, pp. 67–72). In other words, Tong is wondering whether a sexually open culture is equal to civilization. At the same time, he misses the period characterized by a sexually conservative Hong Kong society, as indicated by the lyric that describes having sex with others in a "love hotel" as "doing something very wrong."

In addition, in *Renjian Kaiyan*, Tong analyses an article called *Tokyo Chika No Burakku Majikku* (東京地下のブラック・マジック) (*Black Magic of Underground Tokyo*), written by Haruki Murakami. The article is about the Tokyo subway sarin terrorist attack in 1995, plotted by Aum Shinrikyo, a new religious group in Japan. According to Tong, the relationship among new religious groups, indiscriminate terrorism due to economic inequality and the fall of the legend of getting increased social mobility by gaining high-level education are examined in Murakami's article (Tong 2013, pp. 92–96). Terrorism, inequality and the fall of the legend are portrayed as "ghosts," a metaphor in Murakami's article (Tong 2013, pp. 92–96). Interestingly, Tong said, "Don't you think that Murakami is talking about the story of Hong Kong? The 'ghost' may not necessarily appear as a religious group from underground but it does in your nearby …" (Tong 2013, p. 96). In the foreword, Chan Sui-hung (陳少紅), pen name Lok Fung (洛楓), known as a writer and a former adjunct Assistant Professor in CUHK, commented that Tong takes the metaphor of "ghost" and political power in Hong Kong. "Post-97 city" under a heavy overcast has become a floating city, according to Chan (Tong 2013, p. 14).

Tong's works are typical Japan Narratives which basically do not include discussions or emotional comments about Mainland China. Nevertheless, they still recall Hong Kong's special status and character. Hong Kong's special status as a colony or a special administrative region is different from that of the UK and Mainland China. Japan Hands intellectuals' memory and emotion toward sharing Hong Kong with local readers are shaped by the whole special political, legal, economic, social and cultural system of Hong Kong. Through the practice of the looking-glass self, Hong Kong is repeatedly compared with Japan, a country with which it has no dominant–subordinate or ambiguous political relations. Hence, the special status of Hong Kong and the collective memory, emotion and identity generated have been reverified.

As can be concluded from the above arguments from I to III, widespread Japanese popular culture and the economic interaction between Hong Kong and Japan have provided a foundation for the development of Japanese studies in Hong Kong and prompted the emergence of local Japan Hands intellectuals who, similar to the Hong Kong people, own a collective memory of Hong Kong and its identity. Some Hong Kong people believe that Hong Kong is experiencing strong pressure from the Chinese government in a wide range of areas, such as changes in lifestyle, language and the dialing down of freedom and democratic development. Japan Hands intellectuals express their opinions about Japanese elements through social media or traditional media and share collective emotions with some of the Hong Kong people. These conditions have become the background of the formation of Japan Narratives. The characteristics of Japan Narratives include "othering," "interacting and reproducing" and "reflecting and comparing."

The deeper question we should ask is "What are the historical and institutional reasons behind the abovementioned development of Japanese studies in Hong Kong?" The answer to this question can also provide another perspective in understanding the remote causes of the emergence of Japan Narratives which are related to the identity issue and the relationship between Hong Kong and Mainland China.

Colonial Legacy, Japanese Studies, Chineseness and Hong Kong's Subjectivity

Due to historical and institutional reasons, the British colonial legacies and memory related to Japanese imperialism are one of the keys to understanding the development of Japanese studies in postwar Hong Kong and its relation to Chineseness and Hong Kong's subjectivity.

First, migrant scholars who experienced Japanese imperialism encouraged their students to study about Japan and have become the fountainhead of postwar Japanese studies in Hong Kong. Ch'ien Mu, one of the founders of New Asia College, inspired and helped his student, Tam Yue-him, one of the founders of the Department of Japanese Studies in CUHK, to start his career on Japanese studies. In an interview in 2013, Tam said that for Ch'ien, studying about Japan is worthwhile and necessary because it is one of the important civilizations in Asia (Lin and Tam 2013). Ch'ien also translated certain Japanese books when he was young, according to Tam. Moreover, he was born in 1895, the same year that the Qing dynasty lost in the First Sino-Japanese War and signed the Treaty of Shimonoseki. He also experienced the second Sino-Japanese War. Chow Kai-wing (周佳榮) (2017), a graduate of CUHK, is part of the second generation of Sino-Japanese studies scholars in Hong Kong (Ng 2010, p. 87); he argues that the lyrics of the school song of New Asia College written by Ch'ien are a reflection of Ch'ien's experience from the first Sino-Japanese War to the second one (Chow 2017, Chapter 1). When Ch'ien delivered a speech in Tokyo and Kyoto in 1955, he said that he indeed feels that Japan, from top to bottom, has yet to repent over its invasion of

China (Yan 2008, p. 19). Hence, the memory related to Japanese imperialism is possibly one of the reasons why Ch'ien encourages Japanese studies for the sake of understanding a country that has bonds and enmity with China.

Another example is Zuo Shun-sheng (左舜生), a Professor in New Asia College and a first-generation postwar scholar in Hong Kong studying Sino-Japanese relations (Ng 2010, p. 86). Zuo told his students that Japan is an awful, respectful and hateful nation and that Chinese people must study it (Xiao Si 2018, p. 10). Other first-generation postwar Sino-Japanese relations experts such as Zuo find difficulties in avoiding nationalism while conducting their studies because of the 8-year war experience (Ng 2010, p. 86). Nevertheless, the war experience brought by Japanese imperialism, in another angle, became a crucial motivation for them to study Japan. They established the foundation of Sino-Japanese relations studies, one of the mainstream fields in later Japanese studies, and cultivated the next generation (Ng 2010, p. 87). Ng usually inherits such a genealogy. Conducting Japanese studies improves knowledge about China and how to help China.

However, the genealogy brought by the memory related to Japanese imperialism was not completely unchanged. Ng prefers to use another perspective to see the history of the Imperial Japanese occupation of Hong Kong. For example, Ng said that the military government established guilds for various trades and professions. It helped the development of postwar labor movement, although the military government just did it for their own interests (Chin, Tanigaki and Ng 2018).

Nevertheless, migrant scholars experienced the two sides of Japan and believe that the Chinese must study Japan and try to understand her. Hence, they encourage their students to study Japan and conduct their own Japanese studies in a broad sense. All these efforts have helped the development of Japanese studies in Hong Kong.

Second, British governors allowed migrant scholars to develop academia in Hong Kong despite the implantation of cultural nationalism. In the 1950s, HKU was the only university in Hong Kong. It used English as its medium. For Chinese-medium secondary school graduates, they could not easily enter HKU because of their limited English language proficiency (Chou 2012, p. 87). Likewise, a number of Chinese-medium postsecondary institutions were also unable to meet the demands brought by local students who wanted to continue their studies. Many local students facing insufficient opportunities for higher education entered universities in Mainland China or Taiwan (Chou 2012, p. 87). In addition, the flood of refugees from Mainland China heightened the demand for higher education (Chou 2012, p. 88).

As the Yale–China Association's Hong Kong representative, Charles Long argued with the Department of Education in 1956, saying that "if the educational policy of Government drives thousands of the more intelligent and ambitious young people away from Hong Kong, …" "… the Colony will discover that a great deal of the potential leadership of the Chinese community has been lost to the next generation" (Chou 2012, p. 100). Furthermore, allowing students to leave British Hong Kong and enter the Communist world did not suit the British position in the Cold War (Chou 2012, p. 100). Moreover, in 1950, the Director of Education T. R. Rowell warned that the government should "retain the loyalty of the best of the Chinese middle school students." Otherwise, students who "are subject to well-organised political indoctrination" would "come back to spread more Communistic ideas," and it "would become serious political risks" (Chou 2012, p. 101).

The way to deal with these problems, that is, to establish a Chinese university implementing political denationalization of Chineseness was crucial. Deputy Director of Education L. G. Morgan argued that the government should consider "fundamental psychological and emotional factors" and implied the "denationalisation of local Chinese students" (Chou 2012, p. 106). The government thought of establishing a Chinese university. In fact, Chinese colleges also wanted to gain high official recognition and fought for university status (Chou 2012, p. 129). New Asia College was one of the three Chinese colleges (the other two were Chung Chi College and United College) that cooperated with the government in merging to form one university. A representative example of the political denationalization of Chineseness is the case in which Ch'ien Mu and Tang Chun-I insisted to fly the flag of the Republic of China and celebrate the anniversary of New Asia College in the National Day of the Republic of China. However, their insistence was opposed by the government. The colonial government removed political symbols to avoid the possibility of infiltration from Kuomintang (KMT) and suspicions from the Communist Party of China (CPC). Furthermore, from the bottom of the Chinese-medium education system (primary and secondary schools), political nationalism and cultural nationalism were separated by the colonial government. Traditional Chinese thought, culture and literature were encouraged, whereas modern political issues related to CPC and the relations between CPC and KMT were removed (Wong 2002, pp. 121–122). The establishment of CUHK was just the extension of the political denationalization of Chineseness inside the education system. As one of the reasons, some Hong Kong peoples' Chineseness was therefore rooted in their loyalty to their ideal "China" rather than the actual political entity.

Under the strategy of the political denationalization of Chineseness, CUHK fulfills the cultural purpose of migrant scholars and the political purpose of the colonial government. Moreover, CUHK has become a platform for Chinese migrant scholars, encouraging certain scholars to conduct Japanese studies in the future. With the absence of British nationalism in Hong Kong, the character of denationalized Chineseness of CUHK, as a university which has influence over Hong Kong society, is associated with future identity problems among some Hong Kong elites and the younger generation.

As mentioned previously, Ng insists on his Chinese identity and passion for finding a way to promote Chinese culture. However, he felt lost when the author asked, "Where is China in your heart?" Ng embraces cultural China while being critical to the political aspects. However, the reality that he has been facing is that which involves scandals related to Mainland Chinese citizens in Japan. He feels comfortable and relaxed while he is in Japan or Taiwan, but the same is not true when he is in Mainland China.

However, it seems contradictory that although Ng's Hong Kong identity is obvious, we can see his deep emotions toward China. To the aforementioned question, Ng answered:

"This is a good question. I have no answer. But what I have been expecting is not the present China ... You asked very well. Where is China now? I feel lost. I don't know where is it. Some people think that China is in a flourishing period and everyone should celebrate. But I don't think so. Rather, it is a period of loss and letting people worry. On the surface, the economy seems very good, and the country seems so powerful. However, those problems that have been brought are serious. For example, human rights abuse, supervising people, the problems of pollution, these are all terrible, and the future generation have to bear the responsibility. That's why when you asked me, 'Where is China', I really don't know. I've become much more pessimistic. To some extent, I've become more and more for 'localism'. I know that Hong Kong is in no way independent from China. If China becomes better and gains liberality and democracy, we will also have the same. Hong Kong would become better. If not, it would become worse. I think I am unable to change China so I just have to do my best in Hong Kong. But I feel more and more pessimistic. I found that even in Hong Kong, it is very difficult to do so. The whole Hong Kong, as it were, already fell. We can only do as better as possible in our posts. But I don't know how long it can last. Very pessimistic indeed" (Chin, Tanigaki and Ng 2018).

One of the political and educational backgrounds behind Ng's views is the influence brought by the political denationalization of Chineseness. Meanwhile, cultural nationalism retains its Chineseness in Hong Kong. Hence, his words exude a "traditional Chinese intellectual" aura, that is, the emotions of being pessimistic and lost toward China are expressed while being critical of Mainland China in terms of human rights or environmental pollution. The absence of a British national identity and the growing Hong Kong identity based on her unique political, legal, social and cultural status should also be considered.

Finally, the rebuilding of the economic and cultural relationship between British Hong Kong and Japan after the Second World War contributes to the future development of Japanese studies. In August 1947, just 2 years after the end of the Second World War, the colonial government announced the resumption of trade with Japan (Chan and Yeung 2004, p. 247). In January 1948, information provided by the government showed that Hong Kong ranked second in international trade with Japan, following the United States (Chan and Yeung 2004, p. 251).

In 1949, China Travel Service (Hong Kong) held the first tour to Japan (Chan and Yeung 2004, p. 258). In the same year, Sir Alexander Grantham, the Governor of Hong Kong from 1947 to 1957, and his wife traveled to Japan for around 10 days (Chan and Yeung 2004, p. 256). In 1952, the Japan table tennis team was invited to Hong Kong and played with the Hong Kong team for an exhibition match (Chan and Yeung 2004, p. 263). In the mid-1950s, the interactions of the movie industry restarted, and several Japanese universities have started to enroll Hong Kong students (Chan and Yeung 2004, p. 70).[6]

Given the fact that under the atmosphere of the Cold War, the colonial government, having no millstone of nationalism with Japan, efficiently rebuilt the relations with Japan (the Allied occupation of Japan from 1945 to 1952 and Japan after the occupation) just after the Second World War. Since the 1980s, wide and vibrant economic and cultural interactions between Hong Kong and Japan have gradually become the ground for the future development of Japanese studies in Hong Kong.

Conclusion

As a branch of the development of Japanese studies, this chapter reviewed the link of Japanese studies to Chineseness and Hong Kong's subjectivity. Chineseness was a prime mover of the earlier

---

[6] For instance, in 1956, 70 Hong Kong students enrolled in the Asia University of Japan (Chan and Yeung 2004, p. 70).

development of Japanese studies in Hong Kong. Japanese studies was considered as a tool to reflect and understand China. Moreover, intellectuals believed that understanding Japan, a neighboring country with historical bonds and enmity with China, is necessary. Nevertheless, along with the development of Hong Kong, economic and cultural interactions between Hong Kong and Japan have become vibrant. Hong Kong identity and its special status have also been realized by local citizens. The features of Japanese studies have also become diverse.

As a result of the influential presence of Japan in the society, present-day intellectuals have increased opportunities to communicate with the general public who are interested in Japan issues. This opportunity has turned those intellectuals into Japan Hands intellectuals. Their popular writings unwittingly reverify Hong Kong's special status and character through their incessant comparison between Hong Kong and Japan. Furthermore, in recent years, negative emotions toward Mainland China have been included in some of their popular writings which tend to treat Mainland China as the "other" unintentionally. The replies provided by netizens also contribute to the formation of Japan Narratives.

The relationship between the development of Japanese studies and Hong Kong's subjectivity should not be overgeneralized. The discussion should be considered as a special perspective for the supplementary understanding of Japanese studies in Hong Kong rather than as a general phenomenon in Japanese studies in Hong Kong.

Nevertheless, the relationship between Hong Kong and Japan from the new perspective must be considered. In particular, the issue of people's identity and Hong Kong's special status and character which are always complex and involve different types of significant others who play different roles necessitates adequate exploration.

Finally, colonial legacy, as a political and institutional background, has influenced Japanese studies, Chineseness and Hong Kong's subjectivity. The colonial government sharpened the character of Chinese education. The character of denationalized

Chineseness is associated with the present identity crisis among some Hong Kong people. Under the Cold War, the colonial government efficiently rebuilt the Hong Kong–Japan relations, which became a foundation of gradually vibrant interactions from around the 1960s, particularly after the 1980s. This condition enriched the later development of Japanese studies in Hong Kong. In addition, the memory of Japanese imperialism is heavy for Chinese migrant scholars. Nevertheless, it has transformed into a kind of motivation for the development of the first generation of studies on postwar Sino-Japanese relations, later becoming an important part of Japanese studies.

References

Asahishimbun (朝日新聞) (The Asahi Shimbun). 2013. *Shinsaigo no gienkin, kome to Taiwan ga saita saihinkoku sanjūkakoku karamo* (震災後の義援金、米と台湾が最多、最貧国30カ国からも) (Donations after the disaster, US and Taiwan have the most donations, also from the 30 poorest countries). 4 April. http://www.asahi.com/special/news/articles/TKY201304020473.html (accessed on 7 May 2018).

Cambridge Dictionary. n.d. https://dictionary.cambridge.org/dictionary/english/cantonese?q=Cantonese (accessed on 16 August 2018).

Chan Cham-yi (陳湛頤) (Chen Zhanyi) and Yeung Wing-yin (楊詠賢) (Yang Yongxian). 2004. *Xianggang riben guanxi nianbiao* (香港日本關係年表) (*List of Timelines of Hong Kong–Japan Relations*). Hong Kong: Hong Kong Educational Publishing Company.

Chin Chun-wah, Tanigaki Mariko and Ng Wai-ming, Benjamin. 2018. Getting to Know Benjamin Ng Wai-ming.

Chou Ai-ling Grace. 2012. *Confucianism, Colonialism, and the Cold War: Chinese Cultural Education at Hong Kong's New Asia College* 1949–63. Leiden, Netherlands: Brill.

Chow Kai-wing (周佳榮) (Zhou Jiarong). 2017. *Qianmu shixue daolun: liangansandi chuancheng* (錢穆史學導論: 兩岸三地傳承) (*Introduction to Ch'ien Mu's Historical Science: Spread and Heritage in Mainland China, Taiwan and Hong Kong*). Hong Kong: Chung Hwa Book Co.

Census and Statistics Department, The Government of the Hong Kong Special Administrative Region. 2016. Thematic Household Survey Report No. 59. February.

Honkon daigaku nihon kenkyu gakukei (香港大学日本研究学系) (Department of Japanese Studies, the University of Hong Kong). 2000. *Pekin tenshin honkon nihongo kyōiku nihonkenkyū kaiko to tenbō wākushoppu kaigiroku* (北京・天津・香港日本語教育・日本研究回顧と展望ワークショップ会議録) (Prospect and Retrospect of Japanese Language Teaching and Japanese Studies in Beijing, Tianjin and Hong Kong Workshop Proceedings). Hong Kong: Department of Japanese Studies, the University of Hong Kong.

Wong Ting-hong (黃庭康) (Huang Tingkang). 2002. *Guojia quanli xinggou yu huawen xuexiao kecheng gaige — zhanhou xinjiapo ji xianggang de gean bijiao* (國家權力形構與華文學校課程改革 — 戰後新加坡及香港的個案比較) (State Formation and Hegemonizing Chinese School Curricula in Singapore and Hong Kong, 1945 to 1965). (教育與社會研究 4 期) (*Formosan Education and Society Issue 4*).

Kengopage. 2016. 12 March https://www.facebook.com/kengopage/photos/a.374061035988961.83128.373889722672759/1048677945193930/?type=3&fref=nf (accessed on 7 July 2018).

Lin Shao-yang and Tam Yue-him. 2013. *Tan ru qian jiaoshou koushulishi* (譚汝謙教授口述歷史) (Prof. Tam Yue-him's Oral History).

Masakazu Matsuoka (松岡昌和). 2012. *Honkon no daigaku niokeru nihonbunka nikansuru jugyō no genjō* (香港の大学における日本文化に関する授業の現状) (Current status and issues in teaching Japanese culture at universities in Hong Kong). *Journal of Global Education* 3 (一橋大学国際教育センター紀要 3). Japan: the Center for Global Education and Exchange, Hitotsubashi University.

Ng Wai-ming, Benjamin (吳偉明) (Wu Weiming). 2010. *Taigang de zhongri guan xi yanjiu: lishi, yishixingtai yu yanjiushijiao* (台港的中日關係研究：歷史、意識形態與研究視角) (Sino-Japanese Studies in Taiwan and Hong Kong: History, Characteristics and Problems). *Dangdai shixue shi juan san qi*. (當代史學 10 卷 3 期) *Contemporary Historical Review* 10(3). Department of History, Hong Kong Baptist University.

Ng Wai-ming, Benjamin (吳偉明) (Wu Weiming). 2013. *Honkon ni okeru nihon kenkyu no rekishi, tokushoku oyobi kongo no kadai* (香港における日本研究の歴史、特色及び今後の課題) (The history, character and issues in the future of Japanese studies in Hong Kong). *Kokusai nihon kenkyū no kiso* (国際日本研究の基礎) (*The Foundation of International Japanese Studies*). Taiwan: National Taiwan University Press.

Nippon.heiya (知日部屋) (Zhiri buwu). 2005a. *Fanri hari buru zhiri, jiji dui hua zhongri shuangying* (反日哈日不如知日，積極對話中日雙贏) (To Know Japan rather than Being Against Japan or Being a Maniac:

Active Communication and Win–win for China and Japan). 19 May. http://www.cuhkacs.org/~benng/Bo-Blog/read.php?483 (accessed on 20 May 2018).

Nippon.heiya (知日部屋) (Zhiri buwu). 2005b. *Zhiri buwu de jie shao* (知日部屋的介紹) (The Introduction of Nippon.heiya). 26 May. http://www.cuhkacs.org/~benng/Bo-Blog/read.php?477 (accessed on 7 May 2018).

Nippon.heiya (知日部屋) (Zhiri buwu). 2007a. *Jingdu dishi dui xianggang de qishi* (京都的士對香港的啟示) (Kyoto Taxi and Its Revelation for Hong Kong). 25 July. http://www.cuhkacs.org/~benng/Bo-Blog/read.php?746 (accessed on 7 May 2018).

Nippon.heiya (知日部屋) (Zhiri buwu). 2007b. *Xianggang bixu lifa fanji guang wuran* (香港必須立法防止光污染) (Hong Kong must Legislate and Prevent Light Pollution). 10 September. http://www.cuhkacs.org/~benng/Bo-Blog/read.php?778 (accessed on 7 May 2018).

Nippon.heiya (知日部屋) (Zhiri buwu). 2007c. *Riben tongshike dui xianggang de qishi* (日本通識科對香港的啟示) (Japan General Studies and Its Revelation for Hong Kong). 27 September. http://www.cuhkacs.org/~benng/Bo-Blog/read.php?774 (accessed on 7 May 2018).

Nippon.heiya (知日部屋) (Zhiri buwu). 2008a. *Du jiaozi shijian de guo sheng fanying* (「毒餃子事件」的過剩反應) (The Overreaction from the "Poisoned Dumpling Incident"). 1 February. www.cuhkacs.org/~benng/Bo-Blog/read.php?860 (accessed on 7 May 2018).

Nippon.heiya (知日部屋) (Zhiri buwu). 2008b. *Shui wei Zhongguo xuezhongsongtan* (誰為中國雪中送炭?) (Who provides timely help to China?). 5 February. http://www.cuhkacs.org/~benng/Bo-Blog/read.php?861 (accessed on 7 May 2018).

Nippon.heiya FB (知日部屋 FB) (Zhiri buwu FB). 2014. 30 September. https://www.facebook.com/nippon.heiya/photos/a.608234905866992.1073741827.527394433951040/838091609547986/?type=3 (accessed on 7 May 2018).

Nippon.heiya FB (知日部屋 FB) (Zhiri buwu FB). 2015. 3 July. https://www.facebook.com/nippon.heiya/posts/986128428077636 (accessed on 7 May 2018).

Nippon.heiya FB (知日部屋 FB) (Zhiri buwu FB). 2017. 18 August. https://www.facebook.com/nippon.heiya/posts/1623070257716780 (accessed on 20 May 2018).

Nippon.heiya FB (知日部屋 FB) (Zhiri buwu FB). 2018a. 9 February. https://www.facebook.com/nippon.heiya/posts/1796531033704034 (accessed on 7 May 2018).

Nippon.heiya FB (知日部屋 FB) (Zhiri buwu FB). 2018b. 31 March. https://www.facebook.com/nippon.heiya/posts/1851893838167753 (accessed on 7 May 2018).

Nippon.heiya FB (知日部屋 FB) (Zhiri buwu FB). 2018c. 19 April. https://www.facebook.com/nippon.heiya/posts/1872437969446673 (accessed on 7 May 2018).

Nippon.heiya FB (知日部屋 FB) (Zhiri buwu FB). 2018d. 3 May. https://www.facebook.com/nippon.heiya/posts/1886910584666078 (accessed on 7 May 2018).

Sing Tao Daily (星島日報) (*Xing dao ri bao*). 2016. *Wu Weiming gangri huaijiu* (吳偉明 港日懷舊) (Benjamin Ng Wai-ming, Hong Kong and Japan Nostalgia). 15 January. http://stedu.stheadline.com/sec/sec_news.php?aid=14946&cat=5&subcat=5 (accessed on 7 May 2018).

Song Xinqiao (宋欣橋). n.d. *Qianlun xiang gang Putonghua jiaoyu de xingzhi yu fazhan* (淺論香港普通話教育的性質與發展) (Examining the Nature and Development of Putonghua Education in Hong Kong). https://www.edb.gov.hk/attachment/tc/curriculum-development/kla/chi-edu/resources/primary/pth/jisi4_24.pdf (accessed on 29 September 2018).

Tam Yue-him (譚汝謙) (Tan Ruqian). 2014. *Huiyi laide laoshi yu wode yanjiu daolu* (回憶賴德老師與我的研究道路) (To reminisce Prof. Timothy Light and my way towards an academic career). *Zhuojian mingjia* (灼見名家) (Master Insight). https://www.master-insight.com/回憶賴德老師與我的研究道路/ (accessed on 28 June 2018).

Tong Ching-siu (湯禎兆) (Tang Zhenzhao). 2007. *Mingming Riben* (命名日本) (*Naming Japan*). Hong Kong: Enrich Publishing Ltd.

Tong Ching-siu (湯禎兆) (Tang Zhenzhao). 2009. *Riben zhongdu* (日本中毒) (*Poisoning of Japan*) Hong Kong: Enrich Publishing Ltd.

Tong Ching-siu (湯禎兆) (Tang Zhenzhao). 2012. *Riben jinhua: liuxing wenhua jiedu* (日本進化: 流行文化解毒) (*Evolution of Japan: To Detoxify Popular Culture*). Hong Kong: Live Publishing.

Tong Ching-siu (湯禎兆) (Tang Zhenzhao). 2013. *Renjian kaiyan: cong xiaoshuo yu yingxiang kuishi xialiu Riben* (人間開眼：從小說與映像窺視下流日本) (*Open Eye of the World: To See the Lower Class in Japan from Fictions and Films*). Hong Kong: Enrich Publishing Ltd.

Xiao Si (小思). n.d. CU50•The People. https://www.youtube.com/watch?v=V96C1bwRL5I (accessed on 24 May 2018).

Xiao Si (小思). 1982. *Ri Ying Xing* (日影行) (*Walk with the Shadow of Japan*). Hong Kong: SUNBEAM Publications (HK) Ltd.

Xiao Si (小思). 2016. *Yi Wa Zhi Yuan* (一瓦之緣) (*The Fate of a Piece of Tile*). Hong Kong: Hong Kong Open Page Publishing Co., Ltd.

Xiao Si (小思). 2018. *Ri Ying Xing (xiu ding ban)* (日影行 (修訂版)) (*Walk with the Shadow of Japan (Revised Version)*). Hong Kong: Sunbeam Publications (HK) Ltd.

Yan Gengwang (嚴耕望). 2008. *Qianmubinsi xiansheng yu wo* (錢穆賓四先生與我) (*Mr. Ch'ien Mu and Me*). Taiwan: The Commercial Press.

Zhang Xiaoya (張曉雅). 2014. *Zhuanfang Wu Weiming: zai riben faxian zhonggou* (專訪吳偉明: 在日本發現中國) (An Interview of Benjamin Ng Wai-ming: Discovering China in Japan). http://www.cuhkacs.org/~benng/Bo-Blog/read.php?1436 (accessed on 22 May 2018).

Chapter 10

Colonial Relationality and Its Post-Chinese Consequences: Japanese Legacies in Contemporary Taiwan's Views on China

Chih-yu Shih & Raoul Bunskoek

Department of Political Science, National Taiwan University, Taipei, Taiwan

Introduction

After Japan's defeat at the end of WWII, the Allied Forces returned Taiwan to China, which was at the time represented by the nationalist Kuomintang (KMT). The KMT was then in turn defeated during the Chinese Civil War and retreated to Taiwan in 1949. Consequently, because decolonization did not proceed from an indigenous consciousness embedded in pre-colonial Chineseness (Cummings 2004, p. 279; Chang and Chiang 2012, pp. 28–29), Taiwan became a peculiar post-colonial nation. The exiled KMT, a latecomer to Taiwan, attempted to carry out Taiwanese decolonization from its own perspective of imagined Chineseness. This migrant Chineseness, however, alienated a significant portion of the indigenous population from the decolonization project and induced it to perceive the KMT as the successor of a civilization inferior to Taiwan's colonial modernity (Thiele 2017, Louzon 2017, Chen 2002, Takeshi 2006). Ironically, this colonial modernity indicated enslaved Chineseness at best in the eyes of the KMT.

In the first part of the chapter, we will argue that this irony explains the puzzle why Taiwan differs so much from most other post-colonial societies, where attitudes toward former colonial powers as well as decolonization mark one of the main locations of social cleavage. Under the KMT, attitudes toward a differently imagined China instead have increasingly marked the main social cleavages. The KMT Chinese Civil War agenda, together with its self-imagined "Orthodox China," substituted for decolonization. With the KMT losing the Civil War, reemerging colonial modernity undergirds Taiwan's own identity away from the mainland Chineseness imposed by the KMT. The former colonial relation with Japan has oddly become the dominant intellectual resource to support Taiwan's identity strategy regarding Chineseness.

We will then illustrate how Taiwanese intellectuals born before the end of Japanese colonialism have grown and developed their perspectives on China in later years. We apply the theme of post-Chineseness to complicate the notions of China and Chineseness. Essentially, we will show that those who find Chineseness a challenge to their self-respect allow colonial modernity to constitute either their scholarship or their social relationships (Lee and Chen 2014). In contrast, those who reimagine Chineseness in Taiwanese perspectives are inclined to remain critical to the Japanese influence in their presentations of China.

Colonial Relationality of Modernity and War

Up from colony

The chapter defines colonial relationality as "the conditions of being related through shared colonial history" (Sealey 2018, Shih 2016, Lin 2016). Colonial relationality distinguishes the arriving KMT from the Taiwanese indigenous population, who have either directly experienced colonialism to some extent or internalized indirectly colonial experiences through interaction in later years with those who have direct experiences. Colonial relationality enables discursive congruence among those who once practiced colonial rules, participated in colonial modernity and learned colonial values despite incongruence in their moral assessments toward colonialism (Heller and McElhinny 2017, Harvey 2015, Chow 2014). The most important aspect of colonial relationality for later generations to develop their imagination of China is that a significant portion of the Taiwanese elites accepted the conversion of their own identities into a Japanese one. Wherever the Civil War regime failed to treat their colonial relations with respect, nostalgia to colonial modernity in the postcolonial period was bound to arise (Raychaudhuri 2018). Consequently, images of China would be negative.

We define colonial modernity as "achieving characteristics of modernization that make the colony useful to the colonizer" (Takeshi 2006, Aguir 2011, Shin and Robinson 1999). Some praise it as an instrument to contrast against the backwardness of the KMT or China; others denounce it as mechanisms of exploitation (Morris and Gerteis 2017, Heylen and Sommers 2010). With decolonization, colonialism usually becomes perceived as exploitive, as has been the case in, for example, formerly Japanese Korea and British India. In Taiwan, though, the colonial modernity brought by Japan provides till now an intellectual foundation for those who strive for dignity in front of the disapproving KMT, who at the time of its arrival in Taiwan lacked a similar level of modernity (Barclay 2016, Tsai 2009). On the contrary, for those indigenous people who did not go through conversion or suffered relative degradation due to the arrival of KMT's Civil War regime, a lingering Chinese consciousness may lead to suspicion toward colonial modernity despite readiness to take advantage of it when convenient or strategically beneficial. In fact, the KMT likewise recruited Japanese advisors during its Civil War.

One key development of colonial modernity in Taiwan was the so-called Kominka (Japanization) campaign, which coincided with the beginning of Japan's expansion into China. It included a language campaign and surname reform so that the entire population would eventually enjoy total assimilation. However, the key component of the campaign's cultural aspect was religious in nature (Peng and Chu 2017, Lee, Mangan and Gwang 2018,

Lee 2012). It involved the installation of Goddess Amaterasu as the highest spirit that was fungible for previously worshiped ancestors. Migrants in Taiwan had used to conceive of their own selves as racially Chinese. After Kominka, people officially became Japanese, which was a spiritual thing and, hence (Ching 2001, Henry 2016), arguably, metaphorically similar to the situation the protestants celebrated after winning the Reformation Wars in Europe — i.e. they no longer needed to go through the media of Catholic churches and could now pray directly for God's blessing.

To ensure the absolute loyalty of colonized people toward Japan (Wong and Yao 2011, Chou 1991), the cultural campaigns went hand in hand with material incentives. For instance, the more successfully assimilated families received privileges in education, recruitment for public office and rations. Physically bowing to the emperor at fixed times composed the daily body politics, especially in schools. The post-Kominka situation transformed the earlier designation of the colonized population as "the slaves of the (barbarian) Manchurian nation", which had implicated a status lower even than barbarian. With Kominka, however, they became direct subjects of the emperor. Consequently, as the Pacific War intensified, over 120,000 Taiwanese voluntarily joined the Japanese military to fight against the Allied Forces. Officially serving the imperialist army was considered an honor in general. Even the ultimate defeat could not reduce a sense of pride. This is underscored, for instance, by the fact that even as late as by the 70th anniversary of the end of the war in 2015, pro-Taiwan independence forces in Taiwan insisted that Taiwan only memorize the defeat in order to contrast itself against the self-regarded winner China. They did so to prove that Taiwan is not Chinese (Amae 2011, Liao and Wang 2006).

The KMT after takeover perceived of itself as enacting the role of "liberator" from Japanese colonization (Louzon 2017, Hui 2018, Jacobs 2014, Lo 2002). However, its migrant nature inhibited it from seriously understanding colonization in the Taiwanese context. Therefore, the KMT's decolonization was only superficial, through providing equal citizenship and unifying patriotic education for the post-colonial population. Resistance by those remaining loyal to Japan was mistaken as Communist infiltration or as still a part of the Chinese Civil War. The KMT did not catch the sense of relative deprivation its rule brought upon the indigenous population, which was the result of the following four factors: 1) the population had (partly) internalized the Japanese view that the KMT regime belonged to a lower civilization; 2) it perceived Japan's defeat primarily as a result of American atomic bombing rather than the combat skills of the KMT; 3) the KMT governance was far less efficient and more corrupt compared with the Japanese colonial administration; and 4) the KMT was in itself a loser of the Chinese Civil War. In short, nostalgia for the former colonial identity provided the convenient and effective reference to reverse the KMT Civil War ideology.

Yet, that Japan's legacy remains particularly strong pertains additionally to the fact that the post-colonial Taiwanese population was not held accountable for the war. The defeated Taiwanese soldiers as well as civilian collaborators loyal to Japan received the arriving KMT regime without becoming the objects of war crime trials. As Japan renounced ownership of Taiwan, the population automatically assumed their citizenship of the victorious side — the Republic of China (ROC) — at the moment of defeat. Peculiarly, the returning Taiwanese soldiers felt no military defeat and yet maintained a sense of colonial superiority. As the bizarre winners of the Chinese war against Japan, they escaped the pressure to reflect upon the Japanese war of invasion of which they had been a part. Neither did they jettison the civilizational imagination behind the enthusiasm for war. As a result, 70 years after the end of war, there is the increasingly vociferous assertion that Taiwan should only celebrate the *loss* of war since Taiwan belonged to Japan during the war. In other words, the fact that they officially became "Chinese" citizens provided the pro-independence force in Taiwan with a shield to remain exempted from punishment and a shadow of loss, while also enabling them to comfortably assert an un-Chinese identity.

Practically, though, colonial modernity had its limits (Cheng 1989, Shih 2007). First of all, a vast portion of the population had not gone through Japanization, and this part of the population's nostalgia for colonial modernity was not as powerful (Chu 2016). Second, with the KMT wielding political control in the post-war period, those who had experienced Japanization were able to take advantage of social mobility in economics, education and even public administration. Third, the KMT was able to deliver economic growth for a prolonged period of time to distract from political tensions. Fourth, identificational exits became available in the United States, where educational as well as career opportunities started providing an alternative route to reattain the self-respect lost under KMT rule. Fifth, electoral democratization since the mid-1990s facilitated a rising national consciousness in Taiwan (Jacobs 2013). Last but not least, the KMT engaged in decentralization, indigenization and democratization in the 1980s to accommodate the coming legitimacy crisis that would inevitably emerge with the demise of its first generation (Wang 2009).

In the meantime, the Japanese colonial despise of the "inferior" Chinese civilization was able to find a natural substituting target in communist China, which was economically backward and politically authoritarian. With the last generation of the Japanized population coming to power in Taiwan through the KMT's internal channel (e.g. Lee Teng-hui) and then the next generation following up through winning electoral campaigns (e.g. Chen Shui-bian), colonial modernity, colonial identity and Taiwanese identity reemerged powerfully in Taiwan (Corcuff 2012, Lynch 2004). Ironically, China's rise in the 21st century and confident calls for reunification with the island only bring back memories of the deprivation brought about by the KMT after WWII.

Post-Chinese Possibilities Embedded in Colonial Relationality

(Post)colonial scholarship in general and the writing of China in Taiwan in particular involve strategic choices. For instance, regarding the primary sources and the methodology on which one relies, the language of (re)presentation, and the audiences one intends to address necessarily incorporate as well as affect one's purposes and strategies of research and writing (Smith 2012, Kovach 2010). To the extent that indigenous research anywhere has to be relational in both the social and political sense (Wilson 2009), purposes can evolve and multiply accordingly. This is especially the case when considering that a post-colonial scholar on China can receive educational training in homeland Taiwan, in Japan, an Anglo-European country, in China, as well as in another post-colonial country such as India, Hong Kong or Singapore. Owning some mixed (educational) background is common among scholars, too. In fact, senior China scholars usually received mixed trainings in China, Japan, the United States and Taiwan.

The embrace of particular approaches or the consultation of certain sources implicates one's intellectual and identity distance toward specific audiences (Tanaka 1995). In other words, one can measure the distance of a scholar from China and indicate his or her identity by looking at the methodology he or she adopts and the audience he or she intends to address (Matsumura 2018, Golovachev 2018, Lomová and Zádrapová 2016). If, for instance, one intends to distance oneself from the audience that is at a deliberate distance from China — e.g. by enlisting a supporting Chinese source to interact with a pro-Taiwanese independence audience — one likely identifies more with China than one's audience does. On the contrary, if one uses Japanese sources to mingle with the same audience, one would probably identify less with China. In other words, if one intends to shorten the distance from such a pro-independence audience, one may reflect an implicit purpose of keeping China at bay. However, the identity strategy is more complicated than any universal rule can describe. To name another example, by enlisting a British source or an American methodology, one might intend to take a neutral position between Taiwan and China — i.e. presumably through being "objective." The same style of scholarship could likewise support the quest for higher status in the face of the Taiwanese domestic audience or targets in China, both of whom are arguably less international (Shih 2014).

Taiwan's situation is reminiscent of Hong Kong. Hong Kong is different from other British colonies but comparable to Taiwan in the sense that the main liberator is an external power that failed to appreciate the identity crisis of the former colony. Both Taiwan and Hong Kong face an identity choice between the colonial motherland, Japan and the UK, respectively, on one hand, and the Chinese motherland or the indigenous site on other hand (Hou 2018, Lin 2018, Cheng 2017). This makes the situation in these two localities more complex than the situations in Korea or India. For India, the choice is between the colonial and the indigenous. However, Korea and Taiwan are comparable to the extent that their similar positioning during the Cold War and all-round dependence on the United States add an alternative to their former colonial motherlands (Cho 2015). With regard to facing China through multiple perspectives, the situation in Taiwan seems most complicated. This is particularly the case since Taiwan has the possibility to pursue either a psychologically higher but linguistically neutral scholarship on China embedded in Anglo-American methodology, a higher but anti-China scholarship embedded in the Japanese colonial perspectives or a higher but pro-China scholarship embedded in classic humanistic perspectives. Specifically, the use of Anglo-American methodology, which keeps Chinese voices from intervening, can suit multiple purposes — e.g. it can be used as a tool to move beyond the scope of influence imposed by former colonial Japan, to apply as a standard estranging the presumably politically superior China or to win the respect of fellow Taiwanese who worship the American.

In short, the above can be boiled down to two dimensions: (1) position: whether or not one understands China from a self-imagined internal perspective or an external one and; (2) source: whether or not one allows Chinese perspectives to determine what constitutes Chineseness. As regards the first dimension, there are internal, external and in-between positions where one consciously decides between being Chinese, non-Chinese or partially Chinese (and thus partially non-Chinese). For the second dimension, one can rely on either Chinese sources or allegedly objective sources in order to approach China as well as Chineseness.

The above two dimensions produce 3 × 2 = 6 possibilities of how one can relate to one's China, which we will call post-Chinese possibilities — cultural Chineseness (internal/Chinese), civilizational Chineseness (external/Chinese), Sinological Chineseness (in-between/Chinese), experiential Chineseness (internal/objective), scientific or policy Chineseness (external/objective), and ethnic Chineseness (in-between/objective). The practices or shifts toward a certain post-Chinese identity reflect someone's strategic choice in a context, which implicates upon his or her attitudes and policies on one's China.

The first approach on the source dimension is to rely on those perceived Chinese perspectives. Three categories divided by self-positioning emerge. First, those writers who consider themselves practitioners of Chinese cultural lives in one way or another own cultural Chineseness. Cultural Chineseness could be practiced, for instance, through ancestor worship, specific food diets, advocating patriotism/nationalism, speaking Mandarin/provincial dialects, adhering to the lunar calendar or anything that reproduces a trajectory of relationality shared by other self-identified Chinese. Second, people who are able to mediate between Chinese and other cultural lives possess Sinological Chineseness. Such Chineseness reflects self-confidence in understanding both sides and explaining each to the other. Third, civilizational Chineseness describes an embedded self-consciousness that identifies China as a distinctive other. In this regard, China refers to religious, ideological or cultural resources to be learned or borrowed for exotic purposes on the one hand, and despised and rejected for exclusionary purposes on the other.

The second approach on the source dimension is to adopt a presumably objective standard and divide the post-Chinese possibilities into three in accordance with one's self-positioning. First, experiential Chineseness is owned by those self-regarded insiders who have spent enough time with Chinese so as to practice and support the same pattern as well as stance acquired through experiences from living or working together. Second, ethnic Chineseness contrasts Sinological Chineseness in the sense that people who possess it are not embedded in Chinese cultural or civilizational perspectives. Rather, it comes from awareness of being physically related in one way or another to both the Chinese and the other side. Ethnic Chineseness compels conformity of its owners to expectations from both sides and incurs anxiety of all sides toward undecidable results. Third, scientific/policy Chineseness points to the analytical practices of those self-designated outsiders, who approach and claim knowledge of China based upon certain selected presumably "objective" criteria regardless of how those perceived Chinese under study may respond. These criteria could include size, level of power, type of institution, gene, borders and anything that is functional to define China as an object of a research agenda that makes most sense to the narrators.

Six Illustrative Stories of Colonial Relationality

Hsu Chie-lin's (1935–) practices of cultural Chineseness[1]

Hsu Chie-lin was born in Hsinchu in 1935 and received his primary education at Kitashirakawa Elementary School, a school established in memory of Prince Kitashirakawa Yoshihisa who died during the war of conquest over Taiwan. Hsu later attended a different school to escape from American bombardments. He was bilingual to the point that he wrote his doctoral dissertation in Japanese. After Japan's defeat, Hsu's Chinese teacher was suspected of infiltration and executed by the KMT. Hsu's academic career began at National Taiwan University. During his time there, the professors who impacted upon his intellectual growth the most were mainly the exiled Chinese ones. Although Hsu does not come from a wealthy family, after college, a fellowship from the Japanese government enabled him to enroll in the University of Tokyo to study under the guidance of a leading Sinologist Naoki Kobayashi. Hsu is proud of his training at the University of

---

[1] The following introduction is based entirely on the oral history at http://www.china-studies.taipei/act/tw-7.doc (accessed on 20 February 2018).

Tokyo. Although in his 70s now, Hsu still actively publishes on Manchuria, Taiwan and Japan regularly in Japanese journals.

Hsu's later career demonstrates cultural Chineseness. Despite the deep Japanese influence on his intellectual growth, he still remained critical toward Japan. This was mainly because, coincidentally, the Japanese professors he studied with during his time in Japan were predominantly reform oriented. However, Hsu himself primarily attributes his critical aptitude to the difficult conditions he endured during childhood. Because of his critical stance, he was disappointed at Taiwan's submission of intellectual independence to the US and Japan. He insisted that since Taiwan had officially returned to China in 1945 and in the light of their converging civilization, reunion with China should be the natural path to follow. Hsu's initial agenda in Japan was Taiwan studies, which he intended to be a stepping stone for a longer-term agenda of China studies. Both Hsu's professor in Japan, Naoki, who was a constitutionalist and peace activist, and his professor earlier in college in Taiwan, Sa Meng-wu, who was a reputable institutionalist, had a profound influence on his thinking. This influence was highlighted by the heavy indebtedness to their institutionalist viewpoints in Hsu's doctoral thesis, which answered the question why Japan's Westernization had succeeded but China's failed. Hsu currently still stresses the importance of political thought and argues that China's adherence to classic Chinese thought most powerfully explained its abortion of Westernization. In addition, he finds history extremely important but overlooked by political scientists. He considers his utmost contribution to the Taiwanese academic field his research on the political history of Taiwan.

Hsu's China studies correspond to his cultural Chineseness. For instance, he explains the successes of Deng Xiaoping's reforms mainly through the influences of Deng's thought reforms, which he believes paralleled the thought reforms implemented during Japan's Meiji Restoration. He criticizes the preference for behaviorist methods in social science. Instead, he accepts the Japanese Sinological tradition that relies on the classics. Besides his dissertation, another one of his major projects has been to assess

China's economic conditions through the Japanese academic literature. Here, he owns scientific Chineseness, too. Moreover, he was also the founding father of the China Studies team at NTU's College of Social Sciences. In principle, though, his China studies proceed through the China connections in Taiwan's political history. In this light, he begins his China studies project with the year of Taiwan's colonization by Japan and compares it with that of China during the Opium War so that he is able to see the different influences the UK and Japan have had on China. Over the years, he has invited a good number of leading Sinologists to NTU for exchange programs. Nishida Masaru has been his latest cooperator. They edit a journal together.

Yeh Chi-chengs' practices of Sinological Chineseness (1942–)[2]

Yeh's grandfather was 13 when Japan colonized Taiwan. His many old-fashioned Chinese classic collections fascinated the grandson in his childhood. Yeh's father, though, collected a good number of Japanese books, whose pictures as well as sporadic Han characters likewise attracted young Yeh. The three generations have inherited different civilizational identities, breeding in Yeh liking of both Japanese music and Chinese operas. In school, Yeh met children of the Chinese migrants that had followed the fleeing KMT. Their languages did not mingle well, which often led to fist fights. Yeh therefore became sensitive to the differences in birthplaces very early. He then realized that even Taiwanese had taken multiple paths, with some born or schooled in China during childhood before returning to Taiwan. He also ran into migrant Chinese victimized by KMT rule. After he entered college, his intellectual growth as well as career was heavily indebted to migrant scholars, whose nostalgia for China easily

---

[2] The following introduction is based entirely on the oral history at http://www.china-studies.taipei/comm2/InterviewTW17.pdf (accessed on 24 February 2018).

reminded him of his father's nostalgia for colonial governance. In fact, he noticed his own nostalgia for old times the moment he encountered a Japanese soap opera.

Yeh demonstrates a kind of Sinological Chineseness. For instance, he had the dream to save China while in high school. However, throughout his adulthood he felt alienated from the KMT rule as well as its propaganda and rituals. He acquired a high political consciousness from his father. Yeh feels sympathetic toward migrant Chinese soldiers who ended up in Taiwan often unexpectedly. His critical attitude, career development and scholar engagement benefited enormously from various migrant liberals, some of whom he felt obliged to support despite them generally being against Taiwan independence, which is his wish. Although he is aware of his marginal position, he is ready to criticize both sides for failing to empathize with each other or for their typical hypocritical practices. He uses his coexisting two trajectories of intuitive love for the Japanese songs and Chinese instruments as a metaphor to illustrate how life experiences can be apolitical and yet distinctive. Once politicized, however, the indigenous and the migrant populations in Taiwan are compelled to confront each other.

Yeh's scholarship is accordingly alert to ironies, ambivalence and dialectics. What particularly alerts him is the incapacity of academics to resolve widespread dichotomic incongruences in human society in general and in China as well as in Taiwan in specific. One such incongruence is the one between modernity and tradition, which is obviously a challenge not just for China or Taiwan. Behind this incongruence is the conflict between the West and the East and, more profoundly, between dependence on and fear of the West/East at the psychological end and between being or becoming the West/East at the ontological end. It is unlikely for Taiwanese scholars, Yeh insists, to tackle this issue without themselves being situated both in Western intellectual history *and* engrossed in Oriental wisdom. In order to do so himself, Yeh seeks insight from Newtonian calculus, which originates from the Hobbesian notion of endeavor and produces repercussions in conceptualizing continua in human phenomena. Self-reservation thus contrasts Chinese thoughts. Moreover, Confucian officials of the late Qing period provided Yeh with a contemporary problematiqué, from where he discovered the rationales for Sinicization/indigenization campaigns in social science. This has led to Yeh's ultimate quest for "self-cultivation" as the last resort of transcendence in his own academic discipline — Sociology.

Shih Ming's practices of civilizational Chineseness[3]

Shih Ming was born in 1918. His father had a college degree from Japan and was associated with leading activists promoting political participation for the Taiwanese people. During his childhood, Shih Ming himself went to a private teacher to study the Chinese classics, which his mother also understood well. Although his father was accustomed to the indigenous folk dramas performed for the gathering masses at local temples in Taiwan, he went on to learn music in Japan. Shih Ming was then smuggled to Japan for study when he was 19. He recalls no discrimination against colonized people. He entered Waseda University and enjoyed its liberal style. He mingled well with classmates off school, usually in bars. He also participated in study groups, where he encountered Marxism. Later, he found that Marxism allowed him to understand China in a rather objective way. He was able to travel to China in order to support communism. In actuality, he mainly ended up mingling with the Japanese in Shanghai instead. No Chinese police or Japanese security bothered to watch him because he looked so Japanese. Nevertheless, he sympathized with China and felt regret for not being able to join the fight against Japan when it invaded China.

---

[3] Shih is better known in English as Su Beng, which is his name pronounced/spelled in Taiwanese/Hokkien. The following introduction is based entirely on the oral history at http://www.china-studies.taipei/comm2/InterviewT31.pdf (accessed on 25 February 2018).

Shih Ming's perspective on China increasingly resembles civilizational Chineseness despite him having learned the classics at an early age. This is because his socialist perspective on China romanticizes a future that is neither available in Taiwan nor in Japan. After Japan surrendered, he prepared himself to join the Civil War in China. First, he went to Lianhe University in Beijing where the studies involved serious self-critique sessions as well as the learning of anti-Japanese thought and Marxism. After returning to Japan, Shih Ming began to contact the pro-Taiwan independence organization. He simultaneously reflected upon the meaning of Taiwanese being Chinese from the perspectives of Marxism and materialism. This Marxist view supported the formulation of his theory of Taiwanese nationalism. Japan played an indirect but rather significant initial reference point. It was the contrast with Japan, as well as Japan being the Taiwanese beneficiary of colonial modernity, that Shih Ming used to make sense of the backwardness of China while at the same time conceptually defining China as a "class-based nation."

In his legendary publication — *Modern History of Taiwanese in 400 Years* — he divided the Chinese in Taiwan into five different types according to Marxism: (1) the ruling class that included both the Manchus and later the KMT rulers, (2) the comprador class, (3) the proletarian class in Taiwan during the Qing dynasty, (4) the deceived Taiwanese under the KMT that included those Chinese migrants who followed the fleeing KMT to Taiwan and (5) the sober Taiwanese. For Ming, China is no longer a home of socialism and Japan imposed no suppression on Taiwan after WWII. Rather, China as an entirety contains a suppressive national class (i.e., the ruling class). This explains how the Taiwanese population in its entirety is a suppressed class and why Taiwan necessarily is a separate nation. In this light, the KMT represents the Chinese nation that suppresses Taiwan. In other words, the colonial suppressing class of the KMT has victimized the Taiwanese as a colonized and suppressed class. Hence, for Shih Ming, the appeal to a shared Han identity in China and Taiwan is no more than an illusion.

Chen Peng-jen's practices of experiential Chineseness[4]

Born in 1930, Chen Peng-jen's ancestor followed Ming General Zheng Chenggong (Koxinga) to Taiwan 7 generations ago. During his childhood, Chen knew that he was from Fujian, China. Besides, he remembers that when he noticed that the Japanese emperor had no surname he felt puzzled and perceived himself as absolutely different. As a child, he took courses in Japanese for 6–8 hours a week. He even won a Japanese speech contest in elementary school. However, he was he was not allowed to enter a higher-level competition because his family had kept its Chinese name during the Japanization campaign — even though this was because the campaign had not reached the remote countryside where Chen's family resided. Still, he recalls a neighbor hiding a Buddha statue in a barrel filled with excrements to avoid it from being confiscated and burned by Japanization campaigners. He also points out that those very few who went through Kominka were nicknamed "three-feet-sons," people in between ostensibly four-footed Japanese and two-footed human beings. Nonetheless, Chen later realized that the Japanese teachers were devoted wholeheartedly to education as opposed to the Chinese migrants who had fled to Taiwan and primarily taught for a salary. After his primary education, Chen went to Japan as an adolescent worker, all the while hoping that Japan would lose the war so that he could go home.

Colonial relationality did not lead to a Japanese identity in Chen's consciousness, although he was almost the best-connected Taiwanese among the Japanese high circles, which included a few former Premiers. Rather, very early in his career, he had the luck of encountering a number of senior migrant officials affiliated with the KMT and received their consistent support. Even though Chen did not tour China until it was opened in the 1990s, he attained a strong experiential Chineseness due to his daily life spent with migrant Chinese politicians and intellectuals. Consequently, he understood perfectly well how attached these senior migrant

---

[4] The following introduction is based entirely on the oral history at http://www.china-studies.taipei/comm2/InterviewT%20chen%20pon%20ren.pdf (accessed on 28 February 2018).

politicians were to China, the KMT and its Three Principles of the People. Chen himself even joined the KMT due to his faith in the Three Principles of the People. He was also anti-communist probably because he had internalized this KMT stance. Chiang Kai-shek himself decided that Chen ranked as high as number 4 in the KMT. With regard to Chen's intensive mingling with the KMT elite throughout his career, in particular his relationship with the KMT senior politician Ma Shu-li stood out. Ma, who was in charge of overseas affairs and later became general secretary of the KMT, was very fond of Chen and treated him like a son. Ma later served as Taiwan's representative to Japan for over a decade.

A major contribution of Chen's scholarship is his translated work. In his translations, he was always sensitive to human characters and paid detailed attention to nuances. In his works, a few apparent themes particularly stand out. For example, specific Japanese and Japanese government attitudes toward China, revealed by words and deeds, alerted him. Moreover, he was always prepared to criticize Japanese imperialism, Taiwanese independence and communism. Consistently, these were the enemies of the KMT during the reign of Chiang Kai shek as well as Chiang Ching Kuo. Besides the above, he was preoccupied with storytelling. Among his nearly 200 published books, people and their social relations always made up the core focus of his stories. All this made him most qualified to take up the post of Director of the History Department of the KMT. Chen's achievements during his term included his acceptance of manuscripts submitted from China, the opening up to the public of party historical documents, the raising of funds to establish a civilian foundation and, most importantly, the sending of research delegates to China without the approval of the KMT.

Shih Che-hsiung's practices of ethnic Chineseness[5]

Shih Che-hsiung was born in 1942 and was not formally educated in the colonial system at all. Neither was his family indoctrinated

---

[5] The following introduction is based entirely on the oral history at http://www.china-studies.taipei/act/tw-9.pdf (accessed on 25 February 2018) and also the TV interview at https://www.youtube.com/watch?v=HItzaXEsScM (accessed on 26 February 2018).

under the Kominka campaign. Shih Che-hsiung followed the KMT educational system through college, after which he entered the Graduate Institute of East Asian Studies at National Chengchi University (NCCU) as part of its first cohort. The Institute was the first pedagogical institute of China studies in Taiwan under the KMT. Its mission was to remedy the lack of objective analysis of China, which suffered from serious political biases in the hands of the military and intelligence staff. President Chiang Ching-kuo was so concerned about its development that he even met in person with the first six students the Institute recruited. Shih Che-hsiung would continue his career as student, assistant, lecturer and even Director of the Institute. Along this long career path, he acquired all kinds of interests regarding CCP politics, revolutionary history, ideology, demography, social welfare, the PLA and so on.

Shih Che-hsiung was consciously aware of his position in-between Taiwan and China. However, he has not acted upon any inclination to choose sides. Instead, he stresses the importance for both sides to know each other. His ethnic Chineseness is reflected in his readiness to adjust himself in order to remain connected to both sides. He has a lot of different good friends almost everywhere in China and can always call somebody wherever he goes to China. Moreover, he claims that among his relationships with many of his good friends in China, not a single case of displeasure has occurred. He observes that distrust is used to create problems for academic exchanges. However, he underscores the importance of these exchanges because they are conducive to mutual understanding and making friends. Nevertheless, in times of distrust he still endeavors to keep both sides informed. He does so, for instance, through pointing out directly to Chinese officials that there have been too many restrictions from the Chinese side. Moreover, he recommends that the hosts in Taiwan act straightforward and sincere in order for the other side to gain trust in them. He also highlights the critical importance of taking care of the need for face-saving of both sides.

In his own studies of China, Shih Che-hsiung relies intensively and extensively on field research. Not only did he belong to the first cohort of professors who led graduate students to visit China, but he was also a frequent visitor to various different sites in China himself. One of his famous skills of communication is to deftly recite all kinds of doggerels that he has gathered from villages all over China either to enhance his acceptance at different sites or to provoke the curiosity of his students. Another skill is reflected in his determination to collect a large amount of books each time he goes to China, which enables him to update his perspectives on situations in China socially as well as culturally. During his lifetime, he has been in all 31 provinces in China. His approach primarily takes the shape of humanist geography, since he always begins by investigating the history and ecology of the site that he is visiting. Now at his moment of retirement, he is a little unsure about whether or not his site-oriented scholarship has kept him from developing his own system of China scholarship.

Parris Hsu-cheng Chang's practices of scientific/policy Chineseness[6]

Parris Chang was born in 1936. His father was an appointed county leader during Japanese colonial rule. Now, in the 21st century, the official post of Xikou County leader is still provided by the same family at the same site. Chang is the head of the Xikou association in Taipei. His brother studied agriculture in Japan before returning for college at post-war National Taiwan University. Chang moved to Tainan to attend a better high school. Many of his close classmates at the time — such as Luo Fu-chuan, Hsu Shih-hsian and Trong Tsai — decades later became leading pro-Taiwan independence activists. Hsu encountered Sun Yat-sen thought while being a student in Japan. He recalls that Sun's nation building schemes fascinated him. The KMT executed some of Chang's relatives and neighbors after WWII and his family suffered during

---

[6] The following introduction is based entirely on the oral history at http://china-studies.taipei/comm2/InterviewT%20A.pdf and http://china-studies.taipei/comm2/InterviewT%20B.pdf (accessed on 25 June 2018).

the subsequent land reforms. Moreover, he was able to recollect various stories about the jailing of his acquaintances. Chang learned about politics early because important local political figures came to visit his father frequently. Unlike most Taiwanese families who feel alienated from politics, Chang decided to major in politics. He also passed the diplomats' qualification exams at the age of 20, making him the youngest student ever to do so.

Chang entered the field of China studies through Robert Scalapino, whom Chang was introduced to by a KMT connection because Chang's political position appeared to be anti-communist. However, he formally took China studies as his career path thanks to Doak Barnett. Methodologically, Chang's academic training made him a fervent comparatist. Consequently, he adhered to the method of comparative communism throughout his career. This made him a devoted practitioner of scientific Chineseness. His analyses have continuously been heavily indebted to Harold Laswell's frame of who gets what, when and how. Moreover, Barnett supported him to engage in China watching in Hong Kong. This allowed him to meet with Chinese of various backgrounds escaping from China. Chang was able to establish himself as an expert on Chinese factional politics, which facilitated his worldwide connections including in the former Soviet-bloc nations. Equally informative to scientific Chineseness was his conscious decision not to involve himself in activist campaigns for Taiwan independence. Despite several invitations by close acquaintances, he remained organizationally unconnected to them and contributed to the promotion of Taiwan independence in his own professional way.

Chang's comparative approach enables him to broaden the base of analysis to enlighten his audience from cases otherwise unthinkable. As a member of the first group of overseas scholars who met Zhou Enlai in 1972, for example, he was able to counter Zhou's call for reunification by referring to Switzerland as a model (of neutrality) for Taiwan's future, catching his host completely by surprise. Categorically, this model also differed significantly from other pro-Taiwan independence advocacies, which mainly argued for Taiwan to become part of the US or Japan. Tellingly, he was able to continue his field research in China in the subsequent years, collecting information about the Great Leap Forward and the Cultural Revolution. Another example is that in his testimony at the US Congress, he promoted the "Singapore model" for Taiwan, meaning a Chinese state that did not belong to China. With this he alluded to a softened position on Taiwan's owning of cultural or experiential Chineseness as well as the lack of legitimacy of the KMT to claim representation of China. His comparative scholarship on China has been easily acceptable to think tanks and government agencies in India, the US and Russia, among others.

Conclusion

Colonial relations left by Japan have not targeted Japan as a noticeable reference of contestation in post-colonial Taiwan. Instead, the binary of China and Taiwan as two distinctive political entities constitutes the primary source of division. Colonial relations ironically provide the intellectual resources to support the strategizing of various approaches to a practically undefinable China. We argue that this irony developed because the KMT substituted Chinese Civil War ideology for decolonization and in the process overlooked a significant portion of the Taiwanese whose identity had been constituted by Japanese colonial modernity. The KMT thus neither decolonized the indigenous population nor caused it to apologize for its participation in the Japanese war of invasion. This probably had to do with the fact that the exiled KMT regime once considered Japan's legacy inferior. However, as this chapter has shown, this same legacy has enabled others to own a sense of superiority toward a China often imagined in different ways.

Provided the overwhelming existence of colonial relationality in Taiwan, the post-colonial population can act upon it in various ways. The backgrounds of different people analyzed for this intellectual history project informed their intellectual agency for insistence, resistance and/or reconciliation. In this chapter, we only reflect on the more conspicuous ones among them — Hsu and Chen are relatively critical of Japan, while Shih Ming and Chang are more critical of China; Yeh is critical of both, and Shih Che-hsiung is critical of neither. This underscores that colonial relationality has an overarching impact upon the range of options and the types of identity available within a specific context and thus influences how a post-colonial population understands China, Chinese civilization and Chinese people.

Given that defining and understanding China, rather than Japan, has been the primary source of binary and cleavage in post-colonial Taiwan, we contrived six categories of post-Chineseness in order to complicate China and Chineseness so that writing on China can reveal the agency of writers themselves. However, these are intellectual categories. Actual human beings are able to combine, reconcile and cyclically retrieve them. The notion of post-Chineseness sheds new light on the tentative and strategic nature of the Taiwan–China binary. However, one can anticipate that a specific pattern of behavior ensues once one can trace the emergence of a particular kind of post-Chineseness — cultural Chineseness embraces, experiential Chineseness practices, Sinological Chineseness revises, ethnic Chineseness evades, civilizational Chineseness confronts and Scientific Chineseness objectifies Chineseness. We certainly believe that a more nuanced categorization is possible. In order to provide this, though, more sophisticated types of disposition and behavioral consequences first need to be empirically observed.

References

Aguiar, Marian. 2011. *Tracking Modernity: India's Railway and the Culture of Mobility*. Minneapolis: University of Minnesota Press.

Amae, Yoshihisa. 2011. Pro-colonial or Postcolonial? Appropriation of Japanese Colonial Heritage in Present-day Taiwan. *Journal of Current Chinese Affairs* 40 (1):19–62.

Barclay, George Watson. 2016. *Colonial Development and Population in Taiwan*. Princeton: Princeton University Press.

Chang, Lung-chih and Min-chin Kay Chiang. 2012. From Colonial Site to Cultural Heritage. *The Newsletter* 59: 28–29. Leiden: International Institute for Asian Studies.

Chen, Tsui-lien. 2002. Decolonization vs. Recolonization: The Debate over "T'ai-jen nu-hua" of 1946 in Taiwan. *Taiwan Historical Research* 9 (2): 145–201.

Cheng, Tun-jen. 1989. Democratizing the Quasi-Leninist Regime in Taiwan. *World Politics* 41 (4): 471–499.

Cheng, Yu-shek Joseph. 2017. *Mainlandization of Hong Kong*. Hong Kong: City University of Hong Kong Press.

Ching, Leo T. S. 2001. *Becoming Japanese: Colonial Taiwan and the Politics of Identity Formation*. Berkeley: University of California Press.

Cho, Young Chul. 2015. Colonialism and Imperialism in the Quest for a Universalist Korean-style International Relations Theory. *Cambridge Review of International Affairs* 28 (4): 680–700.

Chou, Wan-yao. 1991. The Kominka Movement [Ph.D. dissertation]. New Haven, CT: Yale University.

Chow, Rey. 2014. *Not Like a Native Speaker: On Languaging as a Postcolonial Experience*. New York: Columbia University Press.

Chu, Feng-yi. 2016. Diverse Facets in Identities and Party Affiliations of Native Taiwanese Elders. *Issues & Studies* 52 (3): 1–24.

Corcuff, Stephane. 2012. The Liminality of Taiwan a Case-study in Geopolitics. *Taiwan in Comparative Perspective* 4: 34–64.

Cummings, Bruce. 2004. Colonial Formation and Deformation: Korea, Taiwan and Vietnam. In Prasenjit Duara (Ed.). *Decolonization: Perspectives from Now and Then*. London: Routledge.

Golovachev, Valentin. 2018. Soviet and Italian Sinologists in China during the Cultural Revolution? *Rivista Degli Studi Orientali* N.S. 90 (Supplemento 2):117–132.

Harvey, Sean P. 2015. *Native Tongues: Colonialism and Race from Encounter to the Reservation*. Cambridge: Harvard University Press.

Heller, Monica and Bonnie McElhinny. 2017. *Language, Capitalism, Colonialism: Toward a Critical History*. Toronto: University of Toronto Press.

Henry, Todd A. 2016. *Assimilating Seoul: Japanese Rule and the Politics of Public Space in Colonial Korea, 1910–1945*. Berkeley: University of California Press.

Heylen, Ann and Scott Sommers (Eds.). 2010. *Becoming Taiwan: From Colonialism to Democracy*. Wiesbaden-Erbenheim: Harrassowitz Verlag.

Hou, Patrick Kuang-hao. 2018. A Mighty River Flowing Eastward: The Formation and Transformation of the Ethnic and National Identities of Situ Hua. *China Report* 54 (1):81–98.

Hui, D. Lai Hang. 2018. Geopolitics of Toponymic Inscription in Taiwan. *Geopolitics*. http://dx.doi.org/10.1080/14650045.2017.1413644 (accessed on 1 June 2018).

Jacobs, J. Bruce. 2013. Whither Taiwanization? The Colonization, Democratization and Taiwanization of Taiwan. *Japanese Journal of Political Science* 14 (4): 567–586.

Jacobs, J. Bruce. 2014. Taiwan's Colonial Experiences and the Development of Ethnic Identities. *Taiwan in Comparative Perspective* 5: 47–59.

Kovach, Margaret. 2010. *Indigenous Methodologies: Characteristics, Conversations, and Contexts*. Toronto: University of Toronto Press.

Lee, Cheng-pang. 2012. Shadow of the Colonial Power: Kominka and the Failure of the Temple Reorganization Campaign. *Studies on Asia Series IV* 2 (2): 120–144.

Lee, Chien-Shing, J.A. Mangan, Gwang Ok. 2018. Taiwan under Japanese Colonial Control: Sport as a Component of Cultural Conditioning, Political Domination, and Militaristic Imperialism. In J. A. Mangan et al. (Eds.). *Japanese Imperialism*. Berlin: Springer, pp. 217–242.

Lee, Shin-yi and Jui-sung Chen. 2014. A Great Citizen Is Still "Under-Construction": The Conflicting Self-Identity in Sayonara 1945. *Journal of Literature and Art Studies* 4 (10): 840–847.

Liao, Ping-hui and David Der-wei Wang (Eds.). 2006. *Taiwan under Japanese Colonial Rule, 1895–1945: History, Culture, Memory*. New York: Columbia University Press.

Lin, Man-houng. 2016. The "Greater East Asia Co-prosperity Sphere": A New Boundary for Taiwanese People and the Taiwanese Capital, 1940–1945 *Translocal Chinese: East Asian Perspectives* 10: 175–206, DOI:https://doi.org/10.1163/24522015-01002002.

Lin, Shaoyang. 2018. Hong Kong in the Midst of Colonialism, Collaborative and Critical Nationalism from 1925 to 1930. *China Report* 54 (1): 25–47.

Lo, Ming-cheng. 2002. *Doctors within Borders: Profession, Ethnicity, and Modernity in Colonial Taiwan*. Berkeley: University of California Press.

Lomová, Olga and Anna Zádrapová. 2016. "The Song of Ancient China": The Myth of "The Other" Appropriated by an Emerging Sinology. In C. Shih (Ed.). *Sinology in Post-Communist States*. Hong Kong: Chinese University Press, pp. 189–211.

Louzon, Victor. 2017. From Japanese Soldiers to Chinese Rebels. *Journal of Asian Studies*. https://doi.org/10.1017/S0021911817001279 (accessed on 20 February 2018).

Lynch, Daniel C. 2004. Taiwan's Self-conscious Nation-Building Project. *Asian Survey* 44 (4): 513–533.

Morris, Andrew D. and Christopher Gerteis (Eds.). 2017. *Japanese Taiwan: Colonial Rule and Its Contested Legacy*. London: Bloomsbury Academic.

Peng, Huan-Sheng and Jo-Ying Chu. 2017. Japan's Colonial Policies — From National Assimilation to the Kominka Movement. *Paedagogica Historica* 53 (4): 441–459.

Raychaudhuri, Anindya. 2018. *Homemaking: Radical Nostalgia and the Construction of a South Asian Diaspora*. Lanham: Rowman & Littlefield.

Sealey, Kris. 2018. Resisting the Logic of Ambivalence: Bad Faith as Subversive, Anticolonial Practice. *Hypatia*. https://doi.org/10.1111/hypa.12404.

Shih, Chih-yu. 2014. China, China Scholarship, and China Scholars in Postcolonial Taiwan. *China: An International Journal* 12 (1): 1–21.

Shih, Chih-yu. 2007. *Democracy Made in Taiwan*. Lanham: Lexington.

Shih, Shu-mei. 2016. Theory in a Relational World. *Comparative Literature Studies* 53 (4): 722–746.

Shin, Gi-Wook and Michael Robinson (Eds.) 1999. *Colonial Modernity in Korea*. Cambridge: Harvard University Asia Center.

Smith, Linda Tuhiwai. 2012. *Decolonizing Methodologies*. London: Zed Books.

Takeshi, Komagome. 2006. Colonial Modernity for an Elite Taiwanese, Lim Bo-seng. In Ping-hui Liao and David Der-wei Wang (Eds.). *Taiwan Under Japanese Colonial Rule 1895–1945*. New York: Columbia University Press, pp. 141–159.

Tanaka, Stefan. 1995. *Japan's Orient*. Berkeley: University of California Press.

Thiele, Wolfgang Gerhard. 2017. Decolonization and the Question of Exclusion in Taiwanese Nationalism Since 1945, *Global Histories* 3 (1): 62–84.

Toshio, Matsumura. 2018. Indonesian Intellectuals' Experiences and China. In C. Shih, P. Manomaivibool and R. Marwah (Eds.) *China Studies in South and Southeast Asia*. Singapore: World Scientific, pp. 65–89.

Tsai, Hui-yu Caroline. 2009. *Taiwan in Japan's Empire-Building*. Oxon: Routledge.

Wang, Sumei. 2009. Taiwanese Baseball: A Story of Entangled Colonialism, Class, Ethnicity, and Nationalism. *Journal of Sport and Social Issues* 33 (4): 355–372.

Wilson, Shawn. 2009. *Research Is Ceremony: Indigenous Research Methods.* Black Point, NS, Canada: Fernwood Publishing Co., Ltd.

Wong, Heung Wah and Hoi Yan Yau. 2013. What Does It Mean by "Being Colonized"? Reflections on the Japanese Colonial Policies in Taiwan. *Journal of Group Dynamics* 30: 342–360.

Chapter 11
The Imaginary of China: Sameness and Otherness from the Perspective of Macau

Cátia Miriam Costa

Centre for International Studies,
Instituto Universitário de Lisboa (ISCTE-IUL),
Lisboa, Portugal

Introduction

Macau embodies two strong cultural and social legacies, the Chinese and the Portuguese. Macau is the product of a negotiated settlement, but it also became a place for other traders from the Portuguese commercial network in the Far East, and afterwards the place where Europeans and North Americans remained until they were authorized to go inland. It has been one of the most internationalized territories in the world for over 500 years.

Well before the creation of the colony of Hong Kong, Macau was a place of co-existence, exchange convergence and newness. Literature and the periodical press had an important role in the circulation of ideas about China, and the colony itself. The publication of fiction, opinion, news, and religious texts in different languages (Chinese, Portuguese and English) characterise the international environment of Macau. This evidence also brings to light the specificity of Macau in the region and within the context of Portuguese colonialism.

The territory had, from the beginning, a particularly characteristic political administration, resulting in a very specific solution. Sovereignty tended to be shared, instead of deploying a straight line, one-directional, top-down colonial template. Instances of this fluid governance model were apparent in the governance of the sea and the coast or in the transit of the Chinese population through Macau, for work or other economic activities. This political coexistence gave rise to a social and cultural interactive coexistence and, at the same time, it occasioned a "communicating hybridity" characterized by syncretism and generative interaction, for which the *Macanese* community is the most representative example.

It was from this coexistence and syncretism that a creative intellectual atmosphere emerged, allowing for the encounter and crossing of diverse perspectives not only on China but on the territory. Starting from the historical perspective, this chapter intends to retrace the convergence and diversity of an imaginary China and Chinese from an intellectual perspective. It will consider the ways in which China and the Chinese were represented in literature and periodical press, from the end of the 19th century to the 1930s. Sameness and otherness coexisted and sometimes mingled, embodying the existing diversity, and becoming central to Macau's character.

"I am afraid of falling in love with it"

This quote is from an unknown author referring to China, and cited by Jaime do Inso, a Portuguese Navy Commander who lived in Macau and wrote about China for Portuguese readers. When writing the preface to Jaime Inso's book *Visões da China* (Visions of China), in April 1927, in Tokushima, Wenscelau de Moraes, a much-respected Portuguese writer who lived for long in China and in Japan, refers to this statement as admirable (Moraes 2006). Wenscelau de Moraes recognizes how difficult it is for the Portuguese public to understand and judge a country like China. Despite the historical relation with China and the possession of Macau, Portuguese readers saw Chinese culture, society, and language as exotic and China was imagined as full of exotic stories.

This image was transmitted to Portuguese readers by Portuguese intellectuals and journalists who lived in Macau. Paradoxically, from a historical perspective, Portugal always played an important role in the circulation of knowledge between the centre of political and economic power and the peripheries of it (Bennett 2015). While Macau was loosing importance in international trade, the East became increasingly remote. The participation in international conferences, mainly those concerning eastern studies, represented Portuguese intellectuals' effort to take part in events where scientific and cultural sociability happened (Pinto 2017).

China and Chinese studies were something out of reach for the common Portuguese. For this reason, Macau became the main place where the Portuguese focused their knowledge about China. Macau was a meeting point for business, knowledge and communication between two very distinct cultures and societies. The choice of Macau as the centre for Chinese studies for the Portuguese is easy to understand, since there was an awareness that Oriental and Chinese studies were a practical scientific discipline (Nepomuceno 2017). For Portuguese readers in Portugal, Orientalism overlapped with Chinese studies (it seems this perspective also occurred in China, see Shih 2003). The perception of the exotic was more attractive than the study of reality. The imaginary picture of China was that captured by metropolitan readers interested in Chinese culture and knowledge. Macau, being the centre of production of this imaginary view, was also the place to develop Chinese studies. The creation of the Repartição do Expediente Sínico, in November 1885, boosts the translation and teaching of Chinese in Macau. Through this decision, Chinese Studies, mostly based in translation work and cultural, social and political knowledge became separate from the Procuratura de Negócios Sínicos (Administration for Chinese Business), a public administration division focused on business between Portugal and China. Chinese language knowledge and translation were the most important basis for Chinese studies through the centuries (Uberoi 2018), and the Portuguese administration of Macau followed this trend.

While developing Chinese studies through Macanese eyes, the Portuguese created a distance between them and the object of study. A more careful reader can find an invisible tension between otherness and sameness, and between support and criticism of the Portuguese administration's actions in Macau. Although the Macanese seemed to need to confirm their otherness in relation to China, they also understood and explained China to others. They assumed the Chinese community in Macau as an essential part of the specificity of Macau. Nevertheless, being the other in relation to China, were they the same as Portuguese? They identified as part of the Portuguese Empire, always recognizing their role as mediators, as being in the middle, not Portuguese. The approval and rejection of colonial regimes by individuals was part of the colonial context and somehow a result of it. Like the Macanese, they are something identified in very different colonial and imperial frameworks (Uberoi 2018). Macanese were at the same time Portuguese citizens and individuals under a colonial regime. This was part of their identity and intellectual production. Some authors defend that Macanese resulted from a transculturation process in which they had to look for understanding with the ethnic exogroup in Macau (the Chinese community). They had to simultaneously promote a rewarding relationship with the local Portuguese elites, take part in local administration, and confirm their difference toward other Chinese people (Romana 2014). In this way, for Macanese people, China represented concurrently self and alterity. China was attractive due to Chinese heritage leadership. At the same time, China repelled because they did not want to have in Macau a cultural and social reproduction of China, or lose their place as mediators between Portugal and China.

Macau, the Place to Communicate Hybridity

Since the start (1557), the Portuguese administration of Macau needed to employ a group of good translators and interpreters. The main goal was the creation of a group of specialized individuals who could mediate the Portuguese and Chinese languages, and facilitate the mutual understanding of Portuguese and Chinese cultures and bureaucracies (Aguiar 2002). The first individuals tasked with this were the missionaries. Working to spread Christianity, they learned foreign languages, including Chinese. The missionaries translated Christian religious books into Chinese. At the same time, they became interested in Chinese literature and philosophy, translating them from Chinese to Latin or other European languages. From Macau, the missionaries ensured that Chinese philosophy and literature were known in Europe. Portuguese maritime connections aided in this endeavor. This was also part of Macau's role mediating between Chinese and European cultures. There was constant interaction between Portuguese and European languages and cultures with the Chinese. However, it was only in the 19th century that a centre for translation was created in Macau. Some European countries formed centres for sinology, integrating Chinese scholars who perfected the style in Chinese languages (Paiva 2008). Nonetheless, the importance of Macau in the relations between Europe and China continued until the British settlement in Hong Kong. Macau maintained its role in Portuguese and Chinese official relationships.

The territory represented the main centre for knowledge exchange, and circulation, which explains the existence of an early printed press in three languages — Portuguese, English, and Chinese. The enduring publication in different languages continues to be one of the most interesting traditions for such a small territory. Text production and reception in different languages was important in the development of the local public sphere. Having significant production in separated collections and printed media and using different languages, suggests the existence of different publics, coexisting in the same place and time. Due to the continued publication in different languages Macau fostered the interactions between diverse discourses and publics, a constant barrage of international communication contexts existed. Although produced in each language for a specific public, the emerging narratives impacted the whole island, through translation and the engagement of multilingual individuals. Macau's role mediating trade and business, and diplomacy and culture, further extended to the flow of separate narratives. Macau attracted people from different origins, serving as a place to rest, or wait for permission to travel to China. This atmosphere made Macau one of the most cosmopolitan places in the region, right from the start of the Portuguese settlement. It was also the most significant weakness of Macau. In order to survive, the territory depended on its role as mediator between China and the Western world. Macau was unable to support itself independently. Food came from China, and income through trade between Western countries and China. Its fragile position made it dependent upon the goodwill of Guangdong Mandarins for the development and extension of relationships between Macau and China. This created a volatile economic and social context, making Macau entirely dependent on its ties with China. Consequently, the Portuguese administration had to adapt to a Chinese-centred Empire (Flores 1993).

The continued dependence was clear to the Portuguese since the start of Macau's occupation. The Portuguese administration regulated the first translator position in 1627, 70 years after the foundation of the Portuguese settlement. The first translators of Macau City were civilians of Chinese origin. They were required to be Christian, and there was a preference for married men. The translators and interpreters were responsible for political and administrative communication, bureaucracy and for explaining to the Portuguese administration the Chinese Empire's traditional approach to politics and business. Chinese authorities objected to Chinese persons' loyalty to individuals to foreigners, like the Portuguese. Chinese authorities referred to them as being "little Portuguese." They suggested that there was a risk of them entering the Chinese mainland (Paiva 2008). The Portuguese relied on these men, calling them "línguas" or "jurubaças," and considered them the city's eyes and ears. The parallel existence of two worlds, separated by language, was one of the main concerns of the Portuguese Administration of Macau. In spite of this, it was only in 1797 that the Portuguese Empire required that the sons of Macau's residents learn Chinese. This must be understood as an acknowledgment of dependence of the colony on the good relations with the Chinese Empire. Although this legislation was important, its real impact on the society of the day is difficult to ascertain. It is difficult to judge in the present whether the recruitment of translators and administrative staff benefited from a change in legislation, or even if it promoted local businesses.

As the connections between Portugal and China increased in complexity, the Portuguese Administration decided to create the first official organization of translators and interpreters in 1865. It had a very small structure but assured the communication between Portugal and China, and between the Portuguese and the Chinese communities in Macau. In 1881, the Procuratura de Negócios Chineses integrated this small division. The number of translators increased. The department remained small, mainly devoted to administrative, judiciary and business affairs. Four years later, and given the importance of translation work, the Portuguese Administration founded the Repartição de Expediente Sínico. This new section specialized in translating and interpreting in Portuguese and Chinese. A full translator needed to know written and spoken Portuguese, Mandarin, and Cantonese, as well as English and French.

By the late 19th century, the recruitment of these translators for the court of Hong Kong or to help French businessmen was still common. The Expediente Sínico de Macau was led by some of the most illustrious sons of the soil, of Macanese origin. Carlos Augusto Rocha d'Assumpção was one of the Macanese who was a "Chief" of the Repartição. He authored the first book with a method for Portuguese speakers to learn Chinese in 1893. Although the presence of Macanese was very important in the Expediente Sínico, other distinct Portuguese sinologists headed the institution. One of the most recognized is Manuel da Silva Mendes, a Portuguese sinologist who became an important Chinese art collector. Most of these individuals knew Chinese language, and culture, but were also the main representatives of Chinese literature and philosophy among the Portuguese community of Macau. A key aspect to consider is the fact Portuguese readers in the metropole knew nothing about the Expediente Sínico's work, nor did they know of the intellectual production of the Macanese and Portuguese leading this public section. Their work and thoughts about Chinese culture stayed in Macau.

Other important organizations from civil society also worked on translation. The most distinguished was the Associação Promotora da Instrução dos Macaenses (Association for the Promotion and Instruction of the Macanese). This Association published manuals and grammar books to learn Chinese. It also translated, and adapted, manuals from Chinese. Furthermore, they were responsible for bringing to Macau the first Chinese from Peking who taught Mandarin at a Macanese public school. These initiatives were very significant as they helped local people prepare for public administration jobs, in which they worked in middle management or as translators. The name of the association suggests the association of Chinese language and culture with the local community, and not the Portuguese community in general, or the Chinese community of Macau. They offered education for Portuguese speakers to learn or perfect Chinese. Classes of Portuguese for the Chinese community were not part of their mission. The situation is similar with the Expediente Sínico. The legal decree creating this public section of Portuguese Administration refers to the Expediente Sínico in Macau, meaning that no other institution in the Portuguese empire would have a similar activity.

As a result, Portuguese sinology converged in Macau, being almost unknown in the metropole. In Portugal, the readers cultivated the imaginary, preferring travel literature, short essays written by Portuguese living in Macau, or novels and poetry written by Portuguese about the Far East. One of the main reasons for this lack of interest from Portuguese readers might be the fact the books edited in Macau were not distributed in Portugal or the Portuguese colonial empire. So, for a Macanese author, the opportunities for writing to the Portuguese readers, were, in general, scarce. A Macanese author had to publish in the local periodical press or with local publishers. Macau was a small territory, with a limited market for press and publishers, meaning that the periodical press constituted one of the main avenues for the sons of the soil to publish. So, Macau and China remained exoticized in Portuguese minds. This was further cultivated by Portuguese authors who wrote about China in Portugal. Macau had the highest concentration of the most important knowledge about China in the Portuguese language, but its dissemination was confined to the territory. Sharing Portuguese language was not enough to create a common public sphere about China and Chinese culture within the Portuguese Colonial Empire. The only newspapers and books circulating resulted from personal connections, and this helped circulate them at a minimum level and improve the intellectual production in the Portuguese language.

The fact that Macau was a centre for international communication contributed to its cosmopolitanism, but also created distinctive public spheres, according to the diverse printed titles published in the territory. Macau progressively lost international importance due to the rising relevance of Hong Kong as a British colony. However, Macau still maintained its reputation for leisure: a place with a special atmosphere, a meeting place between East and West. Portuguese and Chinese were the main spoken and written languages in the territory, yet the English language was also used. In order to make sense of what was considered otherness and sameness, it is important to carefully understand who produced the narratives, for whom it was produced and how it was received. Lotman's semiotic theory, introducing the concept of semiosphere, is adapted to the case we are studying (Lotman 1981). He explores the possibility of coexistence of different semiospheres in the same society and, at the same time, which would explain the interaction of different communities, social classes or ethnic groups, who could communicate among themselves but who also had different identity codes. In the case of Macau, we can say that there were different semiospheres coexisting at the same time and representing different groups: the Portuguese, the Macanese, the Chinese and the foreigners. The Portuguese and Chinese did not communicate directly, but through Macanese mediation became connected.

But Macanese had their own semiosphere, based on their Creole, the Patois, and their traditions (like music or gastronomy), and simultaneously they were able to participate in Chinese and Portuguese society because they knew the languages and cultures.

The semiotic approach can help us understand the complexity and the need for the Macanese to negotiate their identity with the representatives of colonial administration and with the Chinese community. This negotiation was permanent and meant that the key to mediating relations between the Portuguese and Chinese was the Macanese community. This explains why the Repartição do Expediente Sínico in Macau was mainly directed by Macanese intellectuals and why sinology in Portugal depended on the Macanese and on the Portuguese who felt in love with China or Japan. In fact, Portuguese semiosphere at the national level (in Portugal) and transnational level (Colonial Empire) was never engaged in the reception of knowledge about China or the Far East. The evidence is the scarce commitment of Portuguese intellectuals with oriental cultures or involvement in international events and the few focused on the study of these languages and cultures. The Macanese as cultural and linguistic translators and interpreters of China made this work for the Portuguese semiosphere, and Goans did the same for India. In Portugal, Asian or Chinese studies never had an academic tradition nor was a school of thought created, despite the Portuguese being the first to disseminate knowledge about China in Europe.

As mentioned before, Macau was part of the Portuguese Empire but it was also a territory centred on the Chinese Empire. The dependence from China for all the internal decisions in Macau had some direct consequences. The permanent negotiation between Portuguese and Chinese and the growing of an important Chinese community in the territory were determinant to its maintenance. The Chinese community held their own business, and through charity founded their own schools, for education in Chinese language and culture. So, the typical colonial relationship, based on the undisputed supremacy of the colonizer, is not a reality in Macau. Portuguese power and colonial administration continuously navigated the balance of Chinese and Portuguese in the territory, and of the common interests of the Portuguese and Chinese authorities. By the end of the 19th century, the urban space continuously linked the Christian city and the Chinese City. Ferreira do Amaral, the Portuguese governor of Macau (1846–1849), ordered the destruction of the wall separating both communities. The streets became connected, and people could go from the Portuguese city to the Chinese city without any control. This changed the relations between both communities. People were closer and had to cooperate inside the same public space. Business between both communities blossomed. Portuguese authorities recognized the most important Chinese individuals, such as businessman or intellectuals, who the Macanese government invited for official celebrations. This new situation gave Macau its cosmopolitanism back, allowing for new cultural projects. Macau was once more the place where different cultures met. This hybridity promoted by on-going cultural exchange and contact was one of its characteristics.

How can we describe Macau by its hybridity, and then explain that there were different semiospheres which supported diverse public spheres? It seems a contradiction, but it is not. Semiospheres are usually not isolated, and the same individual can participate in more than one semiosphere, which was typically the case of the Macanese individuals. The role of the Macanese as mediators was associated with the Portuguese administration's need to have good connections with Chinese authorities and businessman, as well as with international traders, and increased the communication in different languages. The concentration of the very few Portuguese sinologists in Macau also contributed to this situation. We can even identify a sort of hybridity based on cross-readings through translations, yet based on the consciousness of identity and otherness. The Macanese community, themselves biologically mixed (Portuguese, Chinese and other peoples for Southeast Asia) were the group who generally assured and communicated this hybridity. As a result of this circumstance, Macau was also a place for progressive Chinese ideas. Intellectuals from Guangdong visited Macau several times and even had family relations within the territory. Anarchists, Nationalists and Republicans arrived at the territory and developed contacts with Macanese and the few Portuguese intellectuals living in Macau. Some recent studies have revealed that the heads of the Repartição Expediente Sínico de Macau knew many Chinese intellectuals, most of whom were involved in these new progressive ideas. One of these examples is Manuel da Silva Mendes (Botas 2017).

Echo Macaense is an example of the convergence between the communities existing in Macau. The newspaper created in 1893 and directed by a Macanese, Francisco Hermenegildo Fernandes, was one of the projects brought up by the Macanese and Chinese community, also involving some individuals from the Portuguese community. *Echo Macaense* was the first bilingual newspaper, in the Portuguese and Chinese languages. Until the end of the colonial period, this project remained the sole bilingual newspaper. The Macanese director and founder of the *Echo Macaense* was a journalist and a translator who frequently went to Hong Kong to work. In one of these voyages, it is said he met Sun Yat-sen during a court session where Fernandes was serving as translator. The context was the judicial hearing of Sun Yat-sen because of the port workers strike. The Chinese doctor and politician visited Macau frequently, and developed contacts there. Francisco Hermenegildo Fernandes turned into one of these contacts, and Sun Yat-sen joined the newspaper's project. When beginning the analysis of this newspaper, my main idea was that this project resulted from the will to bring Portuguese and Chinese communities together. But after the development of common research with a Chinese colleague, Agnes Lam, studying the Chinese part of the newspaper, and a careful content analysis followed by a discourse analysis of the Portuguese part, my conclusion was that the Portuguese edition and the Chinese edition were completely different. Each edition had its own news and could reach the public separately, as it did from the 21st February until the end of the newspaper in 1899.

In the first editions in Portuguese, the *Echo Macanese* had specific sections dedicated to the translation of articles from the

Chinese version. We took some examples from the newspapers to demonstrate our argument. One of the most relevant is in the third edition of the newspaper, dated from 1st August 1893. The article is the translation of Dr. Sun's letter to Chiang-keng-keng, a former Ambassador of China in the United States, and now living in Heang-shan, the homeland of both. This letter was publicly released, and defended public policies for education, economy and the fight against opium consumption in the Chinese territory. In the same edition of *Echo Macaense*, a Portuguese article was partially translated into Chinese. The article referred to the need for Portuguese and Chinese communities to work together in order to improve the government of the city. In the fourth edition, the main article was about the silting of Macau's harbor. In its sixth issue, dated 22nd August 1893, in the Chinese section there's only one article about the floods in North China with the note: (apart from this article) "the section comes with other news, but there is nothing of particular interest that deserves to be translated for our Portuguese readers." This means that the newspaper's editors decided whether the news should or should not be translated. This is evidence of the existence of different spheres and semiospheres reading the same newspaper, and someone (in this case the newspaper) taking the role of mediator. In its seventh edition, the Chinese Section highlights Chinese emigration to Brazil. In the tenth issue, from 19th September 1893, the Chinese section states: "This section comes full of local and foreign news." We could give further examples, but we think this little sample is clear enough for us to understand the complexity of translation and of interesting readers from different semiospheres in the same topic. Despite the effort to continue the project, the *Echo Macaense* announced the separation of the Portuguese and the Chinese editions on 21st February 1894. The bilingual edition had only survived for seven months. For then on, each section became a separate newspaper, printed in the same typography, the one owned by the *Echo Macaense*. The separation was never explained to the readers, but the fact of sharing the same typography seems to show that there were no conflicts within the direction of both sections.

One important aspect that must be highlighted is that both editions, in Portuguese and in Chinese, of the *Echo Macanese* reflected the same ideological orientations. Republican and progressive ideas, defending education, public health and citizen's participation in the political system, inspired both editions. The joint publication allowed for the testing of the reception of a newspaper in Chinese. It also guaranteed the availability of a typography available for the edition. The costs of an edition might have been lower with joint production. However, there is no information on the economics of such a project. For this kind of project, it is necessary to see beyond a simple periodical press business.

Another significant aspect is that the *Echo Macaense* contributed to the public debate on the Macanese role in society. In issue 12 of the newspaper, dated 4th October 1893, the need for Macanese individuals to know various languages is emphasized. They should be able to communicate with different communities, if they want to continue to live in the Far East and achieve a comfortable life. In this case, the newspaper represented the local community as an intermediary who needed to contact, and participate in different semiospheres. But still, the Macanese had to choose between being a typical Chinese, stay a Macanese or become into a metropolitan Portuguese. And sometimes they just chose to be all three.

From Macau to Portugal: Different Ways of Reading China

The reception of China was particularly different in Portugal (metropole) or in Macau. The production of discourse was also different from one place to the other. In Portugal, people read travel literature, poetry and novels that were written based on the author's experience. Nevertheless, there was no interest in replacing the imaginary with some practical knowledge. The discourse production about China was based on the writings of Portuguese authors, among them writers, poets or intellectuals who had lived in China. The Portuguese printing houses knew the literary tastes of their readers, offering them the kinds of books they would buy and read. It is curious how rare were translations from Chinese literature or philosophy for the Portuguese market. If someone wanted to study these areas of knowledge, they should look for French or English translations from the Chinese, or travel to Macau where they might be able to find something. Once again, it was introduced as a new kind of mediation, now through a foreign language. Unlike Portugal, in Macau, there was a practical interest in Chinese culture and language, followed by an aesthetic attraction toward Chinese philosophy and literature.

In this research, we analyzed the contents and discourses of different authors, paying attention to the biography of the writer that might constrain the production of the text and to the conditions of reception of the text. We chose texts published between 1898 and 1941, avoiding the more studied authors. Within these authors, there are two Portuguese and one Macanese, and the texts are published in Portugal, Macau, Shanghai and Hong Kong. Our main objective was to have some diversity in the texts sample and to exemplify the diversity according to who was writing and where it was being published. The chosen authors are Jaime do Inso (1880–1967), J. Heliodoro Callado Crespo (1861–1921) and C. A. Montalto de Jesus (1863–1927).

Jaime do Inso was a Portuguese Navy Officer who lived in Macau and traveled in China and Japan. The author published several books regarding Macau and China as a topic (Pereira 2015). He also published under an author edition in Portugal, the novel *A Caminho do Oriente* ("In the way to East") which received the prize for Colonial Literature. But his literary interest was diversified and included the translation of the novel *Mr. Wu*, published in 1918, in New York, which became a Hollywood film in 1927, and a Portuguese translation in 1936. He collaborated with newspapers in Lisbon and Macau. Jaime do Inso felt seduced by China, and it is his inability to totally understand Chinese culture that makes him describe it as exotic or mystic. After leaving China, Jaime do Inso creates, and literally describes what he calls "My Chinese room," demonstrating his love for Chinese culture and the need to maintain this connection even after living in Lisbon. The author wrote most of his texts in Macau or China, and the writing of the texts was much previous to its publishing in Portugal. In his book, *Visões da China* ("Visions of China"), published in 1933, the date of the texts varies between 1924 and 1932. In his writings, he refers to the ignorance of most Portuguese about Macau, including people working in public administration, who do not know that Macau is in China and not in India (Inso 1933).

He wrote about China and Macau, describing the latter as a part and a viewpoint to China (Inso 1941). In his writings about Macau, it is clear the opposition the author creates between the Christian and Portuguese city and the Chinese city, closer to the sea (Inso 1941). The Portuguese city, on higher ground, is described as sleepy and in decline after the loss of most of the important trade to Hong Kong, and does not capture the attention of Inso. By contrast, the Chinese city, defined as full of life with permanent movement, seduces the author for a cultural voyage through its streets and shops. While walking along the streets, the author describes what he observes and takes the opportunity to introduce a cultural or social topic for each description. When he sees a temple, he describes Chinese religions. While observing a dead man in his house, he explains the rituals connected with death in the Chinese culture. The author uses the description of the landscape to inform the reader about the cultural or social significance of the element observed. In this way, the reader travels with the author, who shares his experience directly with him. Similarly, the reader is introduced to the turbulence associated with the modernization of China, the way it impacted literary production, and how the West benefited from this to get informed about Chinese traditions. When arriving at the theatre, the author describes the building, but also the specificity of the Chinese performance, calling the readers' attention to the difference between that and a European theatre. Inso also uses some events to reveal Chinese culture, like the Chinese New Year, the popular Chinese celebration that he most describes. Macau's descriptions include demographic information, but again focused on the

Macanese and Chinese communities. Inso also retrieves the idea of the Macanese community lacking employment opportunities and that local public policy should design a solution. It is interesting how Inso agrees with the Macanese newspaper *Echo Macaense* published more than 40 years before his writings, which evidences that the Macanese community situation had not progressed in a positive way.

Inso was focused on Macau and China, and the Portuguese community of Macau almost disappeared from his texts. When he addresses the Portuguese community, it is with the aim of reinforcing the idea of friendship between the Portuguese and Chinese, pointing out the difference between the Portuguese and the other Europeans while regarding the Chinese, their culture and political problems (Inso 1929, Inso 1933). On the other hand, Inso also highlights the fact that the Chinese looked to the Portuguese in a different way from the other Europeans, and proved it quoting an influent communist from South China: "all the foreigners must get out of China, but the Portuguese will be the last to go." It is interesting to keep in mind that in 1999, the Portuguese were the last foreigners to leave, which seems to correspond to this idea of friendship between the Portuguese and the Chinese that Inso had. The aim of reinforcing the good relations between Portugal and China is also present in the way the author describes the relations between the Chinese businessmen and the Portuguese administration. Taking the example of Lu-Lim-Ioc, a very important Chinese businessman who passed away during the period Inso lived in Macau, he describes his funerary ceremonies, and the action of this Chinese from Macau in the benefit of the city. Lu-Lim-Ioc is still remembered today as the garden he created is public, and remains in the style it had during its founder's life. It is also during the ceremonies of the burying of Lu-Lim-Ioc in Guangdong that Inso witnesses the taking of Guangzhou by the Communist troops in 1928. Despite heavy combat, Inso finds ways to extol local culture and to view the Chinese as non-violent people, saying that Chinese were better traders than warriors. While watching the fighting from Shamine, he feels sorry for the Chinese, and suggests

Guangzhou is changing too fast, not only on the streets but also in terms of people's behaviors. When leaving the city in a turbulent ambience, he thanks the unknown Chinese man who saved his life, recognizing in him the good characteristics Chinese had. He was also critical about the Western role in all the problems China was facing, accusing these countries, and their peoples, of laughing at what was happening in the country and despising the Chinese. In order to strengthen this statement, he says the Portuguese were not the "San-Kuai" (the Western devils).

Inso returns to Portugal, but he goes on writing for Macanese newspapers, and maintains his publishing activity on Macau in the following years. The author tries to get Portuguese readers' attention to subjects concerning Macau and China, but it is obvious that the readers too have a preference for travel literature, fiction and some newspaper articles concerning Portuguese external policy. Nevertheless, Inso always underlines the complexity of Chinese culture, emphasizing the role of translators, and the difficulty of translating the semiosphere and not only the words. If we look at Inso's literary production, we can find he understood much more than he thought about Chinese culture, even when he uses an orientalist discourse to underscore Chinese specificities. If comparing Inso with the following author, who was also of a military bent, one can find many differences between the way both understand the Chinese semiosphere.

J. Heliodoro Callado Crespo was one of the officers writing about Macau and China, and publishing the same in Lisbon. The author published *Cousas da China* ("Things of China") in 1898, referring to his book as non-literary or scientific, but as the gathering of some notes about China. Crespo notes that he will accept as true the dates and facts as told by the Chinese who informed him and as found in Chinese books he could access. This statement by itself shows us the perception the author has. He accepts the facts and dates regardless of veracity, meaning he does not trust his sources or that the information he had access to does not distinguish reality from fiction. If we compare this approach to other perspectives on colonial semiospheres, we will confirm that the colonized are generally described as less rational than the colonizer. As for the errors the book might have, the author recognizes that is the task of writers to correct the errors of the previous ones. Again, the author seems to only take into consideration the intellectual product created on his semiosphere or a similar one as sources of knowledge. His description of Guangdong only characterizes the streets and shops, concluding that so many pieces of information and movement tires the eyes of the observer. While Inso saw in this movement and streets a proof of life and dynamism, Crespo saw a perpetual exhausting movement. The author also describes Shiamen and how Europeans lived there, considering it monotonous. The "floating city," disappearing in the period Inso visited Guangzhou, existed, and Crespo visited it. Crespo saw it as a place where everyone could go, and have tea or sleep. He also mentions the very interesting habit of the intellectuals giving speeches in these places, also used by musicians, actors and singers. Where Inso observed beauty and exotism, Crespo witnessed a decadent and obscure culture. Only in one thing did they share the same opinion: Macau depended on China to survive, and the relation between the Portuguese authorities and The Mandarins of Guangdong was a determinant factor.

Besides *Cousas da China*, Crespo published another book in Lisbon, also about China. The title was *A China em 1900* ("China in 1900"), and the author writes about the contemporaneous situation in the country, including the revolts and the relations between China and Western countries (Crespo, 1901). Crespo justifies the interest of this book with the fact of Portugal holding a colony in China. The author also declares the way he got the pieces of information and how they are useful and significant to serve Portuguese Administration interests. Curiously, he does not publish the book in Macau, and prefers the metropole where the high colonial policies were drawn. In this work, he tries to inform the reader about some Chinese history, the secret societies, or the big revolutions. The author demonstrates that he studied several facts from the political point of view, but never got interested in understanding Chinese political culture, or entering the Chinese semiosphere. Otherness, not by exotism/Orientalism, but by exception is always present in his writings. Crespo was not seduced by China, neither did he feel that the Chinese culture was too complex for him. In his perspective, China represented the other, by opposition to the "us," which never could be merged. Maybe this is the reason why Crespo chose to write about China, having little detail on Macau. The knowledge he produced is practical, but focused on the exterior perspective of China and never admitting the role of Macanese as translators/mediators or a perspective where the Portuguese and the Chinese had to mingle. It is possible that Crespo did not know so much about the Macanese intellectual production, which is difficult in such a small territory. But it is also possible that he decided to erase Macanese intellectual contributions from his books, similar to the ones form the next author, Montalto de Jesus.

Carlos Augusto Montalto de Jesus was a Macanese born in Hong Kong, who lived in Shanghai, Portugal and Hong Kong. He was a fellow of the Geographical Society of Lisbon and a member of the China Branch of the Royal Asiatic Society, which shows his recognition as an intellectual interested in Asian topics. In 1902, Montalto de Jesus published the book *Historic Macao*, in Hong Kong, with the help of a commercial printing house. This is the first book on the complete history of Macau published by a Macanese or Portuguese. The decision to publish it in Hong Kong may be due to the fact Montalto de Jesus was living and working there and had good relations at the administrative and political level, as well as in the intellectual arena. The author read Portuguese and Chinese sources and, for the first time, took both narratives to look for the truth about the settlement and maintenance of the Portuguese in Macau. His work gathers information about the main previous works on Macau, including sources in English, alongside Portuguese and Chinese works. The author explains the decline of Macau, and how other nations took and surpassed the role Portugal had in China through Macau. At the same time, he presents the Macanese community to the reader as a "mixed but legitimate and Christian race being a characteristic feature of

Portuguese colonisation" (Jesus 1902). In this way, the author recognized some specificity of the Portuguese colonizer and distinguished the Macanese ethnic group from the Portuguese and the Chinese. A significant part of the book concerns the decay of Macau, and subsequently of the Macanese community. The author expresses his apprehension for the fact that the "international rivalry in colonial expansion" might compromise the future of Portugal as a colonizer, and the future of Macau as a Portuguese colony in a Chinese context. Montalto de Jesus defends a proactive attitude from the Portuguese authorities, as well as from the Macanese, in order to maintain the colony as a place with its own identity. The Macanese community in Macau and out of the territory received the book with enthusiasm. Even the Portuguese administration was interested in it.

In 1909, Montalto de Jesus published the book *Historic Shanghai*, edited by a local printing house (Montalto Jesus 1909). The book is based on the historical dynamics of a city/territory, and, like in *Historic Macau*, it studies the influence of the foreign communities and the role of the extra-territorial municipalities. Although the Shanghai administration model was different from the one in Macau or Hong Kong, the author explains the impact the internationalization of the city had on its economic activities and political relations. Once again, the book was well accepted, and it had some favorable impact in the Macanese community around the world. Following the success of these books, Montalto de Jesus decided to publish an updated version of *Historic Macau* as a joint edition with collaboration between the Salesian Printing Press and the Tipografia Mercantil (Montalto Jesus 1999). The editors released the edition in 1926, the year the Military Dictatorship ended the First Portuguese Republic in Portugal. The book contains three more chapters than the English version published in 1902. The author introduced an important reflection on the Portuguese and Chinese republics, which took power almost simultaneously (1910 and 1911/1912), and the problems both regimes faced. Montalto de Jesus tries to explain why the Chinese Communist Party gathered so much support within the Chinese population and how the international conjuncture played an important role in this situation. But the author goes even further and explains why when fighting for the Republic, the Portuguese and the Chinese had so much in common, and the reason the shared objectives of both Republics got separated during the Republican regimes. The international humiliations Portugal and China suffered, served as an element of cohesion for their Republican parties in their fight against the Monarchy and the Empire respectively (Spooner 2009). After the Republicans took the power, Macau became a sensitive subject between both republics. For the Portuguese to maintain the colonies meant regaining internal and external respect. For the Chinese, to finish every colonial situation inside the country meant the fulfillment of the main political promises of the regime that was to free China from international exploitation. Besides the relationship between Portugal and China, the author also describes the internal situation of Macau, with a glimpse of hope, and refers to the important role of the Chinese community in Macau's trading activity. Then, Montalto de Jesus points out all the failures, and goes so far as to outline a set of solutions for the public policies of Macau.

His critical look of Portuguese administration was crucial in what happened next. The Portuguese Administration banned the book in an act of censorship, and destroyed all existing copies. The author was politically and socially persecuted, and died the following year. Only the copies offered to friends or bought out of Macau survived. In 1984, the Oxford University Press Hong Kong came out with an edited second edition of the original book, and in 1999, the year of the Handover of Macau, the publisher Livros do Oriente edited a second edition of the censored book. Both editions recognize the contribution that Montalto de Jesus made regarding the knowledge of Macau, its specificity and the problems faced in the first decades of the 20th century. Montalto de Jesus' aim was to influence the local public policies and also to stimulate the civil society to action. Although he did not write about identity, he defended the need for the Portuguese, Chinese and Macanese to find common solutions for the local problems, and he identified the Macanese as a mixed community, able to communicate on both semiospheres, and having a role to play as a connector between the Portuguese Administration and the Chinese authorities and community.

Combining Sameness and Otherness

Where sameness and otherness encounter

Macau was a privileged meeting point between different cultures and semiospheres. Even when mediated, the interaction between sameness and otherness was always present in Macau's daily life. Its hybridity resulted from the convergence of different peoples and cultures into the same territory and the need they had to communicate and imagine solutions for the maintenance of Macau as an international place. The dependence of Macau on China led to the need for this permanent interaction between different actors. The Portuguese Administration of Macau soon recognized the need for understanding the Chinese semiosphere, through the eyes of the translators, and the inevitability of negotiating with the Chinese authorities. Hence, the colonial situation of Macau was never clear, it did not reveal a strong stratification of the society with the Portuguese having the dominant upper hand and the Chinese being dominated. The presence of the Chinese population in the Christian city relied for a long time on the Mandarin's authorization. The consent for trading with Mailand China depended on Chinese authorities, forcing the Western traders to stay in Macau until it was given. The existence of prominent Chinese businessmen in the Macanese society put them at the same level as the Portuguese administrators. The Portuguese Administration kept a permanent dialogue with the rich Chinese community to govern the territory. The inability to have this this dialogue had heavy consequences for a Portuguese governor, João Ferreira do Amaral, who tried to administrate the territory in a fully colonial style, and he was thus summarily assassinated by the Chinese near the Gate of Siege on the Chinese side.

Under these conditions, sameness and otherness had to meet. But this meeting had other results like the creation of a new ethnic group — the Macanese — who assumed themselves as mixed, Christians and mostly bilingual. The Macanese had a significant role as the translators and mediators of the Portuguese and Chinese semiospheres, maintaining a permanent dialogue between the Portuguese administration and the Chinese government. The fact of being biologically and culturally mixed also led to some issues arising, like the ones connected with identity and ethnic belonging. The Macanese were experts in Portuguese and in sinology, and so they were the most prepared to understand and interpret Chinese thought and culture. The fact that Macau was the centre for Portuguese sinology cannot be separated from the hybrid origin of the Macanese and their role as mediators. This role is particularly important in some public institutions like the Repartição do Expediente Sínico de Macau or when receiving and trying relationships with Chinese intellectuals, mostly since the 19th century.

Denying sameness to construct otherness

The Macanese were an ethnic group always in presence of exogroups, the Portuguese and Chinese communities, and seemed to be between these groups. Although always accepting their difference in relation to these communities, they also had a kind of continuity with them. In this way and while identifying themselves with the characteristics of the exogroups, they had the need to claim a particular identitary status for themselves. As the Chinese presence was overwhelming in Macau and the closeness to China could compromise their autonomy and specific identity, they tried to create mechanisms for constructing otherness when referring to the Chinese community. At the same time, they saw themselves as Portuguese citizens who were not ethnically Portuguese. They defended the autonomy of Macau, both from China as from Portugal, which forms a significant part of the arguments exposed by them during their participation in the local periodical press. Their aim was to maintain the balance between Portuguese administrations and the Chinese government, ensuring the survival of the Macanese identity, and make sure that the territory did not bear complete resemblance to either Portugal or China.

For the Macanese to survive, they traced a strategy of denying sameness and constructing otherness while collaborating with the Portuguese Administration and negotiating with the Chinese community. There were examples of Macanese intellectuals who severely criticized the Portuguese Administration in order to improve local governments and to have better cooperation with Chinese authorities. But in each of these cases, the Portuguese Administration strongly punished the authors of these initiatives. To survive, the Macanese community had to tolerate Portuguese Administration and take Portuguese culture as one of the elements for differentiation toward the Chinese — the centre from where the balance of Macau always depended.

References

Aguiar, Manuela Teresa Sousa. 2002. Tradução e interpretação em Macau. *Administração* 15 (57): 1069–1089.

Bennett, Karen. 2015. Translation on the Semi-Periphery: Portugal as Cultural Intermediary in the Transportation of Knowledge. In *How Peripheral is the Periphery? Translating Portugal Back and Forth: Essays in Honour of João Ferreira Duarte*. Cambridge: Cambridge Scholars Publishing, pp. 3–20.

Botas, João. 2017. *Biografia de Manuel da Silva Mendes 1867–1931*. Macau: Instituto Cultural do Governo de Macau.

Crespo, J. Heliodoro Callado. 1898. *Cousas da China: Costumes e Crenças*. Lisboa: Imprensa Nacional.

Crespo, J. Heliodoro Callado. 1901. *A China em 1900*. Lisboa: Manuel Gomes, Editor.

Flores, Jorge Manuel. 1993. Macau e o comércio da Baía de Cantão (séculos XVI e XVII). In *As relações entre a Índia Portuguesa, a Ásia do sudeste e o extremo norte: actas do VI seminário internacional de História indo-portuguesa*. Macau: FO; Lisboa: CNDP, pp. 21–48.

Inso, Jaime do (De colaboração com a Comissão Executiva encarregada da representação de Macau na Exposição Portuguesa em Sevilha 1929). 1929. *Macau: a mais antiga colónia Europeia no Extremo Oriente*. Macau: Escola Tipográfica do Orfanato.
Inso, Jaime do. 1933. *Visões da China*. Lisboa: Tipografia Elite.
Jauss, Hans Robert. 1993. *A Literatura como provocação*. Lisboa: Veja.
Lotman, Iuri. 1981. Um modelo dinâmico do sistema semiótico. In Iuri Lotman, Boris Uspennskii, and V. Ivanóv (Eds.). 1981. *Ensaios de Semiótica Soviética*. Lisboa: Livros horizonte, pp. 67–86.
Montalto de Jesus, C. A. 1902. *Historic Macao*. Hong Kong: Kelly & Walsh, Limited.
Montalto de Jesus, C. A. 1909. *Historic Shanghai*. Shanghai: The Shanghai Mercury, Limited.
Montalto de Jesus, C. A. 1999. *Macau Histórico*. Macau: Livros do Oriente (Re-edition of the 1st edition of 1926 which was seized by Portuguese authorities; the original edition is from the Salesian Printing Press and Tipografia Mercantil).
Moraes, Wenceslau de. 2006. *Ó-Yoné e Ko-Haru* (Organization and Introduction by Tereza Sena). Lisboa: Instituto Camões/Imprensa Nacional Casa da Moeda.
Nepomuceno, Alexandra. 2017. Les brumes de l'orientalisme: brève historie d'une reencontre fantomatique. In *Bérose — Encyclopédie internationale des histories de l'antropologie*, Paris: IIAC-LAHIC, pp. 1–5.
Paiva, Maria Manuela Gomes. 2008. *Traduzir em Macau. Ler o outro — para uma história da mediação linguística e cultural*. Dissertação de Doutoramento em Estudos Portugueses Especialidade de Estudos de Tradução. Lisboa: Universidade Aberta.
Pereira, José Carlos Seabra. 2015. *O Delta Literário de Macau*. Macau: Instituto Politécnico de Macau.
Pinto, Marta Pacheco. 2017. Mapping Portuguese Orientalism: The International Congresses of Orientalists (1873–1973). In Marta Pacheco Pinto (Ed.). *The Orient in Translation: Asian Languages, Literatures and the Luso Space*. V. N. Famalicão: Húmus/Centro de Estudos Comparatistas, pp. 167–197.
Reis, Célia. 2017. A ação de um governador: aspetos do governo de Maia Magalhães em Macau. *Revista de História da Sociedade e da Cultura* 17. Coimbra: Imprensa da Universidade de Coimbra.

Romana, Maria da Conceição Correia Salvado Pinto Barras. 2014. *Para uma Literatura da identidade Macanese Autores/Atores*. Tese de Doutoramento apresentada à Universidade da Covilhã, Covilhã: Universidade da Covilhã.

Shaoyang, Lin. Hong Kong in the Midst of Colonialism, Collaborative and Critical Nationalism from 1925 to 1930: The Perspective of Lu Xun and the Confucius Revering Movement. *China Report* 54 (1): 25–47.

Shi, Chih-yu. 2003. *Navigating Sovereignity World Politics Lost in China*. New York: Palgrave Macmillan.

Spooner, P. D. 2009. *Macau: The port for two Republics* (thesis). Hong Kong SAR: University of Hong Kong.

Uberoi, Patricia. 2018. Preface Special Issue on "Hong Kong: Identity, Intellectual History and Culture." *China Report* 54 (1): 1–14.

Chapter 12

A Research Note of the French Legacies in Indochina's Scholarship: A Review on École française d'Extrême-Orient's Publications and Contributors on Sinology

Tran Tien Nguyen

Department of Oriental Studies, Vietnam National University, Hanoi, Vietnam

Background

Historically, Vietnam and China have had a close relationship, given the fact that the two countries share a common border and that the Viets (or Yueh people, as the Chinese know them) originally came from Southern China for a period of 1,000 years (111 B.C to 10th Century A.D.). Vietnam, which then consisted mainly of the area covered by the present North Vietnam, was under the complete political domination of China. During this period, the Vietnamese borrowed much from Chinese culture and civilization in terms of language, social and political organization, religion and agricultural techniques. Although the Vietnamese maintained and preserved a distinctly Vietnamese spoken language, the Vietnamese script was Chinese, and Mandarin and remained the court language until the French colonization of Indochina (Salabert 2008).

Chinese and French Trails in Vietnam

A long period of domination led to the Chinese belief systems and culture becoming entrenched in medieval Vietnam. In the early history, northern Vietnam was colonized by China's Han dynasty. Vietnam also served as a destination for Chinese people who fled political upheavals in other parts of the Chinese Empire. One wave of refugees came in the turmoil preceding and following the fall of the Han dynasty in 220 AD (Buttinger 1972, p. 35). Traditionally, each considered itself the center of its regional civilization. China thought of itself as "All under heaven." Vietnam occasionally called itself the "Middle Kingdom," (Zhongguo, 中国, Trung Quốc), though Vietnam was part of a larger galaxy of which China was the acknowledged center (Womack 2006, p. 12).

From the 18th century, a steadier process of Chinese immigration started, which, at the outset, was not directly connected with political events in China. China's influence has been far reaching. They designated it as its southernmost province and imposed Chinese language, laws, culture and values on the Viet people. After centuries of resistance to China's rule, the Vietnamese people overthrew their Chinese rulers and became independent.

France gained control over northern Vietnam following its victory over China in the Sino-French War (1884–1885). French Indochina was formed on 17 October 1887 from Annam, Tonkin, Cochinchina (which together form modern Vietnam) and the Kingdom of Cambodia; Laos was added after the Franco-Siamese War in 1893. Before the French came to Indochina, these were independent countries. There are no specific population figures available pertaining to the Chinese in Vietnam prior to the arrival of the French. The Ming refugees during the 17th century and the Chinese migrants arriving from the 18th century onwards settled mainly in Cochinchina. They were active in the commercial and agricultural sectors of the Vietnamese society, and the Chinese settlers played an important role in expanding Vietnamese control over the Mekong delta region. From the early 20th century, the number of Chinese citizens is available from the three parts of Vietnam (Cochinchina, Annam and Tonkin). With the French colonization of Indochina, the number of Chinese residing in Vietnam increased considerably. The Chinese in their traditional roles as traders, retailers, usurers and middlemen served well the economic and political interests of the French. Economic growth under a colonial system attracted new waves of Chinese immigrants from poverty-stricken provinces of Southern China in the late 19th and early 20th century. By the time of the Geneva Conference in 1954 whereby Vietnam was partitioned at the 17th parallel, there were rough estimates of 100,000 ethnic Chinese living in Cholon-Saigon (Carino 1980). By the time the French arrived in the mid-19th century, Hoa held a controlled and dominated the indigenous Vietnamese majority in trade, mining and every urban market sector in addition to prospering under the colonial *laissez-faire* market policies enshrined by the French colonialists (Chua 1998).

The French colonization in Vietnam officially started from 1887 to 1954, even though the French and other European groups had already arrived and started to influence events in Vietnam as early as 1516 (Shackford 2000, p. 181). Portuguese ships bringing missionaries and traders were the first to arrive in Vietnam, and soon afterward French missionaries followed. The French missionaries were a "mission civiliatrice" that was supported by the French intellectuals (Le 2011, p. 132). The French fleets captured the port of Tourane (present Đà Nẵng) in 1858 and Saigon in 1859. Subsequently, Vietnamese emperors were compelled to grant the French control of several provinces, the first three in 1861, followed by more southern provinces. They were also coerced into granting legal status to the Catholic missions, as well as commercial concessions, which facilitated the opening of the ports to enable commerce with the West (Cima 1989, p. 24).

Also, China colonialism had a deep impact on the Vietnamese, and so the French tried to erase the influence of China colonialism (Le 2011, p. 132). This view was later redefined, and now the "mission civiliatrice" also had to break Vietnam's links to China. That is, French colonial officials became "convinced that to achieve permanent colonial success required harsh curtailment of Chinese influences." Hence in their view, to eliminate the Chinese language was simultaneously "to isolate Vietnam from its heritage and to neutralize the traditional elite" (Marr 1984, p. 145). Those activities have been done by the French in their efforts to conquer Vietnam. They tried to implant their hegemony in the Vietnamese mind and in the way they live.

The Treaty of Huế or Protectorate Treaty (often known as the Patenôtre Treaty) was concluded on 6 June 1884 (three weeks after the conclusion of the Tientsin Accord with China, which implicitly renounced China's historic suzerainty over Vietnam) between France and Annam (Vietnam), and this formed the basis for the protectorates of Annam and Tonkin, and for French colonial rule in Vietnam during the next 70 years; this was negotiated by Jules Patenôtre, France's minister to China. The French have traditionally taken great pride in what they call their *civilisation Français*. This includes the language, religion, literature of France, as well as its culture and laws,[1] and also the government and educational system and technological achievements. One of the reasons the French gave for expanding their colonial empire throughout the world was to spread this civilization to inferior native peoples.

This movement of delinkage with China also took place through a new system of education of the Mandarinal elites, removed from the Chinese model. Gradually, the Latin transcription, more accessible for the French officials, and now the local population, was imposed as the tool for writing, at the expense of Chinese characters. The Franco-local schools replaced Confucian schools, and the last imperial examination in Hue was held in 1919. The indigenous teaching systems in Tonkin and Annam were well organized upon the arrival of the French. Primary education for

---

[1] The contribution of France to the legal system played a role in the fact that the Vietnamese claims against China after 1974, when China seized the Paracels by force, were based on international law, using universally accepted concepts such as proximity, or actual and continuous occupation. China, where no substantial theoretical basis was built for the establishment of the rule of law, relied then upon, and still relies today, on the less valid argument of "historical rights," supported by the use of force and a favorable balance of power. See also: Ferrier (1975).

Annamites was free and lay, rather than religious, and this approach came from Chinese tradition.

As with almost all colonization process, one cannot reject the positive aspects of imposed development, albeit recognizing the profound inequalities and discriminations related to it. Under French colonization, Indochina experienced rapid economic development, around mining industries (tin, coal) and agriculture with the system of large plantations of rubber, rice and tobacco. The development of public work and infrastructure was also impressive. Indochina had one of the most extensive networks of roads and bridges in Asia, at the service of course of the economy and the evacuation, to the sea, of agricultural resources (Aurousseau 1926, p. 26).

Following the complete conquest of Indochina, France slowly lost interest in obtaining raw materials from China. France's attention now turned from exploration of Indochina to the creation of a colonial administration (Ennis 1936, p. 57). During this period, the French colonial administration acted on behalf of the Southern ruler (Nam Trieu) in diplomatic relations and ensured Vietnam's sovereignty and territorial integrity. Since the term of the Governor General of Indochina Paul Doumer (1897–1902), the colonial exploitation process throughout Indochina in general and Cochinchina in particular continued on a large scale and with impressive speed of investment and exploitation. Paul Doumer paid special attention to the reform of the administration, fiscal policy and taxation, in order to mobilize huge investment capital and labor force to build infrastructure for the colonial economy. Doumer thus was able to expand his public works program and obtain a large loan that helped with the building of hospitals and schools. Doumer witnessed the establishment of the Ecole Francaise d'Extreme-Orient, which first appeared in Saigon in 1898, to offer opportunity for elite education (Cottrell 2009, p. 28). Under him, the infrastructure system in Indochina was built. He built a trans-Indochina railway that now had connections with Yunnan (China). Nguyen Canh Binh, the Director of Vietnam Center for Intellectual Cooperation, has deeply evaluated the activities that Paul Doumer carried out in Indochina. He thought that the Governor General was not only a ruler but also a scholar, statecraft man and an ambitious politician who wanted to turn Indochina into a French in the Far East." (Hien Do 2016).

In order to serve the rule, the French set a goal of destroying Confucianism, Chinese characters and Nom scripts so as to abolish and replace them with French and have a national script with a Latin alphabet. The feudal examination system was canceled. The French did take certain steps to modernize Vietnam. Under French administration, the traditional Chinese scripts, or the Nom script, in education were replaced by the romanized alphabet of the Vietnamese language (now called Vietnamese). Administrators introduced Western educational practices and theories but ultimately offered such instruction only to members of the Vietnamese elite, and then only haphazardly at best. The large majority of citizens generally failed to acquire even that kind of exposure to Western culture (Cottrell 2009, p. 29).

To accomplish this, the French colonialists should have eliminated the Confucian education system, but it is not easy to apply French education in Vietnam. In the early years, the Cochinchinese government encountered many difficulties when the Confucian school system dissolved. The Confucius teachers left their posts to the free zone of the Hue court to continue their posts. Many students stopped their studying and joined the army forces.

In 1874, Admiral Krantz, the governor of Cochinchina, signed a decree to reorganize the educational discipline, applied it on March 1879, and regulated the education system as having two levels, i.e., primary and secondary. At the primary school, students practice reading and writing the national language, Chinese characters (chữ Nho) and French; elementary grammar; elementary math; elementary geometry; measurement concept and an overview of history and geography. In 1879, the decree of reforming Cochinchina education (Nam Ky) was issued, dividing the main curriculum into three levels. The primary-level study consists of a three-year term where the students are taught French, the national language (Quốc ngữ) and Chinese literature (Han literature).

The secondary school has a three-year term, and each week two hours will be spent for studying the Chinese characters and the national language, with the rest of the time allotted for French. On July 8, 1917, colonial officials established the Office of Higher Education to supervise the growth of and examine the political and economic impacts of Indochinese universities. The office closed all schools that did not hire teachers or teach curricula previously approved by the French. As a result, the colonists outlawed Sino-Vietnamese schools because they adhered to traditional teachings instead of the new required curriculum.

The École française d'Extrême-Orient

Edward Said's 1978 Orientalism has, in fact, cast a very long shadow over the relationship between Europe and East Asia (Boutin and Emery 2016). This issue seeks to highlight much more active 19th and early 20th century French relationships with the Extrême-Orient (particularly China, Japan and Korea) in which cultural, economic, political and creative exchanges blurred cultural and geospatial borders, thus leading to what many scholars and diplomats refer to as "privileged links" with Asian countries.

Unlike the 16th–17th centuries, the new imperialists set up the administration of the native areas for the benefit of the colonial power. During the course of the late 19th century, the study of Asia saw significant changes. The development of science entailed new research facilities. The methodological approach changed the processing of materials on the Orient. On the other hand, to study the architecture, epitaphs and inscriptions, to investigate ethnology, language, etc required the colonial scholars to be present in Asia itself (Rageau, p. 9). The gathering and preservation of artifacts and materials also required complicated conditions, and hence the necessity of setting up local research institutes.

The French School of Asian Studies (The École française d'Extrême-Orient or French School of the Far East, EFEO) was founded in 1898. Its mission was to carry out interdisciplinary research and training in the civilizations of South, Southeast and

Northeast Asia. The main fields of study included history, anthropology, archaeology, art history and linguistics. The emphasis was on primary sources (archaeological, written or oral) and fieldwork in Asia. In 1898, the leading French scholars of India submitted a project to establish Institut de Chandernagore, the first French settlement in India, but they did not gain the attention of authorities (Rageau, p. 10). Paul Doumer later returned to this project, but proposed to establish a research institute in Indochina. EFEO became the first research center to conduct their research on the Orient. The mission of the EFEO in the first phase consisted of the archaeological survey and research activities of the Indochinese Peninsula, and then contributing to the scholarly study of neighboring regions and civilizations such as India, China and Malaysia.

In Indochina, EFEO was an associated college of PSL University dedicated to the study of Asian societies.[2] It was founded in 1900 with headquarters in Hanoi in what was then French Indochina. After the independence of Vietnam, its headquarters was transferred to Paris. Its main fields of research ere archaeology, philology and the study of modern Asian societies. Also in 1900, the EFEO released its first publication entitled "Ancient currency of An Nam." One year later, EFEO published four journals (three months each) printed in a 431-page volume with 75 illustrations and three maps (Rageau, p. 11). These initial studies cover the areas of religion, Cham architecture, Vietnamese folklore, archeology in Laos, Campuchic customs, etc. Also in these volume are two publication on Chinese and Japan studies. In 1902, Seraphin Couvreur introduced a Latinized method of Chinese characters. This system is similar to the Chinese Pinyin that was widely used until the middle of the 20th century.

The library of the EFEO was established in Hanoi in 1903. The development of the library is evidence of the research achievements

---

[2] The following information was acquired from *La bibliothèque de Paris*. EFEO. http://web.archive.org/web/20090416044841/http://www.efeo.fr:80/documentation/bibliotheque.shtml and *La photothèque de Paris*. EFEO. http://web.archive.org/web/20070814110544/http:/www.efeo.fr:80/documentation/phototheque.shtml (accessed on 15 December 2018).

of the EFEO. During the EFEO period in Hanoi and Phnom Penh, from 1900 to 1957, the EFEO library gathered many printed and handwritten works related to Indochina and China. In 1944, the library in Hanoi gathered 80,000 books, including handwritten works, of which half were documents in European languages. At the end of the colonial period, according to the agreements between the EFEO and the Indochina nations, documents written in European languages belonged to the EFEO while other records written in local language belonged to Indochina. The EFEO made copies of these records and sent them to Paris. More than 12,000 books, mostly in Southeast Asia, became the nucleus of the library in Paris, opened in 1968.

The photograph archives of EFEO are very rich in materials (archeology, architecture, art, history, etc.) and spread across many countries (Vietnam, Laos, India, China). The first photographs of the excavations conducted by the EFEO since the beginning of the 20th century are also available. Other important records are gifted by Dalet, Bacot, Boulbet and Bénisti, to name a few. Many photographs are evidences to testify the past historical events that now — due to war — have been changed and/or destroyed. Others records are those that have been excavated and restored by the EFEO for more than a century. For Japan and China, the library has around 11,000 monographs, of which 75% are in the local language. Besides, there are 175 periodic publications in Japanese, 185 in Chinese and 70 in European languages. This collection is the richest in Buddhism, followed by Taoism and Shintō. There are also has more than 2,000 books in the art and archeology field. Scientifically, the EFEO has seen great achievements. With a field of specialization of geographic research, EFEO does not go into every culture. But for that reason, EFEO has become an ideal meeting place for specialized research. After more than a century of operation, the institute is also the cradle of training typical French scholars on oriental studies.

The other significant element inherited from the French colonial past in Indochina is cartography. As early as 1885, after the Sino-French war about Tonkin, the border with China has been precisely delimited by military topographers and ratified by bilateral agreements in 1886, thus imposing the concept of the delineated border over the vaguer notion of unprecise margins, always contestable, which was that of the Chinese Empire: A Chinese Empire that conceived, in theory, no limits to its suzerainty over all the world "under the sky."[3]

Along the same line, we can also note another permanence of the Chinese conception of the law, which is the refusal of international arbitration in the name of sovereignty and non-interference. On three occasions, (1932, 1937, 1947) France, in conflict with the Republic of China on the question of the Paracels and the Spratleys, proposed to use international arbitration; this was, however, systematically rejected by Beijing. In Indochina, France contributed to the building of "national identities" with a contradictory dual movement. On the one hand, there was the construction of a unified "Indochina," and, on the other hand, the construction, revival or strengthening of new nations in Cambodia, and in Laos, particularly in Laos where the modern national identity feeling is quite recent and has been encouraged by the French.

Contributors in French Indochina on Sinology

Vietnamese civilization is as complicated as that of its powerful northern neighbor China, from where it drew many of its influences under a thousand-year domination. Later came the French and the humbling period of colonialism from which Vietnam was not to emerge until the second half of the 20th century. French–Vietnamese relations started during the early 17th century with the arrival of the Jesuit missionaries. As far as we know, in the 18th century, the French involvement in Vietnam was

---

[3] France, through its colonial offensive in Indochina, built the cartography of precisely delineated borders between the French protectorates of Annam and Tonkin and China. Things, however, were less evident in the case of maritime territories, which are at the heart of tensions in the South China Sea. Today's negotiations between China and Vietnam as well as with other countries with claims in the South China Sea are still founded on the treaties signed by France at the end of the 19th century, and, most importantly, on the archives, maps and treaties kept at the French National Library, the Ministry of foreign affairs archives and the archives of the Ministère d'outre-mer.

confined to trade, as the remarkably successful work of the Jesuit missionaries continued. Although books on Vietnam are plentiful, there is relatively little recent scholarship on Sinology in colonial Indochina. Writings about China during the French colony that do exist were written mostly by European contributors at the height of the French Empire with a strong pro-colonial bias as the French sought to justify their actions abroad.

European writings on China began in the 16th century with Catholic missions from Spain, Italy and France, followed by trade and diplomatic delegations from various powers. Therefore, compelled by ideological and commercial aims, Chinese studies had multinational and multidisciplinary beginnings. As a field of academic study in Europe, Sinology was a latecomer and was given an institutional home only in the 19th century when France created a "Chaire de langues et littératures chinoises et tartares-mandchoues" at the Collège de France in 1814. France also has the distinction of being one of the first countries to teach colloquial Chinese at the École des langues orientales vivantes.

One of the first contributors on Sinology was Henri Cordier (1849–1926). However, Cordier was not a product of either the academic training or its more practical version. Unschooled in Chinese, he was sent by his father to pursue a career in business, beginning at the American trading firm Russell and Company, in Shanghai, at the age of 19 (Cagnat 1929, p. 5; Aurousseau 1925, pp. 279–286). Cordier arrived in 1869 and stayed until 1876.

Henri Cordier was a linguist, historian, ethnographer, author, editor and Orientalist. He was President of the Société de Géographie (French, Geographical Society, Paris) and a prominent figure in the development of East Asian and Central Asian scholarship in Europe in the late 19th and early 20th centuries. Though he had little actual knowledge of the Chinese language, Cordier had a particularly strong impact on the development of Chinese scholarship, and was a mentor of the noted French Sinologist Édouard Chavannes. As an accidental Sinologist, acting in his leisure time as a voluntary librarian of the North China branch of the Royal Asiatic Society in Shanghai in 1872, he had the idea of compiling Western writings on China over the centuries. His very premise was Eurocentric, focused on Western study without concern for its Chinese reception. This approach went hand in hand with the fact that he never acquired proficiency in reading or writing Chinese or other Asian languages (Chang 2016).

Cordier was not an employer, nor did he seek financial gain through his publications. He acted out of intellectual curiosity, first as an amateur Sinologist and later as a professional. Living through the heyday of Western imperialism, his advocacy of French colonial expansion was unstinting. Cordier's practices thus integrated two ideological frameworks, combining a research culture of shared knowledge production with European empire building (Chang 2016). In 1876, he was named secretary of a Chinese government program for Chinese students studying in Europe (Aurousseau 1925, pp. 279–286).

In 1878, the first volume of Cordier's *Bibliotheca Sinica* appeared in Paris, after he had left Shanghai. It was awarded the Stanislas Julien prize in Sinology in 1880, named in honor of the second Professor and Chair of Chinese at the Collège de France. Cordier would never revisit China, but he eventually became the most respected in the field of Asian studies, teaching at the École des langues orientales vivantes as well as the École libre des sciences politiques in Paris. Cordier, as the *Bibliotheca Sinica*, is sometimes affectionately referred to, is the standard enumerative bibliography of 70,000 works on China up to 1921. We examine the cross-cultural currents that led to the formation of the philological foundations for the field of Asian studies as we know it today (epitomized by Henri Cordier's *Bibliotheca sinica*, discussed by Ting Chang) (Boutin and Emery 2016); Endymion Wilkinson also praises Cordier for including the full titles, often the tables of contents and reviews of most books (Endymion Wilkinson 2013, p. 986). For the *Bibliotheca Sinica*, a vast bibliographic dictionary of European writings on China that put him in the canon of Western sinology, Cordier relied on an international network for information and improvement.[4]

---

[4] Henri Cordier, *Bibliotheca sinica: Dictionnaire bibliographique des ouvrages relatifs à l'Empire chinois* (Paris: Ernest Leroux, 1878–1895). Starting in 1904, Cordier brought out an enlarged and corrected second edition, *Bibliotheca sinica: Dictionnaire bibliographique des ouvrages relatifs à l'Empire chinois* (Paris: E. Guilmoto, 1904–1908) (rpt. Hildesheim: Georg Olms Verlag, 1971).

Along with Gustaaf Schlegel, he also co-founded and co-edited an international journal of Asian studies, *T'oung Pao* [通報], begun in 1890 and continuing to date. Among his many honors was his election to the Académie des Inscriptions et des Belles-Lettres of the Institut de France, in 1908. One of the significant publications of Henri Cordier (1883)[5] dealt with the conflict between France and China, with deep research carried out on colonial history and international law. He used his private correspondence with a vast international network of diplomats, administrators, missionaries, writers and scholars of every field of Asian studies between the 1870s until his death in 1926 to produce knowledge about China. Indeed, his unpublished correspondence, housed in the Bibliothèque de l'Institut de France in Paris, demonstrates a collaborative knowledge production on a global scale long before the digital revolution. Moreover, Cordier's letters further show his correspondents giving him guidance or professional mentoring at a crucial moment in the development and professionalization of European Sinology (Chang 2016).

As noted before, missionaries were among the first and most important contributors to Sinology. Cordier drew upon this knowledge community early on, finding other informal teachers in addition to Wylie such as the French Jesuit Aloys Pfister, based at Siu ca-wei, the Jesuit mission outside Shanghai. Cordier later exchanged letters with Séraphin Couvreur (1835–1919), another Jesuit missionary. Couvreur's groundbreaking achievement was a phonetic romanization system for Chinese that was adopted by the EFEO to replace the dominant English system of Wade–Giles. Cordier's older correspondents were succeeded over the years by new generations of scholars, diplomats and colonial administrators, many of whom had been his students at the École des langues orientales and the École libre des sciences politiques in Paris. They were asked for contributions to the new edition of his bibliographical dictionary underway as well as for issues of the journal *T'oung Pao*.

---

[5] This book may have occasional imperfections such as missing or blurred pages, poor pictures, errant marks, etc. that were either part of the original artifact or were introduced by the scanning process. See also: Cordier (1883).

With help from his ever-expanding international network, Cordier published an expanded second edition of the *Bibliotheca Sinica* that contained some 70,000 multilingual bibliographic entries.

Letters from Paul Demiéville (1894–1979), who eventually become a Professor of Chinese at the École des langues orientales and the Collège de France, and also a co-editor of *T'oung Pao*, indicate the progress of academic sinology since Cordier began his work. In a letter form 1920, Demiéville reported to "Monsieur et vénéré maître" on his research at the École de l'Extrême-Orient at Hanoi in terms that show his rigorous education: "Je me propose de choisir un des poètes qui illustrèrent la grande époque T'ang, le règne de Ming houang, et de grouper autour de ce personnage, de son oeuvre et de son histoire des études aussi variées et aussi complètes que possible" (MS 5451 pièce 52, April 7, 1920). Demiéville showed that he had acquired not only skills in Chinese language, literature and history but also a sense of how to construct an in-depth study. After expressions of gratitude to his former teacher, he concluded, "mon voeu le plus ardent est de réussir dans la tâche qui m'a été confiée. Oserai-je compter sur votre indulgence si la route est longue et la marche difficile?" (MS 5451 pièce 52, April 7, 1920). Through his polite formulation, Demiéville suggested that research and correspondence would continue to play central roles in their knowledge production. Cordier had passed the baton to the next generation of sinologists.

Apart from Henri Cordier, there have some other French Indochina contributors to the field of sinology, and their researches focus on French Indochina in its relations with China. Gabriel Devéria (1844–1899), a diplomat, sinologist and professor at the l'École des langues orientales, also had good command of the Chinese and worked as Chinese language interpreter and a specialist in epigraphy and history of China and Central Asia. He was a member of the de l'Académie des inscriptions et belles lettres (1897). In the late 19th century, the unfamiliar script of some inscriptions and coins that had been found in China began to incite the interest of a number of European orientalists. It was identified as Tangut (Xi xia) script by Gabriel Devéria in 1882, but in fact earlier in the century, unbeknown to Western sinologists, a Chinese scholar named Zhang Shu 張澍 had already made the identification (Morisse 1904, pp. 313–316).

In *Histoire Des Relations De La Chine Avec L'annam-Viêtnam Du Xvie Au Xixe Siècle: D'après Des Documents Chinois Traduits Pour La Première Fois Et Annotés — Primary Source Edition* (French Edition), Gabriel Devéria has mentioned about how China was under Mongol rule in 1252, Annam had to pay tribute every three years, etc. Under the Ming Dynasty, the regulations for payment of tribute by Annam were altered (Devéria 1880).

In *La frontière Sino-Annamite: Description géographique et ethnographiqued'après des documents officiels chinois traduits pour la première fois*, Gabriel Devéria has described the Cartographies de la frontière sino-annamite (Cartographies of the Sino-Annamite Border). To paraphrase his words: In the southern part of the Celestial Empire live non-Chinese tribes who are all the more important to know that many of them are in contact with us in Tong-king, that the names given to them by the Chinese are far from having an ethnic meaning, and that they may even vary with localities while designating individuals of the same race, we have thought that, in the absence of more precise information, the descriptions of these tribes drawn from Chinese sources may offer some interest. This image of the tributary peoples has no less than nineteen different peoples in the eight Chinese prefectures whose territories are confined to the northern Tong-king, and we have not attempted to classify them in an ethnic manner. Later on, their better-known history and their philology may permit them to be grouped methodically, and we have taken into account in the classification of their descriptions only the places occupied by these peoples on the Sino-Annamese frontier (Devéria 1886).

Apart from these above sinologists, Henri Castonnet des Fossés (1846–1898), a historian, geographer and specialist in the history of India also spent time working in Indochina. In his talk Les Relations de la Chine et de l'Annam (Extrait du Bull. de la Société Académique indochinoise, S.l : S.n) extracted from the *Indochina Academy Society Journal*, at the meeting section dated

July 31, 1883, he opined that Vietnam is not dependent on relations with China and considers it appropriate to history.

Albert Billot (1841–1922), as a diplomat, spent some time researching diplomatic history of the establishment of protectorate on Annam and the conflict with China, 1882–1885, in his *L'affaire du Tonkin : histoire diplomatique de l'établissement de notre protectorat sur l'Annam et de notre conflit avec la Chine, 1882–1885, par un diplomate* (J. Hetzel et Cie, éditeurs, Paris, 1886). This book is a reproduction of an important historical work. However, the text may have a number of errors. Indeed, the text mode of this document was generated automatically by an optical character recognition (OCR) program. The estimated recognition rate for this document is 98.84%. Albert Billot noted in his memoirs that, before 1879, France did not exercise its rights in Annam. It was after the French colony and protectorate of Tonkin that L'Affaire Tonkin or Đông Kinh was named on March 1885. This was a major French political crisis that erupted in the closing weeks of the Sino-French War which effectively destroyed the political career of the French Prime Minister Jules Ferry and abruptly ended the string of Republican governments inaugurated several years earlier by Léon Gambetta. The suspicion by the French public and political classes that French troops were being sent to their deaths far from home for little measurable gain, both in Tonkin and elsewhere, also discredited French colonial expansion for nearly a decade.

Auguste Antoine Thomazi (1873–1959) was a naval officer, journalist and historian of the French navy. He studied the military history of French Indochina and Tang Jingsong who played an important role in the Sino-French War and during the period of undeclared hostilities that preceded it. Thomazi wrote on L'Affaire Tonkin his La conquête de l'Indochine. To paraphrase Thomazi: The Affair (as most French political scandals are still termed), was triggered on 28 March 1885 by the controversial Retreat from Lạng Sơn. The retreat, which threw away the gains of the February Lạng Sơn Campaign, was ordered by Lieutenant-Colonel Paul Gustave Herbinger, the acting commander of the 2nd Brigade, less than a week after General François de Négrier's defeat at the Battle of

Bang Bo (24 March 1885). The Chinese forces advanced in three large groups, and fiercely assaulted our positions in front of Ky Lua. Facing greatly superior numbers, short of ammunition, and exhausted from a series of earlier actions, Colonel Herbinger has informed me that the position was untenable and that he has been forced to fall back tonight on Dong Song and Thanh Moy. All my efforts are being applied to concentrate our forces at the passes around Chu and Kép. The enemy continues to grow stronger on the Red River, and it appears that we are facing an entire Chinese army, trained in the European style and ready to pursue a concerted plan. I hope in any event to be able to hold the entire Delta against this invasion, but I consider that the government must send me reinforcements (men, ammunition, and pack animals) as quickly as possible (Thomazi 1934, p. 259).

In 1882, Tang Jingsong was sent by the Qing government to Vietnam to assess the ability of the Vietnamese government to resist French expansion in Tonkin. During his stay, Tang Jingsong was able to persuade Liu Yongfu to take the field against the French with the Black Flag Army. Liu's intervention resulted in the French defeat in the Battle of Cau Giay on 19 May 1883, in which the French commandant supérieur Henri Rivière was killed. In the wake of this disaster, Jules Ferry's government committed substantial military and naval forces to Tonkin (Thomazi 1931, pp. 55–58).

Another contributor, Charles Dominique Maurice Rollet de l'Isle (1859–1943), a hydrography engineer of the French navy, in his *Au Tonkin et dans les mers de Chine* (Charles 1886), states he accompanied Admiral Courbet to the Extrême-Orient and witnessed the capture of Hue. On the southern coast of China, in Formosa and the Pescadores Islands, he carried out numerous hydrographic surveys and returned to Europe in 1885.

Charles Robequain is a French geographer. In 1924, he was admitted to the EFEO and left for Hanoi. He remained there for four years and wrote his thesis on the province of Thanh Hóa. He then joined the documentation service of the Economic Agency of Indochina, before leaving for Poitiers as a lecturer. In his book

(Robequain 1944), he discusses colonial economics, another subject necessary to understanding the failure of the colony. This work focuses on the changes in the local economy and on the local peasants as the French instituted new industries and farming methods to increase production and profit. This book promotes pro-colonial propaganda to the general public and French administration. Robequain conveys the civilizing mission message throughout, as he consistently reinforces the humanitarian aid and improvements brought in by the French. With funding from the Ministry of National Education, the Ministry of the Colonies and the Government-General of Indochina, Robequain was fortunate to travel to Indochina and gather the most up-to-date information about the colony from the French point of view. His work helped the readers understand the value and importance of Indochina to the French economy, and conversely, the importance of France to the well-being of Indochina.

In summary, centuries of Chinese rule did a great deal to shape Vietnam's culture, language and religion. But even though China had an intense influence on the development of Vietnam, it never erased Vietnam's unique sense of identity or its desire for independence from foreign rule. Vietnam once again came under the control of France. The introduction of French cultures and scholarship in Indochina created many benefits for the Vietnamese, and much of what we currently know of Vietnam and China studies come from the École française d'Extrême-Orient and French colonial contributors in academic fields.

References

Aurousseau, Léonard. 1925. Henri Cordier. *Bulletin de l'École française d'Extrême-Orient* 25: 279–286.

Aurousseau, Léonard. 1926. A.A. Pouyanne: les travaux publics de l'Indochine. *Bulletin de l'Ecole Française d'Extrême-Orient* 26: 370–385.

Boutin, Aimée, Elizabeth Emery. 2016. France-Asia: Cultural Identity and Creative Exchange. *L'Esprit Créateur* Volume 56, Number 3, Fall 2016, pp. 1–13. https://doi.org/10.1353/esp.2016.0027 (accessed on 20 December 2018).

Buttinger, Joseph, 1972. *A Dragon Defiant: A Short Story of Vietnam*, Newton Abbot Devon: David & Charles Limited.

Cagnat, René. 1929. *Notice sur la vie et les travaux de M. Henri Cordier*. Paris: Firmin-Didot.

Carino, Theresa C. 1980. *Vietnam's Chinese minority and the politics of Sino-Vietnamese relations*. https://www.ibiblio.org/ahkitj/wscfap/arms1974/Book%20Series/TheImageOfGodIM/IOGIM-vietnam.htm. (accessed on 5 January 2019).

Chang, Ting. 2016. *Crowdsourcing avant la lettre: Henri Cordier and French Sinology, ca. 1875–192)*. http://eprints.nottingham.ac.uk/34447/1/Chang_L%27Esprit_createur.pdf (accessed on 10 January 2019).

Chua, Amy L. 1998. Markets, Democracy, and Ethnicity: Toward A New Paradigm For Law and Development. *The Yale Law Journal* 108, p. 93.

Cima, Ronald J. (Ed.). 1989. *Vietnam: A Country Study*. Washington: GPO for the Library of Congress.

Cordier, Henri. 1878–1895. *Bibliotheca sinica: Dictionnaire bibliographique des ouvrages relatifs à l'Empire chinois*. Paris: Ernest Leroux.

Cordier, Henri. 1883. *Le Conflit entre la France et la Chine: Etude d'histoire coloniale et de droit international*. Paris: Léopold Cerf.

Cordier, Henri. 1904–1908. *Bibliotheca sinica: Dictionnaire bibliographique des ouvrages relatifs à l'Empire chinois*. Paris: E. Guilmoto) (rpt. Hildesheim: Georg Olms Verlag, 1971).

Cottrell, Robert C. 2009. *Vietnam*. New York: Infobase Publishing.

Devéria, Gabriel. 1880. *Histoire des Relations de la Chine avec l'Annam-Vietnam, du XVI au. XIX siecle*. Paris, Ernest Leroux.

Devéria, Gabriel. 1886. *La Frontière Sino-Annamite Description géographique et ethnographique d'après des documents officiels chinois traduits pour la première fois*. Paris, Ernest Leroux. https://www.chineancienne.fr/19e-s/dev%C3%A9ria-la-fronti%C3%A8re-sino-annamite/.

Ennis, Thomas E. 1936. *French Policy and Development in Indochina*. Chicago: The University of Chicago Press.

Ferrier, Jean-Pierre. 1975. Le conflit des îles Paracels et le problème de la souveraineté sur les îles inhabitées. *Annuaire Français du Droit International* No. 21.

Hien Do. 2016. *Paul Doumer: Người kiến tạo hay thực dân bóc lột Đông Dương (Paul Doumer: The Constructor or Colonist exploitor in Indochina)*. https://news.zing.vn/paul-doumer-nguoi-kien-tao-hay-thuc-dan-boc-lot-dong-duong-post640107.html (accessed on 20 December 2019).

Journoud, Pierre. "*L'Indochine et ses frontières, 1940–1954*. Entre zones d'échanges, espace de confrontation armée et instruments de légitimation politique" in Frédéric Dessberg, Frédéric Thibault (Eds.), *Sécurité Européenne, Frontières, Glacis et Zones d'influence*. Rennes: Presses Universitaires de Rennes.

La bibliothèque de Paris. EFEO. http://web.archive.org/web/20090416044841/ http://www.efeo.fr:80/documentation/bibliotheque.shtml (accessed on 15 December 2018).

La photothèque de Paris. EFEO. http://web.archive.org/web/20070814110544/ http://www.efeo.fr:80/documentation/phototheque.shtml (accessed on 15 December 2018).

Le, LONG S. 2011. Colonial and Postcolonial Views of Vietnam's Pre-history. *SOJOURN: Journal of Social Issues in Southeast Asia* 26 (1): 132.

Marr, David G. 1984. *Vietnamese Tradition on Trial, 1920–1945*. Berkeley: University of California Press.

Morisse, Gérard. 1904. 'Contribution préliminaire à l'étude de l'écriture et de la langue si-hia [sic]'. Mémoires présentés par divers savants à l'Académie des inscriptions et belles-lettres de l'Institut de Paris, première série, 11.

Rageau, Christiane Pasquel. 1989. *Bulletin d'informations de L'Association des Bibliothécaires Français*. N.0140, Ier Trimestre 1989. http://www.hannom.org.vn/web/tchn/data/8902v.htm#rc7 (accessed on 10 December 2018).

Robequain, Charles. 1944. *The Economic Development of French Indo-China*. Translation by Isabel A. Ward. *Supplement, Recent Developments in Indo-China: 1939–1943*. By John R. Andrus and Katrine R. C. Greene. Issued under the auspices of the International Secretariat, Institute of Pacific Relations. New York: Oxford University Press.

Salabert, Juliette. 2008. "*Faux et usage de faux, Sur le bilinguisme chinois de René Leys*" Trans 5 at https://journals.openedition.org/trans/221.

Shackford, Julie and Jason Jones. 2000. *Vietnam An Historical Perspective*. Honolulu, Hawaii: The Henry Luce Foundation, Inc.

Thomazi, Auguste. 1931. *Histoire militaire de l'Indochine français*. Hanoi: Imprimerie d'Extrême-Orient.

Thomazi, Auguste. 1934. *La conquête de l'Indochine*. Paris: Payot.

Wilkinson, Endymion. 2013. *Chinese History: A New Manual*. Cambridge, MA: Harvard University Asia Center, Harvard-Yenching Institute Monograph Series.

Womack, Brantly. 2006. *China and Vietnam: The Politics of Asymmetry*. (Cambridge:) Cambridge University Press.

Part III

Emerging Pluralist Relations — In the Eyes of Autonomous Self

Chapter 13

The Anglo-Japanese Inter-imperial Relations and Ideas on the Future of the Japanese Empire

Hiroyuki Ogawa[1]

Department of Area Studies, University of Tokyo, Tokyo, Japan

Introduction

The Anglo-Japanese relationship in the first half of the 20th century was largely inter-imperial partnership and rivalry. In 1902, Japan and Britain signed the Anglo-Japanese Alliance. By this alliance, Japan tried to prevent Russian advances into Manchuria and the Korean Peninsula, while Britain intended to obtain a counterweight against Russia's southward expansion, which was considered to be the gravest threat to the British Empire. It was also a means of burden sharing, as Britain's need to station large forces in East and Southeast Asia was reduced. The Anglo-Japanese Alliance was renewed twice in 1905 and 1911, and lasted until 1923. Especially by the renewal in 1905, it covered a wider area including India, which was "a cornerstone of the British system of worldwide economic, military, and political power" (Brown 1999, p. 421). In return, Japan's claim to its control over Korea was acknowledged

---

[1] The author would like to thank the organizers and participants of the conference at Chulalongkorn University in Bangkok on 1–2 June 2018, and Tomohito Baji, who kindly read the manuscript, for many helpful comments and suggestions.

by the British. In 1914, Japan entered the First World War as Britain's ally against Germany and occupied Shantung (though eventually returned to China after the war in 1922) and islands north of the equator in the Western Pacific (which would become the South Seas Mandate under the League of Nations), both of which had been previously under German control but became indefensible once the war broke out in Europe. The Anglo-Japanese Alliance was a major buttress of British and Japanese imperial strategies in Asia and the Pacific at least until World War I.

Nevertheless, mainly as a result of growing American objection, the Anglo-Japanese Alliance was finally terminated and replaced by the vague Four-Power Pacific Treaty without military obligations, signed by the United Kingdom, the United States, Japan and France in 1921. After the termination of the bilateral alliance, the Anglo-Japanese relationship gradually deteriorated in the 1920s and 1930s. Finally, they went to war against each other on 8 December 1941, when Imperial Japanese forces took advantage of the war in Europe and started their campaign against the British colonial possessions in Southeast Asia by first attacking Kota Bharu on the northeastern coast of the Malay Peninsula. Hong Kong — defended by British, Indian and Canadian forces — fell into the power of the Japanese Imperial Army on 25 December 1941, and British, Australian and Indian troops in Singapore surrendered to Japan on 15 February 1942. Winston S. Churchill, the then British Prime Minister, famously described the fall of Singapore as "the worst disaster and largest capitulation in British history" (Churchill 1951, p. 81). The British Empire in East and Southeast Asia was once almost totally lost.

However, the Japanese invasion of British India met with a severe setback at Imphal and Kohima in 1944, and the Japanese Imperial Navy suffered seriously against the Americans in the Pacific theatre. Finally, the Japanese Empire, which once expanded — indeed, apparently overexpanded — from the Far East to large parts of Southeast Asia and the Pacific, entirely collapsed as the Japanese government accepted the Potsdam Declaration and surrendered to the Allied powers in the summer of 1945.

After World War II, the British Commonwealth Occupation Force, which was formed by Britain, Australia, New Zealand and British India, joined the occupation of Japan from February 1946. In September 1951, the United Kingdom, together with 47 countries including the United States and several Commonwealth partners, signed the Treaty of Peace with Japan in San Francisco to terminate the state of war and the allied occupation. After Indian and Pakistani independence in August 1947, Britain gradually gave independence to its colonies, protectorates and trust territories. According to John Darwin, "[o]ne of the most remarkable features of the dissolution of the British imperial system was its rapidity: in the twenty years after 1945 it contracted almost to vanishing point, in stark contrast to the durability of other senescent empires in world history, like the Byzantine or Ottoman" (Darwin 1991, p. 52). By the 1960s, the Anglo-Japanese relations not only further normalised (the Treaty of Commerce, Establishment and Navigation was signed between Britain and Japan in 1962) but also became a relationship between two island nations on the opposite sides of Eurasia, both of which had lost most or all of their former colonial territories.

The Anglo-Japanese inter-imperial relations in the first half of the 20th century had not only diplomatic and military aspects but also intellectual and ideological dimensions. The purpose of this chapter is to deepen our understanding of history of the Japanese Empire, mainly through examining discourses of Japanese intellectuals on *intra*-imperial relations within the Japanese Empire, through a historical analysis of the *inter*-imperial relationship with other European empires. Particularly, it will pay attention to British *inter*-imperial legacies in Japanese policy studies toward its formal and informal colonial possessions, including Taiwan and other "Chinese" regions in Asia and the Pacific.

In the existing studies, much attention has been paid to the political thought of Tadao Yanaihara (矢内原忠雄). It is notable that two monographs have been published in English on Yanaihara's thought on imperial and colonial affairs (Townsend 2000; Nakano 2013), and it cannot be denied that Yanaihara was the most prominent among inter-war Japanese liberal intellectuals who worked on the study of empire and colonial policy. However, of course, there were many other liberal and critical scholars of colonial policy in inter-war Japan, such as Miono Yamamoto (山本美越乃) and Akira Izumi (泉哲). This chapter attempts to analyze the scope and limits of political thought of these Japanese liberal intellectuals of colonial policy studies in the inter-war period.

On inter-imperial legacies in colonial policy studies in pre-war Japan, Tetsuya Sakai dealt with the attitudes of some Japanese liberal intellectuals who considered the British Empire as an example to reform the Japanese Empire (Sakai 2007, Ch. 5; Sakai 2010). However, inter-imperial relations were not confined to the one between Britain and Japan. Although this chapter mainly deals with the Anglo-Japanese inter-imperial relations, it also looks at Japan's relations with other imperial or "post-imperial" powers such as France and the Soviet Union, the latter of which could be described as "post-imperial" because it — while ardently criticized imperialism — actually inherited much of the vast territory and multi-ethnic society from the Russian Empire. Furthermore, in addition to these *inter*-imperial legacies in Japan's colonial policy studies on its *intra*-imperial relations, it also explores the *intra*-imperial influences and interactions within the Japanese Empire, such as those between Taiwan and Manchuria.

The Origins and Expansion of the Japanese Empire and "Greater China"

While the British Empire was by far the largest empire in the world, Japan also established its own empire in Asia and the Pacific from the 1890s onward. After the Meiji Restoration in the late 1860s, Japan first pursued a policy of "defensive modernizations" alongside with a few other independent Asian and African nations such as Thailand, Afghanistan and Ethiopia. These diverse groups of states somehow managed to maintain their independence in the face of fierce Western imperialist advances. China could also avoid being divided up fully by great powers, although it was kept in the form of a semi-colonial status, as dozens of foreign concessions and leased territories were made mainly along its coastline, and Manchukuo was eventually established by Japan in northeastern China[2] (Westad 2005, p. 78).

Following the models of European and American great powers, Japan pursued a plan for building up "a rich country with a strong army." Partly in order to overcome unequal treaties imposed by Western imperialist powers which gave them extra-territorial and economic privileges from the mid-19th century, Japan embarked on constitutional developments such as the establishment of the Meiji Constitution and the Imperial Diet in 1889 and 1890, respectively. In the process of pursuing these policies, Japan not only succeeded in overcoming unequal treatment by Western great powers but also followed their lead by obtaining its own colonial and semi-colonial territories in Asia and the Pacific. Some of the regions of "Greater China" such as Taiwan and Manchuria were included in these Japanese colonial and semi-colonial possessions.

By the Treaty of Shimonoseki which ended the Sino-Japanese War of 1894–1895, Japan obtained Taiwan, including the Penghu islands (Pescadores), as its first overseas colony, while Okinawa (the former Ryukyu Kingdom) and Hokkaido (the former Ezo where the Ainu lived sparsely and were subjected to the Matsumae domain based in its southernmost tip) were more or less colonized by Japan as its "internal colonies."[3] By the Treaty of Portsmouth

---

[2] John Darwin regards Afghanistan as part of Britain's "spheres of interference" formed by countries and regions such as Iran and the Persian Gulf as well (Darwin 2009, p. 1). While maintaining its independence, Thailand had to sign unequal treaties with Western powers and eventually conceded the southern part of its territory to Britain in 1909. This became four northern states in British Malaya (Kelantan, Terengganu, Kedah and Perlis), which formed Un-Federated Malay States with Johor in the southernmost tip of the Malay Peninsula. All of the Un-Federated Malay States were placed under Britain's indirect control through British Advisers.

[3] Contemporary arguments on "internal colonies" largely originated in Michael Hechter's socio-historical analysis of Scotland, Wales and Ireland (Northern Ireland after the partition of 1922) as "the Celtic Fringe" or "internal colonies" in the United Kingdom (Hechter 1975). As Hechter pointed out in the new edition of his book, the concept of "internal colonialism" dated from the late 19th century when it was initially coined by Russian populists (*Narodniki*) to describe the exploitation of peasants by urban classes. It was later adopted by Antonio

which ended the Russo-Japanese War of 1904–1905, the Kwantung Leased Territory, which had been originally leased by Russia from the Qing Empire and included the strategically important Dalian and Port Arthur (Lüshun), and Southern Sakhalin (Minami Karafuto) were added to the Japanese Empire. Based on the concessions given by Russia stipulated in the Treaty of Portsmouth, Japan also took over the southern branch line (from Changchun to Port Arthur with its sub-branch lines) of the Eastern Chinese Railway which had been constructed by the Russians. Then, the South Manchuria Railway Company was established in 1906. It is usually abbreviated as the "Mantetsu (満鉄)" in Japanese. The Mantetsu was one of the largest companies in the Japanese Empire and largely an instrument of Japan's "national policy" of extending its economic and military control over northeastern China. Japan also took over from Russia the South Manchuria Railway areas (which means the areas annexed by the Mantetsu) along the railway lines in which the Company had extra-territorial rights and could exclude Chinese involvement.

The vision of the Mantetsu held by its first president, Shimpei Goto (後藤新平), was modelled after the British East India Company, which had been a driving force for British colonial rule in India. The Mantetsu was practically a state machinery which played a leading role in pursuing Japan's continental policy, though it was often embroiled in faction-fighting within and between political, bureaucratic and military elites in Tokyo. Before he became the first president of the Mantetsu, Goto (originally trained as a doctor in Japan) was the advisor on public health, and then chief of the Public Welfare Bureau, of the Office of the Governor in Taiwan from 1896 to 1898 and from 1898 to 1906, respectively. As a colonial administrator in Taiwan under the governorship of Gentaro Kodama (児玉源太郎), he was not only proactive for economic and social development but fiercely oppressive against local insurgents. After Japan occupied a large part of Manchuria as a result of the

---

Gramsci, Vladimir Lenin, Yevgeny Preobrazhensky and Nikolay Bukharin to characterize the persisting economic underdevelopment of certain Italian and Russian regions (Hechter 1999, pp. xiii–xiv). For the latest historical analysis on "domestic colonies," see Arneil 2017.

Russo-Japanese War, Goto was persuaded by Kodama, who had become the Chief of the General Staff of Japan's Manchuria Army in 1904, to become a president of the Mantetsu. Goto accepted the offer after much hesitation. As the first president of the Mantetsu, he was expected to apply his expertise based on his experiences for colonial modernization in Taiwan. The first vice-president of the Mantetsu, Korekimi Nakamura (中村是公), also moved from the Office of the Governor in Taiwan. Nakamura was to become the second president after Goto's resignation to be the Minister of Communications and Transportation in Tokyo in 1908. Nakamura was then transferred to the Governor of the Kwantung Leased Territory in 1917. When he was in Taiwan, Goto directed a large-scale academic investigation into indigenous customs, conducted a census and proposed to establish an institute to do research on industries and hygiene as a basis for making policies of colonial administration. Within the Mantetsu, the Research Department (満鉄調査部) was established in 1907 by Goto based on his experiences in Taiwan, in order to lay intellectual foundations for colonial administration by doing research on general economics and traditional customs of Manchuria. The Research Department of the Mantetsu based in Dalian was to have more than 2,000 researchers (including liberals and even Marxists) at its peak and become the most renowned "think tank" in pre-war Japan. It was also to deal with other countries and regions such as the Soviet Union, of which Masayoshi Miyazaki (宮崎正義) became a leading expert within the Research Department. The Research Section was established at the office of the Mantetsu in Harbin ("a strategic point of transportation connecting Asia and Europe") to conduct research on the Soviet Union as well. In addition, the Research Bureau of East Asian Economics (東亜経済調査局) was set up at the Tokyo Branch of the Mantetsu for the purpose of doing research on politics, economics and societies, not only of Manchuria but also across Asia[4] (Kato 2006, pp. 27–33, 36, 58, 76, 81–82, 159, 195).

---

[4] On Goto in Taiwan and Manchuria (including the establishment of the Research Department of the Mantetsu), see also Kobayashi 2006, pp. 29–40.

During the course of the 1900s, Korea was forced to become a Japanese protectorate through three Japanese–Korean Treaties signed in 1904, 1905 and 1907, and finally annexed by Japan in 1910. In addition, islands north of the equator in the Western Pacific, which had been under German control before the First World War, became Japan's mandated territory under the nominal supervision of the League of Nations founded in 1920. Japan's South Seas Mandate was one of the Class C mandates and could be administered as an integral part of Japan. Some of the other former German-held territories were also categorized as Class C mandates and assigned to Britain and three Dominions of the British Empire: New Guinea (northern half of today's Papua New Guinea, assigned to Australia), Nauru (assigned jointly to Britain, Australia and New Zealand), Western Samoa (today's Samoa, assigned to New Zealand) and South West Africa (today's Namibia, assigned to the Union of South Africa).

The Establishment of Colonial Policy Studies in Japan

As the Japanese Empire became larger and anti-colonial movements in formal and informal colonies stronger, some liberal Japanese intellectuals tried to find the ways in which they could make intra-imperial relations more equal and mutually cooperative. Some of them also maintained that "group personalities" of the constituent parts of the Japanese Empire should be respected. Tadao Yanaihara was probably the most prominent and well known among these liberal Japanese intellectuals in the inter-war years. From 1923 to 1937, he lectured on colonial policy at the Faculty of Economics of Tokyo Imperial University, the predecessor of the University of Tokyo. The Professorship of Colonial Policy at Tokyo Imperial University was founded in 1908 by the initiative of Shimpei Goto. As already mentioned, Goto was a colonial administrator in Taiwan from 1896 to 1906, and then the first president of the Mantetsu from 1906 to 1908. Goto's colonial experiences in Taiwan and Manchuria for 12 years seem to have led him to think that serious and systematic colonial studies were indispensable for further advancing colonial modernity and Japanese interests in its expanding formal and informal empires.[5] Yanaihara was once a student and eventually became a successor of the well-known liberal internationalist Inazo Nitobe (新渡戸稲造), who was the first holder of this professorship.[6]

Nitobe was originally a scholar of agricultural administration who was educated and then gave lectures at Sapporo Agricultural College established in Hokkaido in 1876. Sapporo Agricultural College was established in order to educate students to become future leaders of development and cultivation in Hokkaido, by inviting three foreign academics and educators, including William Smith Clark as its first vice-principal, from Massachusetts Agricultural College. Among graduates of Sapporo Agricultural College, there were some leading figures who were engaged in colonial administration and research in Japan's overseas colonies.

---

[5] Similarly, some colonial and Dominion politicians, administrators, businessmen and organizations, particularly those active in Southern Africa, played significant roles in establishing colonial, imperial and Commonwealth studies in Britain. The Beit Professorship of Colonial History at the University of Oxford was founded in 1905 by Alfred Beit, "the mining magnate" from Africa, shortly before he died. It was the first chair of colonial history in Britain and has existed until today as the Beit Professorship of Imperial and Commonwealth History. Three other senior named professorships of the subject in Britain are the Vere Harmsworth Professorship of Imperial and Naval History at the University of Cambridge (established in 1919 as the Vere Harmsworth Professorship of Naval History and, following a campaign by the Royal Empire Society, renamed in 1932), the Rhodes Professorship of Imperial History at King's College London (established in 1920 by the Rhodes Trust which was founded by the will of Cecil Rhodes, a colonial administrator and mine magnate in Southern Africa) and the Smuts Professorship of Commonwealth History at the University of Cambridge (established in 1952 as the Smuts Professorship of the History of the British Commonwealth), the last of which was "part of a national memorial to Jan Smuts," a Cambridge graduate and renowned military and political leader in colonial and postcolonial South Africa. On three chairs at Oxford and Cambridge, see Hyam 2010, pp. 342–343, 509, 512–514, 517. On the Rhodes Trust's grants to "academic causes with an imperial aspect" to several British universities, including the setting up of the Rhodes Chair of Imperial History at King's College London, see Kenny 2001, p. 19.

[6] In 1901, when he was a professor at Sapporo Agricultural College, Nitobe accepted an invitation by Shimpei Goto to be a technical expert, and eventually the chief of the Sugar Industries Bureau, of the Office of the Governor in Taiwan (sugar was one of the most important industries in colonial Taiwan). Afterward, Nitobe gave lectures on colonial policy as a professor at Tokyo Imperial University from 1909 to 1920, before being appointed as the Under-Secretary General of the newly established League of Nations in 1920. He held that position in Geneva until 1926.

For example, Minoru Togo (東郷実) was a graduate of Sapporo Agricultural College and, after entering the Office of the Governor in Taiwan, was sent to Germany and studied colonial policy at the University of Berlin for three years from 1909. Togo eventually became the head of the Research Department at the Secretariat of the Office of the Governor in Taiwan. Togo's attitude toward empire and colonies was rather eclectic. Indeed, while he severely criticized Akira Izumi for supporting Taiwanese nationalism (as examined below), he opposed the policies of assimilation and argued in his book in 1925 for "coexistence and co-prosperity" between the mother country and colonies by invoking Peter Kropotkin's *Mutual Aid* published in 1902. Some of the origins of Togo's argument for "coexistence and co-prosperity" could also be traced back to the inclusion of terms related to "altruistic interests" such as "coexistence" and "co-prosperity" as well as conventional strategic and commercial "special relationship" in Japan's political statements toward China in early 1917 (Wakabayashi 2001, p. 100; Sakai 2007, p. 227).

Sapporo Agricultural College was incorporated into the newly established Tohoku Imperial University as its School of Agriculture in 1907, and then became the predecessor of Hokkaido Imperial University established in 1918 and today's Hokkaido University founded in 1949. Sapporo Agricultural College can be considered as Japan's first "colonial" college, as its main purpose was to produce human resources to facilitate "internal colonization" of Hokkaido. Indeed, the term "internal colony" was commonly used in pre-war Hokkaido studies, because Hokkaido studies was started largely as colonial studies. In Japan, the first lecture of colonial studies was started by Shosuke Sato (佐藤昌介) — an agricultural economist who had been taught and deeply influenced by Clark together with other students like Nitobe and Kanzo Uchimura (内村鑑三) — at Sapporo Agricultural College in 1890, and the first course of colonial studies (as a course of agricultural administration and colonial studies) was set up when Sapporo Agricultural College was briefly incorporated into Tohoku Imperial University as its School of Agriculture in 1907 (Imanishi 2007, p. 20).

When Hokkaido Imperial University was established in 1918, Sato became its first president and held that position until 1930. Like Sato, Nitobe also took up a position as a full professor at Sapporo Agricultural College in the 1890s. Nitobe's colonial policy studies — later lectured at Tokyo Imperial University — had their roots in his early study, research and teaching on agricultural administration and development in "colonial" Hokkaido.

In 1920, Yanaihara was invited to become an associate professor lecturing on colonial policy at Tokyo Imperial University, only three years after he graduated from the Department of Political Science, the Faculty of Law, of the same university in 1917. In the early 1920s, Yanaihara studied in the United Kingdom and Europe for a little over two years, before taking up a full professorship in Tokyo in 1923. Before he came back to Japan from Europe via the United States, he visited Ireland and the Middle East (Townsend 2002, pp. 227–228). Yanaihara's *Teikokushugi ka no Taiwan* [*Taiwan under Imperialism*] published in 1929 by Iwanami Shoten, a Tokyo-based liberal publisher, was hailed as a "bible" among Taiwanese people, especially its middle-class intellectuals, who longed for liberation from Japanese imperial rule. Indeed, it was considered to be so liberal that it was immediately banned in Taiwan by the Japanese authority. Yanaihara was even forced to resign from his job as a professor at the Faculty of Economics of Tokyo Imperial University in December 1937, after he published an article titled "Kokka no riso [The Ideal of State]" which indirectly criticized Japan's militarism after the outbreak of the Sino-Japanese War in July 1937. In this article published in Chuokoron magazine (September 1937), he insisted — though using rather abstract terms — that Japan's military operation in China could not be approved based on the consideration of "the ideal of state." Yanaihara maintained that strong states should not violate the rights of other states, particularly those of weaker ones, in order to achieve their own "ideal" and "justice" (Yanaihara 1982; Yanaihara 1988; Sumiya 1988, pp. 285–290).

Miono Yamamoto gave lectures on colonial policy at the Faculty of Economics of Kyoto Imperial University (predecessor of Kyoto University). He first belonged to the Faculty of Law from

1912 to 1918, and then moved to the Faculty of Economics. According to Kyoji Asada, both Yanaihara and Yamamoto evidently represented Japanese academics of colonial policy studies based at national universities in the inter-war years (Asada 1990, p. 714). Largely after the Russo-Japanese War, colonial policy studies was established in Japan as a serious academic subject, mainly through the adoption of Western academic achievements. In the early years of colonial policy studies in Japan, Yamamoto started his lectures on colonial policy at Kyoto Imperial University in 1914 and became one of the central figures on this subject. He continued to give lectures to his students at Kyoto on the same subject until his retirement in 1933 (Wakabayashi 2001, pp. 88–89).

After World War I, with Yamamoto as one of their forerunners, other liberal or critical Japanese academics of colonial studies followed, such as Akira Izumi, Tadao Yanaihara and Karoku Hosokawa (細川嘉六). In this descending order, their criticisms against the colonial policy of the Japanese government became stronger (Wakabayashi 2001, p. 88). For some of these Japanese scholars of colonial policy studies, Paul S. Reinsch, Professor of Political Science (1901–1913) at the University of Wisconsin, had a substantial influence through his lectures and writings based on his liberal and internationalist thought against assimilation of colonies[7] (Sakai 2007, pp. 208–210). Indeed, Yamamoto and Izumi both attended Reinsch's lectures at the Department of Political Science of the University of Wisconsin, when they studied abroad in the United States. According to Izumi himself, his book titled *Shokuminchi tochi ron* [*A Study of Colonial Administration*], which was published in Japan in 1921, "owes much to lectures and books of my former respected professor, Dr. Paul Reinsch" (Izumi 1924, explanatory notes). Reinsch's most influential books on colonial policy were *Colonial Government* and *Colonial Administration*,

---

[7] In 1913, Reinsch was appointed as Minister to China by President Woodrow Wilson. He held that position until 1919. After his resignation as Minister, he continued to work for China, first as a legal counsellor from 1919, and after his failed campaign for US Senate as a Democratic candidate in 1920, as an adviser on fiscal reform for the Chinese government until he died in Shanghai in 1923.

published in 1902 and 1905, respectively (Reinsch 1902, 1905; Pugach 1979).

Models for Colonial Reforms

As a newly emerging colonial power, it was quite natural for the Japanese to seek a model (or models) among European great powers which had already accumulated substantial colonial possessions. There were great empires in the East, such as the Qing Empire and the Mogul Empire, but those were seriously declining or had even collapsed by the late 19th century. For most Japanese political, military, economic and intellectual leaders in the late 19th and early 20th centuries, modernization largely meant Westernization. Most modern Japanese intellectuals could be categorized as what Theodore H. Von Laue called "the Westernized non-Western intelligentsia" which was created as "a new category of cultural half-breeds" as part of the general pattern of Westernization (Von Laue 1987, p. 29).

Especially for Japanese critical academics of colonial policy studies (except for Hosokawa who was an ardent Marxist), the British Empire and the British Commonwealth of Nations offered the most important example to follow in order to reform the Japanese Empire into a more equal and mutually supportive one. Yanaihara argued in 1930 that Dominions such as Canada and Australia "now departed from the status of Britain's dependent territories and gained the status as autonomous nations completely equal with the United Kingdom internally, externally and militarily. Moreover, they constitute the British Empire, freely (in other words without enforcement) associated with Britain." He emphasized that it must be called as "an entirely new form of union between political groups" (Yanaihara 1963, p. 420).

Japanese liberal intellectuals tended to criticize colonial policies of subjugation (従属主義) and assimilation (同化主義), and advocated policies of autonomy (自治主義or自主主義) to be adopted in Japanese colonial territories. The British Empire and the British Commonwealth of Nations were considered to be a leading case of the policies of autonomy, while Japan's actual colonial policy rather resembled the French model of assimilation. Indeed, *kominka seisaku* (皇民化政策), a policy of imposing Japanese culture, language, religion (Shintoism) and social institutions on its colonial subjects, was forcefully pursued in the 1930s and early 1940s. In particular, Koreans were notoriously forced to change their names to Japanese ones by the Office of the Governor in Korea during 1940–1945. At least from critical or radical point of view the precedents for *kominka seisaku* could be observed in Japanese assimilation policies (part of its "internal colonial policies") toward indigenous population in Okinawa (called as the Okinawans or the Ryukyuans) and the Ainu in Hokkaido.

According to Izumi, who advocated policies of autonomy rather than those of assimilation, Japan had "unconsciously" adopted policies of assimilation since the acquisition of Taiwan (Izumi 1924, p. 245). Like under the French policy of assimilation which was pursued at least until the mid-1950s, any possibility of independence was totally excluded, even in a long run, by the Japanese government for its colonial possessions. In early 1944, at the beginning of the Imperial Conference held in Brazzaville by the French Committee of National Liberation (which was established at Algiers under the leadership of Charles de Gaulle in the previous year), a political principle in line with French colonial traditions was laid down as follows: "The aims of France in her civilizing work in the colonies exclude any idea of self-government, any possibility of development outside the French Empire; the formation of independent Governments in the colonies, however distant, cannot be contemplated." The rapporteur of the conference in Brazzaville said that "[w]e visualize the Empire in the Roman sense of the word, not in the Anglo-Saxon sense" (Julien 1950, p. 493).

It is true that there were some arguments in favor of self-government even in France, especially in the midst of the transition from the pre-war French Empire to the post-war French Union. For example, Pierre-Olivier Lapie, who had been the Governor of Chad from 1940 to 1942, wrote in 1944 that René Pleven (de Gaulle's commissioner for colonies) and Henri Laurentie (the director of political affairs in the Colonial Commissariat) had "a clearer realization than ever before that the colonizing nation's sole aim is to transform the colonized areas into states which will some day be its own equals," and ultimately might be "freed from their link to France, if such is their wish" (Kratoska 2003, p. 12). However, France's actual policy toward its colonies within the framework of the French Union established under the Constitution of the Fourth Republic in 1946 eventually followed the traditional line of assimilation and largely denied colonial self-government, let alone independence. The granting of internal autonomy to Tunisia in the summer of 1954 was a crucial turning point in the overall French colonial policy away from assimilation and the denial of autonomy and independence toward decolonization (the process of granting of autonomy and eventual independence) (Ikeda 2016). In June 1956, the French government under the premiership of Guy Mollet devolved internal autonomy to the individual territories within the French Union through the *loi-cadre* (Byrne 2013, p. 104). In other words, in both French and Japanese colonial policies (in the former case, at least until the mid-1950s), not only independence but also self-government was basically out of question.

For Japanese Marxist scholars of colonial and ethnic policy studies, the Soviet Union's ethnic policy, both internal and external, offered a model of (at least officially) equal treatment of all ethnic groups. Internally, the Soviet Union, which largely inherited the vast territory of the Russian Empire, was supposed to treat equally all constituent republics and other smaller ethnic minorities. In reality, the conditions imposed upon ethnic minorities in the USSR were often no less ruthless than those in tsarist Russia. It was uncovered in great detail by Timothy Snyder that Iosif Stalin deliberately starved more than three million people in Soviet Ukraine to death in 1933. It was nothing less than "a political famine." From 1933 to 1945, some fourteen million civilians and prisoners of war (including more than five million European Jews who were victims of the Holocaust) were killed by either Nazi Germany or the Soviet Union in "the bloodlands," which covered

Poland, the Baltic States, Belarus, Ukraine and western Russia. Three major methods of murder were starvation, shooting and gassing[8] (Snyder 2010, pp. vii–viii, x–xi, xiv, 379–380, 388, 394–395). In addition, for Stalin, "[t]he secret of collectivization…was that it was an alternative to expansive colonization, which is to say a form of internal colonization" (Snyder 2010, p. 159). However, the reality of the internal ethnic policy of the Soviet Union was strictly concealed in many cases, and Marxists all over the world (including those in Japan) tended to overlook the inconvenient truth in any case. Moreover, under the "atheistic" Communist regime, various religious groups in the Soviet Union (not just religious minorities such as Muslims, Jews and Catholics, but also majority Orthodox Christians) were oppressed at least in public, though people could more or less maintain their religious practices in private.

Externally, since the days of Vladimir Lenin, Soviet leaders advocated self-determination overseas and opposed the continuation of Western imperialists' colonial rule. After the Russian Revolution of 1917, and especially after many anti-colonial leaders were bitterly disappointed as the victorious powers of the Great War did not honor the slogans of self-determination at the post-war peace conferences, the Soviet Union attracted much attention from colonized peoples. "Not only did the Bolsheviks condemn colonialism and offer alliances to those who resisted it, but they also showed the way, it was believed, toward a nonexploitative form of modern society" (Westad 2005, p. 80).

Karoku Hosokawa was a pioneer of and probably the most prominent among Marxist scholars of colonial and ethnic policy studies in Japan. Hosokawa was a researcher at the Ohara Institute for Social Research based in Osaka from 1920 to 1936. After 1936, he moved to Tokyo and continued to publish articles that severely criticized Japanese colonial rule in Asia from the standpoint of anti-imperialism and anti-fascism, first as a temporary researcher, and

---

[8] However, Richard J. Evans criticized that Snyder excessively concentrated on ethnic minorities and sidelined "the fate of the millions of Russians who died at Stalin's hands" (Evans 2015, p. 393).

then as the head of the China Research Division of the Tokyo Branch of the Mantetsu. The China Research Division of the Mantetsu was closed down in 1941 as a result of the "Sorge Incident" in which one of its temporary researchers and renowned commentator on Chinese affairs, Hotsumi Ozaki (尾崎秀実), was arrested because of his collusion with Richard Sorge, a German-born communist and Soviet spy. Sorge (disguised as an American journalist named Johnson) and Ozaki first met and started to cooperate in intelligence activities in Shanghai in 1930, when the latter was a foreign correspondent of the *Asahi Shimbun* newspaper. After the outbreak of the Sino-Japanese War in 1937, the Research Department (*Chosabu*) of the Mantetsu in Dalian experienced substantial expansion to become the so-called "larger Research Department" established in April 1939. However, there occurred the "Mantetsu Chosabu Incident" in 1942–1943, in which the Kwantung Military-Police Unit arrested substantial numbers of researchers of the *Chosabu* on the pretext of wiping out a group of communists. As a result of the incident, the *Chosabu* received a fatal blow and was scaled down significantly. Hosokawa was also arrested in September 1942, because his article titled "Sekaishi no doko to Nihon [The Trend of World History and Japan]," which once passed censorship by the Information Board and was published in *Kaizo* magazine (August-September 1942), was regarded as camouflaged communist propaganda by the Press Section of the Japanese Imperial Army. His arrest marked the beginning of the "Yokohama Incident," the largest suppression of freedom of speech and thought based on fabricated evidences in wartime Japan. Although four prisoners were tortured to death (in prison or soon after their release), Hosokawa was finally released in October 1945, two months after the end of World War II. Ozaki and Sorge were sentenced to death and executed on 7 November 1944[9] (Asada 1990, pp. 6, 520–521, 716–718; Kato 2006, pp. 172–174, 181, 196).

---

[9] "Sekaishi no doko to Nihon" was reproduced in Hosokawa 1972.

The British Commonwealth of Nations and Japanese Liberal Intellectuals

Between the two world wars, the British Commonwealth of Nations was defined by the Balfour Report of 1926 and formally established by the Statute of Westminster of 1931. According to the definition stipulated by the Balfour Report, Britain and the six Dominions (Canada, Australia, New Zealand, Newfoundland, the Union of South Africa and the Irish Free State) were "autonomous Communities within the British Empire, equal in status, in no way subordinate one to another in any aspect of their domestic or external affairs, though united by a common allegiance to the Crown, and freely associated as members of the British Commonwealth of Nations" (National Archives of Australia 1926).

The "White Dominions" of Canada, Australia, New Zealand and Newfoundland obtained internal self-government well before the Balfour Report and the Statute of Westminster. Some British settler colonies in North America and the South Pacific advanced constitutional development by establishing "responsible government" based on the parliamentary cabinet system (the so-called Westminster system), which originated in the United Kingdom, from the mid-19th century onward. The Dominion of Canada, the Commonwealth of Australia, the Dominion of New Zealand and the Dominion of Newfoundland were created as Dominions with the right of internal self-government in 1867, 1901, 1907 and 1907, respectively. The British Commonwealth was gradually formed as these British settlement colonies first became internally self-governing and then (mainly after the First World War) externally autonomous within the British Empire, while other British colonies such as India, which "[f]or climatic and economic reasons … never became a colony of white settlement" (Brown 1999, p. 423), remained tightly under British control. Lord Milner, who had been the High Commissioner for South Africa from 1897 to 1905, observed in 1906 that there were "two empires," one white and self-governing, and the other non-white and dependent (Louis 1999, p. 7).

After the South African War of 1899–1902, the Union of South Africa was formed in 1910 as a fifth Dominion largely underpinned by massive gold production, owing to the British decision to cooperate with "moderate" Boers (Afrikaners) represented by Louis Botha and Jan Christiaan Smuts (Darwin 2009, pp. 251–254, 280–281). Botha and Smuts became prime ministers of the Union of South Africa in 1910–1919 and 1919–1924, respectively. In addition, Smuts was to become one of the leading advocates of a British Commonwealth of Nations, in which each Dominion would enjoy self-government while enhancing cooperation within the British Empire and maintaining allegiance to the Crown. On 15 May 1917, Smuts made a speech at a banquet held in the Royal Gallery of the House of Lords in honor of himself, shortly before he became the only Dominion politician to be a member of Britain's War Cabinet in June 1917. Smuts devoted most of his speech to a definition of the Commonwealth and its affairs, with Milner (also a member of the War Cabinet) sitting by his side. Smuts maintained that the British Empire was "a system of nations." "We are not a State, but a community of States and nations." He then described Dominions as "independent in their government, which have been evolved on the principles of your free constitutional system into almost independent States, which all belong to this community of nations, and which I prefer to call 'the British Commonwealth of Nations'" (Smuts 1952, pp. 187–191). During the Imperial Conference in 1921, Smuts raised fundamental questions such as equality of sovereignty between Britain and the Dominions, but "[a]fter sitting for seven weeks the Conference decided that it would not after all define the mysteries of Dominion Status, preferring plasticity to precision" (McMahon 1999, p. 150). However, this eventually led to the devising of the definition of the Commonwealth stipulated by the Balfour Report five years later.

Smuts' ideas of Commonwealth as well as the Union of South Africa seem to have stemmed from his holistic vision, or holism (Smuts 1926). According to Smuts' son who published his biography shortly after his father's death, it was "perhaps the holistic concept of an integrated whole being larger than the sum of its constituent parts that gave him this idea. No less was it this holistic vision that brought about the integration we now know as the Union of South Africa" (Smuts 1952, p. xiv). Indeed, Smuts went on to say in his aforementioned speech in May 1917 that the British Empire was "a whole world by ourselves, consisting of many nations, of many States, and all sorts of communities under one flag" and referred to "this world which is comprised in the British Empire" (Smuts 1952, p. 189).

From South Africa, there also emerged a small group of British elites who had an important, if not straightforward, influence on the development of the idea (or at least the label) of Commonwealth. In the aftermath of the South African War, Milner recruited a dozen or so young Oxford graduates, the so-called Milner's "Kindergarten," for the administration of South African colonies. As a notable example, Lionel Curtis worked on post-war reconstruction and in the movement that led to the formation of the Union of South Africa. The South African experience led them, including Curtis (who was to become the Beit Lecturer in Colonial History at the University of Oxford) and Philip Kerr, to take up Milner's call for "organic union" of Britain and the self-governing Dominions and form the core group of the Round Table movement. The Round Tablers, meeting together as a "Moot," did not have any formal constitution nor more than about two dozen members. They argued persistently, though elusively, for "organic union" of Britain and the Dominions by using the idealized concept of "Commonwealth," based on their belief that Dominion autonomy and voluntary cooperation were insufficient for security of the British Empire. However, their idea of tightly constituted "organic union," or federation, lost most of its momentum, when the Resolution Nine of the Imperial War Conference of 1917 called for definition of the Dominions as "autonomous nations of an Imperial Commonwealth." However, at the same time, the Round Tablers made a great contribution to stimulate debate about the concept of "Commonwealth," largely through their anonymous articles in the quarterly magazine, *the Round Table*, which was first published in 1910 (McIntyre 2009, pp. 28–31, 87–90).

Unlike other settler colonies of the British Empire, Ireland was annexed to the United Kingdom in 1801. In Ireland, there were increasingly bitter disputes over "Home Rule" (or self-government), particularly from the late 19th century onward. However, the Irish Free State was finally established as a sixth Dominion by moderate Irish nationalists led by W. T. Cosgrave in 1922 after experiencing the Easter Rising of 1916 and the Anglo-Irish War of 1919–1921, although Ireland was partitioned and Northern Ireland remained in the United Kingdom. In the run-up to the adoption of the Balfour Report at the Imperial Conference in 1926, Canada (under Prime Minister William Lyon Mackenzie King), the Union of South Africa (under J. B. M. Hertzog, the Prime Minister in 1924–1939) and the Irish Free State (under the leadership of Cosgrave) played a significant part in persuading the British to accept equal partnership between Britain and the Dominions.

Even in India, provincial autonomy centered on Legislative Councils in provincial capitals was gradually introduced by two Government of India Acts for constitutional reform in 1919 and 1935, although the Viceroy based in Delhi (capital of British India after 1911) largely maintained its control over All-India imperial governance of the Raj. In February 1937, elections of provincial Legislative Councils were held "under the radically democratized system" and the Indian National Congress formed the governments in seven provinces. Then, "provincial autonomy was fully operative for two years after the 1937 elections," before World War II broke out in September 1939 (Brown 1999, pp. 425, 430, 432).

In the Dominions within the British Empire, Dominion parliaments were central to their internal and external autonomy. Indeed, the arguments for establishing colonial parliaments within the Japanese Empire were largely modelled on this British lead. In this inter-imperial perspective, the meaning of Yamamoto's and Yanaihara's arguments for setting up colonial parliaments in Korea and Taiwan, for instance, can be better understood in its historical context.

Yamamoto, who advocated policies of autonomy, argued in his article in 1919 that Korea should be allowed to be a self-governing colony and its future relations with Japan should be made harmonious by making it like those of Britain with Canada, Australia and South Africa. According to Yamamoto, Korea should be allowed to have a parliamentary system and "responsible government" and its inhabitants should have rights to participate in the legislative process. Though rather paternalistically, Yamamoto thought it essential that Koreans could be "trained" toward self-government by strengthening the function of *Chusuin* (中枢院), the consultative assembly for the Governor in Korea, the members of which were Koreans except for its speaker and chief secretary, and establishing local administrative councils largely composed of popularly elected members. In addition, when Yamamoto made an inspection of Taiwan for the first time in 1921, he was disappointed by the Japanese population there but impressed by Taiwanese intellectuals. Therefore, in his article published in 1925, Yamamoto expressed his support for establishing a colonial parliament in Taiwan without considering it as "premature" any more (Wakabayashi 2001, pp. 92, 95, 127).

Yanaihara's theory of colonization owned much to Adam Smith's *Wealth of Nations*, which was published in 1776. According to Smith, Britain should voluntarily abandon its colonies and devise commercial treaties that would guarantee free trade. Smith indicated that this might dispose colonists to respect the mother country and become valuable allies for Britain. In addition, Yanaihara argued that granting autonomy to colonies was not necessarily undertaken at the expense of the metropolis, based on the experiences of Britain's self-governing colonies from the 19th century onward. He maintained that the adoption of policies of autonomy and the recognition of the right of the peoples in Taiwan and Korea to participate in the political system through the establishment of colonial parliaments were a "requirement of justice." In addition, he advocated "responsible cabinet government" for Korea and Taiwan along the lines drawn up in Lord Durham's *Report on the Affairs of British North America* submitted to the British Parliament in 1839 (Townsend 2000, pp. 80–82; Townsend 2002,

p. 229). Lord Durham was one of the leading figures of the liberal wing of the Whigs and had played a major role in drafting the Reform Bill of 1832 for parliamentary reforms in Britain. He was sent to British North America (part of today's Canada) as the Governor-General in 1838 with the responsibility of investigating the situation after the rebellions by the radicals in 1837. The so-called Durham Report of 1839 recommended that internal autonomy and "responsible government" should be introduced in British North America, and therefore indicated (at least in retrospect) the direction toward granting self-government in British settlement colonies.

In Japan, there were a number of Taiwanese students who were engaged in the movement for establishing a parliament in Taiwan. There were a relatively large number of such students at Meiji University in Tokyo. Cheng-lu Lin (林呈禄), Shi-hu Cai (蔡式穀) and Song-yun Zheng (鄭松筠) were some of the leading figures among those Taiwanese students who were not only influenced by but also gave influence to Akira Izumi. Izumi lectured on international law, political science and colonial policy at the School of Law and the School of Political Science and Economics of Meiji University from 1914 to 1927, first as a lecturer and then as a full professor. He eagerly supported the petitionary campaign for establishing a Taiwanese parliament. This campaign was "a characteristic nationalist movement in colonial Taiwan," which started in 1921 and lasted until 1934. However, in the early 1920s, Minoru Togo at the Office of the Governor in Taiwan attacked and even threatened Izumi's ardent support for Taiwanese nationalism and his criticism against Japanese colonial rule in Taiwan. The Office of the Governor considered Izumi's argument as instigating the idea of self-determination among Taiwanese people (Wakabayashi 2001, pp. 96, 98–101, 341).

In 1927, Izumi was appointed to Professor of International Law at the Faculty of Law and Letters of Keijo Imperial University in Seoul (called Keijo under Japanese rule), which had been established in 1924 as the first imperial university outside the Japanese metropole (then, Taihoku Imperial University was founded in Taipei in 1928).[10] Izumi's professorship at Keijo Imperial University in Seoul lasted until his retirement in 1935, after which he moved to northern China to work for the Mantetsu. Before taking up a professorship in Seoul, Izumi was one of the most eminent Japanese scholars of colonial policy studies based at private universities (as against Yanaihara and Yamamoto based at national universities) in the inter-war period, although a substantial part of his publications dealt with international law (Asada 1990, pp. 5–6, 16, 715). Before he started to give lectures at Meiji University in 1914, Izumi, who was born in Hokkaido and 11 years younger than Nitobe, first left Sapporo Agricultural College without finishing the course and then went to the United States to study subjects such as agricultural economics and international law for as many as 16 years.

Yanaihara argued, in his *Teikokushugi ka no Taiwan* [*Taiwan under Imperialism*] published in 1929, that Taiwanese society would be modernized following the example of Ireland. According to Yanaihara, although Taiwan did not have a single daily newspaper of its own and Taiwanese people were not given any franchise at that time, perhaps its middle-class intellectual citizens (which he considered as a powerful force in Taiwanese society) would lead their struggle for political liberty. He argued that this course was shown in Irish history and seemed to be a law of political development in colonial territories (Yanaihara 1988, p. 198). However, on the other hand, Yanaihara's attitude toward Ireland, which gained Dominion status after serious violent struggles, was rather ambiguous, in contrast to his largely positive attitude toward Britain's other self-governing colonies. In the late 1920s and early 1930s, Yanaihara wrote a series of articles in which he severely criticized British colonial policy in Ireland as well as in India. When he added one of these articles as an appendix to *Teikokushugi kano*

---

[10] In the Japanese Isles, Tokyo Imperial University (1877), Kyoto Imperial University (1897), Tohoku Imperial University (1907), Kyushu Imperial University (1910), Hokkaido Imperial University (1918), Osaka Imperial University (1931) and Nagoya Imperial University (1939) were founded. Together with those in Seoul and Taipei, there were nine imperial universities in total within the Japanese Empire.

Indo [*India under Imperialism*] published in 1937, Yanaihara pointed out that, while Ireland had obtained Dominion status and was no longer a colony dependent on the metropole, India was still in the midst of struggles for gaining that status (Yanaihara 1937, preface).

Unlike Yamamoto who was not ready to support the independence of the colonies of the Japanese Empire, both Yanaihara and Izumi argued for the possibility of eventual independence of the colonies. Yanaihara foresaw that possibility quite clearly, though it was thought to be a long process. According to Susan C. Townsend, "he regarded the Japanese empire as a fait accompli and his approach to colonial reform was essentially gradualist. Where he differed from many other colonial reformers either in Japan or in Britain, however, was in the fact that he looked forward to the inevitable, complete and peaceful cessation of the colonial relationship in the distant future" (Townsend 2002, pp. 229, 232). However, Izumi, if not Yamamoto, expressed a similar opinion at least in the 1920s. He maintained, though rather paternalistically, that it was "a divine mission for civilized colonizing powers" to promote happiness of peoples in their colonies and guide their cultural development. Then, Izumi argued, and indeed he "sincerely hope[d]," that it would finally no longer be necessary to possess colonies, if "international morality and sense of justice" were developed and the "natural right" of migration was not prohibited by any men and countries all over the world (Izumi 1924, p. 328).

Conclusion

However, Japanese liberal intellectuals of colonial policy studies were increasingly faced with difficulties after the Manchurian Incident and the outbreak of the Sino-Japanese War in the 1930s. Under the Great Depression, the Japanese government and armed forces sought to obtain "special interests" in Manchuria and Mongolia, like Nazi Germany tried to secure *Lebensraum* (living space) in Eastern Europe or "a frontier empire in the East" (Snyder 2010, p. 215). After the Manchurian Incident of September 1931,

established College of Arts and Sciences — largely modeled on American liberal arts colleges — at the University of Tokyo in 1952. Although Japanese liberal intellectuals faced substantial difficulties and were forced to change their opinions or lost their jobs during the 1930s and early 1940s, the trajectories of imperial universities, Yanaihara and colonial policy studies, for instance, demonstrated Japan's transformation from the pre-war and wartime militaristic Pan-Asianist empire to the post-war "liberal" pro-Western ally of the United States.

References

Arneil, Barbara. 2017. *Domestic Colonies: The Turn Inward to Colony*. Oxford: Oxford University Press.

Asada, Kyoji. 1990. *Nihon Shokuminchi kenkyushi ron* [*A Study of the History of Colonial Studies in Japan*]. Tokyo: Miraisha.

Brown, Judith M. 1999. "India." In Judith M. Brown and Wm. Roger Louis (Eds.). *The Oxford History of the British Empire, Vol. IV: The Twentieth Century*. Oxford: Oxford University Press, pp. 421–446.

Byrne, Jeffrey James. 2013. "Africa's Cold War." In Robert J. McMahon (Ed.). *The Cold War in the Third World*. Oxford: Oxford University Press, pp. 101–123.

Churchill, Winston S. 1951. *The Second World War, Volume IV: The Hinge of Fate*, 2nd ed. London: Cassell.

Cullather, Nick. 2013. "The War on the Peasant: The United States and the Third World." In Robert J. McMahon (Ed.). *The Cold War in the Third World*. Oxford: Oxford University Press, pp. 192–207.

Darwin, John. 1991. *The End of the British Empire: The Historical Debate*. Oxford: Basil Blackwell.

Darwin, John. 2009. *The Empire Project: The Rise and Fall of the British World-System, 1830–1970*. Cambridge: Cambridge University Press.

Evans, Richard J. 2015. *Third Reich in History and Memory*. London: Little, Brown.

Hechter, Michael. 1975. *Internal Colonialism: The Celtic Fringe in British National Development, 1536–1966*. London: Routledge & Kegan Paul.

Hechter, Michael. 1999. *Internal Colonialism: The Celtic Fringe in British National Development*, with a new introduction and a new appendix by the author. New Brunswick, NJ: Transaction Publishers.

the Kwantung Army occupied entire Manchuria within five months and Manchukuo was established in March 1932. While Puyi (溥儀), the "last emperor" Xuan-tong (宣統帝) of the Qing dynasty in 1908–1912, was recognized as its head of state, Manchukuo was a puppet regime or an informal empire controlled almost entirely by the Japanese. More than one million Japanese civilians emigrated to Manchuria, along with the stationing of the Kwantung Army, which was "the ruler of Manchuria"[11] (Kato 2006, p. 63).

As mentioned above, Yanaihara did not abandon his criticism against Japanese militarism and finally lost his job as a professor at Tokyo Imperial University. On the other hand, Izumi's attitude was more eclectic and indeed full of anguish. After the Manchurian Incident, the Japanese government opposed the proposal to invite the United States to the Council of the League of Nations as an observer, insisting on the necessity of a unanimous decision. On this point, Izumi, who was a professor of Keijo Imperial University in Seoul at the time of the Manchurian Incident, indirectly criticized the Japanese government on the ground that the question was just a procedural matter which did not require unanimity. This was a rather exceptional opinion, because most Japanese scholars of international law at that time endorsed the arguments made by the government. However, Izumi gradually came to argue in favor of the government's policy. In February 1933, the General Assembly of the League of Nations adopted a resolution which did not recognize Manchukuo by 42 votes with only one objection (Japan) and one abstention (Siam). In turn, the Japanese government officially notified its intention to withdraw from the League of Nations. On the adoption of the resolution, Izumi criticized the League of Nations on the ground that recognition of states should be left to the spontaneity of each state and it was unreasonable to adopt a resolution of non-recognition among many states with different interests. According to Sakai, "Izumi gradually changed from a cautious attacker against the Manchurian Incident to a typical defender" (Sakai 2007, pp. 215–216).

As the Japanese Empire expanded and became more aggressive in the 1930s, the arguments by Japan's liberal intellectuals to reform the Japanese Empire along the lines of the British Commonwealth of Nations lost much of the momentum. In reality, the Japanese Empire did not become like the Commonwealth and instead expanded from Manchuria and Mongolia to the rest of Mainland China. Particularly after the outbreak of the Sino-Japanese War in 1937, the ideology of Großraum (great space)[12] was pursued based on certain versions of Pan-Asianism such as a "New Order in East Asia" (1938) and then a "Greater East Asia Co-Prosperity Sphere" (1940). In these versions of Pan-Asianism, the Japanese government and its right-wing ideologues considered Japan as a ruling nation in Asia, while they often advanced a more inclusive and idealistic slogan of "the whole world under one roof (八紘一宇)."

After World War II, Japan's seven imperial universities were closed down and replaced by new-system universities such as the University of Tokyo and Kyoto University, which are still informally called as the "seven ex-imperial universities." Yanaihara returned to Tokyo Imperial University (called as it had been until 1949) under the US-led allied occupation (1945–52) and, after being appointed as heads of several faculties and institutes between 1946 and 1951, was elected to be the President of the University of Tokyo during 1951–57. In post-war Japan, chairs of colonial policy studies at universities were abolished and replaced by those of new subjects such as world economy and development economics. In addition, Yanaihara made a significant contribution to establishing Japan's first programme of international relations within the newly

---

[11] Migration to Manchuria was facilitated by the Great Depression, by which Japanese rural communities, in particular those dependent on a single crop like silk, were most severely hit even to the degree of starvation (Cullather 2013, p. 196). When Japan was defeated in 1945, there were approximately 1.5 million Japanese in Manchukuo (Kato 2006, p. 186).

[12] In Germany, Großraum was famously advocated by Carl Schmitt, when he championed Nazi Germany's external policy, which was practically intended to rule Europe. In Italian Fascism, Lebensraum — what the Italians called spazio vitale — was also pursued, but they retained essentially "nationalist" principles of rule as opposed to "thoroughly racialized visions" of the Nazis (Müller 2011, pp. 120–124, 239).

Hosokawa, Karoku. 1972 [originally 1942]. "Sekaishi no doko to Nihon [The Trend of World History and Japan]." In *Hosokawa Karoku Chosakushu* [*The Collected Works of Karoku Hosokawa*], III. Tokyo: Rironsha, pp. 321–386.

Hyam, Ronald. 2010. *Understanding the British Empire*. Cambridge: Cambridge University Press.

Ikeda, Ryo. 2016. "Tunisian Internal Autonomy and the Transformation of the French Colonial Empire." *International Journal of Francophone Studies* 19 (1): 15–27.

Imanishi, Hajime. 2007. "Teikoku nihon to kokunai shokuminchi: 'Naikoku shokuminchi ronso' no isan [Imperial Japan and Internal Colonies: The Legacies of the 'Debates on Internal Colonies']." *Ritsumeikan gengo bunka kenkyu* 19 (1): 17–27.

Izumi, Akira. 1924. *Shokuminchi tochi ron* [*A Study of Colonial Administration*]. Expanded and revised edition. Tokyo: Yuhikaku.

Julien, C. A. 1950. "From the French Empire to the French Union." *International Affairs* 26 (4): 487–502.

Kato, Kiyofumi. 2006. *Mantetsu zenshi: "Kokusaku gaisya" no zenbo* [*A Complete History of the South Manchuria Railway Company: The Total Picture of a "National Policy Corporation"*]. Tokyo: Kodansya.

Kenny, Anthony. 2001. "The Rhodes Trust and its Administration." In A. Kenny (Ed.). *The History of the Rhodes Trust 1902–1999*. Oxford: Oxford University Press, pp. 1–99.

Kobayashi, Hideo. 2006. *Mantetsu chosabu no kiseki, 1907–1945* [*A Trajectory of the Research Department of the South Manchuria Railway Company, 1907–1945*]. Tokyo: Fujiwara Shoten.

Kratoska, Paul H. 2003. "Dimensions of Decolonization." In Marc Frey, Ronald W. Pruessen and Tan Tai Yong (Eds.). *The Transformation of Southeast Asia: International Perspectives on Decolonization*. Armonk, NY: M. E. Sharpe, pp. 3–22.

Louis, Wm. Roger. 1999. "Introduction." In Judith M. Brown and Wm. Roger Louis (Eds.). *The Oxford History of the British Empire, Vol. IV: The Twentieth Century*. Oxford: Oxford University Press, pp. 1–46.

McIntyre, W. David. 2009. *The Britannic Vision: Historians and the Making of the British Commonwealth of Nations, 1907–48*. Basingstoke: Palgrave Macmillan.

McMahon, Deirdre. 1999. "Ireland and the Empire-Commonwealth, 1900–1948." In Judith M. Brown and Wm. Roger Louis (Eds.). *The*

Oxford History of the British Empire, Vol. IV: The Twentieth Century. Oxford: Oxford University Press, pp. 138–162.

Müller, Jan-Werner. 2011. *Contesting Democracy: Political Ideas in Twentieth-Century Europe*. New Haven: Yale University Press.

Nakano, Ryoko. 2013. *Beyond the Western Liberal Order: Yanaihara Tadao and Empire as Society*. New York: Palgrave Macmillan.

National Archives of Australia. 1926. National Archives of Australia, Canberra, A4640/32, E129, Report of the Inter-Imperial Relations Committee, Imperial Conference.

Pugach, Noel H. 1979. *Paul S. Reinsch: Open Door Diplomat in Action*. Millwood, NY: KTO Press.

Reinsch, Paul S. 1902. *Colonial Government: An Introduction to the Study of Colonial Institutions*. New York: Macmillan.

Reinsch, Paul S. 1905. *Colonial Administration*. New York: Macmillan.

Sakai, Tetsuya. 2007. *Kindai nihon no kokusai chitsujo ron [The Political Discourse of International Order in Modern Japan]*. Tokyo: Iwanami Shoten.

Sakai, Tetsuya. 2010. "Hankei to shite no eiteikoku: Kindai nihon no kokusai chitsujo ron no ichi keifu [The British Empire as a Model: A Genealogy of the Political Discourse of International Order in Modern Japan]." In Yoichi Kibata and Harumi Goto-Shibata (Eds.). *Teikoku no nagai kage: Nijyusseiki kokusai chitsujo no henyo [Long Shadow of Empire: The Transformation of International Order of the Twentieth-Century]*. Kyoto: Minerva Shobo, pp. 25–47.

Smuts, J. C. 1926. *Holism and Evolution*. London: Macmillan.

Smuts, J. C. 1952. *Jan Christian Smuts*. London: Cassell.

Snyder, Timothy. 2010. *Bloodlands: Europe between Hitler and Stalin*. New York: Basic Books.

Sumiya, Mikio. 1988. "Kaisetsu [Commentary]." In Tadao Yanaihara, *Teikokushugi ka no Taiwan [Taiwan under Imperialism]*. Tokyo: Iwanami Shoten, pp. 285–303.

Townsend, Susan C. 2000. *Yanaihara Tadao and Japanese Colonial Policy: Redeeming Empire*. Richmond: Curzon.

Townsend, Susan C. 2002. "Yanaihara Tadao and the British Empire as a Model for Colonial Reform." In Gordon Daniels and Chushichi Tsuzuki (Eds.). *The History of Anglo-Japanese Relations 1600–2000, Volume 5: Social and Cultural Perspectives*. Basingstoke: Palgrave Macmillan, pp. 227–245.

Von Laue, Theodore H. 1987. *The World Revolution of Westernization: The Twentieth Century in Global Perspective*. New York: Oxford University Press.

Wakabayashi, Masahiro. 2001. *Taiwan konichi undo shi kenkyu* [*A Study of the History of Anti-Japanese Movements in Taiwan*], expanded edition. Tokyo: Kenbun Shuppan.

Westad, Odd Arne. 2005. *The Global Cold War: Third World Interventions and the Making of Our Times*. Cambridge: Cambridge University Press.

Yanaihara, Tadao. 1937. *Teikokushugi kano Indo* [*India under Imperialism*]. Osaka: Daido Shoin.

Yanaihara, Tadao. 1963 [originally 1930]. "Shokuminchi kokumin undo to eiteikoku no shorai [Colonial Nationalist Movements and the Future of the British Empire]." In *Yanaihara Tadao Zenshu* [*The Collected Works of Tadao Yanaihara*], *IV*. Tokyo: Iwanami Shoten, pp. 416–437.

Yanaihara, Tadao. 1982 [originally 1937]. "Kokka no riso [The Ideal of State]." In Tadao Yanaihara, *Kokka no riso: Senji hyoronshu* [*The Ideal of State: Wartime Essays*]. Tokyo: Iwanami Shoten, pp. 361–384.

Yanaihara, Tadao. 1988 [originally 1929]. *Teikokushugi ka no Taiwan* [*Taiwan under Imperialism*]. Tokyo: Iwanami Shoten.

Chapter 14

China Studies in Aotearoa/New Zealand: Moving Beyond Postcolonialism

Pauline Keating

School of History, Philosophy, Political Science, and International Studies,
Victoria University of Wellington, New Zealand

From Monoculturalism to Biculturalism

By the late 18th century, the British crown had drawn sobering lessons from mistakes made in Australia and its North American colonies, and that can explain what seems to have been a less assertive approach to its colonisation of New Zealand. Significant European settlement of New Zealand's north and south islands began in the 1830s, and settlers were given self-government rights in 1853, just 12 years after New Zealand was formally made a colony separate from New South Wales (Australia). Furthermore, in 1840 the British had signed a treaty with the leaders of Maori tribes, a treaty that purportedly established a "partnership" between the colonizers and the indigenous people. And in the first decade of the 20th century, in 1907, the colony's elevation to the status of "dominion" within the British Empire is commonly seen as the beginning of decolonization and the growing independence of a New Zealand nation.

Many analysts, however, take issue with the assumption that British colonisation of New Zealand was relatively gentle and benign. Historian James Belich, for example, describes the 1840s to

1880s as a "traumatic but dynamic era of colonization, in which settlers attempted the mass conversion of nature and natives." And that was followed, he says, by a "re-colonisation" from the 1880s to the 1940s, which saw "the tightening of links with the metropolis, against the grain of expectations about the steady development of national maturity and independence." In Belich's argument, decolonization did not begin until the 1940s, and it occurred only "erratically and incompletely" (Belich 2011, p. 2).

The meanings and significance of the 1840 treaty, the Treaty of Waitangi, are also vigorously debated. Disagreements about what the Treaty said (the English and Maori versions of the Treaty said different things) began in the 1840s and continue till today. For the British, the treaty was, most importantly, the means by which they asserted their sovereignty. For the Maori, writes Claudia Orange (Orange 1987), the treaty confirmed their rights to land, fisheries and *taonga* (prized possessions), and it guaranteed "a degree of genuine autonomy within the mainstream of New Zealand life." Orange notes that "there has seldom been a meeting of minds between Maori and non-Maori" (Orange 1987, p. 2). Even so, the decolonization that gained traction after World War II did feature some significant participation of pākehā (European) New Zealanders in an increasingly assertive Māori protest movement and in the urban-based Maori renaissance movement that gave sustenance to the struggles for indigenous rights (see, for example, Hill 2012).

The Treaty of Waitangi Act, passed by the Labour Government in 1975, and the Waitangi Tribunal established by the Act are two of the most significant achievements of the mid-20th century Maori rights movement. And since the 1985 amendments to the Act that extended the Tribunal's powers, the Waitangi Tribunal has played a central role in race relations. James Belich and Lydia Wevers contend that "(n)othing has changed the way New Zealanders interact and conduct their social lives in the last twenty years as much as the Treaty and what it stands for" (Belich and Wevers 2008, p. 11). The Tribunal has by no means righted all of the wrongs against the Maori, but it has helped to put violations of the Treaty under public scrutiny and gives legitimacy to Maori protest. A consequence is that the issue of race relations is now firmly embedded in the public discourse about New Zealand's "national identity." Another major consequence is the broad acceptance of a *bicultural* identity, a biculturalism rooted in the partnership agreement in the 1840 Treaty.

New Zealand still has its monoculturalists — people who insist on the primacy of a national identity rooted in the white settler culture of the mid-19th century, variously symbolized by gumboots, sheep or number 8 fencing wire (symbol of the pioneering ingenuity and "can do" resourcefulness of the Kiwi farmer). But a more significant challenge to biculturalism comes from those who celebrate multiculturalism and who welcome the diversity that migrants from Asia and other parts of the non-Western world are bringing to the country. Almost at the same time as amendments to the Treaty of Waitangi Act extended the Tribunal's reach and clout, the government's revised immigration policies in 1987 and 1991 opened New Zealand's door much more widely to migrations from Asian countries (McKinnon 1996; Grief 1995); New Zealand's Asian population today is growing more quickly than any other ethnic group.[1] Of the national population in 2018 (4.7 million), ethnic Asians constitute about 14 percent; they constituted less than 1 per cent 30 years ago.

The radical increase in the country's Asian population is resulting in a very significant demographic change. In fact, as a result of Asian immigrations, the ethnic-Asian population is growing more quickly than the Maori, and it is possible that Asians will soon be the largest minority, larger than the Maori.[2] The growing visibility of Asian people in New Zealand has also

---

[1] Relatively small numbers of Chinese and Indian migrants arrived in New Zealand in the late 19th century, and the populations grew slowly through the 20th century. Data we have for Chinese settlers show that they numbered less than 20,000 in 1986, about 147,000 in 2006, and 171,411 in 2016. The Indian community was smaller than the Chinese before 1987, but is now growing more quickly. From the 1990s, there were migrations from a number of other Asian countries; for example, by 2013, there were 40,350 Filipinos, 30,000 Koreans, 14,188 Japanese (Statistics New Zealand; for more details see http://archive.stats.govt.nz/Census/2013-census/profile-and-summary-reports/ethnic-profiles.aspx?request_value=24726-24726).

[2] Projections are that in 2018 the Asian population, at about 14% of the total, is now just slightly less than the Maori, at 15%. The European population, at about 71% of the total,

triggered a revival of xenophobic and racist attitudes that have deep roots in New Zealand's colonial past. Just as anti-Chinese bigots in the late-19th and early 20th centuries deliberately stoked fears of an invasive "yellow peril," a new wave of racism has greeted migrants from Asia who have been settling in New Zealand since the 1980s. Polemicists in the 1990s tried to stoke fears of an "Asian Invasion," and the New Zealand First political party has campaigned since its founding in 1993 for a reduction in the numbers of migrants from Asian countries (Hannis 2009).

But history does not repeat itself. New Zealand society today is very different from the white settler society of the 19th century. For one thing, the rising relevance (some might say "reinvention") of the Treaty in the late 20th century is making a difference. Treaty discourse has brought to light a long history of racism in New Zealand, and the Tribunal has been addressing and dealing with both explicit and incipient racism for more than 30 years now. Belich and Wevers point out that, as a consequence of "what has been happening around the Treaty of Waitangi …, New Zealanders have discovered we are more racist — and certainly more ethnocentric — than we like to believe in our national self-mythologising." And they ask this telling question: "would the apology to Chinese New Zealanders over the poll-tax have happened when it did without the Treaty?" (Belich and Wevers, p. 9).

Nevertheless, there is not yet a broad consensus among New Zealanders about how biculturalism might be reconciled, or made compatible, with multiculturalism.

The Beginnings and Growth of Chinese Studies in New Zealand

A push to introduce the formal study of Asian at tertiary level in New Zealand began in the late 1940s, during the latter phase of what James Belich calls New Zealand's "re-colonisation." I can

---

is declining. For details, see http://archive.stats.govt.nz/browse_for_stats/population/estimates_and_projections/NationalEthnicPopulationProjections_HOTP2013-2038.aspx.

find no evidence that any of the four university colleges considered introducing the study of Asia before 1948.[3] New Zealand's political and educational leaders at the time were certainly not subservient to Britain, but many of them, even if not explicitly, tacitly endorsed the colonisers' dream of making New Zealand a "better Britain." The university system was based on the British model. Its curriculum was strongly Eurocentric, and promising students were typically encouraged to apply for scholarships that would fund postgraduate study in Britain. A large proportion of the universities' humanities graduates who chose to do doctorates were sent to study at Oxford, Cambridge or the University of London.

Predictably, Maori Studies was also virtually absent from the tertiary curriculum in the first half of the 20th century. In the 1920s and 1930s, attempts were made at Auckland College to have Maori language included as a "foreign language" in the BA programme. Although the university senate in 1929 approved its inclusion, nothing happened. Until the 1950s, any study of Maori language and culture was possible only through adult and community education programmes. The first Maori language lecturer was appointed to Auckland's Department of Anthropology in 1951. The other universities, including the newly founded Waikato and Massey universities, began to introduce Maori Studies programmes in the 1960s and 1970s.

New Zealand's political leaders had little enthusiasm for "engagement with Asia" in the immediate post-war years and certainly did not see their country as "part of Asia." Participation in security alliances such as ANZUS and SEATO did not, at first, result in closer ties with Asian nations; advice from Britain was that New Zealand, unlike Australia, did not need to build ties in Asia

---

[3] In the 1940s, New Zealand had four universities (although three of them were called "colleges" until 1962). The oldest, the University of Otago, was founded in 1869. The University of New Zealand was established by an Act of Parliament in 1870, and by 1897 managed four colleges: Otago (which continued to use "university" in its title); Canterbury (in Christchurch), founded in 1873; Auckland (1883) and Victoria (Wellington) established in 1897. There are now eight universities. Two new universities, Massey and Waikato, were founded in 1964. And then Lincoln University in 1990 and Auckland University of Technology in 2000.

for the sake of meeting threats from its "Near North" (Tarling 2010, pp. 11–12). In this context, the positive connections that resulted from New Zealand's participation in the Colombo plan proved to be particularly important.[4] Celebrating its 15th anniversary in 1967, Prime Minister Holyoake declared that "the two-way traffic between New Zealand and Plan countries has done much to develop an understanding and respect between Asians and New Zealanders." Nicholas Tarling gives the Plan some of the credit for the seeding and growth of Asian Studies at the University of Auckland in the late 1960s (Tarling 2010, pp. 13–17).

As early as 1947, however, Presbyterian ministers who worked among war refugees from China were advocating the introduction of Chinese studies into the tertiary curriculum. The Reverends McNeur and Davies had a meeting that year with Prime Minister Peter Fraser at which they recommended, among other things, the establishment of a chair in Chinese Studies at one of New Zealand's University Colleges (Hyslop 2018). A year later, in 1948, Victoria College in Wellington submitted a request to the University Grants Committee (UGC) for funding to establish chairs in music, geography, philosophy and "Asiatic studies." In that quinquennial round, only the bid for a chair in Asian studies failed (Barrowman 1999, p. 188). Nevertheless, that Victoria put "Asiatic Studies" on an equal footing with three other major disciplines in the humanities is noteworthy, and the UGC's short-sightedness is lamentable.

Victoria's Asian Studies push did not wither after this setback. The College's Professorial Board set up an Asian Studies Committee in 1953, and in 1956 the Committee convened a series of six public lectures on Asia-related topics, one of which was delivered by Arnold Toynbee.[5] By the mid-1950s the issue was not whether

---

[4] New Zealand joined the Plan in 1951, and it soon took the form of a student exchange. It was "novel" because "the universities — and the community — found 'Asian' students in their midst" (Tarling 2010, p. 13).

[5] The title of Toynbee's lecture was "The Resurrection of Asia and the Role of the Commonwealth." In it, he argued the need "to establish and maintain friendship on a footing of psychological as well as individual equality between people of Western and non-Western civilisation" (Toynbee 1956, p. 102).

Asian Studies should be in the curriculum but which regions of Asia should be studied. Professor James Bertram, most famous for his reporting of the kidnapping of Chiang Kaishek in Xi'an in 1936 and his interview with Mao Zedong in 1937, led Victoria's "China lobby."[6] His academic position at Victoria was in English Literature, but he was one of the College's key champions of Asian Studies and strongly argued for a focus on East Asian Studies, at the centre of which should be language studies.[7] The Southeast Asian faction disagreed; its protagonists pushed for the appointment of Southeast Asian specialists, and favored an area-studies approach in which language study was included but not made central. The very small Department of Asian Studies that was set up in 1957 (headed by an Associate Professor who was its only lecturer), and which became a Centre in 1960, explicitly adopted the "area studies" and social sciences approach favored in America; a few years later, that approach was to be recommended by the 1961 Hayter Report in Britain (Hayter 1961). The BA Asian Studies major, first offered at Victoria in 1961, was an "area studies" major that did not include any Asian language study (Victoria did not teach an Asian language until 1969).

In 1963, all four universities submitted applications to the University Grants Committee for grants to fund Asian Studies

---

[6] After completing a Masters degree in English Literature at Auckland College, Bertram won a Rhodes Scholarship to study at Oxford. When he finished at Oxford in 1936, he traveled to Japan and China on a Rhodes Trust Traveling Fellowship, and with commissions to freelance for *The Times*, *Manchester Guardian* and *The Independent*. He reported from Xi'an in December 1936, and in 1938 published *First Act in China: The Story of the Sian Mutiny* (1938). His second book, *North China Front*, was about the five months he spent with the CCP's 8th Route Army. His interview with Mao in November 1937 is included in Volume 2 of the *Selected Works of Mao Zedong* 毛泽东选集: 第二卷. He wrote in detail about his China years (1936 to 1947, including a period in Japan as a prisoner of war) in *Capes of China Slide Away* (1993). In 1947, he accepted a position as lecturer in the English Department at Victoria College of Wellington, and was promoted to professor in 1971.

[7] Both Diana Bridge and Duncan Campbell were taught by Bertram when studying English literature at Victoria University, and remember him well. See Diana Bridge Interview (2017): http://www.china-studies.taipei/comm2/DianaBridge.pdf, pp. 3–4; Duncan Campbell Interview (2017): http://www.china-studies.taipei/comm2/InterviewNZ%20Duncan%20Campbell.pdf, p. 6.

initiatives. Rachel Barrowman, in her history of Victoria University, says that "the committee was briefly concerned about a possible proliferation of Asian Studies development" (Barrowman 1999, p. 198), but anxieties were eased when Canterbury and Otago withdrew their applications. The Committee was satisfied that the Auckland and Wellington proposals were sufficiently different to warrant serious consideration of both. Victoria was committed to the American area-studies approach; Auckland proposed a more traditional sinology programme, one that focusses on languages, literatures and civilizations. Also, by now Victoria was favoring a Southeast Asia emphasis, while Auckland's choice was East Asian studies.

The Asia programmes at both Victoria and Auckland moved forward in fits and starts, and with little involvement of the national government. Victoria's Centre of Asian Studies collapsed in 1975 and a Chinese language programme developed despite the Centre's failure. Auckland's Asia programme grew in the 1970s and 1980s and is today New Zealand's strongest. In these early years, any noteworthy progress of Asian studies tended to be the result of entrepreneurial individual efforts to get Asia into lecture theatres and classrooms and to conduct Asia-related research. This applied at all universities in the 1950s to 1960s. Ian Catanach began teaching Indian history in the University of Canterbury's History Department in 1960; he built a solid foundation for South Asian studies during his 37 years at Canterbury. Hew McLeod, a specialist in Sikh history, did the same at Otago University from 1970 to 1997. Southeast Asia specialist Nicholas Tarling took up his position in the History Department at the University of Auckland in 1965; he played a major role in establishing and shaping the teaching of Asia-related subjects at Auckland and also nationally. He was a key figure in the founding of the New Zealand Asian Studies Society, in 1974, and remained a mover and shaker within the society until his death in 2017 (Clark 2017).

Keith Buchanan at Victoria College was one of the earliest China studies pioneers in New Zealand. Appointed foundation professor of geography at Victoria in 1953, he is perhaps best

(Buchanan 1970; Watters 1998) known as the author of *The Transformation of the Chinese Earth*. S.A.M. Adshead was another pioneer; he had studied European history at Oxford and, when first appointed as a lecturer in history at Canterbury College in 1960, taught European history. But then, to fill what he judged to be a gap in the History Department's programme, he began teaching Chinese history (Moloughney 2016). From the beginning, says Brian Moloughney, Adshead's study of China "was not an end in itself, but a way into a broader understanding of the world" (Adshead 1988).

In summary, therefore, we can say that in the 1950s and through the next 30 years or so, there was growing "talk" about the need to develop Chinese studies in New Zealand, and some piecemeal action. The talk was important. To a major extent, the early initiatives at Victoria were rooted in the belief — the belief of liberal educators — that a humanities education needs to be broad-based and should introduce students to worlds well beyond the British Empire. In fact Alexander Hunter, Professor of Philosophy and Psychology and a prominent administrator in Victoria College's early decades, asserted in 1949 that in proposing to introduce "the study of the civilisation of China, India or Japan," New Zealand was already "probably at least thirty years late" (Barrowman 1999, p. 196). Also, the Asian Studies advocates of the 1950s usually endorsed postcolonial world views that had become mainstream after World War II. Arnold Toynbee's 1956 Wellington lecture was quickly published by Victoria's School of Political Science and Public Administration. In it, Toynbee had told his Wellington audience that they were witnessing "the resurrection of Asia," and that "people of Western origin are going to take, once more, their normal position in the world — a position of equality with the rest of mankind, and not one of dominance." This will make possible, he said, "the world's return to normality" (Toynbee 1956, pp. 102–103). It followed that New Zealand universities had the responsibility to disseminate among New Zealanders a sound and solid knowledge of Asia.

Post-colonial discourses were also, of course, highly relevant to Maori struggles for equality and indigenous rights. It is no coincidence, therefore, that at the same time as the push for Asian Studies was gaining traction in New Zealand universities, the decades-long attempts to introduce the study of Maori language and culture was also bearing some fruit. But the similarities stop there. I know of no instances of any links between, certainly not any mergings, of the Maori and Asianist causes in the 1950s and 1960s — no intellectual exchanges nor any kind of coordinated action. And it is unlikely that either side thought that there should be. A key premise of the drive to develop studies of Asia was that Asia was the home of some of the world's great civilizations, and a study of these civilizations should be firmly rooted in the curricula of all universities. Worth noting in this respect is Moloughney's point, that S.A.M. Adshead, a Europeanist, became interested in Chinese history "because it had the depth and breadth of European history" (Moloughney 2016, p. 598). No one in the 1950s attempted to promote the study of Maori culture on these grounds. On all college campuses at this time, the push for Maori studies came from anthropologists. The first non-Maori scholars to defend the rights of the Maori people on the grounds that they are *tangata whenua* (lit: people of the land) tended to be anthropologists, and they were key protagonists in the drive for teaching programmes that could disseminate more informed, nuanced and sensitive understandings of Maori history and cultures.

China Studies in New Zealand from the 1970s to the Present

Chinese studies moved forward somewhat feebly and falteringly in the 1950s and 1960s, but a foundation of sorts was laid. In 1950, China was virtually invisible in the universities' calendars. By the early 1970s, two universities (in Auckland and Wellington) had Chinese language programmes. Auckland's History Department recruited its first China historian, Chan Hok-lam, in 1967; Robert Taylor, the first China specialist in Politics, arrived in 1969. From 1971, courses in Chinese politics were being taught by Dov Bing at Waikato University. Keith Buchanan had established Chinese geography as a speciality of Victoria's Geography Department, and S.A.M. Adshead was enthralling students of Chinese history at the University of Canterbury. Bill Willmott took up a professorship in Sociology at Canterbury in 1973 (Willmott Interview 2017), and his teaching about China at both undergraduate and postgraduate levels added more lustre to Chinese Studies at Canterbury.

Two major developments in the 1970s caused New Zealand's political, education and business leaders to sit up and notice China, and eventually to concede that knowledge of China should be regarded as a "national asset." First, the establishment of diplomatic relations between New Zealand and the PRC in 1972–1973 seeded an economic relationship that expanded rapidly from the mid-1980s, a relationship on which the New Zealand economy now heavily depends.[8] The growth and energizing of the study of Asia in New Zealand's universities and schools in the 1990s is a direct consequence of the burgeoning economic relationship. The second important event was Deng Xiaoping's launching of China's "reform and opening" era in 1978. As well as being a premise on which the trading relationship rests, the "opening" of China since the 1970s has made Mainland China more accessible to foreign scholars, has expanded their research agenda and has enabled collaborations between PRC and foreign scholars to an extent that was not possible in the Mao years.

Almost all of the 12 New Zealand-based China specialists who were interviewed for the Comparative Epistemologies project began their engagements with China in the 1970s (the exceptions are Manying Ip, the only ethnic Chinese to be interviewed for the New Zealand project so far, and Bill Willmott).[9] Six of the interviewees grew up in New Zealand; four of them are academics and the other two built their careers in diplomacy and New Zealand

---

[8] By December 2017, New Zealand had a $3.5 billions goods and services trade surplus with China. For more details, see Statistics New Zealand at https://www.stats.govt.nz/news/new-zealands-two-way-trade-with-china-more-than-triples-over-the-decade.
[9] Bill Willmott was born in Chengdu in 1932 and lived there off and on until 1949. Manying Ip was born in Hong Kong and completed a B.A. at the University of Hong Kong 香港大学 before moving to New Zealand.

Trade and Enterprise. The other six relocated from their home countries to take up academic positions in New Zealand; two came from Canada, and the others from Britain, the USA, Hong Kong and Australia. Except for Bill Willmott and Manying Ip, none had much interest in China nor did they have any Chinese language training until they were young adults. Richard Phillips, Rosemary Haddon and Ellen Soulliere completed BA degrees in Chinese at Cambridge, the University of British Columbia and Wellesley, respectively, and their degrees served as launching pads into postgraduate degrees in Chinese literature and history. How each of the other seven interviewees acquired Chinese language skills resulted from happenstance as much as anything. Chris Elder was selected by the then Department of External Affairs to be trained as a China specialist, and was sent to Point Cook in Australia for intensive language training (Elder Interview 2016). Diana Bridge's China journey began in the late 1960s when a cloisonné vase that she had purchased in Kuala Lumpur led her to a lecture at the British Museum; in response to her question about how she could learn more about Chinese painting, the lecturer (Basil Gray) suggested that she should "learn the language."[10] So she enrolled in evening classes at the Holborow Community College (Bridge Interview 2017, pp. 2–4). Alan Young, who was teaching in a secondary school while completing a Masters in Geography in the early 1970s, found that resource material on China was "pretty woeful," and that is why he jumped at the chance to study in China offered by the newly established China Exchange Programme (CHEP) (Young Interview, 2016). At much the same time, Duncan Campbell was staying with his father in Kuala Lumpur when Dr Elyas Omar suggested that he "might enjoy studying a bit of Chinese" and pointed him in the direction of Government Chinese Language School (Campbell Interview 2017). Paul Clark in 1973 had decided to apply for a doctoral scholarship, and on the application form put China as his field of study because, for one thing, "China has a lot of history"; he had to be told that

---

[10] Basil Gray was head of the British Museum's Oriental Department at the time.

"you really need to study language first" (Clark Interview 2018). Brian Moloughney, having being inspired by S.A.M Adshead to do postgraduate research in Chinese history, asked Bill Willmott if he could put him touch with a Chinese student who could help him to begin learning the language (Moloughney Interview 2017, p. 3). I also had become fascinated with Chinese history as an undergraduate and, as a way of picking up enough language to qualify for a China study scholarship, I chose to work as an English teacher in Beijing in 1978–1979.

Particularly important for five of the interviewees was the language-learning opportunities provided by the student exchange programmes negotiated with Beijing in 1972–1973. The China scholarships provided New Zealand and Australian students with two years study in China. Paul Clark was one of the three students who formed the first New Zealand contingent in 1974. Duncan Campbell and Alan Young took up their scholarships in 1976, and Brian Moloughney took up his in the mid-1980s. I was awarded one of the Australian scholarships in 1980. Four of the five of these interviewees did not really have a "working knowledge" of Chinese language before enrolling in Chinese language classes in Beijing (Duncan Campbell is the exception), but all five would go on to build careers in the China field — one in diplomacy and NZ–China trade, and the other four as academics in New Zealand universities. This underlines the importance of those scholarships for in-country study in China in the 1970s and 1980s.

The rise of China (the "China miracle") and the expanding New Zealand–China relationship from the 1970s onwards seemed to bode well for a development and deepening of Chinese studies in the country's tertiary institutions and secondary schools. Politicians began to acknowledge the importance of learning about China. The Asia 2000 Foundation (now Asia–New Zealand Foundation) was founded as a "crown entity" by the national government in 1994, and for more than two decades has played an important role in, among other things, developing education-about-Asia programmes outside the formal education sector. Asian Studies scholars have worked closely with the Foundation on several of its programmes, and Manying Ip is a Trustee Board Member. There are now a number of other semi-government or non-government bodies that have been established to foster both the public and private sectors' relationships with China. Most, but not all, focus on the commercial relationships. The New Zealand China Council was founded in 2012 as part of the New Zealand Government's NZ China Inc Strategy. Its membership is almost exclusively business people and former diplomats. New Zealand Trade and Enterprise (NZTE) is a key player in advancing New Zealand's trade relationship with China and helps private businesses to get footholds and prosper in the China market. It has had the good sense to deploy the China skills and experience of Alan Young, someone who, as well as having served as a diplomat on and off since 1982 and as the government's Trade Commissioner in Canton, has been actively engaged in both public and private commercial enterprises in China for almost 40 years now. Local governments were particularly quick to form strong links with China; Wellington City Council, for example, signed a "sister relationship" with Xiamen in 1987, and other municipal and regional Councils were quick to follow. The sister-city arrangements typically give more emphasis to cultural exchanges (the building of Chinese gardens, for example) than do the linkages forged by the central government and private enterprises.

In the education sector, the "rise of China" has had significant ramifications for Chinese studies. Education leaders, along with politicians and business leaders, now proclaim the value of China learning more loudly than they have ever done. Victoria University in 2008 announced that it was making China one of its nine key focus areas, and the founding of the New Zealand Contemporary China Research Centre in 2009 is pointed to as evidence of this commitment. The existing language programmes at the universities of Auckland and Victoria recruited new staff in the 1990s and were able to expand their course offerings as a consequence. Chinese language programmes were introduced where they had not existed before. Seven of the country's eight universities now teach Chinese. Chinese language was first offered at Massey University in 1989, and at both Waikato and Otago universities in 1990; it was reintroduced at Canterbury in 1993.[11] Both Auckland University of Technology and UNITEC (also in Auckland) introduced three-year programmes in Chinese Studies; most focus on language. And now Confucius Institutes in every major city are helping to expand Chinese language learning at all levels of the education system. In 1989, Victoria University created a new position in Chinese History, and so did Otago University in 1993. The Politics and International Relations programmes at the universities of Auckland and Wellington established new positions for political scientists who specialise in China. Faculties of Law, Commerce (or Business) and Education have also made room for the study of China. Developments in the 20th century's last decade, therefore, were very promising.

More than half of the academics interviewed for the Comparative Epistemologies project gained their positions at New Zealand universities during the expansion that began after China's reform and opening. By the 1990s and 2000s, the country's strengthening ties with China were obvious, and the new appointees tended to presume that an academic interest in China would grow apace. In other words, they were cautiously optimistic about the future growth of Chinese studies in New Zealand.

The new enthusiasm for growing and spreading knowledge of China was occurring at the same time as New Zealand's ethnic Chinese population was radically growing, the result of the "new wave" migrations sparked by the government's immigration policy changes in 1986–1987 and 1991. And a consequence of the growing visibility of Chinese immigrants was a rise in anti-Asian racism. It goes without saying that the xenophobia and bigotry made life difficult for the newcomers. It also troubled many non-Chinese New Zealanders, among whom were the scholars and diplomats who have made a lifelong commitment to learning about and disseminating knowledge of China. Anti-Asian racism

---

[11] There were some Chinese language courses on offer at Canterbury in the 1970s, but that initiative fizzled when the lecturer teaching the courses left the university.

became a subject of public debate in New Zealand, and at a time when the broader debates about race and identity — debates about the significance of the Treaty of Waitangi — were intensifying. The amendments to the Treaty of Waitangi Act in 1985 helped energize those debates, and celebrations in 1990 of the 150th anniversary of the Treaty's signing gave them new intensity.

To what extent have New Zealand's China specialists contributed to debates about "national identity" and be allowed to play an active role in nation-building endeavors in post-colonial New Zealand? The final section of this chapter will attempt to answer these questions.

Biculturalism, Multiculturalism and Chinese Studies in New Zealand

We must begin by noting the significant weaknesses and inadequacies of Chinese studies programmes in New Zealand universities in past decades and at present. First, the numbers of China scholars on all university campuses is and always has been very small, and New Zealand's very small population (less than 5 million in 2018, and less than 2 million in 1950) can partly explain this. In fact, it could be said that, since the expansion of China Studies after the 1970s, the numbers of China specialists employed by New Zealand universities is disproportionately high relative to the number of experts in other "area studies." Even so, the small number of New Zealand-based China scholars with specialist knowledge in a subject area that is as vast and complex as "China" are very likely to find that they have little in common other than an interest in, and familiarity with, "China." The research specialities of the 10 academics interviewed for the Comparative Epistemologies project illustrate this point. Their areas of expertise, in broad terms, can be said to be as follows: the Chinese diaspora in Southeast Asia and the Pacific; Chinese literary and material cultures of the late imperial period (1500s–1900); Chinese historiography in the 20th century; imperial women in the Ming Dynasty; Chinese films and popular culture in the 20th and 21st centuries; rural China during the Republican period; Chinese nativist literature in Taiwan and the PRC; China–Japan relations in the Republican period; classical Chinese poetry; Chinese New Zealanders and Maori–Chinese interactions.

Effort has been put into building "communities" of Asian scholars on university campuses and nationally (the NZASIA Society, in particular). But the small number of China scholars and their very disparate interests has discouraged attempts to organize as a collegial body. Instead, they have tended to make a particular effort to forge and sustain strong connections with China scholars outside New Zealand, and do not aspire to be pioneers of some kind of "New Zealand sinology." Maintaining transnational connections was not easy before the age of the Internet; New Zealand is a long way from Western centres of Chinese studies. This meant that new appointees from the UK or North America were likely to feel quite isolated when they relocated to New Zealand in the 1970s and 1980s, cut adrift from the schools in which they had done their doctoral research. The Internet and the digitalisation of archival sources have been seized as lifelines; this is true of all the interviewees, not just those who have come from overseas.

Most of the scholars who took up positions in New Zealand universities late last century soon realized that the study of China existed at the margins of the university curriculum and had shallow roots. This realization is a factor that drove the organization of groupings of Asianists on several campuses (the Asian Studies Institutes at Victoria and Otago, the NZ Asian Institute at Auckland). Almost all Asia-related courses were as insecure as, perhaps more insecure than, China studies, and Asianists recognized the need to organize as a solid body that could lobby for an expansion of Asian Studies and a body from which they could draw some sustenance. And so China scholars saw themselves as China specialists first, and then Asianists, and many felt that their professional lives were situated on the margins of New Zealand society. Of course the two diplomats interviewed for this project, Chris Elder and Alan Young, were very deeply engaged in an enterprise of critical "national" importance — the New Zealand's government's expanding relationship with China. But many of the other interviewees felt that, among their departmental colleagues, university managers and the wider public, they had to struggle to establish the relevance of their China knowledge to New Zealand society, and this remains true even after China's rise to superpower status and its becoming New Zealand's most important trading partner.

Two observations are worth making here. First, only a few of New Zealand's senior China scholars have been active participants in the public sphere outside the universities at which they held appointments. Second, the hopes, back in the 1990s, that the flourishing New Zealand–China relationship would have significant flow-on effects for China Studies have been disappointed.

The first observation needs some qualification. The media and government bodies have called on China scholars for advice and commentaries when they have judged that informed advice or opinion is needed, but usually with the caveat that academics should not be "too academic." The Asia New Zealand Foundation, in particular, has valued scholarship and has commissioned Asia scholars to write articles and booklets for publication on its website. In recent years, government departments have commissioned China specialist to run courses on China for government personnel. The kind of expertise that the 10 scholars interviewed for the Comparative Epistemologies project have to offer, however, is not much valued in the public sector, and only when those scholars were ready to move outside their areas of expertise has the knowledge they offer been valued. To a large extent, the academics who regularly contribute to China training programmes are *contemporary* China specialists with expertise in the fields of commerce, business, law and national security, and most of them have been recruited to university positions fairly recently.

The second observation also needs to be qualified. The "China boom" has certainly helped increase numbers enrolling in Chinese language courses.[12] The keenness to hitch rides on the China bandwagon is understandable, but we must regret the assumption among university decision-makers that only certain types of China knowledge are valuable. They nod when told that the study of Chinese literature, religions, history, geography, philosophies and such are intrinsically important, but they have become unwilling to make appointments in those fields. An assumption is that "history and culture" can be taught by language lecturers, and it does not matter if a "once over lightly" approach is used. In early 2017, Victoria University's School of Marketing and International Business mounted an advertising drive with street hoardings and a web page headed "Conquer Asia," and it used an image of the Great Wall under the caption: "It was designed to keep people out ... Here's how to get your business in." When some of us protested, the "Conquer Asia" heading was changed to "Unlocking Asia," also smugly orientalist; the image and its caption are still there, and "Conquering Asia" is still in the web page address.[13] The promotion of Chinese studies today is based on a rationale completely different from that underpinning the push for Asian Studies in New Zealand during the 1950s and 1960s; as noted earlier, the idea then was that because China is one of the world's great civilisation, China studies should be embedded in the curricula of a university's Arts, Humanities and Social Science programmes. For many senior managers in universities today, the rationale for China Studies today is rooted in New Zealand's economic relationship with China, which took off in the 1980s.

While linked to that economic relationship, the radical growth since 1987 of New Zealand's Chinese population is raising a different set of issues for China scholars. Very importantly, it is bringing in from the cold the history of early Chinese settlements in this country. Descendants of the early settlers were among the

---

[12] Nevertheless, the language learning boom has not often resulted in the creation of new lectureship positions. The workload of existing lecturers has increased, and the student overflow is catered for by contract instructors and Hanban 汉办 teachers provided by the Confucius Institutes.

[13] For details, see https://www.victoria.ac.nz/capital-thinking/conquering-asia.

first to research this early history (for example Ng Bickleen Fong 1959). And then came the monumental work of James Ng, who arrived in New Zealand as a five-year-old during World War II, and who published a four-volume history in the 1990s titled *Windows on a Chinese Past* (1993–1999). Two of our interviewees have also made important contributions to this subject, Manying Ip and Brian Moloughney.[14] Ip, in particular, has made this subject her primary research focus, and has also done important pioneering work on interactions between the Maori and Chinese settlers during both the early and later waves of Chinese migration.

The resurfacing of anti-Chinese hostility and bigotry became a matter of concern for all of us who were teaching courses about China in the 1990s. In fact, it is fair to say that all China scholars, from the beginning of their teaching careers in the China field, were very conscious of a responsibility to "de-exoticise the Orient" in the minds of Western students and to challenge stereotypical understandings of China. Young people love to dismantle stereotypes, and in university classrooms we tended to feel we were making a lot of headway. But what could be done about the racism rooted in ignorance in the homes and on the streets?

The New Zealand–Chinese community is playing a critical role here, and even more especially the "poll tax generations" — people who suffered the indignity of paying the poll tax legislated by the colonial government in 1881, increased in 1896, and not abolished until 1944. A number of associations and bodies representing the established community agitated for decades for a redress of this wrong; their efforts culminated in the Prime Minister's apology in 2002 and the payment of 5 million dollars "as a gesture of reconciliation in support of the formal apology" (New Zealand Government 2018). In a number of other ways, Chinese

---

[14] See the "Selected Publications" at the end of the transcribed interviews with Manying Ip (http://www.china-studies.taipei/comm2/ManyingIp.pdf) and Brian Moloughney (http://www.china-studies.taipei/comm2/BrianMoloughneyInterview.pdf). Moloughney's 1999 and 2006 articles are examples of his work on this subject. All but one of Manying Ip's selected publications are about Chinese New Zealander history and Maori–Chinese interactions.

New Zealanders have worked at countering prejudice and seeking reconciliation with the prejudiced. Helene Wong's work is an example; born in 1949 to immigrant Chinese parents, she has used her theatrical and writing talents to tell the stories of Chinese New Zealanders, including her own, and to make arguments in favour of equity and diversity (Wong 2016). Another example is the documentary film *New Faces, Old Dreams*, the result of collaboration among a range of people that included members of both the established and new Asian communities and academic Manying Ip (Bates 2004). The film's central theme is the resurfacing in the late 20th century of the xenophobia and prejudices endured by Asian immigrants, especially the Chinese, more than a century ago.

Probably the most important way in which academic China specialists can engage in the Chinese communities' struggles for redress and equity is as supervisors of postgraduate projects related to the Chinese diaspora in New Zealand. Several of our interviewees have been doing very good work here. Bill Willmott, supervisor of Charles Sedgwick's doctoral thesis, describes Sedgwick's thesis as "the best study we have on the history and sociology of the Chinese community in New Zealand." (Willmott Interview 2016, p. 6 ; Sedgwick 1982). An important development is the growing number of ethnic Chinese doing postgraduate research on the Chinese diaspora in New Zealand. Lynette Shum's MA thesis, on Haining's Street, Wellington's Chinatown, was supervised by Duncan Campbell at Victoria University; Lynette has become an activist in the endeavor to bring the history of Chinese New Zealanders into mainstream narratives of New Zealand history and into the debates about national identity. Phoebe Li's doctoral thesis, supervised by Richard Phillips at Auckland University, is a critical analysis of Auckland-based Chinese-language media, and was published by Brill as a book in 2013 (Li 2013). Liangni Li, another Auckland doctoral student, wrote her thesis on recent Chinese immigrants in New Zealand, and has taken up a lectureship in Chinese at Massey University.

New Zealand now has considerable number of ethnic Chinese scholars whose studies of the Chinese in New Zealand have required that they also study New Zealand history. They are, therefore, better qualified to participate in the nation-wide debates about racism, identity and multiculturalism than were the earlier generations of China scholars. They bring to their scholarship a knowledge of the ways in which Chinese settlers have been discriminated against and marginalized for more than a century, and they take it as a given that ethnic diversity and multiculturalism should become part of a definition of "New Zealandness" in the 21st century.

A conference in 2005 at Auckland University on "Human Rights, the Treaty and Asian Communities" went to the heart of the matter. Most of the paper presenters were ethnic Asian postgraduate students from the university's School of Asian Studies. Manying Ip, who was the conference convenor, presented a paper titled "Our Treaty Too?" Some of the papers were later published in *The Dragon and the Taniwha: Maori and Chinese in New Zealand* (Ip 2009).

Conclusion

As noted earlier, the big expansion of New Zealand's Chinese population and the growing loudness of Chinese voices in defence of their rights was occurring at the same as a heightening of Maori assertiveness and demands that biculturalism should define all aspects of national life and culture. Maori nationalists (but by no means all Maori) tend to be suspicious of multiculturalism, seeing it as a threat to the Maori movement for autonomy and sovereignty. By the same token, Chinese New Zealanders who are aggrieved about past injustices and the anti-Asian racism they suffer today tend to be resentful of the Maori insistence on biculturalism; they see it as a continuation of old prejudices and habits of exclusivity that, since the late-19th century, have pushed Chinese settlers to the margins of New Zealand society.

This chapter has documented the unsteady and uneven progress of Chinese studies in New Zealand universities since the 1950s, and the high hopes of significant leaps forward as a consequence of China's post-Mao reform and opening. Although there has indeed been some increase in the numbers of academic China specialists in certain disciplines and an increase in Chinese language student numbers, a concomitant of the enthusiasm for China at high levels of government and in business circles has been a "dumbing down" of the study of China — a focus on just the knowledge that can be deemed relevant and useful to New Zealand's commercial relationship with China. The high hopes among China scholar in the 1990s have been disappointed.

This could change in the long run. In the meantime, China scholars have the option of engaging in what many judge to be a more important sphere of public engagement, the politics of multiculturalism and movements against racism. And it is in this sphere that Chinese people and their friends can join hands with the Maori. When film director Taika Waititi recently described New Zealand as a "racist place," we can imagine a great number of Asian New Zealanders nodding their heads (Hollywood Director 2018). Most Maori people strongly feel that they are not yet fully emancipated from the white colonial yoke imposed on their ancestors at the time of white settlement in the early 19th century, and the Chinese attribute at least some of the ostracism and hostility they suffer today to an anti-Chinese racist tradition with roots in the late 19th century. In this respect, therefore, the Maori and Chinese New Zealanders can make a common cause. And there is a challenge for China scholars here. Racism derives from and feeds on ignorance. Educators, therefore, have a major role to play in eliminating it.

Is the principle of biculturalism, a principle cherished by the Maori, an obstacle to cooperation between the Maori and the non-European minorities? Debates about the compatibility of biculturalism and multiculturalism have rumbled on in New Zealand for decades, and resolutions of the debates often rest on semantics. For example, Eric Kolig says that New Zealand is "formally bicultural, institutionally monocultural…and demographically, to some noticeable extent, multicultural" (Kolig 2015, p. 173). There is a growing willingness, however, to allow individuals to have multiple identities; the multiple identities idea complicates biculturalism more than it does multiculturalism. Historian Anne Salmond, drawing on the Maori concept of *whakapapa* ("dynamic networks of complementary relations"), suggests that "there is no need to regard oneself as purely Maori, or Pākehā, or Pasifika, or Asian." Instead, she says, "an individual is made up of all the relationships in which they participate." They have "different *taha*, or 'sides'" which enable them to turn from one network to another, and this makes them "able to adapt to the diverse and rapidly changing world in which we dwell" (Salmond 2012). Salmond offers a vision of racial harmony that goes a good deal further than what has so far been achieved in postcolonial New Zealand.

References

Adshead, S.A.M. 1988. *China in World History*. New York, NY: St Martin's Press.

Author n.a. 2018. "Hollywood Director Taika Waititi says New Zealand is Racist." *The Guardian* (9th April). https://www.theguardian.com/world/2018/apr/09/hollywood-director-taika-waititi-says-new-zealand-is-racist.

Author n.a. 2009. "Human Rights, the Treaty and Asian Communities," Conference held at the University of Auckland in 2009. http://www.scoop.co.nz/stories/ED0511/S00011/human-rights-the-treaty-and-asian-communities.htm.

Barrowman, Rachel. 1999. *Victoria University of Wellington, 1899–1999: A History*. Wellington: Victoria University of Wellington Press.

Bates, Karen. 2004. *New Faces, Old Fears*. https://www.nzonscreen.com/title/new-faces-old-fears-2004.

Belich, James. 2011. "Colonization and History in New Zealand." In Robin Winks. (Ed.). *The Oxford History of the British Empire*, 5, *Historiography*. Oxford Scholarship Online http://www.oxfordscholarship.com/view/10.1093/acprof:oso/9780198205661.001.0001/acprof-9780198205661-chapter-10 (accessed October 2011).

Belich, James and Lydia Wevers. 2008. *Understanding New Zealand Cultural Identities*. Discussion Paper prepared for the Stout Research Centre for New Zealand Studies, Victoria University of Wellington, p. 9.

Bertram, James. 1993. *Capes of China Slide Away: A Memoir of Peace and War 1910–1980*. Auckland: Auckland University Press, 1993.

Buchanan, Keith. 1970. *The Transformation of the Chinese Earth: Aspects of the Evaluation of the Chinese Earth from Earliest Times to Mao Tse-tung*. London: G. Bell & Sons.

Clark, Paul. 2017. "In memoriam: Nicholas Tarling, 1931–2017." http://www.nzasia.org.nz/Nicholas%20Tarling.html.

Grief, Stuart William. 1995. "The Interweaving Themes of New Zealand Immigration". In Stuart Greif (Ed.). *Immigration and national identity in New Zealand: One people, two people, many peoples?* Palmerston North: Dunmore.

Hannis, Grant. 2009. "Reporting Diversity in New Zealand: The 'Asian Angst' controversy." *Pacific Journalism Review* 15 (1): pp. 114–130.

Hayter, William. 1961. *Report of the Sub-Committee on Oriental, Slavonic, East European and African Studies*. London: University Grants Committee.

Hill, Richard. 2012. "Maori Urban Migration and the Assertion of Indigeneity in Aotearoa/New Zealand, 1945–1975." *Interventions: International Journal of Postcolonial Studies* 2 (14): 256–278.

Hyslop, Connie. 2018. "Fleeing Canton: Aotearoa's Welcome." https://presbyterianresearch.atavist.com/fleeing-canton-aotearoas-welcome.

Ip, Manying. (Ed.). 2009. *The Dragon and the Taniwha: Maori and Chinese in New Zealand*. Auckland: Auckland University Press.

Kolig, Eric. 2015. "Whither Cultural Acceptance? Muslims and multiculturalism in New Zealand." In Gautam Gosh and Jackie Leckie. (Eds.). *Asians and the New Multiculturalism in New Zealand*, Dunedin: Otago University Press, pp. 159–192.

Li, Phoebe H. 2013. *A Virtual Chinatown: The Diasporic Mediasphere of Chinese Migrants in New Zealand*. Leiden: Brill.

McKinnon, Malcom. 1996. *Immigrants and Citizens: New Zealanders and Asian Immigration in Historical Context*. Wellington: Institute of Policy Studies, Victoria University of Wellington.

Ministry of Foreign Affairs and Trade. *Opening Doors to China: New Zealand's 2015 Vision*. https://www.mfat.govt.nz/en/trade/nz-inc-strategies/china-strategy/.

Ministry of Justice. Year n.a. "Waitangi Tribunal." https://www.waitangitribunal.govt.nz/.

McCarthy, Greg and Xianlin Song. 2018. "China in Australia: The Discourses of Changst." *Asian Studies Review* 42 (2): 323–341.

Moloughney, Brian. 2016. "S.A.M. Adshead on China, World Institutions, and World History." *Journal of World History* 27 (4): 595–617.

New Zealand Government. 2018. "Community Matters: Chinese Poll Tax." https://www.communitymatters.govt.nz/ask-us/?q=Chinese+Poll+Tax.
New Zealand Legislation. "Treaty of Waitangi Act 1975." http://www.legislation.govt.nz/act/public/1975/0114/95.0/DLM435368.html.
Ng, Bickleen Fong. 1959. *The Chinese in New Zealand: A Study in Assimilation*. Hong Kong University Press, Hong Kong.
Ng, James. 1993–1999. *Windows on a Chinese Past*. 4 vols. Dunedin: Otago Heritage Books.
NZ Ministry of Foreign Affairs and Trade. 2012. "NZ Inc China Strategy." https://www.mfat.govt.nz/en/trade/nz-inc-strategies/china-strategy/.
NZ Trade and Enterprise and Ministry of Foreign Affairs and Trade. 2012. *Opening Doors to China: New Zealand's 2015 Vision*. https://www.tpk.govt.nz/_documents/nz-inc-china-strategy.pdf.
Orange, Claudia. 1987. *The Treaty of Waitangi*. Wellington: Bridget Williams Books.
Salmond, Anne. 2012. "Beyond the Binary — Shifting New Zealand's Mindset." First Sir Paul Reeves Memorial Lecture, Radio New Zealand. https://www.radionz.co.nz/national/programmes/reeves/20121022.
Sedgwick, Charles. 1982. "The Politics of Survival: A Social History of the Chinese in New Zealand." Doctoral Dissertation, University of Canterbury, Christchurch.
Statistics New Zealand. http://archive.stats.govt.nz/browse_for_stats/population/estimates_and_projections/NationalEthnicPopulationProjections_HOTP2013-2038.aspx.
Tarling, Nicholas. 2010. *Imparting Asia: Five Decades of Asian Studies at the University of Auckland*. Auckland: New Zealand Asia Institute.
Toynbee, Arthur. 1956. "The Resurrection of Asia and the Role of the Commonwealth," *Political Science* 8 (2): pp. 93–103.
Watters, Ray. 1998. "The Geographer as Radical Humanist: An Appreciation of Keith Buchanan." *Asia Pacific Viewpoint* 39 (1): pp. 1–28.
Wellington City Council. Year n.a. "Xiamen, China," https://wellington.govt.nz/about-wellington/international-relations/sister-cities/xiamen.
Wong, Helene. 2016. *Being Chinese: A New Zealander's Story*. Wellington: Bridget Williams Book.

Interviews

All transcripts for the following interviews are found under "New Zealand" at http://www.china-studies.taipei/act02.php.

Duncan CAMPBELL
Diana BRIDGE
Paul CLARK
Chris ELDER
Rosemary HADDEN
Manying IP
Pauline KEATING
Brian MOLOUGHNEY
Richard PHILLIPS
Ellen SOULLIERE
Bill WILLMOTT
Alan YOUNG

Chapter 15

A British Legacy or Modern University Crisis? Chinese Studies in Australian Universities

Shirley Chan

Chinese Studies, Department of International University, Macquarie University, Sydney, Australia

Introduction

Chinese Studies as an intellectual discipline in Australia has been a colonial phenomenon since its first establishment in the mid-20th century. At the same time, Chinese Studies in Australian universities has undergone a process of reconstruction and adjustment over the decades under the modern university system. Since Australia's independence from Britain in 1901, the dynamics of modernity and historical reality of post-colonial conditions, the contemporary political, socio-economic environments, and its cultural relationships with countries in Asia, Europe and America are constantly shaping Australia's nationhood beset with complexity in its evolution. This complexity has been understood in different ways — politically, economically and culturally — which have influenced questions of our individual and collective identity and our sense of belonging; questions which are crucial for understanding the development of Chinese Studies in Australia in the last few decades. This chapter provides a brief trajectory about Chinese Studies in Australian Universities in the context of the British colonial legacy; how such a legacy is fading, so is the traditional Sinological studies of taking China as a culture or civilization to be understood, and how the tradition is being replaced by contemporary China Studies seeking solutions for, or understanding of, China as a "political" or "economic" power to be tackled by the West.[1]

From British Colony to Independent New Nation

Australia is a modern nation state, but vestiges of coloniality still remain. The majority of the country's population is of European — mainly British — pedigree and cultural orientation, with an increasing influx of migrants drawn from many other societies across the globe since the 19th century.[2] During the early settlement, the British government was the source of political legitimacy for the European settlement of Australia; militarily, Australia has been part of the Western Alliance, in particular, with America since the 50s; economically speaking, it is integrated into Asia with the 21st century, witnessing China becoming the first trading partner

---

[1] This paper is by no means an exhaustive study of the construction history of intellectual discipline of Chinese Studies in Australia, It only provides a general discussion based on previous studies, and some of the experience from scholars and professionals in the field. I would like to thank academic colleagues whose opinions and experience both as students and later as professionals in China-related careers will serve as a reflection on the development of Chinese Studies in Australia. I thank all the interviewers and interviewees who contributed to the interviews organized by Dr Pauline Keating of Victoria University of Wellington, New Zealand, for the "China Knowledge Project" led by Prof. Shih Chihyu from National Taiwan University, although due to limited scope of this paper and other constraints, only a few scholars experience were mentioned in this articles. They are Dr Stephen FitzGerald, Professor Jocelyn Chey and Professor Jon Eugene von Kowallis — not the least I would express my admiration and respect for all the scholars for their outstanding contribution to Chinese Studies and China knowledge in Australia over the years. I also benefit from past research papers and reports about Chinese Studies in Australia.

[2] Australians of British and other European ancestries are the dominant majority in Australia, estimated at around 92% of the total population. This compares to 4% of the total population that has Chinese ancestry (1.2 million people of Chinese ancestry of an estimated population of 24.77 million as of 2018). Historically, European immigrants had great influence over Australian history and society, which resulted in the perception of Australia as a European country.

of Australia; culturally, the continent is moving from purely the Anglosphere to a multi-cultural Southern Hemisphere nation wrapped in a Western Liberal tradition.

The continent-cum-country moved from colonial to independent status in 1901, becoming a nation within the Commonwealth with the task of building a national identity through self-governance, education, culture and social development on all levels. The question of who and how many should live there is never dissociated from the cultural and political agenda as it continues to point to fundamental issues with regard to Australian identity. As in most other countries influenced by the global flows of migration, the Australian society has clearly moved and continues to move toward a multicultural reality in demographic terms; however, the ongoing conflict between the values derived from the notion of White Australia from the British colony and those generated by the multicultural reality continues to define the ideological climate, while immigrants from regions outside the Anglo-Celtic sphere, in particular Asia, are now gradually becoming more socially and economically integrated.[3]

Politically, complexity was added after the Second World War. Before WWII, the British Government handled most of Australia's foreign policy. Britain's cosmopolitan role in world affairs became increasingly limited during the first half of the 20th century with the decolonization of the British Empire through increased self-governance of its territories establishing "free and equal" member states of the Commonwealth. Member states are united by language, history, culture and their shared values of democracy, human rights and the rules of law. Since 1941, United States has been the most important ally and trading partner of Australia. Over recent decades, Australia has sought to strengthen its relationship with Asian countries, establishing this as the focus of the country's network of diplomatic missions. Foreign relations of Australia are influenced by its position as a leading trading nation and as a significant donor of humanitarian aid. Australia's foreign policy is

---

[3] See Larsen (2017).

guided by commitments to multilateralism and regionalism and strong bilateral relations with its allies. Key concerns include free trade, terrorism, refugees, economic cooperation with Asia and stability in the Asia-Pacific. Australia is active in the United Nations and the Commonwealth of Nations. Evidently, its history of starting and supporting important regional and global initiatives has been described as a regional middle power par excellence.[4]

The official relationship between Australia and China commenced in 1909 when the first Chinese consulate in Australia was established, and diplomatic relations were recognized in 1941. Australia continued to recognize the Republic of China government after it lost the Chinese Civil War and retreated to Taiwan in 1949; however, it switched recognition to the PRC on 21 December 1972. The relationship between China and Australia has grown considerably over the years, with increased economic, cultural and political engagement through numerous organizations such as APEC and East Asian Summit. In recent years, China is Australia's largest trading partner in numerous areas, such as the mining industry and, recently, the education sectors. For the first time in its history, Australia's most important economic relationship is with a nation of rather different governance, politics and values.[5] However, relations between the two countries began to deteriorate since 2017.[6] The increase of Chinese investments and Chinese population in Australia, in conjunction with the rise of China as an economic and political power has been perceived by many as a threat to regional security in the Asia Pacific.

In short, the complexity of modernity and historical context, of post-colonial conditions, realities of migration as well as contemporary political and socio-economic and cultural relationships between Australia and countries in Asia, Europe and America, makes Australia a complex continent in an evolving

---

[4] See https://en.wikipedia.org/wiki/Foreign_relations_of_Australia, for more details.
[5] In the past, Australia's dominating economic relationships had been with the British Empire, the United States and Japan.
[6] See Chey (2018).

space. This complexity has been understood under various headings, politically, economically and culturally, in the more than one hundred years since 1901, an independent Australia, and these differences have influenced questions of individual and collective identity and belonging, questions which have been crucial for understanding the development of Chinese Studies in Australia in the last few decades.

Australian Universities

Along with parliaments and policy, the idea of a university was imported with European settlers. This colonial inheritance was expressly British in character. Colonial records suggest "little interest in developments such as the new research universities of Germany or the land-grant institutions of the United States. Instead, local debate focused on a different concern — which British traditions would work best for an Australian university?"[7]

Legislation creating the University of Sydney was passed in 1850. From its inception, the University of Sydney borrowed from across British tertiary practice. In appearance, the influence of Oxford and Cambridge was clear. Nowadays, people are still attracted to the University by its Oxbridge-British atmosphere and appeal, as well as the university system transplanted from Britain. Yet, Sydney drew also from the newer universities of Britain in curriculum and aspiration. The university offered entry without religious qualification to those who passed an examination.[8] Classes were organized around the lecture and tutorial model familiar to Scotland and Ireland, with professors rather than tutors as the principal teachers. As in Scotland, the university opened admission to a wider social demographic, typically living at home and traveling to campus for classes. As in Ireland, the new institution would develop in time to strengthen professional programs in medicine, law and engineering.

---

[7] Davis (2012).
[8] *Ibid*.

The model informing the University of Sydney offers an amalgam of universities from Edinburgh and London to Dublin, with architectural hints of Oxford and Cambridge in its design and motto (*sidere mens eadem mutato*) to stress continuity with British origins.[9] This new institution would become the model for all later Australian higher education — an autonomous, professional, comprehensive, secular, public and commuter university. Today, the teaching style, academic career path and examination structure of the academic year remain a largely British-styled system. Academic staff have been recruited mainly from Europe and America, and English remains the official language throughout the system.

Each university was established by legislation based on the now dominant Australian model. The new university would be given land and funding by the state to support a non-sectarian and self-governing institution. Though residential colleges would be established in time, most students would commute to campus, complete an undergraduate degree and leave for a life in corresponding professions. From the late 19th century, research became an established part of the university mission. Australia may have adopted British notions of a university, with an academic career focused on teaching, but in time, the important technological innovations of German and American institutions and a rising international interest in scientific research, proved influential. Laboratories appeared around campus from the 1870s. Research would become universal, adopted by every institution as part of the standard Australian model.[10]

For Australian universities, three factors have kept the system on a single path: national policy, the aspirations of students and academic values. Australian universities have worked simultaneously in two worlds for more than two decades — "one public, highly regulated, and deeply constrained, the other international and more like a private market. The first is the world of domestic undergraduates,

---

[9] *Ibid.*
[10] *Ibid.*

where Canberra sets strict rules about price and entry. The second is the market for international students, where universities can make choices about where to recruit, what to charge."[11] How and in what way universities and their academics and policymakers can make knowledge disciplines benefit the community, the students and the country in the challenges of modern university system, are questions that are consistently faced by many.

Chinese Studies in Australia

Chinese Studies in Australia as a British Colony has been a colonial phenomenon since its first establishment in the mid-20th century.[12] In Australia, the impacts of British colonial legacies in Chinese Studies have decreased in recent decades, shifting from traditional Sinology to contemporary Chinese Studies under a modern university system which is profit-oriented and managerialism based; the scholarship of Chinese Studies is losing concentration as a discipline in some universities with the curriculum design and budget planning largely affected by various factors such as political preference, country-to-country relationship, government funding, the university administration's policy or even personal preference of the administrators.

While there is still influence from the British colonial legacy in terms of the use of English language, the academic system and

---

[11] *Ibid*.

[12] Professor Shih Chih-yu has provided the definition of colonialism as "processes of occupation and control for the purpose of exploitation," and of colonial legacies to be "forces that have originated with colonialism to impact upon contemporary understandings and practices," with both the colonizing and the colonized in mind. (Shih Chih-yu). Strictly speaking, my chapter does not talk about occupation, control and exploitation, which are meant for the Australian aborigines as the colonized. Rather here, the focus is on British legacies and the European settlers who are themselves the colonizers at the periphery copying the systems of empire. In this chapter, this refers to the British colonial legacies (or impact of European traditions) on Australia with their influence on political and socio-economical system, the relationship with other countries such as America and China, the university system and the White Australia policy and thus the construction process of Chinese Studies in Australia. Some of these impacts are decreasing and some are increasing the China–Australia relationship and Chinese Studies in Australian universities.

examination structure in the universities, the American influence becomes more prominent through the United States' notion of area studies and its politics and economics in the region after the WWII.[13] Scholars and academics continue to face the challenges posited by internal and external tensions and political, economic and social conflicts. There is general acknowledgment of the importance of the study of China in Australia and that it is crucial to provide access to and to foster the knowledge and education as a national asset. Yet, there are still challenges to overcome in order to make contingent plans and programs available.

The academic life and work experience of the key figures and pioneering scholars in Chinese Studies is a reflection of the journey of Chinese Studies being a construction process of knowledge discipline in Australia by the social and political influence of the countries. At the same time, these dedicated people were playing an active role in contributing to Chinese Studies and China knowledge as part of the construction process of human experience. The interviewees in this study who studied and worked between the 1960s and 1980s, as students and China experts and academics, although different in their specialties and having written their theses on different topics in Chinese Studies, studied the Chinese language, both modern and classical, reading a broad range of Chinese texts, from the Confucian Classics to Lu Xun's works; they developed deep knowledge in various fields in Chinese Studies with firsthand experience in studying and working in North America, Hong Kong, Taiwan, Japan and China as well as in Australia.

Chinese Studies in Australian Universities

The influence of the European tradition on Sinology in Australia is observable in its early years of establishment when the University of Sydney was the first Australian university to establish "Oriental Studies." The first chair of Chinese Studies came in 1955 as part of

---

[13] Coughlan (2008, p. 65).

Oriental Studies, later than Japanese Studies which had its first chair back in 1918, with professors posted from England.[14] Coming from the European traditional training of Classical studies, almost without exception, professors of Oriental Studies in the early years were trained and obtained their qualifications in the classics and oriental languages in England, and were versatile scholars with knowledge of history, classical and modern literature, art, philology, archaeology and antiquities of the pre-specialist era.

In 1955, after consulting the Professorial Board, a selection committee, meeting under the Deputy Vice Chancellor, the late Professor C.R. McRae, decided to appoint A.R. Davis (1924–1983) from Cambridge University as the Chair of Oriental Studies at the University of Sydney. Davis was described by his principal referees, A.C. Maule and Arthur David Waley (1889–1966), as one of the most brilliant and promising men of his generation in the field of Oriental Studies.

Davis founded the Department of Oriental Studies from scratch. At the time of his death in the early 1980s, it was a flourishing institution of high standing in the language, literature and history of both China and Japan, with an emerging interest in Korea. Before coming here, Davis had some interesting correspondence with the Registrar, Margaret Telfer, about the range of his work. He was asked, in effect, whether a scholar in Classical Chinese would really be capable of developing the kind of department that the University wished to see. His answer is itself a classic:

> There is no question that a university course in Chinese requires a substantial amount of teaching in Classical Chinese even though the emphasis of that course is primarily directed towards

---

[14] The first Chair of Oriental Studies was established in 1918 when James Murdoch (1856–1921) was appointed Professor in Japanese at the University of Sydney. Murdoch attended the University of Aberdeen in 1875 and graduated with an M.A. with first-class honours in classics in 1879. Prof. Arthur Lindsay Sadler (1882–1970) succeeded Murdoch in 1922 until he retired in 1947. Sadler was knowledgeable in Japanese history, classical and modern literature, art, philology, archaeology and antiquities. He taught most of the curriculum himself.

modern China and modern Chinese. Teaching solely in Modern Chinese could only produce a practical training, not properly consistent with University standards. This is the general view in European universities and one to which, I believe, the Faculty of Arts would subscribe.[15]

Professor Davis' view on Chinese studies showed his commitment to a high standard of training in the traditional European universities during that time. Davis's firm devotion to scholarship and training benefited the University immensely.[16]

As a scholar, Davis's interests were wide and his knowledge has been described by a colleague as encyclopedic, with abiding interests in the poets and poetry of both ancient and modern China and of modern Japan.[17] Davis had an impressive list of publications during the last 30 years and was often in service also as a scholarly editor. He was Founder and President for many years of the Oriental Society of Australia established in 1956. The Society still continues with its *Journal of the Oriental Society of Australia,* which is the oldest journal published in Australia concerned mainly with China, Japan, South East Asia, and South Asia, but articles have also covered Korea, Mongolia, Tibet, Burma, Cambodia, the Middle East and Sri Lanka.

After Sydney University, the Chinese Studies program came to existence at Melbourne University followed by the Australian National University. Professor Harry Felix Simon, originally from London, was appointed Foundation Professor of Oriental Studies at the University of Melbourne in 1961 until he retired in 1988. He was the Dean of the Faculty of Arts in the 1970s and also a great supporter of the East Asian Collection. At Melbourne University, he played an important role in the establishment of teaching and research in the discipline of Oriental Studies (which later changed its name to East Asian Studies), including the teaching of Chinese

---

[15] Penny (2014).
[16] *Ibid.*
[17] *Ibid.*

and Japanese languages.[18] The Australian National University (ANU), in Canberra, Australia's capital city, has an extensive track record in China Studies.

Relatively young and yet energetic, Chinese studies in Australia has built a great reputation internationally for its teaching and research on China in the 1970s, 1980s and 1990s. The country is not short of a name list of well-known and revered world-class Sinologists or Chinese Studies scholars. Apart from A. R. Davis, we should mention the late Pierre Ryckmans (1935–2014). Also known by his *nom de plume* Simon Leys, Ryckmans was a Belgian-Australian Sinologist and translator whose many works included a translation of the *Analects* of Confucius (1997). Having taught in both Australia National University and the University of Sydney, Pierre Ryckmans was a defender of humanities education and was sharp in criticizing the modern university model and how managerialism had undermined intellectual creativity and benighted tertiary institutions both in Australia and abroad.[19] For Ryckmans, the failure of modern

---

[18] http://www.alra.org.au/newsletter1007/1007_yeung_2.pdf. In 2009, the Melbourne University library has been presented the Harry Simon Collection. According to the library website, this Collection consists of around 1030 books published in classical Chinese from the 1880s(?) to the 1980s, which comprises the private research collection of Professor Emeritus Harry Felix Simon. See http://cat.lib.unimelb.edu.au/record=b5051134~S30 for further information.

[19] In 1986, higher educational reforms were introduced by the Labor government education minister John Dawkins. The universities became more profit driven and vocational in nature, with many degrees catered for employability and technical skills. It is believed that these reforms gradually changed the role of the universities. The reforms "would transform the underlying philosophy of university education, introduce a model of quasi-business competition between and within institutions, impose a system for measuring teaching and research summed up by crude metrics and establish a nationwide system that handed the scrubbing brush to the *Hutudans* of academia while empowering a growing caste of university administrators. Hailed by *bien pensant* reformers for economic pragmatism, for opening access to higher education to the greatest number for a practical cost, and for unseating elitism, the reforms were but part of what is globally recognised as the 'neo-liberal turn' that has transformed liberal democracies into market-driven economies." Barmé, Geremie. "An Educated Man Is Not a Pot: On the University," *China Quarterly* (http://chinaheritage.net/journal/an-educated-man-is-not-a-pot-君子不器/). According to a recent survey, after 30 years of constant expansion some complain that universities "have become too vocational in nature — too focused on jobs, not enough on the art of inquiry." Ironically, more university degrees mean "more university graduates would fail to find a job after

universities was not just making places of higher learning and research bloated vocational institutions training students, seen by many people as practical and useful. It was also because people failed to see the essence of university education. He quoted the Daoist philosopher Zhuangzi (third century BCE) to sum up the paradox between what in life may seem impractical but in essence is absolutely essential.[20] After all, this sort of "uselessness" is the very ground on which rests all the essential values of our common humanity. For the same reason, Ryckmans was a strong advocate of traditional Sinology or "generalist approach,"[21] who believed that China should be studied as a "multidisciplinary humanistic undertaking."[22] This view of traditional Sinology was shared among Liu Tsun-yan 柳存仁 (1917–2009), David Hawkes (1923–2009) and John Minford (1946–present).[23] These scholars argued

---

graduation. Part-time work, casualisation and under-employment are widespread. Graduate salaries have not improved for years. Increasingly, students, particularly the most advantaged, turn to postgraduate education to boost their chances in an overcrowded jobs market, raising questions over credentialism. All of these do little to correct an imbalance in skills entering the jobs market. Too many lawyers does not balance out a shortage in IT experts or agricultural scientists. Worse still, all of these come at a cost to debts owed by students under the Higher Education Loans Program (formerly HECS) and the taxpayer's money." Some suggest, perhaps, it is time to "include a return to a tripartite public education and training system, which includes TAFE, teaching-only polytechnics and research-intensive universities." See Stephen Parker, "The UK is rethinking university degrees and Australia should too," (in The Conversation, https://theconversation.com/the-uk-is-rethinking-university-degrees-and-australia-should-too-82963).

[20] People all know the usefulness of what is useful, but they do not know the usefulness of the useless. 人皆知有用之用。而莫知無用之用也。See Geremie Barmé, "An Educated Man Is Not a Pot: On the University," in China Quarterly. http://chinaheritage.net/journal/an-educated-man-is-not-a-pot-君子不器/ Also see Leys (2011).

[21] The term "generalist approach" with an emphasis of the needs to study Chinese civilization with a broad-based cultural or historical background as a whole, is used to contrast the "disciplinary/specialized approach" which often applies Western "disciplines" to focus on a particular area of study of China, such as economics, politics or language. Frederick Mote in the US was one of those who argued that using a Western disciplinary approach to study China "is an act of the provincialization of the understanding of China." For details of the debate between the two camps, see Coughlan (2008, pp. 142–151).

[22] Coughlan (2008, p. 144).

[23] Hawke completed his doctoral dissertation on The Songs of the South in Oxford. His work attracted the attention of the pre-eminent Chinese scholar and translator, Arthur Waley, who became his mentor and friend, and named him as his literary executor. Elected to the chair

that traditional Chinese studies or good Sinology needs to maintain the very things one should strive "to retain at the centre of our curriculum: a sense of cultural continuity and actuality, of the past in the present, and of the present in the past; a sense of the interconnectedness of literature, history and philosophy, of the lively links between scholarship and life."[24]

Liu Ts'un-yan was a typical traditional Sinologist. He was a Chinese scholar familiar with many branches of Chinese literature, classical and vernacular, and in many varieties of the Chinese language — Mandarin, Cantonese and Shanghai dialect. A graduate from Peking University and with a Ph.D. from the University of London, Professor Liu was the bearer of a great tradition (an attribute shared by both the European and Chinese traditional learning). His deeply humanistic vision of Chinese Studies was spelled out most eloquently in his own inaugural lecture, delivered on 5 October 1966:

> As a product of Western civilisation the modern university had its origin in medieval European ecclesiastic education. Its objective was to produce an all-round man rather than to give technical and professional training... In the Humanities we still respect this great tradition. This is precisely what is meant by the Chinese classical saying: 'The accomplished scholar is not an utensil' *junzi buqi* 君子不器 (*Analects of Confucius*). That is to say, a scholar of moral integrity does not regard himself merely as an instrument.

---

of Chinese in 1959, Hawkes spent a dozen years building up a fine department, where literary and classical studies flourished, and where modern China was by no means ignored. He rapidly acquired an enormous international reputation as a scholar who was rigorous in his methods, encyclopedic in his reading and humane in his mode of expression. John Minford was born in Birmingham, UK, in 1946. He studied Ancient Greek and Latin literature. He entered Balliol College, Oxford, in 1964 on a classical scholarship and obtained first class honors in Chinese Literature in 1968. He completed his Ph.D. at the Australian National University in 1980 under the supervision of Professor Liu Ts'un-yan. In 1970, John Minford and Hawkes began their collaborative 5-volume translation for Penguin Classics of the great 18th-century novel *The Story of the Stone*, otherwise known as *The Dream of the Red Chamber*, which was finally completed in 1986. See http://www.chinaheritagequarterly.org/features.php?searchterm=019_vale_hawkes.inc&issue=019 for more details.

[24] See http://www.chinaheritagequarterly.org/features.php?searchterm=019_vale_liu_minford.inc&issue=019 for further information.

> What students of Chinese are learning appears to be an instrument. But it is an instrument only in the sense that it is a medium through which advanced studies in much broader fields may be made. A mere knowledge of the language does not in fact constitute the real understanding of that language. In order to understand the feelings expressed in the Chinese language one must be acquainted with at least some of the many rich works of literature and philosophy which have been written in Chinese... We are concerned not only with a language and a literature but, through the learning of that language and literature, with something more lasting, a deeper, and hence more intimate and even sympathetic, understanding of the people whose language and literature we are studying.[25]

As acknowledged by many, during his own lifetime, Liu Ts'un-yan and his colleagues made ANU a place in which Sinology was able to flourish and a great place for both academics and students for research collaboration and deep engagement of China knowledge.

The cases of both Sydney University and ANU and their pioneering academics and scholars in Chinese Studies between the 1950s and 1980s illustrate the influence of the European tradition of Sinology and classical studies in Australia. With their classical training and encyclopedic knowledge in broad areas of Chinese Studies, these scholars played a major role in establishing and shaping Chinese Studies in the leading Australian universities before the 1980s and defending the value of traditional education and the mission of what a university should have. The commitment to tradition from both the Western and Chinese learnings provided academic vigor and training for students not only in both classical and modern Chinese languages, but a deeper understanding of Chinese culture, history, literature and philosophy and humanity as a whole. While we cannot generalize elsewhere the phenomena found in Sydney University and ANU, the reputation of world-class traditional Chinese Studies and Sinology during that time in

---

[25] Minford (2009).

these two leading institutions speaks to the high benchmarking and recognition they have set and received for Australia. Like Sinologists in Europe in learning about China until the Second World War, these scholars' knowledge of the relevant languages and cultures gave them the power to write on a range of topics and to criticize the mistakes of other scholars, from Confucianism to Daoism, Buddhism and popular religion, as well as art, mythology and the history of science.

Sinology and Chinese Studies

Traditional Sinology and Oriental Studies in Europe originally had the purpose of studying and understanding another culture and another people; China was seen as a civilization that was to be studied and understood by the Western countries, by people such as the missionaries or scholars who had interest in knowledge regarding China in its history, people, language, literature and culture, in particular the Confucian classics and classical Chinese texts that have enduring influence on the life of Chinese people. The strong commitment to and defence for a traditional Sinological approach to studies of China since Professor Davis' time and later by Professor Liu Ts'un-yan and Professor Pierre Ryckmans did not come without a reason.

After the establishment of the People's Republic of China in 1949, the study of China developed along diverging lines. The rise of Area studies, the role of China watchers and the political environment had changed the role of Sinology. The Area studies approach, especially in the United States, challenged the dominance of classical Sinology in Europe. Scholars in the US have stirred up a Chinese Studies vs. Sinology debate after the event which John Fairbank at Harvard University promoted as the "study of China within a discipline," an approach which downplayed the role of philological Sinology, and focused on issues in history and the social sciences.[26] It was not Fairbank's original intention to

---

[26] Zurndorfer (1995).

altogether abandon the traditional Sinological approach of studying China. In fact Sinology continued to be part of the Harvard curriculum where "modern Chinese Studies" was added to focus on investigation of contemporary politics, institutions, economic history and the social life of Asia.[27]

Nevertheless America in the 1970s saw a strong promotion of China areas studies in American institutions, with more than half of the research funding utilized by contemporary China studies when studies and research on post-1949 China was considered lacking. Nowadays, in Europe, Sinology is still known as Chinese Studies, whereas in the United States, Sinology is a subfield of Chinese Studies. Elizabeth Perry, Professor of Government at Harvard University observed in her article "The PRC and American China Studies: Fifty Years" (1999), that the US model for the study of China based on the social science areas studies on China were born out of a Cold War mentality to "know one's enemy" and that "the contemporary China field was more oriented towards up-to-the minute intelligence analysis and policy punditry."[28] This view seemed to echo Said's (1978) who argued that "the study of the cultures of the Middle East and Asia by Western scholars was motivated by a desire to enforce the political, economic, and cultural dominance of the West."[29]

In his *Orientalism*, Said's view of Asia as otherness to be dominated by the West may not be shared by many in traditional Sinology, including Ryckmans who believed that China should be studied as a civilization with an essentially holistic character. In Ryckmans' view, as far as Sinologists are concerned, Chinese civilization "presents the irresistible fascination of what is totally 'other' which can inspire the deepest love, together with a strong desire to know it" — in other words, not an "other" to be conquered or defeated. In this sense, Ryckmans rejected the existence of Orientalism in Sinology.[30] On the other hand, one can hardly deny

---

[27] Ibid. (p. 35).
[28] Quoted from Coughlan (2008, p. 148).
[29] Said (1978).
[30] Coughlan (2008, pp. 151–152).

the influence of political environment and political motivation on the construction of a realm of knowledge such as Chinese Studies, as argued by Perry.[31] The debate of Sinology vs. modern Chinese studies started in America, and the notion of Area studies and the impact of it has also hit Chinese Studies and Asian Studies in Australia. Chinese Studies in Australia was shaped by the political and socio-economical relationship with China and Asia.

Chinese Studies in post-colonial Australia is a testimony of Australia's national identity in the tension between its socio-economic and political relationship with Asia on the one hand and its Western allies on the other. We need to mention Dr. Stephen FitzGerald who was Australia's first ambassador to China (1973–1976). FitzGerald had made very important contributions to Chinese Studies in Australia as well as the building of a good relationship between the two countries after Whitlam's Labour Party won the election in 1972. FitzGerald's first-hand experience of studying and working in Hong Kong, Taiwan and China shaped his thinking and the way he contributed to building the Australia–China relationship in the 1970s. During the late 1970s and 1980s when China had opened the door, there was huge interest in China, and FitzGerald became a consultant educating and helping people understand China and the various reforms that went on:

> Business people wanted to go and see what business opportunities there were. Others like universities were interested, state governments were interested. There's this intense interest in wanting to do things in China so I became a consultant. I still kept my active involvement with the Asian Studies Association. But from then on, for, intensively over the next decade, the decade of the eighties, I was almost a commuter to China. I would go to China eight or nine or ten times a year with different clients. I had

---

[31] Although the Cold War is over, China–US relationship since Obama and now Trump continues to evolve in a complex mix of intensifying diplomacy, growing international rivalry and increasingly intertwined economic and technological competition. As long as Australia is closely following Washington's direction, the Australia–China relationship is also complex.

clients from almost every industry, from iron and steel to the sugar industry all the way through to brewing beer, the lot.

At the same time in Australia, FitzGerald became more and more involved in the movement to try to get the study of Chinese and China as well as other Asian societies into schools and into universities. As the chair of a committee at the beginning of the 1980s, he produced a report for the Association of Asian Studies on how to get Asian studies into schools. He was also the Chair of the Asian Studies Council set up by the government back in 1956 and helped develop a strategy for the study of Asian languages and societies throughout the education system, in schools and in universities. At the end of the 1980s, FitzGerald was a consultant of the Queensland government and they were wanting to introduce Asian languages as compulsory in schools across Queensland. He traveled the length and breadth of Queensland, going to tiny little schools, big high schools and so on, talking about this to teachers, talking to parents.

A report entitled "Asian in Australian Education: Report of the Committee on Asian Studies to the ASAA" was published in the early 1980s. The report emphasized the essential rationale for studying China and Asia in Australia and has considered it as "being in Australia's long term interest" at the geopolitical level; then in the late 1980s and mid-1990s Australia under the Hawke and the Keating government was considered part of Asia and that Australians could benefit from trade and economic relationship with its Asian neighbors.[32] Chinese Studies and China knowledge therefore has been important to Australia for political and economic reasons in the past decades. The Asian economic miracles were followed by the China boom since the 1990s. Australia benefited from the economic miracles due to its geographical location and proximity to China and other Asian countries. Chinese Studies has been promoted as Asia knowledge and needs to be equipped in order to better the relationship between the two countries for

---

[32] Coughlan (2008, pp. 118–119).

China's rising role as an important economic power. As the Liberal government in Australia moved away from the enthusiasm about Asia in the Keating era since 1996, funding for Asian-related programs "has been progressively cut short or not continued."[33] In the 21st century as China rises as a world economic power and becomes Australia's most important trading partner, America's political influence and Eurocentrism continues to resurrect in the political sphere in Australia and the relations between Australia and China began to deteriorate in 2018.

At the same time, the teaching of Chinese in Australian universities made considerable progress in the 1990s with an influx of Chinese immigrants and students with Chinese heritage background (e.g., from Hong Kong, Taiwan, Malaysia and Singapore). In the non-language sphere, the range of disciplines being taught within Chinese studies has expanded throughout the decade. Teaching in most of the Chinese Program is informed by staff research in a wide variety of different fields, including Chinese language teaching and many aspects of contemporary and traditional China. While traditional Sinology subjects such as Classical Chinese are still taught in the more established universities, interest in contemporary China has added new vigor to the Chinese studies offerings.[34]

As Australian scholarship on China is changing from the European tradition of sinology to a mainstream process, influenced by area studies and the need to understand contemporary China, the debate on what Chinese Studies or "New Sinology" should be continued in the last two decades.[35] Professor John Minford wrote in the announcement for a forum on "Sinology Old and New: A Forum" on 19 April 2009 when Anthony C. Yu, Emeritus Professor

---

[33] Coughlan (2008, pp. 128–129).
[34] Fitzgerald *et al.* (2002).
[35] While "Sinology" seemed to be outdated in Australia, scholars who have had sinological training continue to have the respect for having the possession of such linguistic and cultural capital in the skills of classical Chinese. Coughlan (2008, p. 163).

of University of Chicago, was visiting the ANU at the invitation of John Minford and The China Institute:

> Whither Chinese Studies?
> Professor Anthony Yu's visit to the ANU offers an opportunity for reflection on some of the challenges facing those of us who teach courses and conduct research on China — in its many aspects: from the Oracle Bones of the Shang dynasty, to the latest Chinese antics on the Internet. Does Chinese Studies actually mean anything? Does Chinese have to become a sub-division of Business Studies? Can a graduate in Chinese studies manage without at least a grounding in literary Chinese? Does Song-dynasty poetry matter? Is the Three Kingdoms relevant to modern China? Is there a valid rationale for a holistic 'New' Sinology, one in which a knowledge of the Chinese tradition informs a perception of China today, and one in which an engagement with present-day China enlivens our perceptions of China's traditions?

In other words what are Chinese Studies? Or what kind of knowledge and experience should Chinese Studies in a university offer to our students? We probably can find an answer in Pierre Ryckmans's memorial speech for Professor Liu Ts'un-yan (1917–2009) which provided a definition of Sinology and explained how Professor Liu was a great example of traditional Sinologist:

> Chinese studies were formerly called "sinology" — a word that lately fell into relative disuse, as many students in our field now prefer to define themselves by their respective specializations — and they would call themselves (let us say) historians, or linguists, literary historians, sociologists, political scientists — whatever. They rightly feel that, if they were to call themselves "sinologists," this would imply an almost absurd ambition– as if they could be conversant with the totality of four thousand years of Chinese culture. In Western terms this would be as if scholars of classical Greece, or of English literature, or of French history, would present themselves as "Europeanologists." It seems indeed as if a learning which would encompass *all* the main aspects of Chinese civilisation

through the ages should be, by definition, beyond the grasp of any individual mind, as it would entail an intellectual storing capacity that is simply superhuman. And yet — this is precisely what was accomplished in China by a small elite of highly educated scholars. Professor Liu was one of the last representatives of what was truly a generation of intellectual giants.

...

He obviously cultivated a rich inner life. Though we naturally had no direct access to this, we could measure its quality by its fruits: the serene equanimity of his mood, the constant kindness he extended to all. His spiritual philosophy was (I think) the product of a natural convergence: he fulfilled his social and professional duties according to Confucian ethics. He controlled his motions and maintained inner calm through the practice of meditation and Taoist discipline. All forms of religious experience interested him — and not only from a scholarly point of view. (I know for instance that he had read the Christian Gospels with attention and respect.) The spirit of Buddhist compassion constantly inspired his actions. He achieved a quality of integrity, detachment and serenity that should remain an example for all of us.[36]

Ryckmans's view about Chinese Studies and the need for traditional Chinese Studies shared a parallel with others who expressed concerns that Asian Studies with "area" based approach to research and teaching in Asian studies in Australia may generate in-depth expertise in a particularly narrow field of knowledge — say the tax laws of Indonesia — but they may lack knowledge about the wider historical, cultural and political context of those tax laws.[37]

Scholars and China experts were adamant on the widespread expedience of university administration clinging onto the practical side of teaching only modern language which will not benefit the community nor make our next generation better equipped with the required knowledge of China. The curriculum design with an

---

[36] Ryckmans, Pierre.
[37] Fitzgerald *et al.* (2002).

emphasis on being "pragmatic" and "strategic" of the courses has caused the loss of the meaning of "education" and changed students' attitude of learning Chinese. Speaking to an interviewer in an oral history project about Western sinologists, the American Chinese literature scholar Jon Eugene von Kowallis, who has been teaching in Australia since 1996, compared an elite American college's approach in teaching Chinese Studies with a European university that still followed the traditional approach system:

> At the time, in the States there was this notion, particularly at Williams and it got worse, it was this idea that you have to make Chinese more practical. In other words, don't teach Chinese literature, don't teach classical Chinese, teach business Chinese because their students want to go to China to do business. Well, some do and some don't. Just because you learn Chinese literature doesn't mean you can't do business. Just because you learn business Chinese doesn't mean you'll be a successful business person in China. But the administrators in the US were not thinking that far. What I got out of teaching at Charles University in Prague in the early 1990s, what impressed me the most, was the students' attitude. And that was, 'We're here for an education. What we do afterwards, is another question entirely. We'll figure that out after we get our first degree'. And it was a very, very good attitude. 'We're here to learn. We have these five years to learn. Afterwards, we'll worry about that afterwards'. They're great and they had more opportunities than some American students simply because there were a lot of employment opportunities for Chinese-Czech interpreters in Prague. Barmé, it might be eight or ten years ago, came up with a major article advocating the "new sinology." He felt that it was important to revive sinology and by that he meant when students approach China, they need to approach China with a knowledge of language and literature and culture and so on and so forth. He didn't get very far with it though. I think it's mainly because administrations of universities are interested in expediency and what he advocated was not the most expedient thing.[38]

---

[38] Interview with Jon von Kowallis for the China Knowledge Project, 2018.

One of the challenges under the modern university system was that a lot of the decision-making responding to funding shortages, as well as the effect of market forces and government policies in higher education, have resulted in the high price of escalating department/program conflicts, forcing academics to invest their time and energy in defending their disciplines and positions.[39] Fluctuation in fashion and policy, driven by reaction to events, undermines the continuous effort needed to strengthen Australia's Asia/China knowledge base.[40] This happened so often that while Chinese studies enjoyed growth in student enrolment numbers, it is not ultimately benefited by this growth. When Chinese Studies merged with other languages to form a department, the former would be normally operated to bring in income to keep other languages running — sometimes the former were considered as threat or rivalry by the latter. This approach not only sacrifices staffing in Chinese Studies, meaning less staff for more students, but also cuts in Chinese courses that were not considered by the administrators as practical or fashionable and yet are fundamental and essential to Chinese Studies students, not to mention losing the opportunity for the discipline to develop better. Chinese Studies as a knowledge discipline is losing its concentration by being "watered down" by other languages or disciplines that need the enrolment figures. Professor von Kowallis continues:

> When I went to Columbia to begin an undergraduate major in Chinese language and culture, the "core curriculum" was all Eurocentric. My Chinese language and culture courses had to fit around Western humanities, Western philosophy, English literature, Western art history and music. I've never been proud of that. If we had a core curriculum nowadays here at UNSW, there probably would be a course on China. Although, my suspicion actually, is that it might eventually end up being a course on East Asia or Asia and I have problems with Asian Studies. Asian Studies was brought in here by the previous Dean

---

[39] Coughlan (2008, pp. 54–55).
[40] Fitzgerald *et al.* (2002).

who didn't like Chinese Studies for some reason probably because he thought the Chinese language too difficult. He thought that since Asia is bigger than China, ultimately, we'll get more students in Asian Studies. It didn't work that way. Although he favoured Asian Studies, Chinese Studies grew, despite his opposition to it. Because China is an important country. The problem with Asian Studies is it gets to be too watered down. You'd have a week or two on India, a week or two on China, a week or two on Japan, a week or more on Korea, a week or two on Southeast Asia. There's your ten weeks for a trimester right there. It's too watered down.[41]

The risk of teaching Chinese Studies as part of another discipline is its fragmenting and distorting of knowledge about China:

It's like when I went to the Association for Asian Studies Conference in Washington DC a couple of weeks ago (in 2018). I was on a panel called 'Teaching Chinese literature as world literature: Lu Xun as exemplar'. One of the panellists who was a young Chinese woman teaching somewhere in the Midwest in the United States made the point, "I don't want to teach just a little subsection on modern Chinese literature in somebody else's world literature course, where I teach Lu Xun and students go away with the idea that women are oppressed in China." Because, of course, that's not really what Lu Xun is about. But if you teach one story or something like that and the students don't have any context, then they will go away with impressions like that.[42]

The loss of financial independence and concentration on Chinese Studies as an independent knowledge discipline means Chinese Studies does not have the opportunity to develop further even though the discipline brings in larger enrolment numbers and

---

[41] A similar mentality could be observed in another university when Asian Studies merged with European Languages.
[42] Kowallis, China Knowledge Project Interview. 2018.

income. In the past, some universities used to have independent Chinese departments with their own budgets and secretaries and high enrolments and they were able to subsidize the smaller, more specific courses on China that had lower enrolments:

> When departments were ended, and we were all merged into one "School," that has various different names; now- it's called Humanities and Languages, the independence that the Chinese program had was compromised. We're now part of a larger unit. And the problem now is that with our big enrolments, we've gone from subsidizing our own small courses (which were cancelled) to subsidizing other people's small courses... So, we become work-horses for other departments and programs. That's one of the disadvantages of the current system.[43]

Turf wars, self-protection in the department/disciplines as well as managerialism in the modern university system made teaching and research suffer when academics were forced to waste time on unnecessary administration tasks[44]:

> I think that if there is an effect on research quality, it's because we are being urged to produce more quantity. They want to have bureaucratic checks on the quality of the quantity, but the thruster is for quantity and then they will use their standards to determine quality. So, in that sense, I think the research is suffering a bit for that reason. Academics in Australia are forced to waste time on some unnecessary changes or reforms instead of being allowed to build on what they have already through what they call "evaluations" or "program reviews." Years ago, I ran into Glen Dudbridge, who had been Professor of Chinese at both Cambridge and Oxford. At that time, I ran into him at Berkeley. He had just finished doing an evaluation of the School in which Chinese and Japanese were located at the University of Melbourne (in Australia). This must have been at the end of 1996. They'd done an evaluation right before I got there. He was asking me some questions about

---
[43] *Ibid.*
[44] Coughlan (2008, pp. 179–182).

what was going on at Melbourne. I mentioned pressure to get grants and so on and so forth. And he said that the problem with Australian academia is it's kind of like China in that they have one *yundong* 運動 (movement and restructure), then another *yundong*. 運動完了以後, 再等一段時間, 又來一個運動. So, they just go from *yundong* to *yundong*. They're not building on what they have already.[45]

Nevertheless there is a widespread acceptance among Australians at all levels — governments, businesses and parents — that Australian interests are served by deepening and broadening knowledge of Chinese language and culture. Importantly, most Australian universities have embraced the opportunities afforded by the increasing presence of students with Chinese origins on their campuses. In part, this increase is derived from the expansion in the numbers of international students, a significant proportion of whom have Chinese ethnic origins. In addition, the number of Asian-born Australians has nearly doubled in the last 10 years. Both these groups of students seek knowledge of Chinese culture, and many want either to learn or maintain their Chinese language skills. As a consequence, the proliferation of courses designed for "background speakers" has led to a general improvement in the quality and quantity of Chinese courses in universities in the last 10 years.[46]

Toward the end of the century, many of those studying China called for an end to the split between Sinology and the disciplines. The Australian scholar Geremie Barmé, for instance, suggests a "New Sinology," one which "emphasizes strong scholastic underpinnings in both the classical and modern Chinese language and studies, while encouraging an ecumenical attitude in relation to a rich variety of approaches and disciplines, whether they be mainly empirical or more theoretically inflected."[47] Almost no one can deny that students should learn both classical and modern Chinese, both language and culture — not one or another — in order to develop

---

[45] Kowallis, China Knowledge Project Interview. 2018.
[46] Fitzgerald *et al.* (2002).
[47] Barme, (2012).

competent knowledge of China. However whether this can be successfully introduced or sustained in the universities will depend on how the government and the university administrators will support this kind of model which used to be very successful at the ANU. As FitzGerald recalled, the ANU used to be the outstanding place for the study of China in the period since about 1950 where all people in different fields in Chinese Studies came together to make a concentration and mainstream of Chinese Studies:

> ... The ANU set up something called the Australian Centre on China in the World, CIW where you had a whole lot of different scholars, studying different aspects of China. Some contemporary politics, somehow the party works, some studying Chinese film, all of this. Part of the reason why the ANU was so successful (in the past), is because they had these concentrations. It was in one big concentrated school that was called the Research School of Pacific Studies. But in that, they're all together, there were about a hundred academics. You had a huge concentration of China expertise and it kind of became self-perpetuating, and they're all together and it's all kind of mixing up and a great ferment of intellectual activity about China.[48]

As of 2016, there are about 40 universities in Australia with about 22 offering Chinese programs — some of these programs are being offered in the Confucius Institutes instead of inside the Faculties. Research Centres are established in some of the universities depending on availability of funding. Most of these research centres conduct research on contemporary China.

ANU used to be the largest hub for China Studies. More than 50 China specialists taught and conducted research, often through the various centres and institutes within ANU. This included the Contemporary China Centre which began in 1970 as a research facility concerned with scholarly social science analysis of post-1949 China. In 2010, the Centre merged with the Department of Political & Social Change (PSC). It published one of the leading

---
[48] Interview with FitzGerald (2018).

international journals on contemporary China, *The China Journal* (http://www.press.uchicago.edu/ucp/journals/journal/tcj.html). The Australian Centre on China in the World (中华全球研究中心/中華全球研究中心, http://ciw.anu.edu.au/) is another notable research institution with a special interest in advancing an understanding of China on a global scale. All of this activity comes under an umbrella institute, the ANU China Institute (http://chinainstitute.anu.edu.au/), which covers all ANU staff and students, across all disciplines, engaged in Chinese studies.

The University of Sydney's China Studies Centre was established in 2011. According to its website, the China Studies Centre seeks to "contribute to Australia–China cooperation and relations in business development, public health and social change." Press coverage of the Centre when it opened stated that the China Studies Centre was intended to "eventually match the University of Sydney's US Studies Centre in scope and influence." The Vice-Chancellor Michael Spence told the newspaper *The Australian*: "What we are doing is looking at the details of Chinese life and hoping we can make a contribution in some small way to development of solutions to the problems that China faces. This centre will not just have an important academic role but a crucial role, like our US Studies Centre, of providing public and government education."[49]

UTS is home to Australia's China research efforts. The Australia–China Relations Institute is a think tank established in December 2013 through a A$1.8 million donation made by a PRC businessman, Mr. Xiangmo Huang, Founder and Chairman of the Yuhu Group. The think tank's director until early 2019 was Australia's former foreign minister, Bob Carr. University of Melbourne's Centre for Contemporary Chinese Studies describes itself as "promoting an Australian approach in the study of contemporary China" and as being "a source of research-based information on China, Chinese societies and Chinese economies."

---

[49] Sainsbury, Michael. The Australian, 26, October, 2011. https://www.ussc.edu.au/analysis/university-of-sydney-to-open-largest-chinese-studies-centre.

In 2016, the Western Sydney University established the Australia–China Institute for Arts and Culture "as a hub and national resource centre for cultural exchange between Australia, China and the Sinosphere (including Taiwan, Hong Kong, Singapore and other centres of Chinese culture)."[50]

Institutions that have "China" in their name, as the above show, are not the only ones that study China and its various disciplinary facets. There are Confucius Institutes and Chinese Studies programs/disciplines/departments in 20 or so universities. For professional organizations, the Oriental Society of Australia established by Professor A. R. Davis in the 1950s is the oldest professional organization and is still active with the *Journal of Oriental Society of Australia* being published yearly. Apart from the Oriental Society, another professional organization should be mentioned. The Chinese Studies Association of Australia (CSAA, http://www.csaa.org.au/) was established in 1991 as the professional association for China specialists whose disciplinary expertise includes anthropology, economics, geography, history, language, law, linguistics, political science, sociology, literature and other aspects of Chinese society and culture. It convenes a major biennial conference[51] and publishes new appointments, forthcoming conferences and workshops, and campus news. The CSAA advises on the teaching of the Chinese language and culture in the Australian education system and also advises government on research funding requirements. In short, the Association seeks to be influential in shaping policy on Chinese Studies in Australia.

Chinese Studies: Now and Beyond

2018 marked the 200th anniversary of the first Chinese settlement in Australia. The celebration of the year was a reminder of the contribution of the Chinese community to this country in the last

---

[50] See https://www.westernsydney.edu.au/aciac/about for more details.
[51] The 15th CSAA Biennial Conference was held in 2017 at Macquarie University well attended by 180 participants from local and overseas by accepting papers written in both English and Chinese language. The next one will be held in La Trobe University in 2019.

two centuries. Yet 2018 was also a year that reminded us that the Australia–China relationship could be an ongoing challenging and delicate issue with ethnocentrism rooted in Eurocentrism and White Australian policy back in the colonial period that continue to haunt the Australian community.[52] This is especially the case when U.S.-China relationship is at a new low in the Trump era.[53] It is observed by Gareth Evans, former Australian Foreign Minister, that the current government has been "obsessively deferential to Washington."[54] Then there was the parliamentary review of new national security legislation which would "criminalise the simple act of receiving and discussing information deemed harmful to the national interest," particularly targeting China. An important element of the background to this legislation is the debate on Chinese influence in Australia. A paper published in 2018 analyzed how anxiety or China angst arose when China was misread in the Australian public discourse on China:

> China matters significantly to contemporary Australia in terms of trade relations, capital movements, education and global order. Australian public discourse on China, however, inhabits two conflicting parallel universes, one a narrative of economic complementarity, the other of fear and anxiety. The spectre of the rise of China haunts Australian society in and among these two spheres: one in which China's economic rise is to be encouraged as a sign of it joining the capitalist world system, and the other in which China's ascent is regarded as a threat to be contained. …this problematic discourse [is called] Changst [China angst], arguing that it is permeated with a developmentalist logic (Chakrabarty, 2000) that misreads China through the homogenizing history of

---

[52] Polya (2018).
[53] Karabell, (2019), https://www.politico.com/magazine/story/2019/10/15/donald-trump-china-trade-war-hostility-229851.
[54] On October 31, former foreign minister Gareth Evans said in an interview with PRC state media outlet *The Global Times*: "There's also a tendency with this government to be obsessively deferential to Washington and I do worry that with Washington now moving to a very aggressive, hostile, confrontational stance with China, there will be pressure on the Australian government to follow suit. I think that pressure should be resisted." Australia–China Relations Institute (2018).

both capitalism and Eurocentrism. This reading of China as but a copy of Western capitalism evokes anxiety because its distinctive forms of capital flow disrupt the comforting teleology.[55]

On Monday 19 March 2018, a group of scholars of China and the Chinese diaspora submitted a statement to the parliamentary review of new national security legislation. The open letter quoted the following:

> The complex political landscape of Chinese Australia is not reducible to a simplistic 'pro' or 'anti-Beijing' binary. Yet, if the debate continues to be conducted in these terms, with commentators speculating as to the supposedly divided loyalties of Chinese Australians, or contemplating punitive measures to restrict the rights of those identified as 'pro-Beijing', we run the risk of creating just such a polarization. We have in Australia's mature multicultural society the capacity to conduct this important debate with much greater rigor, balance, and honesty than we have so far. We call on all those involved in the debate to work towards this end.[56]

The letter is noteworthy for outlining the background of the current Chinese influence debate and, more significantly, Australia's constant struggle for its national identity between being a Eurocentric ex-colony independent of Britain and part of Western allies, and a young, modern nation with a multicultural society. Having been working as diplomat, academic and consultant, FitzGerald believed that the politicians and the government need to send out the right signal to people on the importance of maintaining good relationship with China and to provide enough funding for learning and research in China:

> ...in brief, I think the resistance is winning at the moment. It was really on the ascent throughout the 1980s and through to the middle of the nineties. And one of the reasons for that is because

---
[55] McCarthy (2018).
[56] Asia and the Pacific Policy Society 2018.

the political leadership in Australia. But they believed in it, encouraged it and they sent out all the right messages. They didn't fund it enough, but nevertheless people were getting the message. So that conveyed itself to people in school, to students who thought, 'well yeah, why not?' The logic was there for learning Chinese for example. Then in the early nineties, there was a meeting of COAG, the Council of Australian Governments. At the meeting at Hobart, at the beginning of the 90s, a proposition was put by the Queensland government that all of these governments should support a new initiative for Asian languages and studies in schools… It became something which was called NALSAS, the National Asian Languages and Studies in Australian Schools. The first chair was Colin Mackerras. Interestingly, a China person was the first chair. That went on, it was given funding but not enough. Then in the second half of the 1990s, the government changed in 1996 and the Keating government was defeated, and the Howard government came in and the messages changed.

In 2003 the Howard government cut the funding for the National Asian Languages and Studies in Australian Schools program. I don't believe it has recovered. When Julia Gillard was prime minister, she had this initiative called the Asian Century. The Asian Century White Paper that was produced, promised a lot in terms of the teaching of Chinese and other languages and studies, but offered no funding. I wrote publicly at the time, I said "This is a delusion," and it's a really sad and cruel delusion because if you don't put money behind it, it's not worth it.[57]

FitzGerald argued that we need to have teachers who can teach our students the language to have access to Chinese culture and Chinese people. More still, we need to have political leaders who appreciate the need for Chinese language and culture and who can put the resources into it. For FitzGerald, to build a people link with China is fundamental:

Greater access to Chinese language education, and thus access to Chinese culture, Chinese people, Chinese history and all of that

---
[57] Interview with Fitzgerald (2018).

huge richness, which, leave the politics aside, is fundamentally important in the same way that if no one in the country spoke any European languages, I would argue that that's a kind of crime. You would have to try to force them to learn one or more European languages to access all of that. So, the first and I think the most fundamental benefit of that would be to be able to access the society and to link up with people there. I mean, you may be a paediatrician, but you can enjoy a relationship with paediatricians in China in their language or maybe you're an actor or a musician or you may just be an ordinary person. I mean, you may not have any special kinds of things.

So that's the first thing. The second is that politically we'd be much better able to understand what this huge giant of a country is. That takes me back to my reaction to the Cultural Revolution. I think we have to be able to understand this country and even more today because of the influence that it has a great big power and a huge economy. So that's the second reason. The third reason, which some would say is the first, but I think it's one of the three, is the economic. I think it would give great economic benefits to us as well and I think we'd be much better at managing ourselves in what I call the Chinese world.

Without being able to speak the same language you won't be able to communicate and understand each other. Unfortunately, the British colonial mentality still influences Australia and not understanding China and not having the right attitude and open mind was one of the reasons that Australia still has the resistance of being part of Asia and has the unstable political approach of siding with America and Britain so much is because of language.

We will need to study the language and have a deep study of some aspect of the culture, preferably history. I would make it compulsory for all students in Australia to study history of some part of the world. So that's really important to have that kind of study which is very deep: If you just had this and it's all superficial, then I think that's a problem. And here is somewhere where we could be employing more people of ethnic Chinese background who have grown up maybe bilingual and who've done, somewhere along the way, they've studied some aspects of Chinese society, but they've also studied some discipline, but they're bilingual and to that extent and in that sense, they can access the society. We should be employing a lot more of such bilingual people in our universities and that's where you can get the mainstreaming.

It should not be possible for anyone in Australia to get from primary school to the end of university, without having studied something to do with China and with the rest of Asia. It should not be possible. So that's my principle and then you have to work it out from there. Studying China should certainly be starting from high school, primary if we can.[58]

As advice to young scholars who are interested in studying Chinese and China, Professor Jon von Kowallis, who is Chair of the Chinese Studies Program in the School of Humanities and Languages at UNSW, said: "Start with learning the language as early as you can, try to learn Japanese or at least get a reading knowledge of Japanese. Try to go to China, spend time in China, develop connections in China, colleagues in China. Realize that things in China are different to things here, but that's not necessarily bad. Chinese do things differently, but sometimes they work out better, sometimes they don't. Be prepared for that."[59]

On the other hand, cultural exchange between Australia and China is ideally a process of mutual understanding and two-way engagement. As we have more international students coming to study in Australia, where we have a situation with Chinese, where

---

[58] Interview with Fitzgerald (2018).

[59] Interview with Kowallis (2018). Professor Jon Eugene von Kowallis studied Chinese language and literature at Columbia University (B.A.), National Taiwan University, the University of Hawaii (M.A.), Peking University and the University of California, Berkeley (Ph.D.). Prior to coming to Australia, he taught at Berkeley, UCLA, Oregon, Williams College and Karlova (Charles) University in Prague, the Czech Republic. In Australia, he has taught at the University of Melbourne and UNSW, where he was recipient of the ARC Discovery grant for a project on Lu Xun's early thought. In 2013, he was named Arch Professor at the University of Georgia and in 2018 elected President of the Oriental Society of Australia. During his interview Professor Kowallis made a remark about his own identity: "I'm glad they consider me as Australian. I am an Australian citizen, but most Australians consider me to be an American. The funny thing then is when I go back to America, a lot of academics call me Australian because my institutional affiliation is here. Which I don't mind but it's just funny. For the purpose of this interview, they can identify me as Australian, that's fine."

both in schools and in universities, we should make this opportunity for cultural exchange. We need to have the right attitude and that people should all come together to make a change, to make an Australian experience available to international students: the locals, the international students, the academic staff, the alumni, all of them. The problem was there was no reaching out. The university has to do it...[60]

Obviously, a deep engagement with China requires a good mindset with a purpose of acquiring the knowledge of a country, a civilization, a culture and a people that is different and yet integral of the same humanity. Therefore, Chinese Studies should be developed and supported as a long-term undertaking. In this sense, Pauline Keating alarms us through mentioning of the risk of "dumbing down" of the study of China — "a focus on just the knowledge that can be deemed relevant and useful to New Zealand's commercial relationship with China."[61]

Dealing with racism and anti-China hostility ingrained and institutionalized in ex-colonies such as Australia and New Zealand could be a long battle, as shown in Keating's chapter in this volume:

> The resurfacing of anti-Chinese hostility and bigotry became a matter of concern for all of us who were teaching courses about China in the 1990s. In fact, it is fair to say that all China scholars, from the beginning of their teaching careers in the China field, were very conscious of a responsibility to 'de-exoticise the Orient' in the minds of Western students and to challenge stereotypical understandings of China. Young people love to dismantle stereotypes, and in university classrooms we tended to feel we were making a lot of headway. But what could be done about the racism rooted in ignorance in the homes and on the streets?[62]

---

[60] Interview with Fitzgerlad (2018).
[61] *Ibid.*
[62] Keating, Pauline, "China Studies in Aotearoa/New Zealand: Moving Beyond Post-Colonialism," in this Volume.

Scholars and China experts interviewed almost unanimously agreed that it is in Australia's best interest to maintain a good relationship with China and nurture a better understanding of China. To provide a deeper engagement with China and develop good knowledge and understanding of the country, it is not just about designing and offering university courses. Some suggest the language learning should start as early as secondary school or even primary school.[63] Furthermore, more than any time ever we need leaders from the government who can send out the right signal to the Australian community. FitzGerald believed that to change the situation it will need to have an effective lobbying of the government:

> Australia should play a role in regional stability by being able to influence China and other big powers by "living in a Chinese world" in the present and the future. It is no more pleasant or unpleasant or whatever than living in an Anglo world. But many people don't welcome that and Canberra listens to Washington far too much and the Howard government and the Turnbull government "stir that nasty Sinophobia and xenophobia, which has got a nasty history in Australia." To reduce this Sinophobia in Australia we have to find ways of influencing the government to explain to them how harmful this is to our interests. Like "China Matters" which is not for profit organization and which has a self-proclaimed mission to get a more sophisticated and nuanced discussion about China in Australia and to get sound policy. We need to think about preventing the aftermath of an international disorder that could come about, how to rebuild the international stability.[64]

Like FitzGerald who has spent most of his life in building and improving the relationship between Australia and China, Jocelyn Chey who was Australian Consul General to Hong Kong between 1992 and 1995, and founding Director of the

---

[63] Interview with Fitzgerald (2018).
[64] Interview with Fitzgerlad (2018).

Australia–China Institute for Arts and Culture, Western Sydney University from 2016 to 2017, is a former diplomat in Hong Kong and Beijing and one of the first graduates in Chinese Studies in Australia. Her training and working experience positions her well to comment on recent developments in the Australia–China relationship. She expressed her concerns regarding international disputes between contending powers and their frequent consequence of persecution of local ethnic minorities and how the contributions of the growing Chinese community to the nation and to our developing relationships with Asia are under-appreciated.[65] She points out that

> How to cope with China is a key question for Australia's future. While there are a handful of doomsayers, forecasting its imminent collapse due to internal political divisions and financial problems, most analysts believe that China will continue to grow and become more technologically advanced and militarily powerful, and we in Australia have to accept this fact. It is not simple or easy. China's competition with the United States is becoming more stringent, marked by trade disputes and flexing of military muscle and it seems the Trump administration has decided that China's rise should be curbed militarily and economically. Chey (2018).

Chey has aptly pointed out that blaming of the Beijing's political interference has ignored the diversity of Chinese Australian community of 1.2 million in Australia (that does not necessarily have ties with Beijing or the PRC) and the fact that many Chinese came to Australia because they cherished Australia's political freedom and democratic system.[66] To Chey, it is an irony that it is a vicious loop that has led to some recent instances of racism affecting Chinese Australians being blamed on the Australian government by their media, and it is increasingly common for

---

[65] Chey (2018).
[66] *Ibid.*

members of this community to say that they no longer feel welcome in this country. As Professor Jocelyn Chey points out:

> Australia [also] needs an Open Door and should not let the parameters of our international relationships or multicultural policies be set by Washington. There are many reasons for Australia to cooperate with China and to expand our trade and diplomatic ties in Asia, and there are many reasons for us to cherish the role that Chinese Australians play in these relationships. Chey (2018).

Conclusion

Chinese Studies and Chinese scholars in Australia universities will continue to play a vital role in building the relationship and bettering the mutual understandings between Australia and China. In the modern university system, we need to think and rethink how to retain Chinese experts and provide support to research, teaching and learning Chinese language and culture, to ensure widely recognized study pathways for our students. It is no longer a matter of whether Australians, especially government leaders, policymakers and opinion-makers, and university administrators, should consider the knowledge of China to be important for national prosperity and survival. Instead it is about how much support Chinese Studies can get from different levels of the Australian government and community to the universities which have to provide sustainable education to our next generation, sustainable education that is not focusing on China as a rising economic and political power, but to develop Chinese Studies to provide and nurture knowledge about China as a different people, different culture with different history and philosophy with a shared humanity, for better human coexistence and survival in an ever more interconnected world. Within the universities, Chinese Studies should provide students the opportunity to study and develop deep engagement with China; should train their students to be more than merely a tool…but a thinker and leader…for the common interests of the peoples and humanity as a whole.

References

Asia and the Pacific Policy Society. 2018. "An Open Letter from Concerned Scholars of China and the Chinese Diaspora: Australia's debate on 'Chinese influence'," https://www.policyforum.net/an-open-letter-from-concerned-scholars-of-china-and-the-chinese-diaspora/.

Australia–China Relations Institute. University of Technology, Sydney. Australia–China Relations Monthly Summary October 2018. *Times*. https://www.australiachinarelations.org/content/australia-china-relations-monthly-summary-october-2018.

Barmé, Geremie. 2012. "New Sinology," The China Story. https://www.thechinastory.org/cot/new-sinology/.

Barmé, Geremie. 2017. An Educated Man Is Not a Pot: On the University. *China Heritage Quarterly*. http://chinaheritage.net/journal/an-educated-man-is-not-a-pot-君子不器/.

Chey, Jocelyn. 2018. Caught in the Middle: Chinese Australians Feel Unwanted. https://johnmenadue.com/jocelyn-chey-caught-in-the-middle-chinese-australians-feel-unwanted/.

Coughlan, Chia-mei Jane. 2008. *The Study of China in Universities: A Comparative Case Study of Australia and the United Kingdom*. New York: Cambria Press.

Fitzgerald, John, Robin Jeffrey, Kama Maclean, Tessa Morris-Suzuki. 2002. Maximizing Australia's Asia knowledge: Repositioning and Renewal of a National Asset. https://researchbank.swinburne.edu.au/items/32dcc93e-c530-470f-bd52-304b2a573c56/1/.

Fitzgerald, John and et al. 2002. Maximizing Australia's Knowledge: Repositioning and Renewal of a National Asset, a Report by the Asian Studies Association of Australia, Inc.

Davis, Glyn. 2012. "The Australian Idea of a University," https://meanjin.com.au/essays/the-australian-idea-of-a-university/.

Karabell, Zachary. 2019. "Don't Blame Just Trump for U.S.-China Hostility," Politico Magazine, 15 October,2019. https://www.politico.com/magazine/story/2019/10/15/donald-trump-china-trade-war-hostility-229851.

Keating, Pauline. "China Studies in Aotearoa/New Zealand: Moving Beyond Post-Colonialism," (Forthcoming, in this volume, 2019).

Larsen, Svend Erik. 2017. *Australia between White Australia and Multiculturalism: A World Literature Perspective. Comparative Literature: East and West*, Vol. 1. https://www.tandfonline.com/doi/full/10.1080/25723618.2017.1339510.

Leys, Simon. 2011. *The Hall of Uselessness*. Melbourne: Black Inc.

McCarthy, G. M. and Song, X. 2018. "China in Australia: The Discourses of Changst," *Asian Studies Review*, 42 (2): 323–341. https://doi.org/10.1080/10357823.2018.1440531.

Minford, John. 2009. Tribute to Emeritus Professor Liu Ts'un-yan. *China Heritage Quarterly*, No.19. September 2009. http://www.chinaheritagequarterly.org/features.php?searchterm=019_vale_liu_minford.inc&issue=019.

Penny, Benjamin. 2014. "Preface to A.R. Davis Reprints," in *East Asian History*. http://www.eastasianhistory.org/38/davis-reprints-preface.

Polya, Gideon. 2018 "Australian Sinophobia and China-bashing from Colonial Persecution and White Australia to Trump America's Asia Sheriff," https://countercurrents.org/2018/01/26/australian-sinophobia-china-bashing-colonial-persecution-white-australia-trump-americas-asia-deputy-sheriff/.

Ryckmans, Pierre. 2009. In Memoriam: Professor Liu Ts'un-yan, AO, (1917–2009 Liu). *China Heritage Quarterly*, No.19. September 2009. http://www.chinaheritagequarterly.org/features.php?searchterm=019_vale_liu_rickmans.inc&issue=019 (accessed 15 December 2018).

Said, Edward. W. 1978. *Orientalism*. London and Henley: Routledge & Kegan Paul.

Sainsbury, Michael. The Australian, 26, October, 2011. https://www.ussc.edu.au/analysis/university-of-sydney-to-open-largest-chinese-studies-centre.

Zurndorfer, Harriet. 1995. *China Bibliography: A Research Guide to Reference Works About China Past and Present*. Hawai'i: University of Hawai'i Press. https://books.google.com.au/books?id=uu5zn7-ImJoC&printsec=frontcover&redir_esc=y#v=onepage&q=Fairbank&f=false.

Chapter 16

Pondering China Studies in the Philippines as an Academic Practice and Scholarly Inquiry

Tina S. Clemente

Asian Center, University of the Philippines — Diliman, Diliman, the Philippines

Recontextualizing China Studies in the Philippines

China Studies in the Philippines is multifarious. First, as an academic practice in tertiary education, it is approached through varied fields and modalities such as, but not limited to, area studies, international relations, cultural/ethnic studies, history, and economics. Second, as a subject of scholarship, it is inclusive in that it covers any aspect of China and its people, the Chinese diaspora, and Chinese in the Philippines as distinct streams of inquiry. This paper attempts to interrogate the field of China Studies in the Philippines by considering the field as a current academic practice and scholarly inquiry. I present areas for particular rumination using my experience at the University of the Philippines (UP), which is considered the Philippines' national university, and in particular, the UP Asian Center, the graduate unit in which China Studies, as part of its degree programs, is formally lodged. In the succeeding discussion, I locate the motivations in studying China in the colonial historical context, the evolution of academic programs and attendant issues, and points for further research.

The Interest in China and the Chinese in Spanish Philippines

There are many connections between the Philippines and China in history that make the former an interesting site for interrogating China Studies and its evolution. Pre-state Philippine polities and China engaged in a thriving exchange of goods during the protohistoric period (Clemente 2012). Such relations have not only yielded artifacts but also documentary evidence from dynastic annals, allowing archaeological, anthropological and historical studies to thrive in the academe.[1] The onset of Spanish colonialism in the Philippines disturbed the trade between the polities with China as well as with Southeast Asia and brought in a new era of international involvement for the Philippines. In the Spanish colonial period, the reorientation of the Philippines' relations with the world was drastically altered. It found itself grafted as the edge of the Spanish empire and a significant conduit to a new era of world trade through the galleons. From the port of Manila, the galleons sailed to the rest of the empire, which awaited the cargo of Chinese goods. The latter were exchanged for silver to assuage China's demand for it. The Philippines became a critical link in the galleon trade, which connected China to Europe and the Americas.

Beyond China's involvement in the galleon trade, the colonial administration was occupied with managing the Chinese traders who streamed into the Philippines.[2] The institutional predation toward Chinese traders was a manifestation of the administration's insecurity with the Chinese trader minority who were difficult to subjugate and who entrenched themselves in the colony's economic life. Accounts on the Spanish period show uneven gathering of population and commercial data — which are supposed to give information on the number of baptized Chinese (i.e., indicating

---

[1] Such studies have also been pursued outside the traditional confines of the academe who study pre-colonial socio-historical connections to underscore the notion of longstanding harmonious relations, predating contemporary perspectives of conflict.

[2] The Philippines is distinct in having the world's oldest Chinatown in Binondo, Manila.

subjugation), how much to tax them and how much commerce was attributed to them. On the other hand, the Catholic clergy, who had a major role in colonial management, had missionary designs on China. It was therefore a natural interest for the clergy to not only gain converts from the Chinese in the Philippines but to also capitalize on them to gain a connection to the Chinese mainland (Clemente 2015).

Hence, reasons for studying China and the Chinese abound, but the administration engaged in endless efforts to control and reduce the numbers of Chinese in the colony while being contested by those who championed Chinese presence as an integral lever of the economy. The liberalization of the Philippine economy and the coming of the merchant houses opened up wholesale and retail trade, which provided an opportunity for the Chinese to become merchants in the buying and selling business, linking local economies to foreign merchants, taking on an evolved middleman role (Clemente 2013). The Chinese who inter-married entered into landholding, while Chinese merchants entered into business ownership. While involvement in the economy has transformed amid the existing socio-political nuances pervading the economic structure at different times, the narrative about the Chinese has somewhat remained in stasis in the view that the Chinese have supplanted the indigenous in their own economy (Clemente 2017a). When the Spanish left, the Philippine economy remained West-oriented but now inclined toward the Americans, the new colonizers. This orientation remained well after the Philippines gained independence.

The interests on China and the Chinese in the preceding exposition and the long tradition of education in the Philippines[3] beg the question why a tradition of Sinology did not materialize. How is it possible that during three centuries of Spanish

---

[3] The Philippines is distinct in having "the oldest extant university in Asia": Pontifical, Regal and Royal University of Santo Tomas, The Catholic University of the Philippines, also known as the University of the Santo Tomas (UST). The latter was instituted in 1611 (Lim-Pe 1973) while other universities were set up after, demonstrating that the tradition of education has long existed in the colony.

colonization, the interest in China did not evolve into a field of study and does not find itself as a dominant strand in institutionalized academic programs in the Philippines today?

Several insights are helpful in exploring answers to the question. First, the colonial administration did not focus on building bilateral relations with China. China's commercial involvement in the galleons was driven by the market, not requiring the colonial administration to apply economic diplomacy. Second, interest in the Chinese in the Philippines or missionary possibilities in China only redounded to efforts in managing the former and strategizing entry in regard to the latter. Such interests did not find space in education. Elsewhere in the Spanish colonies, education, language instruction, religious conversion and intermarriage were integral to hispanization. However, Spanish colonial settlers in the Philippines (including administrators and religious orders) comprised of fewer numbers compared to the indigenous and Chinese put together, creating longstanding concerns for security. Religious conversion then functioned as the flagship instrument to manage the colony while education and language instruction were restricted as they were seen to empower the non-Spanish, heightening concerns on security. To make matters worse, the Philippines was on the edge of the Spanish empire and could hardly survive, financially, making the Chinese connection, whether through the galleons or commerce in the Philippines, all the more important for economic survival. The ensuing social stratification resulted in class structures that served to maintain colonial security. As more and more Filipinos with indigenous ancestry gained access to education, the use of knowledge was directed at problematizing the nation-project, Filipino identity and independence. The rising indigenous educated class deemed that nationalist concerns were more important as a subject of scholarly attention. Colonial interests, which included relations with China, remained an enterprise of colonial rulers. On the other hand, Chinese achievements in the Philippine economy intertwined with the evolving nation-project as flash points of tension.

At present, while China/Chinese-related studies on the Spanish period are prolific, it mainly became the domain of the field of history. Other fields in the social sciences began to focus on research themes related to Chinese in the Philippines beyond the Spanish colonial experience such as diaspora, social networks, commerce, integration and identity. Chinese in the Philippines became an amorphous area of study but did not become a dominant agenda in the current institutionalized practice of China Studies in the Philippine academe.

American Interests, Area Studies and China Studies

Where American colonial influence is concerned, China Studies proceeded from an Area Studies conceptualization. Course descriptions are often thought of as being reflective of American Cold War sensibilities. In the post-American period, the influence of the United States in the Philippines' basic institutions, especially education, remained strong and Area Studies, which has its roots in US interests, started at the University of the Philippines — the country's national university. China Studies then began as an issue-driven field (Clemente 2017b), strongly influenced by its pertinent publics in government, media, think tanks and domestic and international civil society, which are mostly oriented toward immediate concerns rather than theory. Benedict Anderson gives an illustrative characterization in a 2011 interview:

> The first is a problem of audiences. On the one hand there is the audience of professionals in the same disciplines in English-speaking universities; on the other is the audience of bureaucrats, journalists, intelligent common readers. In the first, prestige is assigned to "theory," disciplinary theory, while in the second readability, minimum jargon and theory, and good basic research are primary. So far as I know U.S. national state support of area studies hadn't markedly declined. The bureaucrats know that today's theory is gone in four years' time, and they can't be bothered with impenetrable prose, mathematical calculations, and the like. The second reason is really political. If a country or

region is regarded as a "problem," then area studies gets more airing. China studies fine, to a lesser extent Japan studies. Islamic studies is fine, African studies doesn't matter. Latin America is okay, Central Asia is not. Southeast Asian studies did will from 1950 to 1977 because of the heavy U.S. involvement in the area, communists everywhere, the Vietnam War, and so on (Aguilar et al. 2011, p. 109).

Caroline Hau says it differently, but is equally incisive:

Crucially the institutional setting of American academia, in particular, sets its own limits on what can be studied and how. "Areas" matter insofar as American interests say that they matter — just as Southeast Asian studies were promoted by the exigencies of the Cold War and the Vietnam War, so too Arabic and Middle East studies were boosted by the war in Afghanistan, while programs focusing on Eastern Europe disappeared with the fall of the Berlin Wall (Hau 2014, p. 54).

It was not unexpected that in contemporary Philippine academe, China Studies became more associated with the trajectories from Area Studies *vis-à-vis* traditional Sinology. What underpins what we now see as a *de facto* academic tradition is the fact that in its conception, China Studies, which became a specialization within Asian Studies degree programs, was shaped by political and economic motivations of the Philippines as a state, echoing the interests of the US. In contrast, historical studies, although important, problematize topics that are not considered acutely pertinent to the security of the Philippines. Among the periods of the UP Asian Center's institutional history, the most contentious was during 1973–1979 when the center was then the Philippine Center for Advanced Studies[4] and was perceived as a

---

[4] The University of the Philippines Asian Center's institutional history is described as follows: "...the Asian Center's history is one of the most colorful, if not the most controversial narratives within the University of the Philippines System. Based on a series of changes in name and institutional status, the various periods of the history of the Asian Center may be identified as follows: Institute of Asian Studies, (1955–1968); Asian Center I,

Marcos think-tank. In turn, the Marcos government was seen as a US ally.

China Studies was eventually born as a focus within Northeast Asian Studies in the Asian Studies Masters degree programs. In their current form, the programs have thesis and non-thesis tracks and follow the basic structure as presented in Table 1. The core subjects are the same for all area programs: Northeast Asia, Southeast Asia, West Asia and South Asia. It is through the specialization courses that that student gets to focus on the chosen country. The rest of the courses fall under the sub-specialization category.

It is important to note that the University of the Philippines is known for opposing the Marcos dictatorship, and it has produced a body of perspectives that is critical to the establishment until today. The evolution of a tertiary public education inherited from the United States into one that is nationalist but anti-establishment has shaped the study of China in its China Studies programs in significant ways. While the teaching and content of the courses have evolved, the impression that the program has remained US- or West-oriented still exists. Apart from a lack of emphasis on Mandarin language instruction, some course descriptions still seem reflective of Cold War sensibilities. Scholars who are well versed in the political history of knowledge production will find certain aspects discomfiting. For instance, the framing of dichotomies between the East and West (AS 202) as well as between socialism and capitalism (AS 208) are illustrative. On the other hand, courses on nationalism and national development (AS 203) and industrialization (AS 205) are reflective of the interest in surging Asian nations that had a strong nationalist dimension in its economic ascent. This in itself contributed to the anti-colonial perspective even if the course inception was not deliberately for that. As Winichakul (2014, pp. 881, 883) posits, there is a paradigmatic shift from Cold War Area Studies to a post-Cold War framing of

---

(1968–1973); Philippine Center for Advanced Studies (1973–1979); and, Asian Center II, (1980–Present)..." (Santamaria 2017).

Table 1: Asian studies graduate programs.

	M.A. in Asian Studies (thesis track)	M.A. in Asian Studies (non-thesis track)
Core subjects	12 units	12 units
Area/country of specialization • AS 230 Seminar on Northeast Asia • AS 235.1 Social and Economic Development in China • AS 235.2 Politics and Governance in China • AS 235.3 Culture and Society in China	12 units	12 units
Sub-specialization (electives)[5] • AS 202 The East–West Encounter • AS 203 Nationalism & National Development • AS 204 Agrarian Development & Peasantry in Asia • AS 205 Industrialization & Urban Development in Asia • AS 206 Philosophies & Religions of Asia • AS 207 Arts of Asia • AS 208 Socialism & Capitalism in Asia • AS 211 Security Issues in the Asia Pacific • AS 212 Regionalism and Community Building in Asia • AS 298 Special Problems in Asian Studies	3 units	15 units
Comprehensive exam	YES	YES
Language requirement	YES	YES
Thesis	YES	NO
Total course credit	33 units	39 units

Source: UP Asian Center website, accessed on 15 May 2018.

Asia as a dynamic area of study. In parallel with the recognition that Asian Studies by Asians is important, so did the view that it is important to build China Studies in the Philippines that is informed by Philippine perspectives and contexts.

---

[5] China majors on thesis track can also explore China through one more course within the subspecialization/elective courses while those on non-thesis track can have five of the following courses. Not all electives are available all the time since offerings are contingent on student demand and faculty availability.

The program allows thesis writers among China majors to exercise wide leeway in choosing topics for study, contingent on the availability of faculty who could supervise students on such topics. While the UP Asian Center has produced varied types of China-related research by China majors, the inclination is toward the contemporary period. To widen the glimpse of thematic undertakings, I present a record of theses produced by the University as a whole. The University of the Philippines has produced, through student thesis research in the undergraduate and graduate levels, a wealth of studies related to China and the Chinese. Using the subject search function of the university's online public access catalog, records of theses were pulled up and organized according to year, title and author. Considering search limitations, the studies from 1937–2017 number 89 and span across the varied disciplines. Table 3 presents three groupings of years, and I find that the 2000–2017 grouping yields the most studies of 45 compared to 23 in 1980–1999 and 22 in 1937–1979, indicating that terminal student research reflects the rising prominence of China in various topics. Given the increasing importance of China's economy, it is also not surprising that 12 of the 21 theses with economic content across all years come from the last period.[6]

A classificatory typology was constructed based on four broad categories of China-related subject matter in student research: China, China-other, Philippines–China and Chinese in the Philippines. "China" refers to matters that relate to the politics, culture and people of the People's Republic of China (PROC). "China-other" refers to China as studied in relation to other states, regions, culture and peoples outside of the PROC except the Philippines. "Philippines–China" refers to all matters relating to bilateral relations between the two countries. "Chinese in the Philippines" refers to matters related to diasporic Chinese in the Philippines, Chinese-Filipinos and new migrants. The content analysis reveals that the most frequent China-related subject matter is Chinese in the Philippines (29), followed by China (20),

---

[6] Note that some of these relate to Chinese in the Philippines. Interest in China is often related to issues on Chinese in the Philippines.

China-other (12) and Philippines–China (12). Eleven theses were uncoded owing to vague details on the public record, making it necessary for further investigation. Of the 11 uncoded theses, 5 are related to science, 4 are related to economics and 2 are related to language studies.

What we can observe in Table 2 is that while colonial legacies are present in some topics, the range of topics is wide enough to exhibit diversity in thought and interest in China and the Chinese from multiple disciplines. In the Malaysian context, Sinology, China Studies and Chinese Overseas Studies correspond to civilizational, state and ethnic contexts and are influenced by identity politics (Ngeow *et al.* 2017). The Philippine experience is more amorphous — a kind of ambiguity that reflects the eclecticism pervading the study of China-related subject matter in the Philippines. This is most evident in my study of the community of China experts in the Philippines, where the absence of strict categories in subject matter does not necessarily reveal a crisis but instead shows flexibility and various ongoing negotiations in the knowledge production space (Clemente 2018).

A supplementary vignette on China-related subject matter in research is from the topics accommodated in the *Asian Studies Journal* — the journal of the UP Asian Center. While a journal is not a comprehensive reflection of the institution's direction, it is nevertheless useful to indicate what ideas are accommodated into the conversation within the wide purview of the institution's perspectives. It is therefore noteworthy that 37 among 61 articles on Northeast Asia have content on China or are China-related from 1966 to 2014 (Table 3).

Closing Remarks and Further Research

This chapter sheds light on the academic and scholarly approach of China Studies in the Philippines and contributes to the narrative of the heterogeneity of China Studies by exploring the dynamic involving multi-continuum colonial trajectories, nationalist thought and institutionalization issues in tertiary education. The preceding

Table 2: China-related content in thesis production.

Year	Title	Author
	1937–1979: 43 years, 22 studies	
1937	The development of the primary and middle school curriculum in China	Yang, Szu Chieh
1938	Chinese immigration in the Philippines during the American era (1899–1937)	Hilario, Rafaelita V.
1940	The organization of the foreign service of China	Tan, Yao Eng
1952	The Chinese community in the Philippines	Weightman, George Henry
1954	The status of Chinese secondary schools in the City of Manila	Padilla y Runas, Luz (Dulatre)
1955	A comparative study of the Confucian political thought and Dr. Sun Yat-Sen's three principles of the people	Pua, Chin Tao
1956	China — a Soviet step to world conquest	Powell, Roy B.
1956	Cultural retention and religious affiliation of secondary school Chinese students in Manila	Beltran, Anita Kho Go
1958	The history, ideology, and politics of the post war conflict between Nationalist China and Communist China	Kim, Chil Suk
1959	The case of the overstaying Chinese visitors in the Philippines	Foo Tak Sun
1960	A study of problems involved in the continental shelf contiguous to the littoral state	Kuan-Tsyh Yu, Steven
1961	The question of admission of Communist China to the United Nations	Li, Leroy Chi-tsung
1967	A test of the belief congruence principle in prejudice against Chinese in the Philippines	Bulatao, Rodolfo Andres
1967	The role of export trade in the strategy for the economic development of Taiwan, 1956–1965	Chen, Cheng-shun

(Continued)

Table 2: (*Continued*)

Year	Title	Author
1969	A comparative study of elementary teacher education in the Republic of the Philippines and in the Republic of China	Hsiao, Bernard H. N.
1969	Pakistan-China relations (1962–1968): a Pakistani point of view	Ghayur, Azmat
1970	Communication systems of the Binondo Chinese	Lim, Benito
1972	A study of economic development planning in the People's Republic of China. – 1972.	Constantino, Ferdinand K.
1972	Chinese investments and their effects on Philippine economy 1961–1970. – 1972.	Ang, Pue Tin
1976	The 1950 marriage law of the People's Republic of China: its repercussions on the status of women in Chinese society	Dorros, Sybilla Green
1979	Sample instructional material in selected grammar lessons for grade five using the sector analysis approach	Cayanan, Wilhelmina N.
1979	Sino-African technical cooperation: a case study in cross-cultural communication 1980–1999: 20 years, 23 studies	Javier, Josefina Villarba
1981	The role of Chinese investments in the Philippine economy: 1970–1980. – 1981.	Aldana, Ma. Corazon H.
1982	Pattern of entry into manufacturing: a case study of Chinese entrepreneurs. – 1982	Leh, Richard L.
1982	The 1950 agrarian reform law of the people's Republic of China and the abolition of the landlord class	Mangubat, Benjamin Resplandor
1982	The People's Republic of China's policy towards the overseas Chinese in Southeast Asia 1949–1981	Carino, Theresa Chong
1986	A preliminary annotated bibliography of materials on Sino-Philippine relations available in selected libraries in Metro Manila, 1975–1984	Zhou Kangmei, 1951–

1986	An evaluation of the breast-feeding education program in Shanghai First Maternity and Infant Hospital	Liu, Kejia
1987	Philippine trade with China. -- 1987.	Ebarvia, Maria Corazon M.
1987	The role of the Chinese in the Philippine economy	Arellano, Rosalinda Lopez
1989	Non-intellective factors affecting academic performance of students in Filipinized Chinese high schools in Metro Manila	Sia, Vicente Y.
1989	Sino-Suluan historical relations in ancient texts	Wang, Teh-Ming
1990	Comparacion fonetica, diagnostico y tratamiento de las dificultades de los estudiantes Chinos para aprender Espanol	Mateu, Rosa Orti
1990	Supplementary tutoring in mathematical learning in Filipinized-Chinese primary schools	Chang, Rita Dy
1994	Ang pagsasalin ng Taong Yungib ng Peking ni Cao Yu: mga implikasyong teoretikal ng semantikong salin sa Filipino mula sa orihinal na Tsino ng dulang Beijingren	Miclat, Mario Ignacio
1994	Comparative effectiveness of the conventional Chinese teaching method and Instructional Video (IV) assisted instruction in selected Chinese-Filipino elementary schools in Metro Manila	Chuaunsu, Rebecca Shangkuan
1994	The performance of the Chinese-Filipinos in Philippine commercial banking: an evaluation	Carino, Monica Suyin C.
1995	Political leadership and the Federation of Filipino-Chinese Chambers of Commerce and Industry: continuity and change (1954–1994)	Carino, Theresa Chong
1995	Student activism in the "Diliman Commune" (1971) and the Tiananman democracy movement (1989)	Tang, Marie-Charlotte

(*Continued*)

Table 2: (*Continued*)

Year	Title	Author
1995	The gender question: the changing image and status of women as reflected in selected Chinese stories	Marcos, Sining A.
1996	China's post-cold war security perspectives and strategies: their implications on the Philippines	Magtuloy, Chona Panganiban
1997	A study of the emergence of Kaisa Para Sa Kaunlaran, Inc. as a new Chinese-Filipino socio-political association	Chua, Emma Lim
1998	Development of vocabulary instructional materials for Chinese EFL learners	Huang, Xiaoping
1999	A history of architecture in Binondo, 1594-1898: a socio-historical study of the architecture in Binondo	Del Castillo, Lorelei D.
1999	Development of molecular genetic markers for the giant clam, tridacna crocea 2000-2017: 18 years, 43 studies	Yu, Elizadora T.
2000	Reflective thinking strategies: focus on the study of Filipino among Chinese-Filipino secondary students	Josue, Editha Espino
2001	Historical geochemistry and mineralogical characteristics of sonn cores 114-21, 22 and 23, South China Sea, Western Philippines	Aguda, Nancy Rhoena R.
2001	Population genetics of two marine fish species in the South China Sea and Sulu Sea	Endriga, Marla A.
2002	China's food economy in the early 21st century and its implications for the rest of the world	Li, Ninghui
2002	Communicative language teaching in Chinese EFL classes and students' language proficiency	Huang, Hui Ming
2002	Learning strategies in reading and language achievement of Chinese non-English majors	Lu, Qing Qin

2002	The economic impact of China's entry to the WTO on Philippine trade of industrial manufactures	Gatlabayan, Kristine L.
2003	Calcareous nannoplankton distribution in surface sediments from the eastern and western portions of the South China Sea	Fernando, Allan Gil Salazar
2003	Nutrient fluxes in various coastal ecosystems of the south China Sea perturbed by human activities	Dupra, Vilma C.
2003	Post-cold war China-ASEAN relations: exploring worldview convergence and its security implications	Baviera, Aileen San Pablo
2003	Sage within, leader without: the development of Ru philosophy from Zhou period to contemporary China	Ong, Michelle Q.
2003	The U.S. foreign policy towards China from 1993 to 2000: economic relations and Taiwan issue	Zhang, Ziyu
2004	Analyses of the painting styles and decorative motifs on Ming blue and white ware with references to ceramic cargoes of Lena and other shipwrecks	Esguerra, Arnulfo N.
2004	Bangko po! Chinese-Filipino in the Philippines commercial banking: the statistical significance of ethnicity	Abesa, Jose Maria
2004	Fading red: rethinking the revolutionary model opera films of Mao's cultural revolution	Jiang, Wei
2004	Philippine-China military cooperation: a case study of the Spratlys	Quilala, Bayani H. IV
2005	China's emergence: threat or opportunity for the Philippines	Reyes, Lili-Mae T. Santos, Marie Kristien Moiselle L.
2005	Jackie Chan: Asian screen hero: global phenomenon	Tiu, Arthur Alain C.
2006	Bridges: an illustrated book on the history of the Chinese Filipinos	Marte, John David Z.

(*Continued*)

Table 2: (Continued)

Year	Title	Author
2006	China's 'crowding out' effect: the case of Philippine FDI flows	Diezmo, Katrina Cecilia T.
2006	Chinese college students' English linguistic proficiency, attitude and expository writing competence	Shen Shuxia
2008	China's accession to the WTO: a study of the Philippines' revealed comparative advantage 2002–2006	Allejos, Marianne V.
2008	Physical activity and the Filipino-Chinese high school student	Pituk, Jerrecho R.
2008	Strategies for crisis management: the responses of China to SARS and Avian flu pandemics and the lessons for the Philippines	Clavejo, Lorenzo A.
2008	The Chinese middle class: an analysis of its political influence towards democracy in China.	Wong, Andrea Chloe
2009	Travel motivations of Chinese inbound tourists to the Philippines	Ambrosio, Krystle Mei Go
2010	An Assessment of health decentralization in China: the pitfalls of market reforms.	Santiago, Marifel C. Mendoza
2010	Collection development of non print materials in Filipino Chinese schools in Metro Manila	Singian, Ma. Alma Navarro
2010	Educational administration practices in Chinese Filipino schools	Kotah, Sining Marcos
2010	Four essays on Chinese economic success in pre-hispanic and hispanic Philippines	Clemente, Tina S.
2011	Investigation of the application of the keyword method of mnemonic visual association on enhancing the learning oral Mandarin Chinese to adult beginners	Sarmiento, Nadine D.
2011	Translating selected contemporary short stories from Taiwan: a problem-based approach	Nicdao, Jose Marcelino A.

2012	Hoy! Tsinoy ako!: an ethnographic analysis of the representation of the Tsinoy in Philippine television	Sy, Stanly Galo Claudio
2013	An exploratory study of the interior design of selected Filipino Chinese homes in Metro Manila in relation to their social identity	Po, Eandra Leslie M.
2013	Problem-based learning: effects on critical and creative thinking skills in biology	Orozco, Jason A.
2013	Traditional concepts of space in contemporary Chinese family compounds	Hung, Inah Francesca T.
2015	Motivational and contextual factors in Chinese language learning performance	Tan, Judy G.
2015	Vector autoregression, impulse-response function and forecast error variance decomposition analysis: macroeconomic shocks emanating from the Chinese economy and their regional and global impacts	Cristobal, Bamily S.
2016	A Study on the influence of Chinoy culture on the self-disclosure behavior of Filipino-Chinese families	Tintiangko, Jesselee T.
2016	Cancer[vivors]: understanding cancer patients' perceived psychological and physical effects of Qigong	Mariano, Jihromarie S.
2016	New Chinese migrants in the Philippines: exploring non-economic factors in migration decisions based on personal narratives	Ganadillo, Ivy Marie L.
2017	An Empirical assessment of trade creation and trade diversion effects of the ASEAN-China Free Trade Agreement: has the Philippines become more integrated?	Feliciano, Paul Neilmer M.
2017	Immediate effects of cupping on shoulder range of motion in males	Enriquez, John Laetner M.

Source: This table was processed from University of the Philippines Web OPAC using "China" and "Chinese" as entries in a subject search, accessed on 15 May 2018.

Table 3: China-related content in the *Asian Studies Journal*.

Title	Author	Volume and Year
Articles with content on China		
1. Obstacles to missionary success in nineteenth century China	Ellsworth C. Carlson	ASJ 4:1 (1966)
2. A new concept of law, a study of Dr. Sun Yat Sen's political philosophy	Liu Shia-ling	ASJ 4:1 (1966)
3. Meiji Buddhism: Religion and patriotism	Minoru Kiyota	ASJ 4:1 (1966)
4. Chinese strategy and intent during the Sino-Indian border dispute	Donald R. Hetzner	ASJ 5:2 (1967)
5. The conversion of the Alani by the Franciscan missionaries in China in the fourteenth century	Frank W. Ikle	ASJ 5:2 (1967)
6. Pearl Buck and the Chinese novel	George A. Cevasco	ASJ 5:3 (1967)
7. Soviet and Chinese revolutionary strategy: Comparison and evaluation at the present	Roger Hamburg	ASJ 6:3 (1968)
8. Chinese communities in Eastern Java: a few reviews	C. Baks	ASJ 8:2 (1970)
9. The People's Republic of China as a nuclear power: A study of Chinese statements on global strategy	Leo Y. Liu	ASJ 10:2 (1972)
10. Political culture as a factor of political decay in China and Japan	Yearn H. Choi	ASJ 10:3 (1972)
11. Social change and political legitimacy in warlord China	Anthony B. Chan	ASJ 11:1 (1973)
12. The May fourth movement and the origins of Chinese marxism	Luis V. Teodoro, Jr.	ASJ 13: 1 (1975)
13. Social distance in Iloilo City: A study of anti-Chinese attitudes in the Philippines	John T. Omohundro	ASJ 13: 1 (1975)
14. The great proletarian cultural revolution	Felisa Uy Etemadi	ASJ 13:2 (1975)
15. The theoretical basis of sexual equality and marriage reform in China	Sybilla G. Dorros	ASJ 13: 2 (1975)
16. Evolution of Sino-American economic relations, 1784–1929: A survey	Paratha Sarathy Ghosh	ASJ 14:3 (1976)
17. Contemporary existentialism and the concept of naturalness in taoism and Ch'an (Zen)	Robert K. Lin	ASJ 14:3 (1976)
18. Chang Hsueh-Liang on the Sian incident	Jiu-Hwa Lo Upshur	ASJ 14:3 (1976)
19. Recognition policies toward China: A comparative study	Herbert S. Yee	ASJ 14:3 (1976)

Table 3: (Continued)

Title	Author	Volume and Year
20. The status of women in the People's Republic of China	Sybilla G. Dorros	ASJ 16 (1978)
21. The Status of Woman in China: Yesterday and Today	Soon Man Rhim	ASJ 20 (1982)
23. The Chinese natural religion: Confucianism and Taoism	Paul Chao	ASJ 20 (1982)
24. The Sino-Soviet conflict: Post-Mao period, 1976–1979	R.C. Ladrido	ASJ 20 (1982)
25. States as Managers of International Labor Migration: The Cases of South Korea and Taiwan	Vicente Angel Ybiernas	ASJ 50:2 (2014)
26. Reebok shoes and special economic zones: A case of local autonomy in China	Mario I. Miclat	ASJ 30 (1992)
27. Economic reform in China	Zhongdi Zhu	ASJ 31-32 (1995)
28. Human rights discourse in the Asia-Pacific region: Implications for the Philippines	Daniel A. Bell	ASJ 36: 2 (2000)
29. A comparative study of Chinese education in the Philippines and Malaysia	Ellen H. Palanca	ASJ 38:2 (2002)
30. Chen Shui-Bian and Taiwan-China (Cross-Strait) relations: An initial assessment	Edgardo E. Dagdag	ASJ 39:1-2 (2003)
31. Virtual Spaces for Imaginable Marriages: A Discursive Analysis of Structured Powers for Foreign Brides in Taiwan	Yeong-Shyang Chen	ASJ 40:1 (2004)
32. Rural China: From Modernization to Reconstruction	Tsui Sit and Tak Hing Wong	ASJ 49:1 (2013)
33. Philippines-China Relations, 2001–2008: Dovetailing National Interests	Charles Joseph de Guzman	ASJ 50:1 (2014)
Regional subjects with China-related content		
34. The erosion of the bi-polar power structure in the 1960's: Its impact upon East Asian international politic	Josefa M. Saniel	ASJ 11:2 (1973)
35. Diplomacy in East Asia: An expression of general world views	Frank W. Ikle	ASJ 14:3 (1976)
36. The Eurocentric Worldview: misunderstanding East Asia	Larry Fields	ASJ 19 (1981)
37. Macro-Historical Conditions for a Reconciliation in East Asia: Remaking History in an Age of Civilizational Crisis	Kinhide Mushakoji	ASJ 50:2 (2014)

Source: *Asian Studies Journal* compilation, 1966–2014.

discussion brought out the following points. First, the in spite of Spanish colonial attention on the galleon trade, Chinese presence in the Philippines and religious missions in China, interest in China and the Chinese during the colonial period did not translate into China Studies as a field of study. Nevertheless, historians and, eventually, other social scientists in contemporary times studied these subjects outside of the China Studies field. Second, the colonial Area Studies perspective influenced the contemporary China Studies academic program in the Philippines. While the process of decolonization commenced several decades ago and program content and pedagogy evolved, one cannot deny American influence in China Studies when the Asian Studies program was designed.

As an insight for succeeding research, I raise, for further exploration, the point that the interdisciplinary approach can be a decolonial instrument and a modality that helps tackle subject matter in China Studies. I argue that as a decolonial instrument, interdisciplinarity can be emphasized more in recontextualizing the Area Studies approach of China Studies.[7] In practice, the UP Asian Center already goes by multidisciplinarity (Saniel 1975) as a more inclusive approach to the involvement of more than one discipline.[8] The additive characteristic of multidisciplinarity *vis-à-vis* integrative quality of interdisciplinarity (Choi and Pak 2006) makes the former easier to operationalize given that multiple disciplines are represented without requiring intersection across disciplinal boundaries. The program already promotes three main specialization dimensions, i.e., development, politics and governance, and society and culture. Within this frame, considering interdisciplinarity in tackling subject

---

[7] Certainly, the subject of interdisciplinarity can be a contentious one. First, the tension between Area Studies and the disciplines exists. Reflecting on contemporary China Studies in the U.S. from 1977–2002, Walder (2004) expresses the attendant tensions in two divergent perspectives. On one hand, China Studies is simply an amalgamation of studies on China done by the social sciences. On the other hand, China Studies draws from the distinct academic traditions of area specialists.

[8] The literature makes various distinctions in the level of disciplinarity. For instance, one can view the differences in a spectrum that distinguishes among intradisciplinary, multidisciplinary, crossdisciplinary interdisciplinary, and transdisciplinary (Jensenius, 2012).

matter in each dimension can be further enriching as it promotes reflexivity as well as methodological and ontological diversity (Carolissen *et al.* 2017), which are necessary in decolonial efforts in teaching and learning. A stronger interdisciplinary training where approaches can be more balanced (e.g., at least, a certain discipline does not dominate) in tackling each dimension will certainly dovetail with a problem-based pedagogy that covers empirical and normative discussions in light of how disciplines relate to each other in an interdisciplinary context (Reyers *et al.* 2010).

While Mandarin language proficiency is preferred but not deemed critical to specializing in China, what has been crucial in building specialization in the Philippines is having the grasp of and inputs in current debates. Dialogue, in various molds of scholarly writing and public intellectualism, has been a necessary methodological instrument in problematizing subject matter. In this sense, the interface of the epistemic community and/or community of practice with academic study becomes significant. Also, bringing in the practice of reflexivity deepens and widens the conversation in epistemic communities.

As I end, I return to the beginning. My last point for further research is on the study of pre-colonial commercial relations between protohistoric Philippines and China. This subject is not only helpful in deepening Philippines–China studies but it also challenges the kind of imaginaries that persist in Philippine history — that anything pre-colonial is not worthy of study. It challenges the notion that the absence of the usual civilization markers makes Philippine history less important. I argue that pre-colonial development, unevenness of social change and the conditions for development challenge essentialist, moralist and colonial perspectives in appreciating Philippine history and society.

References

Aguilar, Filomeno, Hau, Caroline, Rafael, Vicente, and Tadem, Teresa. 2011. Benedict Anderson, Comparatively Speaking: On Area Studies, Theory, and 'Gentlemanly' Polemics. *Philippine Studies* 59 (1), pp. 107–139.

Carolissen, R., Canham, H., Fourie, E., Graham, T., Segalo, P., and Bowman, B. (2017). Epistemological Resistance towards Diversality: Teaching Community Psychology as a Decolonial project. *South African Journal of Psychology* 47 (4), 495–505. https://doi.org/10.1177/0081246317739203

Choi, Bernard C. and Pak Anita W. 2006. Multidisciplinarity, Interdisciplinarity and Transdisciplinarity in Health Research, Services, Education and Policy: 1. Definitions, Objectives, and Evidence of Effectiveness. *Clin Invest Med* 29 (6), pp. 351–364.

Clemente, Tina S. 2012. Chinese Trade in Pre-Spanish Philippines: Credit, Hostage and Raid Regimes. *Journal of Southeast Asian Studies* (JATI) 17 (1), pp. 191–206.

Clemente, Tina S. 2013. Guanxi in Chinese Commerce: Informal Enforcement in Spanish Philippines. *Seoul Journal of Economics* 26 (2), pp. 203–237.

Clemente, Tina S. 2015. "Spanish Colonial Policy Toward Chinese Merchants in 18th-century Philippines." In Madeleine Zelin and Yu-ju Lin. (Eds.). *Merchant Communities in Asia, 1600–1980*. London and New York: Routledge, pp. 123–140.

Clemente, Tina S. (2017a). "Loyalty on Trial: Chinese-Filipinos and the West Philippine Sea Dispute." In Chih-Ming Wang and Daniel P.S. Goh. (Eds.). *Precarious Belongings: Affect and Nationalism in Asia*. London: Rowman and Littlefield International, pp. 95–114.

Clemente, Tina S. (2017b). "China Studies in the Philippines: Evolution and Challenges." In Shih Chih-Yu, He Peizhong and Tang Lei. (Eds.). *From Sinology to Post-Chineseness: Intellectual Histories of China, Chinese People, and Chinese Civilization*. Beijing: China Social Sciences Press, pp. 131–161.

Clemente, Tina S. (2018) "Insights on China Studies as a Community of Practice." In Tina S. Clemente and Chih-yu Shih. (Eds.). *China Studies in the Philippines: Intellectual Paths and the Formation of a Field*. Oxon and NY: Routledge, pp. 4–22.

Hau, Caroline S. 2014. Privileging Roots and Routes: Filipino Intellectuals and the Contest over Epistemic Power and Authority. *Philippine Studies: Historical and Ethnographic Viewpoints* 62 (1), pp. 29–65.

Jensenius, Alexander Refsum. 2012. "Disciplinarities: Intra, Cross, Multi, Inter, Trans." http://www.arj.no/2012/03/12/disciplinarities-2/ (accessed on 13 May 13 2018).

Lim-Pe, Josefina. 1973. *The University of Santo Tomas in the Twentieth Century*. Manila: University of Santo Tomas Press.

Ngeow, Chow-Bing, Ling Tek Soon, Fan Pik Shy. 2017. "Pursuing Chinese Studies Amidst Identity Politics in Malaysia." In Chih-yu Shih. (Ed.). *Producing China in Southeast Asia*. Springer: Singapore, pp. 17–38.

Reyers, Belinda, Roux, Dirk J., Cowling, Richard. M., Ginsburg, Aimee E., Nel, Jeanne L., and Farrell, Patrick. O. 2010. Conservation Planning as a Transdisciplinary Process. *Conservation Biology* 24 (4), pp. 957–965.

Saniel, Josefa M. 1975. Area Studies: A Focus of Multidisciplinary Approach in the Social Sciences. *Asian Studies Journal* 13 (1), pp. 77–88.

Santamaria, Matthew. 2017. Pioneers and Legends: The Rise and Transformation of Asian Studies at the University of the Philippines' Asian Center. *Asian Studies: Journal of Critical Perspectives on Asia* 53 (1), pp. 128–135. http://asj.upd.edu.ph/mediabox/archive/ASJ_53_1_2017/Santamaria.pdf.

Walder, Andrew G. 2004. "The Transformation of Contemporary China Studies, 1977–2002." In David Szanton. (Ed.). *The Politics of Knowledge: Area Studies and the Disciplines*. Berkeley: University of California Press, pp. 314–340.

Winichakul, Thongchai. 2014. Asian Studies Across Academies. *The Journal of Asian Studies* 73 (4), pp. 879–897.

Future Agendas?

Chih-yu Shih

Department of Political Science, National Taiwan University, Taipei, Taiwan

On our future agenda, there are many more questions left than we can possibly touch upon. For instance, we could include an agenda of academic practices to study. So, we would include the following subjects:

1. Institution — how does colonial modernity affect the disciplinary division, academic calendar, incentives for intellectual engagement and other practices in former colonies and facilitate cooperation or exchange with the former colonial powers to shape studies of China?
2. Pedagogy — How are textbooks, post-graduate training and methodology of China/Chinese studies in former colonies reliant on former colonial powers?
3. Migrant scholars — How do postcolonial intellectual migrants in former colonial powers practice scholarship on China differently than intellectual migrants from colonial powers in their former colonies?
4. Visits, grants, and language — How do students of China studies in former colonies rely on various academic resources provided by former colonial powers?

We could, as an alternative, also interrogate the colonial relations of China studies in terms of the subjects of study. So, we could include the following topics:

1. Diffusion — Are the topics and the research agendas in China studies in former colonies acquired from former colonial powers?
2. In-groupness — Do the agendas of China studies among members of the Commonwealth or Co-Prosperity Sphere inform one another?
3. Paradigms — Do paradigm shifts in former colonies mimic the ones in former colonial powers or do they provide answers to anomalies in their own societies or changes in China?

We have discussed in the book how the memory of colonialism can be a relevant issue in the evolution of postcolonial intellectual history. More specifically for the future, in combination with migrant and ethnic studies in Southeast Asia, we could contrive the two comparative sub-agendas of (1) Chinese varieties: How is colonial history being remembered incompatibly at different Chinese communities? (2) Indigenous varieties: How are ethnic Chinese considered differently in indigenous populations due to their different positioning during the colonial past?

The major challenge remains to be the fluidity and undecidability of our identities as an autonomous scholar who studies China as well as someone to be studies as vicarious agents of China or Chinese. We could have numerous points of interrogation — (1) Sources: Which of the colonial and/or Chinese sources are considered strategically convenient to achieve a kind of knowledge on China that can support an identification desired by former colonies? For example, how is the use of colonial perspectives functional to the de/re/construction of a pro-Western identity for former colonies? (2) Dialogues — Who among neighbors, religious groups, former colonial powers, Chinese readers and others composes the major audience of China studies in former colonies and reflects their identification? For example, do scholars publish in English, an indigenous language, Chinese, or, if not English, the language of former colonial powers? (3) Divide I: How do different approaches to China or Chineseness in former colonies reproduce or transcend ethnic divisions naturalized by the colonial past? For example, how does Chinese language education indicate Chineseness in former colonies? (4) Divide II: How do colonial pasts construct the relations between former colonies and China and affect contemporary approaches to China in former colonies? For example, how does the use of personnel of former colonies to staff colonial governance in China affect contemporary views on China? (5) Divide III: How did the colonial/hegemonic use of identity or control strategies to divide different former colonies provoke China's dilemma toward them and their views on China today? For example, how does the division of British South Asian colonies affect contemporary views on China in each former colony?

Index

A
1953 Asian Studies Committee, 344
Adshead, S.A.M., 347–349
Ahok, 139–140
Anglo-Irish War of 1919–1921, 327
Anglo-Japanese relations, 307–309
Anthony Yu, 386
Arab–Chinese relations, 61
Asian Invasion, 342
Asian studies graduate programs, 414
Asiatic Studies, 344
Atif, Pervin, 86

B
1927 Brussels Conference of Oppressed Nationalities, 38
Barrowman, Rachel, 344, 346
Belich, James, 339–340, 342
Belt and Road Initiative (*see also* BRI), 76
Bertram, James, 345
Bibliotheca Sinica, 296, 298
Billot, Albert, 300
Black Hole of Calcutta, 5

Boxer Rebellion, 5
British East India Company (*see also* BEIC), 4, 7, 73, 312
British English language legacy (*see also* BELL), 72
Buchanan, Keith, 346, 348

C
Campbell, Duncan, 345, 350–351, 359
Carr, Bob, 394
Cecil Clementi, 168–169
Chandra, Lokesh, 20
Charles Dominique Maurice Rollet de l'Isle, 301
Chatterjee, Partha, 5
Chen Junbao, 172
Chey, Jocelyn, 402, 404
China boom, 356, 384
China Exchange Programme (*see also* CHEP), 350
China miracle, 351
China–India *Bhai–Bhai*, 26, 40
China–Japan relations, 355
China–Pakistan relations, 71
Chinese Medium Instruction (*see also* CMI), 187

435

Chinese University of Hong Kong (*see also* CUHK), 108, 173, 183, 193
Chinese-Arab Cultural Legacy, 53
Christiandy Sanjaya, 139
Churchill, Winston S., 308
Clark, Paul, 350–351
Cold War Area Studies, 413
Colloquial Novels, 168, 170
Conquer Asia, 357
Cornelius de Houtman, 126
Cosgrave, W. T., 327
Council of Australian Governments (*see also* COAG), 398
Cultural Cold War, 106–108
Cultural Revolution, 175–176, 251, 399
Curtis, Lionel, 326

D
Davis, A. R., 375–377, 381, 395
defensive modernizations, 310
Deng Xiaoping, 64, 241, 349
Dewey, John, 37, 54
Ding Wen Jiang, 56
Discovery of India, 40
Divide et Impera, 122
Doumer, Paul, 289

E
Easter Rising of 1916, 327
Echo Macanese, 268, 270
Elder, Chris, 350, 355
Encyclopedia on India–China Relations, 14

English Medium Instruction (*see also* EMI), 188
English-ization, 113
enlightenment intellectuals, 54, 152

F
Fairbank, John, 381
Ferreira do Amaral, 267, 279
Ferry, Jules, 300
FitzGerald, Stephen, 368, 383
Foreign Affairs Support Movement, 56
Fouad Muhammad Shibl, 54
Francisco Hermenegildo Fernandes, 268
French–Vietnamese relations, 294

G
Gandhi and New India, 18
Gilgit–Chilas–Khotan route, 4
Gitanjali, 37
Glimpses of World History, 40
Great Leap Forward, 251
Greater China, 311
Greater East Asia Co-Prosperity Sphere, 333

H
Haddon, Rosemary, 350
Hau, Caroline, 412
Hawkes, David, 378
Herbinger, Paul Gustave, 300
Historic Macao, 276
Historic Shanghai, 277
Holyoake, 344
Home Rule, 327

Homi Bhabha, 61
Hong Kong–Japan interactions, 200, 225
Hotung, Robert, 165
Hu Jintao, 65, 76
Huang Yaokun, 188
Hunter, Alexander, 347
Huntington, Samuel, 62
Hussein, Taha, 54

I
India and China in the Colonial World, 16
India–China exchanges, 3
Indian National Army (*see also* INA), 11, 18, 41, 43–44
India–Pakistan relations, 72
Industrial Revolution, 29, 72
Ishiku Hori, 36

J
Jaephil Suh, 153
Jamsetjee Jejee Bhoy, 6
Japan Hands intellectuals, 194, 201–202, 209–210, 212, 214, 224
Japan Narratives, 202, 208, 212, 218, 224
Japan's Orient, 150
Japanese–Korean Treaties, 314
Joko Widodo, 142

K
Kalimpong, 11–12, 31–32
Kalla, Jusuf, 139
Karoku Hosokawa, 318, 322
Keating, Pauline, 401
Kerr, Philip, 326
Khotanese Saka, 4

Kipling, Rudyard, 55
Kiranbala, 37
Kokab Khawaja, 87
Kolig, Eric, 361
Korekimi Nakamura, 313
Kotnis, Dwarkanath, 40
Krantz, 290
Kwantung Leased Territory, 312–313

L
Lai Jixi, 167, 169
Laswell, Harold, 250
Lee Kuan Yew, 100, 110, 115
Lenin, Vladimir, 322
Liang Qichao, 17
Liangni Li, 359
Lieus Sungkharisma, 138
Lord Durham, 328–329

M
Mantetsu Chosabu Incident, 323
Maori–Chinese interactions, 355
Market dominant minority, 129
Masayoshi Miyazaki, 313
Maule, A. C., 375
May Fourth Movement of 1919–1920, 36, 168
May Riot, 125, 137
McLeod, Hew, 346
McRae, C. R., 375
Meiji Restoration, 153, 241, 310
Minford, John, 378, 386
Minoru Togo, 316, 329
Miono Yamamoto, 310, 317
Mira Sinha Bhattacharjea, 9
mission civiliatrice, 287
Mollet, Guy, 321

Moloughney, Brian, 347, 351, 358
Monk Feng Tzu-kai, 20
Morgan, L.G., 220
Muhammad Ali, 56
Muhammad Yusuf Hamka, 138
Muhib Al-Din Al-Khatib, 62

N
1971 Nixon–Mao dialogue, 158
Nanyang University Students Union (*see also* NUSU), 110
Near North, 344
Nehru, Jawaharlal, 18, 38
New Sinology, 385, 388, 392
New Zealand sinology, 355
New Zealand Trade and Enterprise (*see also* NZTE), 352
New Zealand–China relationship, 351, 356

O
Oei Tjong Hauw, 132
Omar, Elyas, 350
Open Door Policy, 179
Opening of China, 349
Opium Trade, 9
optical character recognition (*see also* OCR), 300
Oriental Studies, 293, 374–376
Orthodox China, 232
Ou Dadian, 167, 169
Oxbridge-British atmosphere, 371

P
Panikkar, K.M., 15
Parris Chang, 249
People's Action Party (*see also* PAP), 100, 109
People's Republic of China (*see also* PRC), 158, 165
Pfister, Aloys, 297
Philippines–China studies, 427
Phillips, Richard, 350, 359
poll tax generations, 358
Portuguese Administration of Macau, 259–260, 262, 279
Pratibha Patil, 38
Pribumi, 129
problems of another, 21

Q
Qiu Shuting, 188

R
Ramayana in China, 19
Rayson Huang, 106, 112
Red Star Over China, 18
Reform and Opening Up, 88
Resurrection of Asia, 347
Riben Jinhua, 215
Richards, John F., 8
Rise of China, 33, 70, 75, 351, 370, 396
Robequain, Charles, 301
Russel, Bertrand, 37
Russian Revolution of 1917, 322
Russo-Japanese War of 1904–1905, 312
Ryckmans, Pierre, 377, 381, 386

S
Said, Edward, 56, 291
Scalapino, Robert, 250
Self-Support Movement, 56
Shosuke Sato, 316
Singapore Model, 251
Smith, Adam 328

Snow, Edgar, 18
Soulliere, Ellen, 350
Stein Collection, 4
Sun Yat-sen, 18–19, 30, 35, 39, 45, 186, 249, 268
Swami Vivekananda, 14
Sylvain Levi, 36, 38

T

Tagore, Rabindranath, 14, 34
Taiping Rebellion, 5, 17, 27, 31
Tan Cheng Lock, 104
Tan Kah Kee, 102
Tan Lark Sye, 101–102, 106
Tan Yun Shan, 17, 38, 46
Tanaka Kankuei, 124
Tang Jingsong, 300–301
Tansen Sen, 4, 34
Tarling, Nicholas, 346
Thakur Gadadhar Singh, 5
Thampi, Madhavi, 11, 16
Third space, 61, 66
Thirteen Months in China, 6
Thomazi, Auguste Antoine, 300
Tiong Hoa Hwee Koan, 130–131
Tionghoa, Persatuan, 133
Townsend, Susan C., 331
Toynbee, Arnold, 344, 347
Treaty of Waitangi 1840, 340
Treaty of Waitangi Act 1975, 340

U

U.S.–China relationship, 396
Unlocking Asia, 357

V

Valckenier, Adrian, 127
von Kowallis, Jon Eugene, 388, 400

W

Wahid, Abdurahman, 138
Waitangi Tribunal, 340
Waley, Arthur David, 375
Wang Gungwu Report, 112
Wellington Delegation, 168
Weng Songran, 179
Wevers, Lydia, 340
White Dominions, 324
White Man's Burden, 73
Wilkinson, Endymion, 296
William Lyon Mackenzie King, 327
Willmott, Bill, 349–351, 359
Windows on a Chinese Past, 358

X

Xiangmo Huang, 394
Xu Zhimo, 37

Y

Yang Dazhao, 13
Yellow Peril, 342
Yokohama Incident, 323
Young, Alan, 350–352, 355, 365

Z

Zheng He, 10, 63
Zhou Enlai, 250
Zhou Jiarong, 188
Zoning System, 128

CPSIA information can be obtained
at www.ICGtesting.com
Printed in the USA
BVHW040037070220
571709BV00005B/5

Published by
World Scientific Publishing Co. Pte. Ltd.
5 Toh Tuck Link, Singapore 596224
USA office: 27 Warren Street, Suite 401-402, Hackensack, NJ 07601
UK office: 57 Shelton Street, Covent Garden, London WC2H 9HE

British Library Cataloguing-in-Publication Data
A catalogue record for this book is available from the British Library.

COLONIAL LEGACIES AND CONTEMPORARY STUDIES OF CHINA AND CHINESENESS
Unlearning Binaries, Strategizing Self

Copyright © 2020 by World Scientific Publishing Co. Pte. Ltd.

All rights reserved. This book, or parts thereof, may not be reproduced in any form or by any means, electronic or mechanical, including photocopying, recording or any information storage and retrieval system now known or to be invented, without written permission from the publisher.

For photocopying of material in this volume, please pay a copying fee through the Copyright Clearance Center, Inc., 222 Rosewood Drive, Danvers, MA 01923, USA. In this case permission to photocopy is not required from the publisher.

ISBN 978-981-121-234-5

For any available supplementary material, please visit
https://www.worldscientific.com/worldscibooks/10.1142/11609#t=suppl

Desk Editors: Aanand Jayaraman/Karimah Samsudin

Typeset by Stallion Press
Email: enquiries@stallionpress.com

COLONIAL LEGACIES AND CONTEMPORARY STUDIES OF CHINA AND CHINESENESS
Unlearning Binaries, Strategizing Self

Editors

Chih-yu Shih
National Taiwan University

Prapin Manomaivibool
Chulalongkorn University

Mariko Tanigaki
University of Tokyo

Swaran Singh
Jawaharlal Nehru University

World Scientific

NEW JERSEY · LONDON · SINGAPORE · BEIJING · SHANGHAI · HONG KONG · TAIPEI · CHENNAI · TOKYO